Paddling
Oregon

Robb Keller

FALCON®

HELENA, MONTANA

A FALCON GUIDE ®

Falcon® is continually expanding its list of recreational guidebooks. All books include detailed descriptions, accurate maps, and all the information necessary for enjoyable trips. You can order extra copies of this book and get information and prices for other Falcon® guidebooks by writing Falcon, P.O. Box 1718, Helena, MT 59624 or calling toll-free 1-800-582-2665. Also, please ask for a free copy of our current catalog. Visit our website at http:\\www.falconguide.com.

1 2 3 4 5 6 7 8 9 0 XX 03 02 01 00 99 98

Falcon and FalconGuide are registered trademarks of Falcon® Publishing, Inc.

Cover photo: Kayakers on the White River,
by Bob Woodward.

Back cover photo: Jolly rafters on the Owyhee,
by Frank S. Balthis.

Black-and-white photos by author, unless otherwise noted.

Library of Congress Cataloging-in-Publication Data

Keller, Robb, 1960-
    Paddling Oregon / by Robb Keller.
        p. cm.
    Includes index.
    ISBN 1-56044-533-5 (pbk.)
    1. White–water canoeing—Oregon—Guidebooks.   2. Rafting (Sports)—Oregon—
Guidebooks.   3. Rivers—Oregon—Recreational use—Guidebooks.   4. Oregon—
Guidebooks.   I. Title.
    GV776.07K45   1998
    797.1'22'09795—dc21   98-23764
                                                                    CIP

CAUTION

Outdoor recreational activities are by their very nature potentially hazardous. All participants in such activities must assume the responsibility for their own actions and safety. The information contained in this guidebook cannot replace sound judgment and good decision-making skills, which help reduce risk exposure, nor does the scope of this book allow for disclosure of all the potential hazards and risks involved in such activities.

Learn as much as possible about the outdoor recreational activities in which you participate, prepare for the unexpected, and be cautious. The reward will be a safer and more enjoyable experience.

 Text pages printed on recycled paper.

I chatter, chatter as I flow
To join the brimming river,
For men may come and men may go,
But I go on for ever.

—Alfred Lord Tennyson
The Brook

Contents

Rivers and their tributaries

		Sectional Skill Levels	Beginner Intermediate Expert

River		Section #1	Section #2	Section #3	Section #4	Section #5	Basin Map
1 Alsea River	Class	I to II					Mid Coast
Page 15	Miles	52					Page 434
2 Breitenbush River	Class	III+(IV)					Mid Willamette
Page 18	Miles	8+					Page 436
3 Brice Creek	Class	IV+ & V	IV & V				Lower Willamette
Page 22	Miles	3.2	3.8				Page 430
4 Bull Run River	Class	III					Sandy
Page 26	Miles	2.5					Page 454
5 Butte Creek	Class	III (IV-)					Mid Willamette
Page 30	Miles	7 to 18					Page 436
6 Calapooia River	Class	II+(III)	I to II (III+)				Mid Willamette
Page 34	Miles	10+	12.5				Page 436
7 Canyon Creek	Class	IV to V					Mid Willamette
Page 37	Miles	7+					Page 436
8 Canyon Creek, Washington	Class	IV+ & V					SW Washington
Page 41	Miles	4					Page 448
9 Chetco River	Class	II to IV	III-IV (V)	I to II			South Coast
Page 45	Miles	14	6	20			Page 446
10 Clackamas, Upper	Class	III (III+)	IV (V)	III (IV)	II		Lower Willamette
Page 49	Miles	7.5	8	10	4		Page 430
11 Clackamas River, Lower	Class	III to IV+	II (II+)	I to II			Lower Willamette
Page 56	Miles	2.5	15	5 to 22			Page 430
12 Clackamas River, North Fork	Class	IV+ (P)	V				Lower Willamette
Page 60	Miles	4	3.5				Page 430
13 Clear Creek	Class	II+ (III)	II (IV)				Lower Willamette
Page 63	Miles	8	12				Page 430
14 Collawash River	Class	V (P)	IV				Lower Willamette
Page 66	Miles	8.5	5.5				Page 430
15 Coquille River, South Fork	Class	III & IV	II (III)	III (IV)	IV (V)	I & II (IV)	South Coast
Page 71	Miles	3.6	3.5	3.1	1.4	22	Page 446
16 Crabtree Creek	Class	III+	I to II				Mid Willamette
Page 76	Miles	10	15.5				Page 436
17 Crooked River, Lower	Class	IV	III (IV)				Deschutes
Page 79	Miles	16 to 18	9				Page 418
18 Deschutes River, Upper	Class	I to II	I to V+				Deschutes
Page 84	Miles	44	14				Page 418
19 Deschutes River, Central	Class	IV to IV+	IV (V)				Deschutes
Page 90	Miles	5	14.2				Page 418

River		Section #1	Section #2	Section #3	Section #4	Section #5	Basin Map
20 Deschutes River, Lower	Class	II (III)	III (III+)	I & II (III)			Deschutes
Page 93	Miles	41	11	44			Page 418
21 Donner & Blitzen River	Class	III (III+)					Malheur Lake
Page 101	Miles	17.2					Page 432
22 Drift Creek (Alsea)	Class	II (III)					Mid Coast
Page 104	Miles	20					Page 434
23 Drift Creek (Siletz)	Class	III (IV, P)					Mid Coast
Page 107	Miles	9 to 11					Page 434
24 Eagle Creek	Class	III (V, P)	III (IV, P)				Lower Willamette
Page 110	Miles	6	8				Page 430
25 Elk River	Class	II (III+)	I & II (IV+)	II (III+)	I to II		South Coast
Page 114	Miles	5.6	3.5	6.7	13		Page 446
26 Fall Creek	Class	III (IV)					Upper Willamette
Page 119	Miles	7					Page 452
27 Fifteenmile Creek	Class	IV & V					Hood
Page 121	Miles	3.5					Page 424
28 Grande Ronde River	Class	II to III	I (III)	II to III			Grande Ronde
Page 124	Miles	25	32	94			Page 422
29 Grave Creek	Class	IV & V	III				Rogue
Page 131	Miles	3.5	12				Page 444
30 Hills Creek	Class	IV+ to V-					Upper Willamette
Page 134	Miles	5					Page 452
31 Hood River	Class	III (III+,P)					Hood
Page 137	Miles	12.5					Page 424
32 Hood River, East Fork	Class	V (V+)					Hood
Page 140	Miles	6					Page 424
33 Hood River, West Fork	Class	IV (V)					Hood
Page 143	Miles	6.5					Page 424
34 Illinois River	Class	IV (V)					Rogue
Page 147	Miles	34					Page 444
35 Imnaha River	Class	III to IV	II & III (IV)				Grande Ronde
Page 152	Miles	38	20				Page 422
36 John Day River	Class	I & II	I & II	I & II (III)			John Day
Page 158	Miles	23	47	69			Page 426
37 John Day River, North Fork	Class	III+ (V)	II to II+				John Day
Page 163	Miles	41	60				Page 426
38 Jordan Creek	Class	III					North Coast
Page 167	Miles	7					Page 438
39 Kalama River, Washington	Class	III (IV)	II (II+)				SW Washington
Page 170	Miles	25.7	10				Page 448
40 Kilchis River	Class	III to IV	I to II				North Coast
Page 174	Miles	7 to 13	5 to 7				Page 438
41 Klamath River	Class	IV (IV+)					Klamath
Page 178	Miles	15					Page 428
42 Klickitat River, Washington	Class	III+	II+				SW Washington
Page 182	Miles	21	17+				Page 448
43 Lake Creek	Class	V to VI	II to II+	III (IV)			Mid Coast
Page 185	Miles	1.5	4	5+			Page 434
44 Laying Creek	Class	III+ to IV					Upper Willamette
Page 189	Miles	5					Page 452
45 Lewis River, East Fork, Washington	Class	IV+	IV+ (V)	IV+ & V	III to IV	I to II	SW Washington
Page 192	Miles	5.5	4.5	5.6	7.4	13	Page 448
46 Little Klickitat River, Washington	Class	IV to V					SW Washington
Page 199	Miles	9.7					Page 448
47 Little White Salmon River, Washington	Class	V	V (P)				SW Washington
Page 202	Miles	2	3.5				Page 448
48 Lobster Creek	Class	IV					Rogue
Page 208	Miles	5					Page 444
49 McKenzie River	Class	V	II & III (III+)	I & II			Upper Willamette
Page 211	Miles	0.4 to 2	42	39			Page 452
50 Metolius River	Class	II & III	III				Deschutes
Page 216	Miles	13	17+				Page 418

River		Section #1	Section #2	Section #3	Section #4	Section #5	Basin Map
51 Mill Creek	Class	IV	II				Mid Willamette
Page 220	Miles	5	7				Page 436
52 Minam River	Class	III					Grande Ronde
Page 224	Miles	22					Page 422
53 Molalla River	Class	III+ (IV)	II				Mid Willamette
Page 226	Miles	14.5	12				Page 436
54 Nehalem River	Class	I	I+ to III	FW			North Coast
Page 231	Miles	53	39	8+			Page 438
55 Nestucca River	Class	III (V)	I (I+)				North Coast
Page 235	Miles	8.3	24				Page 438
56 Owyhee River	Class	II (IV, P)	II & IV (V)	III (IV)			Owyhee
Page 239	Miles	70+	35	60			Page 440
57 Pine Creek	Class	III to III+					Powder
Page 246	Miles	8+					Page 442
58 Pudding River	Class	FW (I+)					Mid Willamette
Page 249	Miles	27					Page 436
59 Quartzville Creek	Class	V	IV+ (P)	IV	III+ (IV)		Mid Willamette
Page 252	Miles	2.9	4.2	3.1	8		Page 436
60 Rogue River	Class	I & II	III (V)	I & II			Rogue
Page 258	Miles	33	34	34			Page 444
61 Rogue River, North Fork	Class	IV+	III+				Rogue
Page 268	Miles	3.7	5				Page 444
62 Row River	Class	II+ to III (IV)	II (III)				Upper Willamette
Page 271	Miles	5	5				Page 452
63 Salmon River	Class	III (III+)					Sandy
Page 274	Miles	7					Page 454
64 Salmonberry River	Class	III+ (IV)					North Coast
Page 277	Miles	9					Page 438
65 Sandy River, Upper	Class	IV+	III (IV-)				Sandy
Page 281	Miles	5.5	13				Page 454
66 Sandy River, Lower	Class	IV	III to III+	I to II+			Sandy
Page 285	Miles	6.5	5	15.5			Page 454
67 Santiam River, Little North Fork	Class	IV+ (P)	II (IV)	II (IV)			Mid Willamette
Page 290	Miles	±7	6.5	6.5			Page 436
68 Santiam River, Middle Fork	Class	III+ & IV	IV				Mid Willamette
Page 296	Miles	14+	2+				Page 436
69 Santiam River, North Fork	Class	III (IV+ & V)	I to II+ (P)				Mid Willamette
Page 300	Miles	12	34				Page 436
70 Santiam River, Upper South Fork	Class	II+ (III)	IV+ (V, P)	III (V)			Mid Willamette
Page 305	Miles	7	5	10			Page 436
71 Santiam River, Lower South Fork	Class	II (IV+)	I+ (P)				Mid Willamette
Page 310	Miles	13	5.6 to 30+				Page 436
72 Sauvie Island & Multnomah Channel	Class	FW					Lower Willamette
Page 313	Miles	Various					Page 430
73 Siletz River	Class	III (IV,V)	III	III	III (IV)	I (II)	Mid Coast
Page 317	Miles	5	4	4.5	7	7.5 to 33	Page 434
74 Siuslaw River	Class	I to II	I to II	II+ to III-	FW		Mid Coast
Page 322	Miles	33	25	23	20		Page 434
75 Smith River System, Oregon & California	Class	III to V					Smith System
Page 326	Miles	Various					Page 327
76 Snake River	Class	II to IV	II (III)				Grande Ronde
Page 336	Miles	32	47				Page 422
77 Squaw Creek	Class	II+ (III)	III & IV (P)				Deschutes
Page 343	Miles	16	12				Page 418
78 Sweet Creek	Class	IV+ (V, P)					Mid Coast
Page 348	Miles	±2.2					Page 434
79 Thomas Creek	Class	III (IV,P)	I to I+				Mid Willamette
Page 351	Miles	13.2	17.3+				Page 436
80 Trask River	Class	III & III+	III (IV+)				North Coast
Page 354	Miles	8	11				Page 438

River	Section #1	Section #2	Section #3	Section #4	Section #5	Basin Map
81 Tualatin River Class	I	I+ (II)				Lower Willamette
Page 358 Miles	21	5.5				Page 430
82 Umpqua River, North Fork Class	II & III (IV)	III (IV)	II (III)	II to II+	I (II+)	Umpqua
Page 361 Miles	19.2	11	7	13	6.5	Page 450
83 Umpqua River, South Fork Class	III (IV+)	III (IV)	II (III+)	I to II+ (III)		Umpqua
Page 368 Miles	10	5	17	59		Page 450
84 Washougal River, Washington Class	IV	IV (V)	III (IV)	II (III)		SW Washington
Page 371 Miles	6	1	7	3		Page 448
85 White River Class	II & III (IV)	III+ (IV)	III (IV,P)			Deschutes
Page 376 Miles	6.5	12	11			Page 418
86 White Salmon River, Washington Class	IV to V	IV+ (P)	V (P)	III+ (V-)	.	SW Washington
Page 381 Miles	9	5.1	5	8		Page 448
87 Willamette River Class	I+ (II)	FW to I	FW	FW	FW	Upper to Lower Will.amette
Page 389 Miles	18	42	69	22	25	Pgs.430,436, 452
88 Willamette River, N. Fork of Middle Fork Class	V	II & III+				Upper Willamette
Page 397 Miles	5	8.5				Page 452
89 Wilson River Class	III+ & IV	III (IV)	I to II			North Coast
Page 401 Miles	8+	15	9			Page 438
90 Wind River, Washington Class	IV+ (V)	IV (P)				SW Washington
Page 405 Miles	6	5				Page 448
91 Yamhill River, South Fork Class	II (II+)	I				Mid Willamette
Page 409 Miles	15	45.6				Page 436
92 Yaquina River Class	FW to II					Mid Coast
Page 412 Miles	36					Page 434

Acknowledgments

Many folks helped bring this book to completion. Without their contributions and expertise, it would have taken me far beyond the time allotted to finish the project and learn of the many boatable stretches of rivers and creeks described. Contributors include Witt Anderson, Jason Bates, Thomas Bell, Jeff Bennett, Field Blackard, Ron Blanchette, Eric Brown, Steve Cramer, Richard Frenzel, Kale Frieze, Brent Mahan, Jens Mullen, Mike Olson, Michael Parent, Jim Reed, Dick Sisson, Morgan Smith, Ron Sonnevil, Bill Tuthill, Jed Weingarten, and Andrew Wulfers. I am particularly indebted to those who contributed several write-ups for their respective parts of the state.

I also am indebted to Jeff Jacob for his great photos and constant paddling companionship. It was Jeff who first enticed me into a hard shell kayak and spent hours teaching me photography, river reading, and rolling skills. If not for Jeff's adventurous spirit and willingness to allow a beginner to tag along, I might never have learned to explore and appreciate the hidden wonders of rivers, creeks, and whitewater.

Many thanks to Jeff Bennett for his legal advice, inspiring guidebooks, and contributions to the text. Jeff is truly a legend in the paddling community. With several books to his name on a wide range of outdoor pursuits, Jeff defines the renaissance man.

Without the aid of Ron Killen, John Francia, Jeff Andre, Jim Philly, Chris Funk, Darren Jacob, and many Lower Columbia Canoe Club members I would never have made it to the river on occasions when I was without transportation. We have floated and struggled through many years of fun and friendship on countless river adventures. Thanks, guys!

Thanks to Jo Miller and all the folks at U.S. Geological Survey, the Bureau of Land Management, the USDA Forest Service, and the U.S. Army Corps of Engineers for providing maps, hydrograph statistics, conversion information, trip requirements, and general river information.

Thanks to Ed Ditto (Grateful Ed on the Internet) for his humorous addition to the often technical writing. Tawltail Creek is a trip that no one should miss.

Special thanks to Falcon Publishing and my editor, Randall Green, for teaching a beginner how to run this Class V project through patient editing, constant encouragement, and extensions of time that I needed.

Thanks, of course, to my parents, friends, coworkers, and fellow paddlers for listening to my long-winded stories of weekend adventures of terror and bliss. My enthusiasm for whitewater and countless river stories often spills out to take over a conversation.

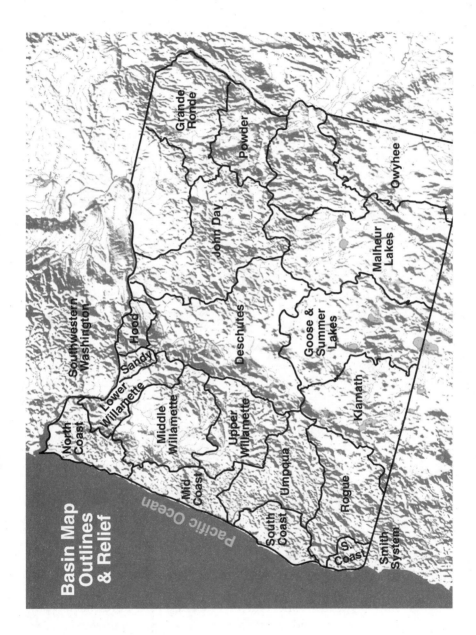

Basin Map
Outlines
& Relief

Pacific Ocean

North Coast
Southwestern Washington
Hood
Sandy
Lower Willamette
Middle Willamette
Mid Coast
Upper Willamette
South Coast
Umpqua
S. Coast
Smith System
Rogue
Klamath
Deschutes
John Day
Goose & Summer Lakes
Grande Ronde
Powder
Owyhee
Malheur Lakes

The Rivers

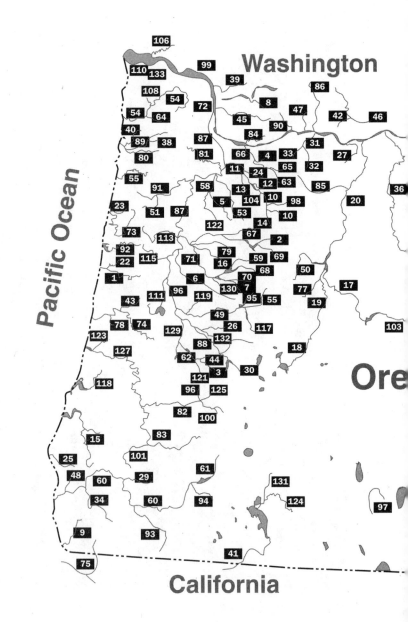

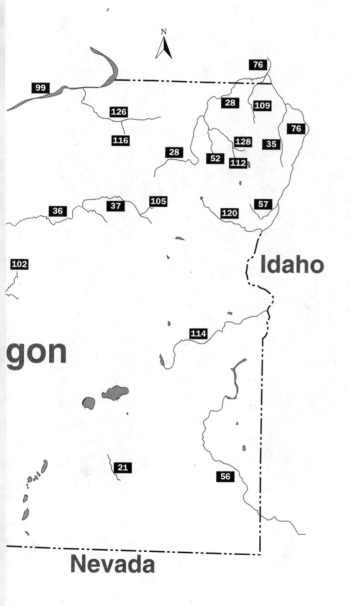

N

99

126

116

28

76

28   109

128   35   76

52   112

120   57

36   37   105

102

Idaho

gon

114

21   56

Nevada

With Mount Hood shining in the background, the Sandy River flows past forest and field. JEFF JACOB PHOTO

Introduction

Oregon is a diverse state containing almost every imaginable climate and type of scenery. Most of its streams are seasonal, dependent on heavy spring and winter precipitation. Other long streams flatten before reaching the Pacific Ocean, fed year-round by springs, snowmelt, and dams along the western slopes of the Cascade Range. The state's northwest corner is heavily vegetated, with thick ferns and tree growth that resemble those of a rain forest. Many coastal areas provide dramatic ocean views, and the surf is always up at several popular beaches that boast big swells. Though most kayakers and canoeists find a good standing wave or wave hole preferable to ocean surf, Oregon offers fun either way.

The state's mountains also are varied. The Cascade Range rises sharply beyond the lower coastal ranges, collecting water that eventually makes its way to the Willamette Valley and the Pacific Ocean. Gentle streams have carved deep, narrow canyons into these high mountains. Steep creeks are common, with many still left to explore for a first descent. The Cascades block much of the precipitation that heads east, creating high desert beyond. Their eastern slopes feed the White, Hood, and Metolius rivers, which find their way to the mighty Columbia River on Oregon's northern border. The Deschutes, John Day, and Crooked rivers all collect water from mountains farther east and from springs that filter mountain water through deep layers of porous, volcanic rock. Cinder cones, fossil beds, and whitewater rapids punctuate the arid, open landscape. The town of Bend and surrounding communities enjoy exceptionally dry and sunny weather in comparison to the often overcast Willamette Valley.

To the southeast, the Steens Mountains rise above the marshy grasslands known as the Malheur Desert, seasonal home to a wide variety of migrating birds. Bighorn sheep, deer, and rattlesnakes thrive among the deserted canyons, spires, and hoodoos near the Owyhee River. The Wallowa and Blue mountains, to the northeast, separate the Grande Ronde, Imnaha, Minam and Snake rivers, as well as Pine Creek, Joseph Creek, and a bucket full of creeks that have yet to be explored. The Snake River drains a huge area, going east beyond the Bitterroot, Sawtooth, Steens, and Teton ranges as it picks up most of the water that drains west from Wyoming, Idaho, and Nevada.

Paddlers enjoy year-round boating in Oregon, as well as in neighboring areas of Washington and Northern California. This guide includes descriptions for all of Oregon's major streams, plus several sections of rivers and creeks in these adjacent states. The region's streams vary from short, steep, Class V, technical nightmares to slow, meandering, scenic daydreams. Long stretches of water through uninhabited areas allow multiday, self-contained trips. Such vast, unpopulated areas make Oregon the country's leader in Wild and Scenic River designations. Yet many of the state's streams are within an hour's drive from metropolitan areas, allowing easy day trips or quick evening floats after work.

This book attempts to disperse the knowledge, pleasure, and spirit of river running. The author and editors have tried to make it the best guidebook it can be, but changes happen quickly. Please help to keep the information presented here as accurate as possible by writing to Falcon Publishing with updates, or by e-mailing the author at riverat@teleport.com. One thing not included in this book is a ranking that lists certain river sections as "better" or "worse" compared to others. All rivers are good runs for someone. The book also does not attempt to help paddlers choose equipment, learn technique, or find someone to take them downstream; look to folks who are in the river running business for your specific needs.

Each paddler has his or her own methods, friends, equipment, and style. I love streams, and think of boating as a personal adventure. As your paddling experience becomes diverse and broad, I hope your experiences on the river are good ones. May the River Gods be with you! Maybe we'll meet one day on a healthy, flowing stream and share a smile.

How to Use this Guide

Paddling Oregon is divided into 92 river entries, numbered and ordered alphabetically. Each entry contains various pieces of information. Overall, a river write-up contains general information regarding the stream as a whole, followed by more specific sectional information that includes ratings, flow, and mileage. The sectional divisions are not intended to suggest separate "runs," but are instead based on differences in stream character. Within any given section there may be more than one day's paddle, though many sections may be used as one-day runs, depending on the length of run desired. The goal here was to allow paddlers to pick their own run length and character by combining sections or using alternate access areas. This may help prevent paddlers from piling up at popular destinations.

Information for each river is divided by the following entries and subheadings:

Stream name and area
The stream name, followed by the upper and lower limits of the stretch discussed. In most cases, this guide covers each stream from some accessible upper location to its confluence with another stream or the ocean.

Character
A short general description of the stream character for all sections. This may include outstanding characteristics or brief notes on the most memorable sections.

Location
A basin map shows the general location of the river in Oregon, for a quick idea of the stream basin and area. The text describes more specifically nearby towns and drainages.

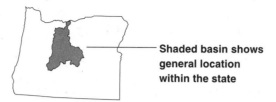

Shaded basin shows
general location
within the state

Class

The general level of stream difficulty along the entire stream for all sections. Class is ranked from I to VI, with some flatwater (FW) sections. A (P) following the class rating indicates a necessary portage. Class designations in parentheses indicate more difficult rapids or portages that occur within a stretch of water.

Skill level

The general level of competence required to run the river.

Craft

The type of boat or craft that works best on each particular stream. People run streams in all sorts of craft. This section distinguishes between streams that can be run only in smaller whitewater craft (canoes and kayaks) and those that have enough water and room for larger craft (rafts, catarafts, and drift boats). "All" craft indicates that open canoes, drift boats, rafts, and even vinyl craft such as pool toys or innertubes can drift the stream in sections. Craft not intended for whitewater use should remain within flatwater or Class I to I+ areas.

Recommended flow

The recommended level for paddling most sections of the stream listed, measured in cubic feet per second (cfs). Those who desire to float beyond the levels recommended, or even at flood stage, do so at their own risk. At higher flow levels, the class and character of the stream may be more hazardous than listed. The gray band on the hydrographs (see below) reflects the general recommended flow. Particulars for each river section and specific flow recommendations are given under "Going with the Flow."

Optimal flow

The best flow level for running most sections listed, measured in cubic feet per second (cfs).

Water source

The origin of water for the stream. Rain, snowmelt, springs, dam-controlled water, or a combination of sources are listed. Giving paddlers an idea of where the water comes from and how regular flow can be, this information aids in determining the paddling season.

Average gradient

The average drop, measured in feet per mile (ft/mi), over the entire stream. On the gradient charts that accompany each description, the gray line running from upper left to lower right represents the average of all gradients shown. The gradient for a particular stretch of stream is represented as a gray bar which extends above or below the average gradient.

Hydrographs

Hydrographs were created using USGS statistical data for the listed streams, based on several years of data. The smaller black lines indicate high and low flow averages over the period of record. (They do not indicate the highest and lowest flows ever recorded.) The darker central line indicates the mean flow averaged over the same period of record. The gray band indicates the range of flow recommended for running some sections of river at any one time. Refer to sectional data for recommended flows for each section.

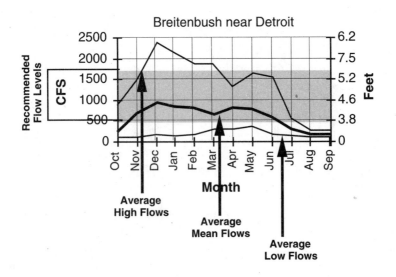

Profile/gradient charts

These charts contain a great deal of information crammed into a single graphic representation. Each chart is a combination of two graphs: one for profile information, with the elevation in feet along the left side; and one for gradient, with the feet per mile axis along the right side. Both graphs share the bottom axis, indicating river miles. In addition to elevation and gradient, additional location markers point to locations (in river miles) along the black profile line. Some abbreviations are used (for example, campgrounds are CG, parks are Pk., and creeks are Cr.) to reduce space.

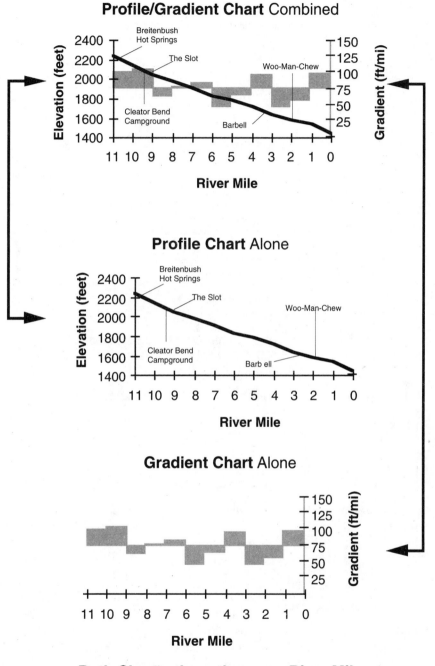

Like the combined profile/gradient chart, each individual gradient chart contains information about the steepness of the river over any given mile. The gray bars rise above and below the average gradient line for the entire river as shown below; as in other charts, they do not indicate the steepest single drop, but merely the *overall* drop in the river over the mile shown. The charts below show gradient distributed over 1 mile with a drop in elevation of 20 feet (a gradient of 20 feet per mile):

Gradient Chart Alone

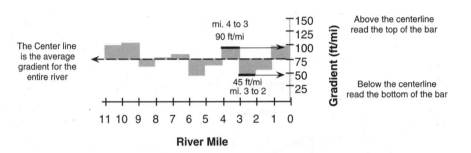

Within the mile or more of river charted the river gradient may not be continuous, but present steeper areas at waterfalls or pool-drop rapids.

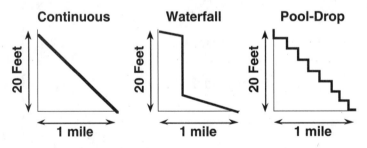

Hazards

A brief list of the major hazards on all sections of the stream listed. Route descriptions under "Going with the Flow" give more detailed information regarding specific hazards for each section.

Overview

A general description of the river, more wide-reaching than the more technical how-to information given elsewhere in the river entry. Some historic, camping, and scenic information is listed here.

Going with the Flow

A mile-by-mile description of each river section, including descriptions of rapids, scouting, and necessary information about how to run the section. Each section has its own header listing class level, recommended flow, and mileage. This information is more specific than the class and flow data given for the river overall.

Class designations

The chart below roughly defines the class ranking structure for paddlers, though many of the terms are vague or subjective, and difficult to interpret. There really is no absolute measure of difficulty for any given set of rapids, since each set can vary with water level, river changes, the condition of both paddlers and gear, and a paddler's experience on the stream. *Paddling Oregon* lists a class rating for each section of river in the book, based upon the level of difficulty as I viewed it, but I have not run all the rapids or stretches at higher or lower water to view seasonal changes. In most cases it is not difficult to imagine what a rapid will do with lesser or greater flows, but in some cases changes could be contrary to the listed suggestions. When in doubt, expect a more difficult classification. Ranking rapids, especially more difficult Class V's, is an art rather than a science.

Class	Level	Obstacles	Rescue	Scouting	Risk
Flatwater	Beginner	Smooth Surface	Self-rescue	As needed	Low
I	Beginner	Riffles and waves	Self-rescue	As needed	Slight
II	Novice	Wide channels, waves, some rock dodging	Some help may be required	Boat scouting and as needed	Some
III	Intermediate	More turbulent rapids with rocks and maneuvering	Aid often required/ exposed swims	Recommended	Moderate
IV	Advanced	Unavoidable waves, holes and routes; required maneuvers	Aid usually required; dangerous swims	Mandatory	High
V	Expert	Complex maneuvers required in turbulent, dangerous water	Team aid necessary; dangerous swims	Mandatory	Extreme
VI	Crazy/lucky/ magical	Nearly impossible routes; extreme turbulence and complexity	Team aid required; sweious swim risks	Are you kidding?	Death or injury very likely

LEAVE NO TRACE

Residents of Oregon have cared enough about their environment to show foresight and courage in protecting popular, sacred, and/or rare areas. Early establishment of state river access laws allowed free passage on Oregon waterways, though today many of these laws are being threatened by industry and private concerns. I hope that Oregonians will keep their environmental spirit in mind, along with recreation and wildlife, despite our state's rapidly changing population. We have the opportunity to set a new standard for river protection. Our larger rivers have suffered dams and pollution, but I am hopeful that we can restore health to our

11

injured systems and keep those that are free-flowing and pristine as wonderful tomorrow as they are today.

Responsible paddlers do their part, and follow no-trace principles as they run our state's rivers and streams.

THREE FALCON PRINCIPLES OF LEAVE NO TRACE
- Leave with everything you brought in.
- Leave no sign of your visit.
- Leave the landscape as you found it.

SAFETY

To ensure a safe and happy boating experience, paddlers should abide by the following rules:

Never boat alone

Always paddle in groups of three or more with at least two craft in case the need arises for assistance. Many proficient paddlers have died on easy stretches where they thought no significant hazards existed. Though solo paddling can be personally rewarding, we can't advise or recommend it. If you are going to do so anyway, stick to stretches with which you are very familiar and to sections that lie well within your boating ability. In addition, you should inform someone of your trip location and expected time of return.

Avoid drugs or alcohol on the river

Save the bottled fun for after the run! Though many paddlers enjoy beer on the river, we don't recommend it. Save the party for off-river, where you are far less likely to endanger yourself or others. It is easier to relax and reflect on a day's experience from a chair beside a fire. Many a knight has been christened "Helmet Knight"—in paddling circles, folks who have overindulged are "knighted" with a river helmet that must be worn for the duration of their last night on the river, then are baptized by a splash of holy river water the following morning. Which brings us to . . .

Never boat a rapid or section that you do not feel up to doing

Though peer pressure can be strong and running many demanding rapids successfully can be good for the ego, follow your heart and stomach as much as your head. When in doubt, opt for the portage or take the day off. Know your ability at the moment, not what you are capable of doing.

And know your ability before you go. Keep in the proper condition to run at the level you are boating.

Use appropriate gear in good working condition

Never use faulty equipment that is too worn or unsuitable for the task. Use only gear that is intended for its purpose, and make sure you have the recommended

Be thoroughly versed in safety and rescue procedures before undertaking technical runs and travel with paddlers who are equally versed. JASON BANKS PHOTO

equipment for the class you are running—and know how to use it. Turn to Appendix A for checklists that can help you collect the appropriate gear for stream run.

Using proper gear also means wearing a life jacket or personal flotation device at all times, and a helmet in all water that ranks Class II and above. Wear proper gear for the weather, terrain, and water temperature.

Scout any drop, bend, or rapid that you cannot see

Avoid surprises: when in doubt, stop and scout! Always make sure you have time to reach safety before committing to any blind drop or unclear route. Debris can shift to new locations without notice! Only commit when you feel secure that you can make the intended line, and have a back-up plan in case you miss your mark. Always consider the consequences of a mistake.

Advance in regular intervals with skilled and trusted company

Avoid jumping too far in the class scale too soon. Take several trips at a given level before you progress to the next step; be comfortable with your current level before moving up the scale. Paddle with people who are capable of running at the class you wish to run and whom you trust to aid you as needed.

ONE LAST THING

Paddling pursuits are enjoyable, but they also are dangerous. Water sports require special skills, planning, common sense, and equipment. This book is intended as an aid to those who wish to run the rivers and creeks of Oregon (plus parts of nearby Washington and Northern California). We include information in this book to help paddlers make informed decisions about the region's rivers. The paddlers themselves still must assume the risk that floating these streams entails.

Be warned in advance that we researched and wrote this guidebook under certain stream conditions. You may encounter something different on the water. Streams are ever-changing entities with constantly moving debris, boulders, and banks. They are not static. They change with varying flow and weather. On every return to a familiar stream I encounter new waves, new or changed rapids, shifting debris, and different flows. Treat every trip as a first descent and be prepared for any conditions you might encounter.

Paddlers should be properly trained by certified instructors or programs before they attempt the runs in this book. In addition, we recommend you always paddle with trusted companions, have proper equipment in good condition, and know rescue techniques. Never paddle alone, and always paddle within your comfort zone and level of difficulty.

Good luck and enjoy!

1 Alsea River

Clemente County Park to Alsea Bay

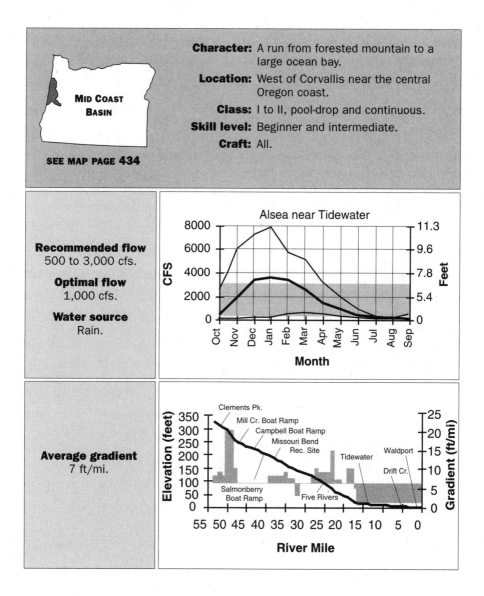

Character: A run from forested mountain to a large ocean bay.

Location: West of Corvallis near the central Oregon coast.

Class: I to II, pool-drop and continuous.

Skill level: Beginner and intermediate.

Craft: All.

MID COAST BASIN

SEE MAP PAGE **434**

Recommended flow
500 to 3,000 cfs.

Optimal flow
1,000 cfs.

Water source
Rain.

Alsea near Tidewater

Average gradient
7 ft/mi.

Hazards: The entire 52 miles of the Alsea River contain few rapids and no obstructions. Trees line the river in all sections, contributing potential log hazards (though no log hazards were observed in late 1996). At low flows the river becomes shallow and rocky.

Access: From Interstate 5 south of Albany, take Exit 228 to connect with Oregon Highway 34 (the Corvallis–Lebanon Highway). Follow OR 34 through Corvallis and Philomath to reach the Alsea's southwest fork. There OR 34 and U.S. Highway 20 separate; OR 34, now called the Alsea Highway, leads to all access locations and connects with U.S. Highway 101 on the south side of Alsea Bay in Waldport.

Overview: The Alsea River meanders for more than 50 miles through Oregon's coastal mountains to Alsea Bay and the Pacific Ocean. Paddlers can view much of the river from OR 34, but the road leaves the river in places. Hillsides are forested with a mixture of evergreen and deciduous trees, with more deciduous trees along the river. Numerous pullouts along the road complement the area's many boat ramps, campgrounds, and parks, allowing boaters to choose from an endless array of access points.

Look for good campgrounds east of Tidewater, especially Slide Campground and Blackberry Campground along OR 34. Paddlers can find additional sites along Forest Road 33 and near Five Rivers to the south (Maples Campground), or along Forest Road 3462 (Canal Creek Campground) before OR 34 crosses the river to the north. Those who can travel self-contained from an upstream put-in can stay overnight at one of the campgrounds, continuing to a downstream take-out the following day.

The Alsea River is a common drift boat stream with good fishing for steelhead, as well as for coho and chinook salmon. Since the fishing season coincides with the boating season, paddlers should stay clear of lines and areas where anglers are working the water. Politely ask where to pass if in doubt. Power boats are common below Tidewater and within Alsea Bay. Low-water channels between tidal flats and marsh areas make navigation difficult for fishing boats, so give them ample room to pass.

Going with the flow

Class: I (II)	Recommended flow: 500 to 3,000 cfs	Miles: 52

The Alsea River is good place for beginning kayakers or canoeists to practice river skills, since it has few rapids or hazards. Watch for small rapids and a small, Class I+ ledge-drop below Blackberry Campground (River Mile 22.6); **Rock Crusher,** containing rocks, channels, and a ledge with small waves, about 0.4 mile below Mike Bower Wayside (RM 21.2); and **Hellion** rapids (RM 19.1), where faster Class II water forces boaters toward the rocky right bank. The rest of the river contains Class I water with small waves, pourovers, eddies, and rocks to dodge. Boaters can avoid all rapids by boating upstream or downstream of the 3.5-mile area between RM 22.5 and RM 19. At flows below 3.5 feet at Tidewater, the river becomes shallow and rocky, making it more difficult to roll and navigate.

The Alsea River splits into North and South forks west of the town of Alsea. Though we do not explore them here, both forks have been run by paddlers and are reported to be Class I and II respectively. See the guidebook *Soggy Sneakers* (Corvallis, Ore.: Willamette Kayak and Canoe Club, 2nd ed., 1990), for details.

Access Area	RM*	Side	Notes
Mill Creek Boat Landing	47.0	R	Covered bridge over the river.
Campbell Boat Landing	42.3	R	After Maltby Creek on the right.
Salmonberry Boat Landing	40.2	L	Bridges above and below.
Missouri Bend Recreation Site	37.6	R	
Fall Creek Park	32.2	R	Private park (fee required).
Digger Mountain Mill Bridge	30.8	L	Private property beyond bridge.
Stoney Point Boat Ramp	29.6	L	
Launching Forest Camp	25.0	L	Park facilities.
Blackberry Campground	22.6	L	Boat ramp and camping.
Mike Bauer Recreation Area	21.2	R	Picnic area.
Quarry Hole Boat Ramp	20.0	R	
Hellion Rapids Boat Ramp	19.0	R	
Barkleys Boat Ramp	17.2	R	
Kozy Kove Boat Ramp	11.2	R	Below Tidewater
Taylors Landing	8.5	R	
Happy Landing	8.4	R	
Oaklands Marina	5.0	L	
Fishin' Hole Trailer Park	4.8	L	
Drift Creek Landing	4.5	L	
King Silver Boat Ramp	4.3	L	

* river mile

2 **Breitenbush River**

Hot Springs to Detroit Reservoir

MIDDLE WILLAMETTE BASIN

SEE MAP PAGE **436**

Character: A river through a lush, forested, rock canyon with hot springs.

Location: North-central Oregon, near Detroit.

Class: III+ and IV, technical pool-drop.

Skill level: Upper intermediate and advanced.

Craft: Kayaks and canoes.

Recommended flow
500 to 1,700 cfs.

Optimal flow
1,000 cfs.

Water source
Rain, snowmelt, and springs.

Average gradient
75 ft/mi.

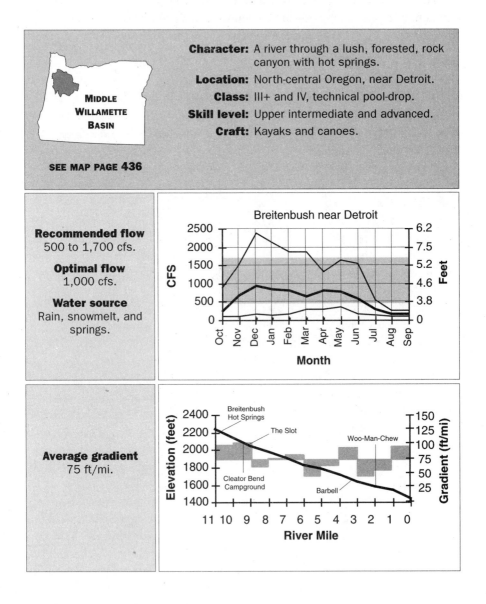

Hazards: Logs are ever present on the Breitenbush River. The water is cold and swift. **Barbell** (Class IV) has a regular hydraulic on the right that could recirculate a boater and gear indefinitely at higher water. Scout **Woo-Man-Chew** on the drive to the river; look for a small roadside pullout on the river's left bank. Scout **The Slot** for debris from Cleator Bend Campground before putting in.

Access: Reach the Breitenbush River from the north by following Oregon Highway 211 to Estacada, then taking Oregon Highway 224 along the Clackamas River to Oregon Highway 46. Signs point east to Breitenbush Hot Springs about 9 miles before OR 46 reaches Detroit Reservoir. Follow the road to the hot springs resort, or take it a short distance farther to a bridge across the river, an alternate put-in. You may have to pay a fee to use the parking lot and/or facilities at the resort if you plan to stay, soak, or eat. Not far beyond the turnoff to the springs on OR 46 is Cleator Bend Campground, which provides another put-in option. If you want a shorter trip, look for a few small pullouts along the highway; these have steep banks where boats could be lined down to the river.

From the south, follow Oregon Highway 22 along the Santiam River to Detroit Reservoir and continue around the reservoir to OR 46 and the Breitenbush River. From Cleator Bend Campground, OR 46 leads west to where signs indicate the road leading to the hot springs resort.

Take out at the stream gage 1 mile up the reservoir not far below Woo-Man-Chew rapids, or at Upper Arm Campground, just 0.5 mile farther. Alternately, you can take out at the town of Detroit, just a short paddle along the reservoir. All take-outs are on river left.

Overview: The Breitenbush River is spectacular, with crystal-blue water coursing through a rocky gorge. Its banks are steep and brushy most of the way, making a climb out difficult. (The road follows the river not far overhead in the case of a necessary carry or hike.) Vegetation is heavy, with logs spanning the water in locations. Log jams have been a problem in years past, but the recent floods have cleared out most of them with the exception of one necessary portage just below Cleator Bend Campground.

The Breitenbush provides ample Class III to IV action from start to finish. It's a great river on which to warm up your Class IV skills and start boating technical Class III to IV pool-drop water. Most of its rapids can be boat-scouted but require technical skill. Paddlers usually run the river during spring runoff, but ample water is available during the fall rainy season and at times in winter as well.

Breitenbush Hot Springs Resort provides vegetarian food, lodging, and hot springs for a nominal fee to supplement your river run experience. Campgrounds are available along OR 46. Don't forget your camera on this memorable trip!

Going with the flow

Class: III+ (IV)	Recommended flow: 500 to 1,700 cfs	Miles: 8+

Don't visit Breitenbush Hot Springs until you're done running the river, or you may not make it in—especially on those cold winter or early spring trips. Below the hot springs, the volume of the Breitenbush River is lower than it is downstream, since several creeks contribute to the flow later on. Scout the rapid known as The Slot, just below Cleator Bend Campground, before running; a log jam may block passage in the upper portion of this rapid. Lower tight slots were free of debris last time we checked, but large logs span the river in several places downstream and could shift at any time. Pools above many of the tighter blind bends allow one to read and run much of the river. Before attempting this run, paddlers should be comfortable maneuvering in tight spots to scout blind corners or drops.

The Breitenbush's upper gorge is quite dramatic, containing deep pools and rounded rock formations that line the banks as paddlers twist their way downriver. This upper portion contains many technical Class III to III+ rapids, each requiring more than one drop or maneuver. The many drops are too numerous to name, occurring every hundred yards. Look for pools toward the bottom of the drops for recovery.

Downstream, the rapids and river spread out. The drops are less complex than those upstream, but steeper. A difficult rapid to portage or scout, Barbell occurs a little more than a mile below the OR 46 crossing. Look for a rock division that channels water into the rapid's upper pool. At optimal or higher flows, run Barbell

Tom Arni shoots "Woo-Man-Chew" on the Breitenbush.

on the left, where a rocky technical slide drops into a pool. The right side contains a keeper regular hydraulic with a feeder eddy on the right. At lower flows one can boof the 6- to 8-foot drop with speed, but at higher flows the rapid, which resembles a manmade weir, could keep a boater and gear.

About 0.5 mile below Barbell is Woo-Man-Chew rapid. Unlike Barbell, it can easily be scouted on river left where there is a cement platform. Most boaters choose the slot left of center, but the 8-foot drop can rear-ender a paddler.

Below Woo-Man-Chew, those ready to take out should look for a trail leading to the road, on river left. Others may continue a short distance to the gage on river left and an easier take-out. Alternately, paddlers may wish to continue to Upper Arm Campground or the town of Detroit. Some report that, at lower reservoir levels, rapids continue to Detroit, though I've never run this section when water was low enough to see them.

Going with the flow
Section 1: Upper Brice Creek to Champion Creek

Class: IV+ to V	**Recommended flow:** 300 to 1,000 cfs	**Miles:** 3.2

Running the upper portion of Brice Creek means beginning with a tricky lead-in to a 15-foot waterfall. The fall is followed by a steep, narrow canyon. Proceed with caution, since logs abound here. Once out of the canyon, the river parallels the road and passes under a bridge. This bridge is a good put-in for a more sane Class IV+ run. Note that the run is much more constricted and pushier than it appears from the road.

Of all the rapids in the next stretch, only **Bubble Trouble** (River Mile 5.3) is hidden from view at a bend in the road. This steep, slanting ledge-drop pours into a boiling pool and is often run on the right. **The Snake,** just below, where a flat boulder blocks the center of the river, is generally run by entering on the right, taking a sharp left turn, then turning back to the right to complete the S-Turn. **Orthodontist's Nightmare** follows in less than a mile, named after a boulder with a nice protrusion at teeth level. It is often portaged or run down the center—if indeed there is a center. Since it is next to the road, scout it on the way up.

Lemans is the next rapid that requires quick turns: after a left entrance, move toward the center and then head back left to make a clean run. In a short distance, Hop-Skip-Splat sneaks up on boaters; eddies above it are few and small. Water cascades over this 12-foot drop onto a series of froth-covered boulders. Paddlers have run it every which way and survived, but the cleanest line is far left, or a portage along the road on the right.

Rick Dickensen maneuvers through a rapid on Brice Creek.

The run eases up somewhat to Champion Creek, which enters on the left signaling the take-out on the right.

Section 2: Champion Creek to Cedar Flats Campground

Class: IV to V	**Recommended flow:** 500 to 1,500 cfs	**Miles:** 3.8

Below Champion Creek, Brice Creek offers a few Class II to III warm-up drops before **Upper Trestle** rapid. This horseshoe-shaped drop is usually run by eddying out just above the drop on the right, then ferrying across the top of the horseshoe and dropping over the ledge on the left. You can scout **Lower Trestle** rapid from either right or left, but it is best to view it and Upper Trestle from the road on the drive up. The 6-foot ledge at Lower Trestle (also referred to as **Arthur's Ledge**) is usually run on the right, angling left. If you point too far right, the boiling waters in the small punchbowl below may redirect you back into the falls.

The next drop, **Pogo,** is easily scouted from the water. Slide up on the smooth rock island and take a look. The usual line follows the rightmost side of the left channel. The shallow lead-in makes for a difficult move at lower water. At low flows some boaters carry to a depression at the lip of the drop and slide in. It is an easy portage around this one. Calmer water allows a breather before reaching **Cheesegrater,** which is best scouted from the road. This long, broad, slanting, shallow ledge is run left of center. Entering too far right will push a paddler to the right, where a small overhang about head level greets the unwary. Also, the right wall is badly undercut, so take precautions!

Scout the next rapid, **Gumdrop,** on the drive up to be sure the left channel is clear. Check for logs in the downstream ledge-drop at the same time. The huge sweet "gumdrop" divides the channel just upstream. Run the ledge just left of center. The two drops here have also been called **Fun** and **No Fun.**

Paddlers encounter several more Class II to III rapids before the final major Class V folding drop known as Elvis's Viewing Room (or **Cedar Creek Falls**). A view from the road will give you an indication of where to pull out in order to scout at water level. A short, swift pool separates a sticky hole from a 15-foot waterfall. The object is to run far left, staying on the ledge and boofing off the end. If you happen to fall into the gyrating hole, there is a good chance you'll see Elvis, as one unlucky boater claimed after being underwater for a good 30 seconds. The upstream end of this hole leads into a 6-foot-long cave. This is a real easy carry; consider it.

The take-out at Cedar Creek Campground is about 0.2 mile downstream on the left. A nice set of concrete steps leads up from the water. The final 1.5 miles are mostly short Class III rock gardens, with some fun eddy-hopping. The next bridge, which marks the trailhead, is another good take-out option. Below it, the creek becomes a shallow gravel bar run with brush and wood to the Row River.

—Jim Reed

![4] Bull Run River

PGE Powerhouse to Sandy River

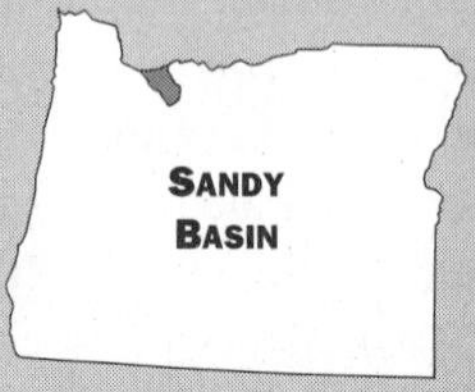

SANDY BASIN

SEE MAP PAGE **454**

Character: A clear river with conglomerate rock and undercut caves.

Location: Northwest Oregon, just east of Portland.

Class: III, pool-drop.

Skill level: Intermediate.

Craft: Kayaks and canoes.

Recommended flow
250 to 2,000 cfs.

Optimal flow
1,000 cfs.

Water source
Rain, diversion- and dam-controlled.

The river is run year-round except occasionally in late summer. Diversion from the Sandy River at Marmot Dam can increase flows.

Average gradient
74 ft/mi.

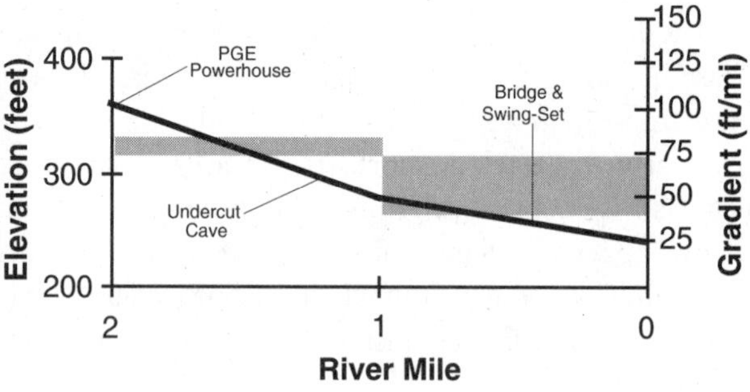

Low summer water on Bull Run. JEFF JACOB PHOTO

Hazards: Technical, Class III pool-drop rapids line the upper mile of the Bull Run River. The powerhouse at the put-in can release water suddenly, so boaters should pass quickly. **Pipeline,** along the lower Sandy River, is a long, hole-filled, Class III rapid often run as part of many trips.

Access: From U.S. Highway 26 just east of Gresham or south of Sandy, turn east on Bluff Road. Follow this road to Hudson Road, also heading generally east. Signs direct you to Dodge Park, which is the usual take-out. To reach the put-in, head east from the Dodge Park bridge and turn left at Lusted Road, following it for about 2 miles. Turn left at Ten Eyck Road, then left again at Bull Run Road. The Portland Gas & Electric Powerhouse is on your left, just across the bridge over the river. A parking lot awaits, and a steep trail follows the fence toward the river.

Overview: The Bull Run River provides the City of Portland with its municipal water supply. The water is taken from the river about 6 miles above the put-in and is supplemented by a diversion channel from the Sandy River for power. Two of the three water tunnels that supply water from the Bull Run were damaged in the 1996 floods, forcing the use of backup well water and limiting city water usage. It was "Water, water everywhere and nary a drop to drink . . . !" The PGE Powerhouse releases water into the lower Bull Run and may change flow suddenly. Boaters should stay clear of this area or pass quickly to avoid injury. PGE allows access down a trail near the parking area at the powerhouse; the path is steep down to the river.

The river is situated in a narrow, rocky canyon with impressive undercuts and large boulders. One particular undercut, about 0.5 mile from the put-in, looks inviting except for the rock that has fallen from its conglomerate ceiling. The riverbed is carved into rock, with little sediment, making the water crystal-clear. Abundant moss and ferns line its steep, lush banks.

The Bull Run can be paddled most of the year.

Going with the flow

Class: III	Recommended flow: 200 to 2,000 cfs	Miles: 2.5

The Bull Run River is a great place to begin boating technical Class III water. One of the best skills to have before attempting this river is a solid brace—don't forget to lean in to those rocks rather than away from them. The first few rapids are difficult to see, but usually have clear paths that zigzag down the middle. Some tight maneuvering is required, especially at low water.

After the first few Class III rapids in the first 0.5 mile, the river gradient eases somewhat and the routes become more straightforward. **Swing-Set** is the only named rapid on this river; it's located about 0.5 mile before the confluence with the Sandy River, just after paddlers pass under powerlines. The rapid was named for the cable crossing just downstream, which is still visible. The rapid contains big waves down the middle, but it is not so large or technical a rapid as those in the upper mile. Hike upriver along the right bank to make additional runs down this fun spot.

Many paddlers do the Bull Run in combination with the Sandy River, continuing for as many miles as desired. If you decide to take the same course, note that Pipeline rapid on the Sandy River, just below Dodge Park after the confluence, is the most significant rapid of the day. Novice boaters should scout the rapid from the park, on the left, before putting on. Oxbow Park is a good take-out for a longer day, containing several more Class II and II+ rapids and an additional 8 miles of paddling. A parking area across from Oxbow Park along the river's right side (where the water bends to the left) is an alternate site that will shorten the trip by 3 miles.

5 Butte Creek
Scout Camp to Pudding River

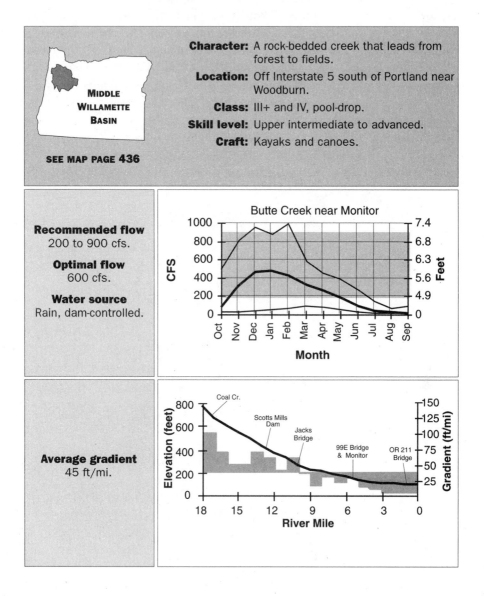

MIDDLE WILLAMETTE BASIN

SEE MAP PAGE **436**

Character: A rock-bedded creek that leads from forest to fields.

Location: Off Interstate 5 south of Portland near Woodburn.

Class: III+ and IV, pool-drop.

Skill level: Upper intermediate to advanced.

Craft: Kayaks and canoes.

Recommended flow
200 to 900 cfs.

Optimal flow
600 cfs.

Water source
Rain, dam-controlled.

Butte Creek near Monitor

CFS / Feet / Month

Average gradient
45 ft/mi.

Coal Cr.
Scotts Mills Dam
Jacks Bridge
99E Bridge & Monitor
OR 211 Bridge

Elevation (feet) / Gradient (ft/mi) / River Mile

Hazards: Scout **Splittin' Hairs** on the drive up to make sure it is free of debris. Two Class IV rapids in the upper section are technical. The first contains **Sucker,** a grabby diagonal hole near the bottom. The second, **Knuckle Buster,** has a technical lead-in to a larger ledge-drop. The rest of the major rapids are Class III pool-drops. Some contain narrow chutes; scout these for debris. Portage the dams at Scotts Mills and 2 miles farther downstream. The lower creek banks are brushy, and debris can collect in braided channels.

Access: To reach the take-outs from Interstate 5, take the Woodburn exit and follow either Oregon Highway 211 or Oregon Highway 214, depending on the take-out desired. Alternately, follow Oregon Highway 99E from the north or south to OR 214, OR 211, or Whiskey Hill Road. Each choice crosses Butte Creek heading east. Take a look to make sure there is adequate flow.

The upper take-outs and put-ins are accessed by following Meridian Road or Oregon Highway 213 to the town of Monitor. From Monitor continue south along Meridian Road to Mount Angel–Scotts Mills Road and turn east. Continue along Mount Angel–Scotts Mills Road for 2.5 miles past OR 213 to Scotts Mills Park, an alternate take-out. From the park, cross Butte Creek and turn right onto Maple Grove Road just a short distance beyond the crossing. Turn right again at Butte Creek Road after only 0.1 mile. Follow Butte Creek Road 4.5 miles to the pullout.

Paddlers may choose to put in above Butte Creek's upper bridges. These bridges are near private property, so obtain permission first. The uppermost put-in on the creek is below a Class VI narrow gorge along a road to the right that leads to a scout camp. Park along the road below the gorge for a scramble down the bank to a rock ledge put-in.

Overview: Separating Marion and Clackamas counties, Butte Creek begins in the forested hills beyond Scotts Mills and can be run to the Pudding River many miles downstream. Photographic scenes along this large creek are dramatic. Upper Butte Creek is also a great place to start boating Class IV rapids, since the rapids here are forgiving, yet technical.

Boaters will find the upper stretches (between the Class VI gorge and the OR 213 bridge) to have the best whitewater. Below the OR 213 crossing are more Class III rapids, but the creek meanders, slowly widens along agricultural land, and embraces many islands and piles of debris as it makes its way toward the Pudding River.

Going with the flow

Class: III (IV-)	Recommended flow: 200 to 900 cfs	Miles: 7 to 18

Above the scout camp along Butte Creek Road, the land and road become private property. Butte Creek gorge marks the beginning of the creek's practical boating area. Below the gorge itself (a turbulent Class VI channel), Class III pool-drop water stretches through beautiful moss- and fern-covered rocky walls. Below the scout camp, a steep climb to a ledge outcropping leads to a good put-in. An alternate put-in is back toward Scotts Mills at a small roadside pullout; look for it after passing some houses. Carry your craft and gear down the steep bank to the creek along a trail.

About 1 mile below this upper put-in is a narrow, Class IV rapid that separates into two rocky chutes we call Splittin' Hairs. The rapid is located at a private bridge downstream and can be viewed before putting on the river. At low water the rapid can be scouted from the creek's central rock island, but at very high flows it may be covered. The usual route through it is along the left side of the right channel, dropping into a narrow slot with a pool at the bottom.

Below Splittin' Hairs the creek continues with Class II water that builds to Class II+ and III. The creek slides down some technical drops with one larger drop that winds through a narrow passage into a small gorge. In another mile, paddlers encounter the creek's first Class IV rapid. Scout it from the left bank and the center island. The rapid snakes through technical, rocky chutes at the top before dropping into a small hole midway into the rapid. This smaller wave-hole is usually not a problem—boaters crash through with a face full of water. After the middle drop the water rushes around a sharp right bend and drops into Sucker, a diagonal hole where water recirculates off of a protruding right bank and tends to grab boats and keep them. I've seen people swim here, getting flushed into the pool below. Run on the far left, hugging the left bank as you round the bend.

Chris Funk lines the drop at Knuckle Buster.

The next Class IV rapid is not far ahead. Known as Knuckle Buster, it follows a short rapid just below the recovery pool for Sucker. After running the small boulder garden, portage or scout Knuckle Buster along the right bank (paddlers can also walk the right bank after Sucker to scout.) The rapid starts with a technical lead-in on the left before dropping over a 5-foot ledge. The ledge-drop is more forgiving than it looks, but the upper technical lead-in has scraped many a knuckle. The creek narrows and drops through a turbulent passage into a narrow pool. Paddlers should have good technical ability before attempting to run this sequence.

Below the two Class IV rapids, Butte Creek keeps your attention with Class II water and a sharp S-turn Class III+ rapid. Scout or portage the latter on the right. Two more miles of Class II water with a couple of Class III horizon line drops lead to Scotts Mills Park and Dam. There are some nice surf waves before the dam; catch them if you can. Walk the dam on the left or run the fish ladder, also on the left. The ladder drops awkwardly down and around a sharp right bend before it enters below the dam. (It also contains low, spiky bushes that almost ruined my dry top.) Class II+ to III- rapids follow in pool-drop fashion for the next 2 miles. After that distance is a second dam. Portage this dam on the left. It is an easy carry.

Steep, rocky banks along forested hills give way to brushy banks and open space below Scotts Mills Park. Below the dams, the creek contains more Class III rapids, evenly distributed between calmer Class I and II water. Before reaching the OR 211 bridge, the creek widens. Islands begin to appear, and paddlers may encounter debris in the various channels. Butte Creek enters the Pudding River just a couple of miles below the OR 211 crossing. Those who wish to do so may continue to the Whiskey Hill Road bridge along the Pudding River for a slower float through an agricultural region. Because the river current slows, its channels are commonly blocked by debris, making occasional portages necessary.

6 Calapooia River
Thirteen-Mile Bridge to Brownsville

Character: A run through clearcut hills to farms and grazing lands.

Location: South of Corvallis near Holley.

Class: II to III, pool-drop; continuous Class I+.

Skill level: Beginner to intermediate.

Craft: Kayaks and canoes.

MIDDLE
WILLAMETTE
BASIN

SEE MAP PAGE 436

Recommended flow
600 to 2,000 cfs.

Optimal flow
1,200 cfs.

Water source
Rain and snowmelt.

Average gradient
13 ft/mi.

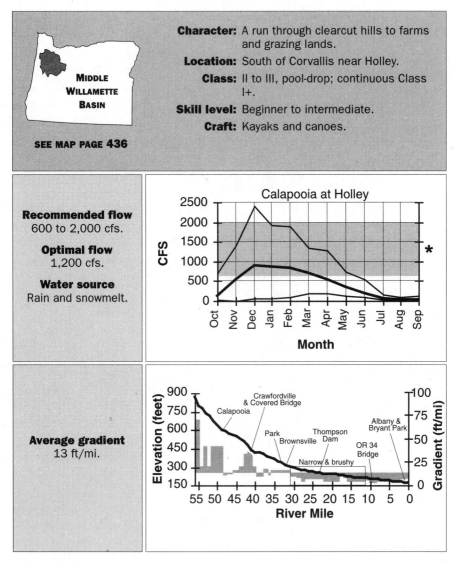

* No depth measurement available.

Hazards: Logs are the major concern on the Calapooia River. Two portages have been required along the upper river since the floods of 1996. Two limbos under logs are also required. Much debris is piled along riverbanks and gravel bars. Rapids are generally straightforward boulder gardens or ledge-drops. The most difficult drops are **Dollar Drop** and **McKercher** rapid. Both are Class III+ at higher water and Class III at lower water. Most beginning paddlers should avoid McKercher Rapid.

Access: From Interstate 5 take the Brownsville exit (Exit 216 near Halsey) east along Oregon Highway 228. OR 228 leads to Brownsville where a city park on river right provides a good take-out just downstream of the bridge. Not far after OR 228 crosses the river to the north, a small riverside pullout allows a good view of McKercher Rapid. McKercher Park is just up the road on river right before you reach the small town of Crawfordsville, allowing good access to the lower section of river. Most paddlers will wish to avoid McKercher rapid by putting in at the pullout downstream.

Farther up OR 228 is the town of Holley. Upper Calapooia Drive leads southeast from Holley along the Calapooia River for upstream access. Bridges and pullouts allow access in several places. A common take-out for the upper stretch of river is just before the Four-Mile Bridge, 3.4 miles above Holley. You'll have to climb up a steep bank with prickly bushes, but it's not too bad. A small side road just beyond the bridge makes a good parking spot.

Scout **Dollar Drop**, about 2.5 miles up the road beyond some small abandoned structures, on your drive up. This is the most difficult of the Class III drops on the river. Continue upstream roughly 9 to 10 miles to a gated bridge over the river (Thirteen-Mile Bridge). Good put-in access is down a trail on the left.

Overview: The Calapooia River winds for more than 60 miles from Albany to foothills of the Cascade Range. Recent clearcuts mar the landscape along the river, but the river corridor is lined with deciduous trees and is still very scenic. The area is diverse, with rocky gorges, gravel bars, sandy beaches, small cliffs, and open farm and grazing lands along the river's lower stretches.

Most of the Calapooia's rapids are on the easier side of the class scale. Routes through them are generally straightforward and easy to read from the boat. The riverbed is wide for a stream of such small volume, hence the need to run the river at flows above 600 cubic feet per second. At lower flows the river is bony in places, and paddlers will find themselves "flintstoning" their way through short shallow stretches. Flows over 800 cfs are sufficient to cover most of the rocks.

Going with the flow
Section 1: Thirteen-Mile Bridge to Four-Mile Bridge above Holley

Class: II+ (III)	**Recommended flow:** 650 to 2,500 cfs	**Miles:** 10+

Some paddlers put in farther upstream for a Class I+ warm-up, but most opt to put in at the upper bridge because of its easy access. From here, the river offers

0.5 mile of continuous Class II+ rapids. Soon the rapids taper off to Class II boulder gardens with an occasional Class II+ area among mostly Class I+ water. This is a great place for advanced beginner paddlers with good Class II skills and experience to begin advancing to Class II+ and III water. Most of the rapids in this stretch are forgiving and generally flatten or pool at the bottom for recovery. Shallow water can make recovery difficult in the event of a flip, but higher water adds the concern of faster current and bigger hydraulics.

The most difficult rapid on this stretch is located across from the abandoned town of Dollar and is called Dollar Drop. It is easily scouted on the drive up near some small buildings along the right, about 2.5 miles from the lower bridge. If you don't like what you see, you can easily portage the drop along the right bank. Below Dollar Drop, a couple of Class II areas break up the Class I+ stretches. Take out above the lower bridge on the right up the steep bank, at easier pullouts along the upper road, or continue to Section 2 and take out at Holley, McKercher Park, or Brownsville.

Section 2: Four-Mile Bridge to Brownsville

Class: I to II (III+)   **Recommended flow:** 650 to 2,500 cfs   **Miles:** 12.5

The Calapooia's lower section is an easier Class I+ float from the Four-Mile Bridge to Holley. The waterway passes through farmlands and offers a couple of Class II rapids. Below the covered bridge at Crawfordsville, a more difficult Class II drop can easily swamp an open canoe. McKercher Park follows in about 1 mile on the right. Take out at the park, since Class III+ McKercher rapid is just beyond!

Pouring through slots formed in the rock, McKercher rapid drops around boulders and pourover ledges. Scout the rapid on the drive up from a roadside pullout just below McKercher Park if you intend to run it. It is the most difficult rapid on the river, and beginning paddlers should avoid it.

Below McKercher Park and rapid, easy Class I water meanders to Brownsville (River Mile 32). Beginners should portage a weir about 3.5 miles below McKercher Park. Take out at the city park on the right in Brownsville beyond the second bridge. Below this point, the river narrows and becomes bushy and overgrown as it loses water to irrigation, making boating impractical. However, the lower stretch near Albany is often a worthy paddle along flat water or Class I water.

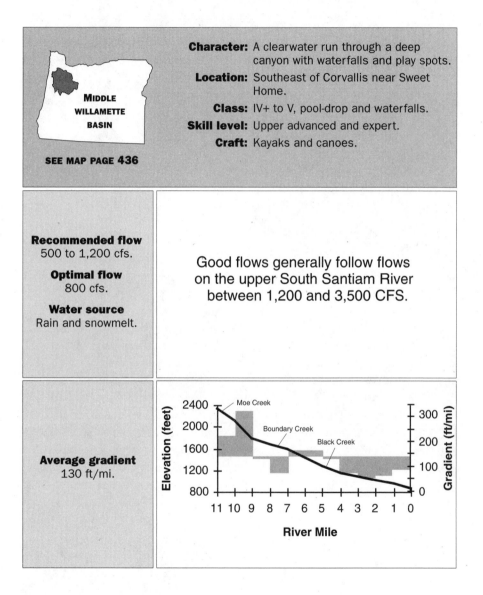 7 Canyon Creek
Seven-Mile Bridge to South Santiam River

Character: A clearwater run through a deep canyon with waterfalls and play spots.

Location: Southeast of Corvallis near Sweet Home.

Class: IV+ to V, pool-drop and waterfalls.

Skill level: Upper advanced and expert.

Craft: Kayaks and canoes.

MIDDLE
WILLAMETTE
BASIN

SEE MAP PAGE **436**

Recommended flow
500 to 1,200 cfs.

Optimal flow
800 cfs.

Water source
Rain and snowmelt.

Good flows generally follow flows on the upper South Santiam River between 1,200 and 3,500 CFS.

Average gradient
130 ft/mi.

David Gilmore runs a drop on Canyon Creek. JIM REED PHOTO

Hazards: Canyon Creek has three primary rapids stretches. These are continuous, moderately steep, and always contain shifting wood. The river pushes hard at high flows when wood hazards are the primary concern. **Judgment Day** rapid contains road construction rock, making the potential for pins greater.

Access: U.S. Highway 20 crosses Canyon Creek about 18 miles east of Sweet Home. Turn north on a short spur road on the east side of the bridge to reach the take-out. Reach the put-in by crossing the US 20 bridge onto Forest Road 2022, continuing 7 miles to the next bridge and put-in.

Overview: The floods of 1996 caused more dramatic changes in rapid structure on Canyon Creek than any stream I have paddled in Oregon and southern Washington since these events. The creek continues to provide technical fun for Class V paddlers despite the changes.

The Canyon Creek drainage has been heavily clearcut, but vestiges of its inherent beauty still shine through. The creek contains many continuous boulder gardens and multipitch drops. A significant amount of wood is always present, so keep your attention glued to the creekbed, especially at higher flows. Forest Road 2022 runs 100 feet above the creek on the right, allowing a grunting hike out if necessary.

Going with the flow

Class: IV and V	**Recommended flow:** 250 to 1,000 cfs	**Miles:** 7+

For the first 0.5 mile of the Canyon Creek run, this quiet, meandering stream greets paddlers with a pleasant warm-up. The fun begins soon after, as paddlers spot the upcoming 100 feet of Class III rapids. The Class III segment ends with a 4-foot pitch into a pool above a tight double drop known as **Chocolate Chips.** One or two boats can get out on the right at the edge of the drop to scout. The hole at the bottom of the second pitch has been known to rear-end boats or toss them around.

What follows next is 300 yards of Class IV boulder garden. Below this is **Chicken Little,** a major rapid composed of several segments. The 1996 floods moved a large number of boulders around in the entrance drop. Run the drop to a pool above a sharp right bend in the channel. Scout the next set of pitches on the left and portage left if wood dictates. Follow the flow through the next three pitches to where the creek bends left at a rock wall. Scout the following boulder garden from either bank, looking closely for existing wood. This boulder garden is a hoot at higher flows, ending with 3- and 4-foot pitches into a canyon. Eddy-scout for wood as you progress.

The creek continues with Class IV, low-intensity rapids to two 6-foot ledges. Eddy-scout for wood and a clean line through. Watch out for holes at higher flows! **Green Demon** presents itself 300 yards downstream. Here the creek narrows to a deep slot; the Demon has been run, but wood can wedge in the slot below the surface. Scout or portage along either bank.

About 0.5 mile of Class III water leads to the sweet boulder garden known as **Terminator.** This rapid and the following one, Judgment Day, are visible along the drive to the put-in at the road's narrowest spot—both should be obvious to those paying attention. Terminator is a roller-coaster ride, and some of its holes have tossed ill-prepared paddlers. A pool immediately below the boulder garden announces Judgment Day. Scout on the right since rock dramatically shifted in the floods, making potential pins a greater concern here. Several initial pitches can be run, but you may want to avoid worse lower pinning spots by portaging. Make your decision when scouting.

Downstream, the boulder action continues for 100 yards to where the creek enters another canyon. A steep pitch leads into the 400-yard canyon, where wood and rock limit your options. Scouting is not easy here, but the center line is usually kind. Several moderate drops entertain paddlers. The recent floods removed a huge log jam. Eddy- and bank-scout as needed.

Flatwater follows for roughly 2 miles. A significant narrowing of the creek signals upcoming **Osprey** rapid. Scout this long, narrow rapid on the right, paying close attention to wood and holes. A 6-foot ledge-drop occurs 200 yards downstream, followed in less than 0.3 mile by a narrow slot-drop. Run the main flow to the left to avoid a hole center-to-right.

A mile of Class III water follows, and the creek gorges up again for some Class III drops. After passing under the US 20 bridge, paddlers should watch for the take-out on the right. You may wish to continue downstream and along the South Santiam River for a longer trip, but the creek itself is usually plenty for a day's effort.

—Jens Mullen

8 Canyon Creek—Washington
Seal-Launch above Fly Creek to Lake Merwin

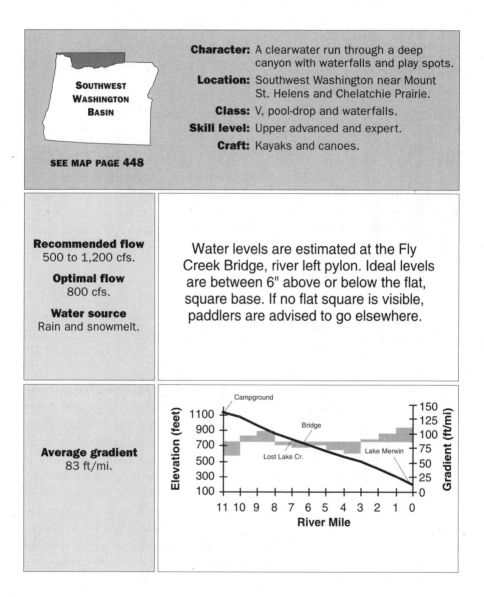

SOUTHWEST WASHINGTON BASIN

SEE MAP PAGE **448**

Character: A clearwater run through a deep canyon with waterfalls and play spots.

Location: Southwest Washington near Mount St. Helens and Chelatchie Prairie.

Class: V, pool-drop and waterfalls.

Skill level: Upper advanced and expert.

Craft: Kayaks and canoes.

Recommended flow
500 to 1,200 cfs.

Optimal flow
800 cfs.

Water source
Rain and snowmelt.

Water levels are estimated at the Fly Creek Bridge, river left pylon. Ideal levels are between 6" above or below the flat, square base. If no flat square is visible, paddlers are advised to go elsewhere.

Average gradient
83 ft/mi.

Hazards: Canyon Creek combines many pool-drop rapids with extended boulder gardens and exciting waterfalls. The rapids and falls can be quite forgiving at lower water, but holes become big and powerful at higher flows. At upper levels the consequences of a missed line will often be extended, out-of-control surfing, followed by a swim. Logs and other debris (such as cars) have a history of moving around in Canyon Creek, so be cautious. When in doubt, scout. Should you find yourself needing to hike out, find a route along the cliffs on river left.

Access: The upper stretch on this creek is not currently accessible from any easy shuttle route due to washouts along the road. Judging by the size of the washouts (huge), it looks as if the road will be out for some time.

To reach the take-out at Lake Merwin, take the 179 Street/Battleground exit off Interstate 5 just north of the Oregon border. Follow signs to Battleground along Washington Highway 502 east. At the outskirts of Battleground, turn north on Washington Highway 503 and follow it past the Mount St. Helens National Volcanic Monument Headquarters to Chelatchie Prairie, marked by the Chelatchie Prairie Store on your right. Continue past the store about 1.5 miles to a single-lane bridge over Lake Merwin with a large pullout on the right. Take out up the steep gully on the same side of the bridge as the pullout.

To reach the put-in, return to the Chelatchie Prairie Store and take a left immediately past it. Follow this road until you reach a single-lane bridge over Canyon Creek, just downstream from the Fly Creek confluence. This is the bridge from which to gage the flow (see recommended flow, above). Either put in here, or continue along the same road for another mile to a large pullout on the right with a faint trail leading down to an exciting seal-launch.

Overview: Canyon Creek combines challenging whitewater with beautiful scenery despite heinous logging along the drainage. This run has it all: boulder gardens, tight gorges, and waterfalls. At low to medium flows, Canyon Creek is an excellent run for those who are just beginning to paddle more difficult creek runs. At high flows, it can humble the best of paddlers. All in all, Canyon Creek is one of the classic runs in southwestern Washington and should not be missed by paddlers with the skill and experience to run it!

Now the bad news: Canyon Creek is presently endangered by a proposed hydroelectric project. The project would take virtually all of the creek's flow into an 11-foot diameter pipe at a point about 0.5 mile below the Fly Creek confluence and bring the water directly to the existing hydroelectric facilities at Lake Merwin Dam. Come paddle this creek and see why it is worth protecting.

Going with the flow

Class: IV+ to V	Recommended flow: 500 to 1,200 cfs	Miles: 4

If you start your day's run at the upper put-in, you'll wake up with a 12-foot seal-launch into Canyon Creek's cold water. Just downstream you will encounter your first rapid, **Final Exam,** named for the last rapid on the impractical run above the one described. If Final Exam feels close to your limit, consider taking out at the bridge just below the Fly

Mike Olsen finds the right spot on Canyon Creek in Washington.
MILAN CHUCKOVICH PHOTO

Creek confluence. Those short on time can also put in at this bridge, but this means missing the seal-launch and Final Exam warm-up. Either way, check the water level on the bridge pylon from your boat to confirm what you saw from the top of the bridge.

Fun Class II to III water brings you to a great play hole known as **The Wheel,** with a big eddy on the left if the level is good. Enjoy this play spot, but don't wear yourself out—the meat of the run is still to come! More Class II to III water leads past a beautiful waterfall flowing in from river left. Next comes the first gorge, where a couple of logs extend from the left shore into the middle of a steep drop and mark the beginning of the real action. Scout this narrow rapid from river right, make sure to check that the gorge below is free of logs. The scenery following this first drop is beautiful and typical of southwest Washington creeks. As you reach a calm pool following the gorge, look up to see a bridge high overhead. It's often used for bungee-jumping, so you may see some jumpers.

Just below the bungee-jumpers' bridge is **Terminator.** A mean diagonal hole at the base of this drop has claimed many swimmers; paddle hard and punch it on the left. This move is best scouted from river right just above the drop. The pool below Terminator is relatively small, so move through it quickly to assist any swimmers. Next is a steep ramp that is difficult to scout; try looking from the left shore and the right eddy directly above the drop. As you come down the ramp, thread your way between a couple of large holes on the right and an overhanging rock on the left.

Relax for a moment and enjoy the scenic springs tumbling in from the cliffs on the left. But don't let up for long. A ledge that cannot be seen downstream clearly marks **Thrasher Prelude;** scout from the left bank. The next drop, **Thrasher,** is also scouted from the left. If the water is high enough, there is a sneak chute on the left. The boulder in the center of this drop has moved in recent years, but the hole below remains burly.

Soon afterward, the river opens up and enters a Class IV to IV+ boulder garden. At the bottom of this boulder garden is a drop with a violent hole. Snag an eddy on the right above the last ledge to scout. A few hundred yards of Class II to III paddling will bring you to an eddy on the right above 18-foot **Big Falls,** which plunge into a large punchbowl formation with undercut walls on both sides. This waterfall drop looks heinous, but generally has been forgiving. That's a very good thing, because there's nowhere to portage!

After a large pool below Big Falls, another Class IV boulder garden and a few Class III rapids bring you to two waterfalls in combination, both of which can be scouted, portaged, and photographed on the left. The first falls, **Champagne** (10 to 12 feet), is normally run off the prow in the center. The next drop, **Hammering Spot** (12 to 15 feet), should be boofed hard on the far right unless you wish to discover that this drop is aptly named. The next big ledge has some boulders hidden in the landing, so keep your nose up to avoid a piton or vertical pin.

One last play spot marks the entrance to Lake Merwin. At the reservoir, a paddle of about 1.5 miles allows time to reflect on the day's run. Stay left to reach the bridge; take out up the left bank on the upstream side.

—Jed Weingarten

◼9◼ Chetco River
Slide Creek to Pacific Ocean

Character: A wilderness run through old-growth forest with rock exposures.

Location: Southern Oregon coast near Brookings.

Class: I to V, pool-drop and continuous.

Skill level: Beginners to advanced and expert.

Craft: Kayaks and canoes; all craft on lower river.

SOUTH COAST BASIN

SEE MAP PAGE 446

Recommended flow
500 to 3,000 cfs.

Optimal flow
500 cfs.

Water source
Rain and snowmelt.

Average gradient
25 ft/mi.

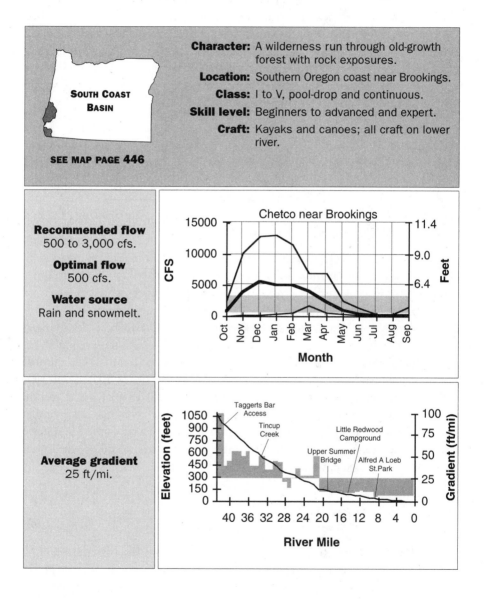

Hazards: The wilderness section of the Chetco River is remote with rapid challenges and hazards that may be difficult to portage. The Kalmiopsis Wilderness contains an abundance of poison oak and extremely steep slopes. The lack of soil along the river makes packing out all human waste necessary; take self-contained gear for overnight trips. Downstream in Section 2, **Chetco Gorge** and **Conehead** contain Class V rapids that must be scouted, with a portage recommended. Other Class III and IV rapids must be negotiated along this section. Below Low Water Bridge the river is easier Class I and II water, but paddlers should note strong upstream winds and tidal influences below Social Security Bar.

Access: Follow U.S. Highway 101 (the Pacific Coast Highway) to where it crosses the Chetco River south of the town of Brookings along the southern Oregon coast. Off US 101 on the north side of the river, the North Bank Chetco River Road heads east. Take this road to reach take-outs at Social Security Bar Boat Ramp and Loeb State Park. To reach the river's upstream put-ins, follow the road farther into the national forest where it becomes Forest Road 1376. Use a Siskiyou National Forest Map for upper road reference.

Overview: The Chetco River offers a wide variety of boating opportunities. The river contains two main runs and a lesser-known wilderness run along its upper reaches in the Kalmiopsis Wilderness Area. Upstream of Loeb State Park, the river resides within Siskiyou National Forest. The scenery here is a spectacular combination of old-growth forest and rock exposures. The whitewater section of river, including the Chetco Gorge, is remote and the wilderness section is even more so.

Salmon and steelhead fishing is excellent on the Chetco, with abundant drift boat and bank anglers. The uppermost wilderness section (Section 1) is rarely run, usually at low water during spring and early summer. The whitewater section (Section 2) is run by kayakers in winter and spring and, less frequently, by rafts. Innertubes or inflatable kayaks are the craft of choice in late spring and early summer, when extensive portaging is required. A variety of craft take to the lower, flatwater section (Section 3) once the water warms up.

Going with the flow
Section 1: Slide Creek to Tolman Ranch

Class: II to IV	Recommended flow: 400 to 800 cfs	Miles: 14

Section 1 of the Chetco River requires carrying your equipment between 3 and 14 miles through the Kalmiopsis Wilderness Area, depending on your selected put-in and condition of your four-wheel-drive vehicle and chain saw. The two possible put-in areas for this stretch are Taggerts Bar and the mouth of Slide Creek. The shuttle can take anywhere from a couple of hours to the better part of a day, and the hike to your chosen launch site can take the better part of a day as well. All but the last 2 miles of this 14-mile Class II to IV stretch are within the Kalmiopsis Wilderness. The run requires a minimum of two to three days to complete under typical low water conditions.

At low water, much of this wilderness stretch is Class II and III water meant for discovery. Anyone attempting to run the upper Chetco during winter and spring should be an expert paddler prepared to portage difficult, rugged terrain. Be prepared for the worst and hope for the best. Take experience, film, and precautions. Leave only footprints.

Section 2: Tolman Ranch to Low Water Bridge

Class: III to IV (V)	**Recommended flow:** 400 to 800 cfs	**Miles:** 6

The upper 1.5 miles of the Chetco River's middle stretch contain Class II rapids and gravel bars where sandstone and shale bedrock have allowed the river to cut a wide channel. Densely forested slopes and a near-wilderness setting are breathtaking and more than make up for the mellow whitewater. The channel narrows where the bedrock changes to a rainbow-hued mixture of red, white, and green chert. This unusual rock is composed entirely of skeletons from microscopic plankton called radiolaria, which lived about 150 million years ago. Even a small piece of chert contains skeletons from tens of thousands of individual plankton.

The chert, which is hard and resistant to erosion, constricts the river channel to create rapids. Over the next 2 miles the rapids are mostly Class III, with two Class IV pool-drops in close succession toward the middle. Scout or portage the Class IV rapids on river left. The channel widens in the next 0.5 mile where Class I and II

Candy Cane Rapid above Conehead on the Chetco. ANDERSON PADDLES PHOTO

water leads toward a steel bridge. The bridge provides a take-out alternative for those who do not wish to enter the gorge 0.5 mile downstream.

The Chetco Gorge begins with a long Class V rapid. Paddlers can make a moderately difficult scout or portage along the right through a talus pile of large, colorful chert boulders. Conehead, a spectacular, house-sized, cone-shaped boulder of rainbow chert, is located a few hundred yards downstream of the gorge's first major drop. Itself Class V, Conehead is easily portaged on the right. Paddlers usually take this option, since this rapid dives into an undercut ledge and holds a good number of logs. Though Conehead has been run, on the right, I don't recommend it.

Below Conehead the bedrock changes to sandstone and shale. The channel widens as the river eases to Class II for 1.5 miles to a take-out on river left at an old low water bridge site. An alternate take-out is 1 mile farther at the mouth of the South Fork Chetco River.

Section 3: Low-Water Bridge to Pacific Ocean

Class: I to II	Recommended flow: 400 to 800 cfs	Miles: 20

The lower Chetco River is gravel-bed, Class I and II water dominated by an aggressive fleet of drift boats, which flock to the river between the first fall rains and early April, when the fishing season ends. Fishing for steelhead is excellent here, but the competition is fierce. River etiquette is important: approach anglers with respect, asking where they would like you to pass, and avoid paddling through their drift.

This section includes several access points. Many boaters put in at the mouth of the South Fork Chetco River on river left. Access is easy here, but a sweeping turn against the left bank immediately downstream of the South Fork can cause trouble for novice paddlers if the current is strong and debris is trapped there. A popular take-out is on the left at Redwood Bar. An upstream, spring-and-summer thermal wind can be strong downstream of Redwood Bar, a popular put-in for boaters who take out at Loeb State Park, downstream on the right.

The quality of the scenery decreases and the amount of wind increases downstream of Loeb State Park as the Chetco flows through private property. Boaters who put in at Loeb typically take out on river right at Social Security Bar, which is the approximate upstream limit of tidal influence. Those wishing to extend their journey to the ocean can take out in the harbor on river left downstream of the US 101 bridge.

—*Ron Sonnevil*

10 Clackamas River, Upper

June Creek Bridge to North Fork Reservoir and River Mill Dam

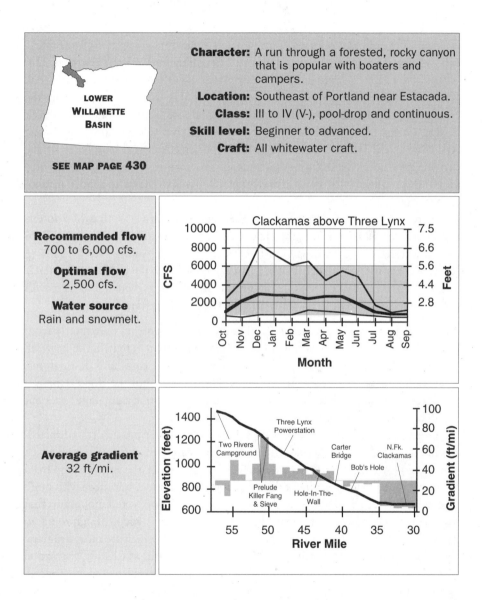

LOWER
WILLAMETTE
BASIN

SEE MAP PAGE **430**

Character: A run through a forested, rocky canyon that is popular with boaters and campers.

Location: Southeast of Portland near Estacada.

Class: III to IV (V-), pool-drop and continuous.

Skill level: Beginner to advanced.

Craft: All whitewater craft.

Recommended flow
700 to 6,000 cfs.

Optimal flow
2,500 cfs.

Water source
Rain and snowmelt.

Clackamas above Three Lynx

Average gradient
32 ft/mi.

Hazards: Cabled logs may still present hazards on the upper river (Section 1). **New Killer Fang, Prelude,** and **The Sieve** require a scout and/or portage. In Section 3, **Hole-in-the-Wall** and **Carter Bridge** rapid are more hazardous and should be scouted by first-time boaters.

Access: To reach take-outs and put-ins from either Interstate 84 or Interstate 5 follow Interstate 205 to Oregon Highway 212 and then to Oregon Highway 224, which follows the Clackamas River. Continue along OR 224 past the North Fork Reservoir to one of many possible access options. The usual access spots are the South Fork Clackamas River bridge near Memaloose Campground, Fish Creek Bridge, Carter Bridge, and Three Lynx Power Station. OR 224 becomes Forest Road 46 beyond Three Lynx, where Two Rivers Picnic Area and June Creek Bridge provide good access to the upper sections. At this writing, the road beyond Three Lynx Power Station was gated at the bridge, but was expected to reopen to two-lane traffic.

To reach the upper sections via an alternate route, drive south on I-5 to Oregon Highway 22 near Salem, then take OR 22 to Detroit Reservoir where FR 46 can be accessed along the Breitenbush River to the north. Another route to FR 46 follows Oregon Highway 26 beyond Sandy and Clear Lake to Forest Road 42. Take FR 42 to Forest Road 58, continuing along FR 58 to where it intersects with FR 46 near Two Rivers Picnic Area and the Ripplebrook Ranger Station.

Overview: The Upper Clackamas River is an Oregon favorite, particularly from Three Lynx Power Station to North Fork Reservoir. Boaters may chose between runs that rank from Class II to Class IV, depending on access and destinations. Access may be interrupted at times above Three Lynx until the flood-damaged road is completely repaired. Traffic currently is allowed along a one-lane road, but it will be restricted during reconstruction of slide areas.

Campsites are plentiful along OR 224 and FR 46, but most Portland metropolitan area paddlers make day trips since the area is just an hour's drive away. OR 224 follows the river closely, but is high enough above the river to keep from intruding. Local paddlers often take the scenery for granted, but those who don't frequent the river will admire the sheer cliffs and steep, fir-covered mountains that line the rocky confines of its clear blue water. The river is wide enough to allow more than one route down many of its pool-drop rapids, which are more dramatic than the average gradient indicates. Most of the river rates at Class II, with good play waves and holes that punctuate calmer stretches. Its rapids are evenly spaced, Class III drops with pools near the bottom. The few Class IV rapids can be avoided by altering your put-in location; see the section descriptions below. Scout the river from the road on your drive up OR 224, but be aware that many rapids are not visible from the road without a scramble down steep banks.

The general character of the river has remained the same since the 1996 floods. Hole-in-the-Wall changed briefly, allowing an easier skirt of the hole on the right, but it is now back to its original character. The famous **Bob's Hole** series of play waves and holes below the river's last Class III rapid was filled in by gravel in the 1996 floods. The wave holes are returning, though, and locals hope that they will once again provide an arena for the Bob's Hole Rodeo, held in May and sponsored by the Oregon Kayak and Canoe Club (OKCC). Also in May, the Northwest Rafters Association sponsors slalom events at Carter Bridge and downriver races for all types of craft below Three Lynx.

This large river provides ample flow throughout the year for a good variety of craft close to the Portland metropolitan area. Rafts have a harder time at flows below 1,200 cubic feet per second when the river becomes shallow and rocky. Rafting Section 2 requires a portage at The Sieve and a mandatory run of New Killer Fang.

Going with the flow
Section 1: June Bridge to Collawash River

Class: III (III+)	Recommended flow: 500 to 3,000 cfs	Miles: 7.5

Paddlers have avoided this section of the Upper Clackamas River in recent years due to logs cabled into the riverbed by the Forest Service. Many of the logs have been washed out or buried over the past few years, allowing a reasonable run of this enjoyable section. Paddlers should remain cautious, however, since logs or cable may still be present.

The upper river volume is less than half that at the Three Lynx Power Station stream gage because the Collawash and Oak Grove forks contribute significantly below Two Rivers Picnic Area. Spring and fall rains, snowmelt, and steady flow from the Olallie Lakes basin provide adequate flows during all but the summer season. The upper river rarely has too much water, and flows above 4,000 cubic feet per second at the Three Lynx stream gage are minimal. Larger flows help to cover logs and provide more space to maneuver, but increase rapids difficulty and speed drift time.

One benefit to paddling this section is the added attraction of Austin Hot Springs, midway between June Bridge and Two Rivers Picnic Area. The privately owned springs steam up from the river left bank. Soaking pools once lined the river's right shore, but these were eliminated in the recent floods. Boaters may relax in the warm water but must not trespass along the private property to the right. Attempts to develop the property have failed so far.

Class III rapids punctuate the steady Class II water below June Bridge. More difficult Class III+ rapids occur 4 and 2 miles above the bridge leading to Forest Road 63, Bagby Hot Springs, and the Collawash River. Both rapids can be scouted from the road on the drive up.

Section 2: Two Rivers Picnic Area to Three Lynx Power Station (Killer Fang)

Class: IV (V-)	Recommended flow: 1,000 to 4,000 cfs	Miles: 8

Often referred to as the "Killer Fang" section of the Clackamas River due to the once-ominous rapid of the same name, Section 2 is the river's most remote run. It is also the most technically demanding area. Logs, landslides, and a serious gradient combine to create ever-changing conditions. Paddlers should assume that the rapids they encounter will be different on each trip, since debris shifts throughout the year.

Paddlers get a good warm-up in the first 2 miles as Class II water separates a few Class III areas. A large boulder fence begins the first section of more difficult water known as **Gates** rapid, followed by **Hole-in-the-River** on the left. Several blind corners follow the latter rapid, where debris and strainers may collect.

A mile farther downstream, the Oak Grove Fork of the Clackamas enters on the right. In another 0.5 mile the river banks sharply right off the left wall at a Class III+ rapid known as **Rocky's** rapid. Alder Flat Campground is up a trail here on the right. Paddlers having difficulty at this point should take out at the trail, since more serious rapids and hazards follow over the next 1.5 miles.

Drop Stopper is the first Class IV rapid just below the campground. Look for it where a large boulder at the bottom of a drop splits the river. A large landslide along the right bank is just upstream. Scout from the gravel bar on the left or along the steeper right bank. The river then eases for a mile or more before reaching Prelude rapid. Watch for a headwall on the left as a signal. Below it, the river is divided into narrow chutes that have pinned logs in years past. Scout or portage both chutes on the right.

Just below Prelude is Killer Fang. I viewed the Fang years ago before a landslide filled it in. At low summer flows in those days, almost all of the water disappeared under a rock ledge before surfacing downstream. It looked positively scary. The rapid has since been filled in by a landslide, but it may wash out and reveal its underlying dangers once again. The bad news is that while the original Fang was filled, a new rapid was created just downstream. This rapid, known as New Killer Fang, is a recommended portage and mandatory scout along house-sized boulders on the right bank. It ranks Class IV+ to V at most flows and is undercut along both walls below the left chute. Portage over and between the huge landslide and boulders on the right.

Just beyond, along the riverbank to the right, is The Sieve. Before the 1996 floods, landslides and a river-wide tree bottled up this boulder garden, making it a mandatory portage. The rapid was clean of debris after the floods, though a portage along the right at an expanded gravel bar is easy. **River's Revenge** is another Class IV+ boulder garden just downstream. It is the last of the big rapids in this section, collecting much of the debris that is washed downstream from the upper river. Take time to scout it on the right before attempting to run it.

The remainder of the trip rates Class II+ to either of two destinations: the OR 224 sandstone bridge in just over a mile, or the upriver side of the Three Lynx Power Station bridge. Both take-outs are on the river's left bank.

Section 3: Three Lynx Power to Bob's Hole

Class: III (IV)   **Recommended flow:** 1,000 to 8,000 cfs   **Miles:** 10

Section 3 is the run referred to as the "Upper Clackamas" by most boaters. It is one of the most frequently paddled sections of river in the Portland metropolitan area. Solo paddlers usually have little difficulty hitching a shuttle ride or connecting with other boaters. Bob's Hole is a popular take-out for runs from either Fish Creek, Carter Bridge, or Three Lynx Power Station. Intermediate-level paddlers can enjoy this section of the Clackamas with proper planning and care. Though it includes a couple of easier Class IV drops, finding the appropriate route makes these hazards less severe. Class II water separates the more difficult, pool-drop rapids described.

The upper put-in at Three Lynx Power Station, just over the bridge on river left, is a good launch site for all types of craft. Soon after passing under the bridge the river divides into a Class III rapid, where most of the flow channels right. The bouncy right path leads to a calm convergence at the bottom. In a short distance Powerhouse rapid bends to the left where a large pillow forms off a jutting right headwall. A recovery pool at the base of the drop follows, with strong eddies at most flows. Pass the powerhouse quickly, since flows may change suddenly.

The Narrows, rated Class III, follows in less than a mile; view from the drive to the put-in. Large diagonal waves build as the river current narrows into a turbulent passage here. Class II+ rapids punctuate the next mile before paddlers reach the

Chris Funk lines up for the Carter Bridge Rapid.

Roaring River. Rapids bend here toward the right where large waves and smaller holes are formed above the confluence with the Roaring River.

The section's first Class IV rapid, Hole-in-the-Wall (or **Headwall**), is roughly a mile below the Roaring River confluence. Several paddlers have died in this whirlpool pocket in the river's left wall, but no deaths have occurred since a ladder was placed in the upstream wall of the pocket in 1980; it leads to a trail that continues downstream to Fish Creek. The floods of 1996 diverted water away from the pocket, dropping the rapid's rating to a Class III, but conditions may change as debris is washed out. The normal route is along the left side of the river, avoiding a midstream hole then moving quickly to the right away from the corner pocket near the bottom. **Fish Creek** rapid is a mile downstream just beyond a bridge where the river divides at an island. Take either route around the isle, but the right side is wider and more visible. **Armstrong** rapid follows in a short distance as a bridge comes into view. Large waves bounce off the left side here toward the bottom.

Boaters often confuse the Armstrong Bridge for Carter Bridge, but Carter awaits downstream. **Carter Bridge** rapid is just around the bend from Armstrong. Scout it along the left shore, or from the bridge on the drive up. The normal route is along the far left after rounding a river-left boulder. Two large holes along the left side can be avoided by staying left of the first hole and paddling to the right just beyond it to miss the second wave-hole. At lower flows the upper hole is fun to play in, but it can be a little sticky.

Class III **Sling Shot** rapid and more Class II water fill the next 1.5 miles below Carter Bridge before paddlers reach **Big Eddy**. Rapids at both the entrance and exit of the large eddy are visible from the road. The rapid narrows and banks toward the right into the eddy, with large waves forming off the left bank. The exit rapid (sometimes called **Rock-and-Roll**) can collect wood, so scout it on your drive up. At high flows the easy left side is available, but the right is more fun; use it to wind down the technical entry to more moderate waves and holes.

In 0.25 mile **Toilet Bowl** rapid leads into waves of increasing size. At higher flows the waves are Grand Canyon sized as they squeeze toward the bottom. Small eddies on both sides allow paddlers to make their way back upstream for some dynamic eddy turns or attempts to surf the huge waves, which are generally too fast to catch. But don't linger too long—better surfing is found just downstream at Bob's Hole. Those who are ready to take out can do so easily just below Toilet Bowl, up a trail to a pullout on the right.

One of the most disappointing results of the 1996 floods was the temporary disappearance of the Bob's Hole series of surf waves and holes. The first of that season's floods deposited a huge gravel bar at the bend where some of the best surfing in the Pacific Northwest had resided, canceling the Bob's Hole Rodeo for 1996. Happily, Round Two of the 1996 floods cleaned out much of the main hole, and other holes also are returning. Paddlers often make a trip to Bob's for a day's practice. While working to perfect their rodeo moves, surfers should yield to traffic from upriver.

Section 4: Bob's Hole to North Fork Reservoir (Memaloose)

Class: II	Recommended flow: 1,000 to 10,000 cfs	Miles: 4

This section of the Upper Clackamas generally is referred to as the "Memaloose" section after the campground and tributary of the same name downstream. Novice rafters and paddlers will enjoy this relatively relaxing Class I trip with occasional Class II rapids at bends in the river. Most boaters on this section put in below Bob's Hole, or just above it at the pullout below Toilet Bowl, where an easier trail leads to the river.

The scenic river is the main focus of attention, with abundant side streams, birds, and enough paddling action to wake one from the dreamy environment during the first half of the trip. The road closely follows the river along this section for easy scouting on the way to the put-in. Lazy Bend Campground, on the right, provides a good take-out for a short run before reaching the slack water below the South Fork Clackamas River. Memaloose Bridge is just downstream for an alternate take-out. Below Memaloose Bridge the character changes to Class I, with the South Fork Clackamas entering on the left in less than a mile.

The canyon walls steepen at Big Cliffs as the road rises above the river, forcing paddlers to continue to Promontory Park and Boat Ramp on the right—an additional 2 miles—to reach an easy take-out. The current is slow once the river reaches the reservoir, so boaters should plan on taking more time to complete the last 2 miles. Several campsites within the Salmon–Huckleberry Wilderness line the left shore of the reservoir, accessible only by boat.

▐11▌ Clackamas River, Lower
River Mill Dam to Willamette River

LOWER WILLAMETTE BASIN

SEE MAP PAGE **430**

Character: A wooded run past parks and rural areas.

Location: Southeast of Portland near Gladstone.

Class: I to II, pool-drop.

Skill level: Beginner and intermediate.

Craft: All.

Recommended flow
700 to 7,000 cfs.

Optimal flow
2,500 cfs.

Water source
Rain and snowmelt.

Average gradient
12 ft/mi.

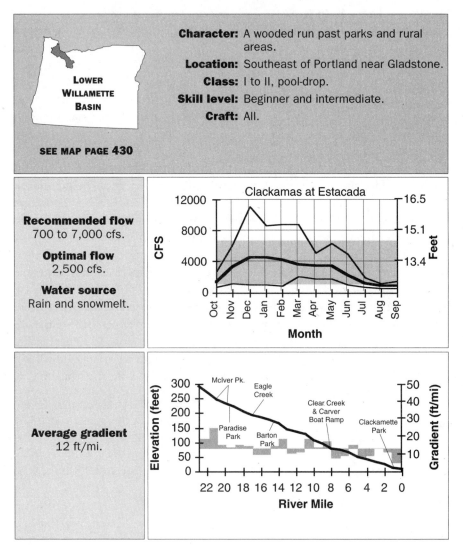

Hazards: The lower Clackamas River has numerous Class II rapids and a high volume that can produce powerful hydraulics, but it holds few hazards for properly prepared boaters. At flood stage many rapids wash out and new ones are created. Between Cazadero Dam and River Mill Dam lie more than 2 miles of Class III to IV+ whitewater. This section dramatically increases in difficulty with volume. Scout the most difficult rapids along the upper portion of this stretch from the road. One hazard along the lower portion of the river is the presence of motorboats.

Access: To reach put-ins from Portland, Interstate 84, or Interstate 5, follow Interstate 205 to Oregon Highway 212. Take OR 212 to Oregon Highway 224, which follows the Clackamas River. At the little town of Carver, turn right across the bridge to put in at the boat ramp on river right. Alternately, continue up OR 224 to Barton. At Barton, turn right. After crossing a bridge over the Clackamas River along Bakers Ferry Road, continue to Harding Road. Turn left and continue to Springwater Road, on the left. Follow Springwater Road to signs that direct you to Milo McIver State Park.

To reach the River Mill Dam or Paradise Park, stay on OR 224 past Barton and Eagle Creek. To get to Paradise Park, take Heipler Road to the right; the dam is farther along OR 224, along Mill Road to the right before you reach Estacada. Paddlers will have to carry craft and gear through a gate to the river at the dam.

To reach the different take-outs, use the above directions or take Oregon Highway 99 from Gladstone to reach Clackamette Park, just over the OR 99 bridge across the Clackamas. If boating the horseshoe loop in McIver Park, use the upper and lower boat launches in the park for a 2.5-mile run.

Overview: The lower Clackamas River is an excellent place to begin whitewater boating. The river is wide at normal flows, quite scenic, and uncluttered despite its popularity. Though people flock to the parks along the river to cool off and play in the water in summer, on the river one can still find a fair amount of solitude. In the section known as High Rocks, just a couple of miles upstream of Clackamette Park, swimmers often jump from cliffs to the deep, narrow river channel below. In places homes are visible along the banks, particularly in the last several miles. Respect the rights of property owners here, since they see a fair amount of river traffic.

Animals come to the river at night. Beaver have left evidence of their presence along the banks in many places. Paddlers often see eagles, blue herons, and osprey. Osprey have become so abundant along the river that fake utility poles had to be erected to transfer nesting sites from the real poles.

Going with the flow
Section 1: Cazadero Dam to River Mill Dam

Class: III to IV (IV+)   **Recommended flow:** 500 to 4,000 cfs   **Miles:** 2.5

This short stretch of the Lower Clackamas River between the dams makes a great ending segment for those who have just come from the upper river, an exciting start to a lower river run, or an enjoyable and scenic jaunt if time is short. The largest rapids are toward the top of the 2-mile stretch. Scout them from the road through the trees on the drive to Cazadero Dam from Estacada, deciding whether the flow is right for your desired excitement level. At higher flows, the rapids difficulty increases from Class II to IV+, and possibly Class V at very high water levels.

The riverbed is open and rocky at the top, slowly converging into a deeper, narrow stream with vertical banks. At low flows later in the season, beautiful, clear pools reveal schools of salmon. After passing under a bridge, the river flattens to River Mill Dam. Paddlers can find a good access area within the town of Estacada behind Sluggo's Diner on the southwestern side of town. The property is private, so obtain permission before parking or taking out.

Section 2: River Mill Dam to Carver

Class: II (II+)   **Recommended flow:** 700 to 5,000 cfs   **Miles:** 15

Access to this section of river can be had as far up as River Mill Dam, but anglers are common between the dam and Milo McIver Park. The river is easy Class II water until a Class II+ rapid presents some challenge for novices just below the McIver Park upper boat ramp. The Class II+ rapid called **The Minefield** by drift boaters is a good practice spot for negotiating larger waves and eddies. With the exception of a rock at the center top of the rapid, it is relatively free of rocks and debris at moderate flows. The current splits as it slams into the riverbank at the bottom. This rapid completely washes out at flood stage and has a fair surf spot at the bottom left at optimal flows.

Other Class II rapids along the river are straightforward but can still catch boaters off guard. Beginners should boat this section first with experienced paddlers, in larger groups, to avoid having a yard sale of equipment. The next two Class II rapids after The Minefield are more difficult than those farther downstream.

Try the river sections below Barton Park as a warm-up for the stretch below McIver Park. An often-run section is the Horseshoe Bend stretch; it runs from upper McIver Park to the park's lower boat launch area, and is an easy stretch to shuttle. This 2.5-mile stretch provides good entertainment for an after-work run close to the Portland metropolitan area.

Below McIver Park, the river continues in Class II character with longer stretches of flatwater. Paradise Park is only 0.5 mile below McIver for an alternate access. Eagle Creek enters the river on the right at River Mile 17.6, but is easily missed since an island separates the river at that point into two channels. Powerlines cross the river in another 1.5 miles, signaling that Barton Park is only 1 mile away. Watch for this section's many new gravel bars and large wood deposits along the banks. Take out at Barton Park on river right or continue to Carver Boat Ramp.

The stretch from Barton Park to Carver Boat Ramp is a popular stretch of river for beginning kayakers and canoeists. Several Class II rapids with obvious routes drop between flatwater floats. In a couple of places the river drops down rocky slides that scrape boat bottoms at lower water but provide nice surfing spots for beginners. The lower river toward Carver makes for a lazy float, giving paddlers the chance to relax and enjoy the scenery. Carver soon comes into view (look for the bridge); the take-out is on river left just after one final Class II drop into a popular fishing eddy. Clear Creek enters the Clackamas River just upstream of the Carver Boat Ramp.

Section 3: Carver to the Willamette River

Class: I to II	**Recommended flow:** 700 to 5,000 cfs	**Miles:** 5 to 22

The Lower Clackamas River eases up a notch from Carver to its confluence with the Willamette River. Some small, Class II riffles can be fun to surf or play on, but for the most part this section is flatwater with some sharp bends. The river narrows near High Rocks, where swimmers often jump from cliffs into the deep water below. More than one death has occurred here: swimmers rarely wear life jackets, the jagged rock entraps unwary feet, and currents are unpredictable.

Clackamette Park provides an easy take-out before the Lower Clackamas empties into the much larger Willamette River. Continuing along the Willamette is not recommended due to the number of speed boats and jet skis. The Willamette in this area is well known and easy to see, but provides little excitement for paddlers or other nonmotorized boats with the exception of morning sculling or paddling practice.

12 Clackamas River, North Fork

Upper Bridge to North Fork Reservoir

LOWER WILLAMETTE BASIN

SEE MAP PAGE **430**

Character: A run through an isolated forested canyon with brush banks and waterfalls.

Location: Southeast of Portland near Estacada.

Class: IV+ and V, continuous pool-drop.

Skill level: Upper advanced and expert.

Craft: Kayaks and canoes.

Recommended flow
250 to 1,000 cfs.

Optimal flow
500 cfs.

Water source
Rain and snowmelt.

Flows are generally estimated by the Clackamas River's Three Lynx Gage. Flows of 3,000 and rising to 6,000 and falling are adequate.

Average gradient
164 ft/mi.

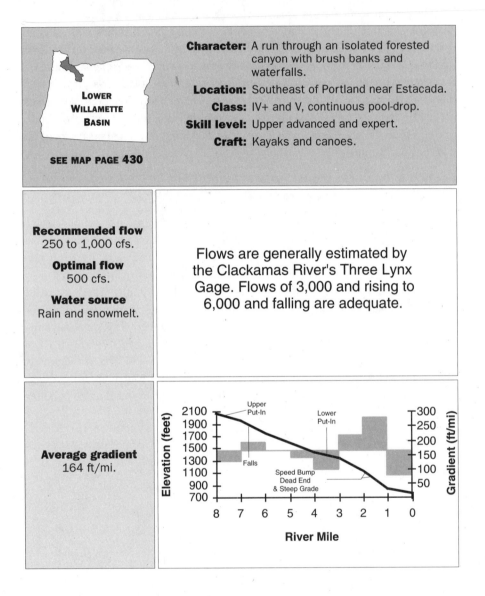

Hazards: Like wood? If not, stay off this river. Log portages, jams, submerged logs, and brushy banks all move wood around after higher than normal water. Expect to pin your boat every third trip. Only paddlers with stamina should attempt this run, since there is also a strenuous 0.25-mile portage with a scary descent around an unrunnable falls. The road, somewhere in the direction of heaven, is a mile from the river anywhere except the take-out. Hunters and anglers pack heavy artillery, and the area is a common four-wheel-drive playground.

Special note: New log hazards since the floods of 1996 and 1997 have moved wood to hazardous locations. Run and scout conservatively if you plan a trip along this exciting stretch.

Access: Follow Oregon Highway 224 from Portland east past Estacada and above the North Fork Reservoir Dam. At the bottom of the grade watch for a turnout on the left, just before the bridge over the North Fork; park here for the take-out.

To reach the put-in, continue east on OR 224 for about another 0.5 mile to a left turn. Follow the steep road to the left until it turns to gravel. After 0.9 mile, park at a bulldozed and blocked road on the left and start walking! The river is 0.75 mile away; you'll have to carry craft and gear.

Alternately, paddlers may put in an additional 4 miles upstream at a bridge and campground area just across the North Clackamas River.

Overview: The North Fork Clackamas River is one of the more difficult and intense rivers in the Portland area. Don't put on without Class V boating skills, good judgment, rescue equipment, and adaptability. The river canyon, heavily wooded with poison oak and blackberries, is incredibly steep; attempts to hike out will never be forgotten.

The river consists of very long, continuous Class III and IV+ boulder gardens, interspersed with 4- to 6-foot ledges; some even have pools after them. There is one great 20-foot waterfall just beyond the mandatory portage around **Dead End.** The last mile of Class III water is relaxing compared to what happens upstream.

Going with the flow
Section 1: Upper Bridge to Main Put-In Road/Trail

Class: IV+ (P)	Recommended flow: 300 to 800 cfs	Miles: 4

Paddlers have run the upper 4 miles of the North Fork Clackamas River, but the gradient is lower than in the canyon below, and fun water is not as continuous. The upper river also offers numerous logs for paddlers to portage and limbo under. Brush lines the banks here, infringing on the river in places. The stretch's three 10-foot waterfalls and one 20-foot fall were run in May 1995 by Michael Parent, Ron Blanchette, and Dave Northrup.

Section 2: Put-In Road/Trail to North Fork Clackamas Reservoir

| Class: V | Recommended flow: 300 to 800 cfs | Miles: 3.5 |

After a pleasant 0.75-mile descending hike to the river, paddlers reach a brushy put-in that introduces 0.5 mile of Class II+ water spiked with a few Class III rapids. Portage the giant cedar that appears in the water after a right-hand bend. Soon after this portage, Class IV+ water begins with **Blind Alley,** a 180-degree left turn against a vertical left wall. A short pool leads to **Manhole,** a 6-foot ledge-drop, immediately followed by a long, Class IV boulder garden with a rocky runout.

The river continues in this fashion for 1 mile, then breaks to the right off a headwall and behind a big log jutting from the right bank. At this point, watch for an old logging road/trail on the left in roughly 150 yards. Shoulder 'em and suffer. Below the trail is a wonderful 12-foot ledge known as **Speed Bump,** but don't run it—doing so makes portage angst increase dramatically. And portage you must, since **Dead End,** a 50-foot unrunnable falls, lies only 25 yards beyond.

When the portage trail descends and flattens, look for a scrappy descent through the trees to the river. Heading back to the water here is the much preferred route when compared to the muddy bank farther down the trail; here, at least, you've got handholds! Once you're in the water again, a few 3-foot ledges lead to the lip of **Steep Grade,** a 20-foot, two-tiered waterfall. Run left, since the first hole throws you back toward the right.

The next mile of river is a continuous Class III+ to VI+ boulder garden. Routes heading left of several islands are usually clear; pins are common in this stretch but rarely life-threatening. If you get pinned, stay in your boat until someone wades out and pulls you free.

Near the end of this wild stretch are a few hazards worth noting. The first is **Storm Drain,** a 6-foot ledge backed closely on the left by a large boulder with wood stuffed under it. Boof hard and flat to the right, since there are shallow shelves here. The next 150 yards run a terrifying gauntlet of wood that, miraculously, is mostly stacked up on the shore. Scout this section just to make sure. About 200 yards farther, a small pool signals the start of **Blind Double Date,** identified by a rock wall on the left and a few giant undercut boulders on the right. Around a sharp left corner are two vertical logs, not quite wedged against the left wall. No one has come to grief here yet, but scout right and listen to your intuition.

Just below the second part of Blind Double Date it's all over, except for a mile of Class III water and a few strainers before the lake. The North Fork Clackamas was run in January 1995 by Doc Loomis, Jeff Bennett, *et al.*

—Mike Parent

13 Clear Creek

Oregon Highway 211 to Clackamas River

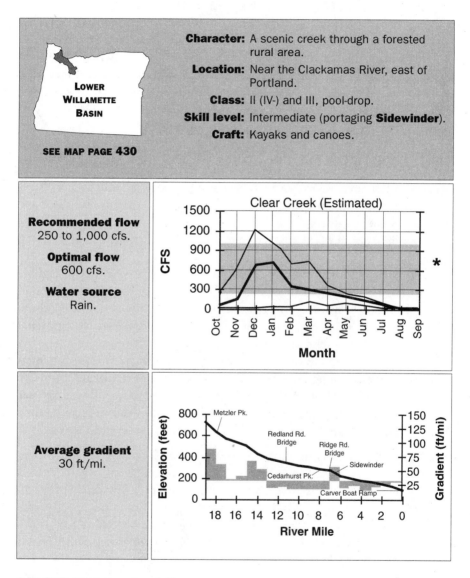

LOWER WILLAMETTE BASIN

SEE MAP PAGE **430**

Character: A scenic creek through a forested rural area.

Location: Near the Clackamas River, east of Portland.

Class: II (IV-) and III, pool-drop.

Skill level: Intermediate (portaging **Sidewinder**).

Craft: Kayaks and canoes.

Recommended flow
250 to 1,000 cfs.

Optimal flow
600 cfs.

Water source
Rain.

Clear Creek (Estimated)

CFS

1500
1200
900
600
300
0

Oct Nov Dec Jan Feb Mar Apr May Jun Jul Aug Sep

Month

*

Average gradient
30 ft/mi.

Elevation (feet)

800
600
400
200
0

Metzler Pk.
Redland Rd. Bridge
Ridge Rd. Bridge
Cedarhurst Pk.
Sidewinder
Carver Boat Ramp

18 16 14 12 10 8 6 4 2 0

River Mile

Gradient (ft/mi)

150
125
100
75
50
25

* *No depth measurement available.*

63

Hazards: Brushy banks, twisting bends, and possible fences are present along Clear Creek. The upper creek contains continuous Class II water with two Class III drops below Metzler Park. **Sidewinder** is a dangerous Class IV rapid in otherwise Class II water along the lower creek. It is located 0.25 mile below the Ridge Road bridge.

Logging in late 1995 along the right side of this creek dropped several logs close to the river, but only one portage was necessary farther down. In three locations along Clear Creek, fences could be drawn across the entire creek; they were pulled back to allow passage on our trips. One such location was just below Metzler Park, with another just after a nice yard on a horseshoe bend. The third fence was located about 2 miles before the Carver Boat Ramp take-out.

Access: From Portland or Interstate 205, turn east onto Oregon Highway 224 and follow it toward Estacada. At Carver turn right and go over the bridge that spans the Clackamas River. Turn left beyond the bridge on Springwater Road, then take the next left to Carver Boat Ramp. This is the take-out for the lower section.

To reach upper access points, return to Springwater Road (or continue along Springwater Road after crossing the Clackamas River) and follow it to Strowbridge Road. Turn right onto Strowbridge Road, which connects with Ridge Road before crossing Clear Creek at an alternate put-in or take-out site. **Sidewinder** rapid is only 0.25 mile below this bridge. Continue up Ridge Road to Four Corners, where Redland Road intersects your route. Take Redland Road left, crossing Little Clear Creek first, to reach Clear Creek for an alternate access.

To reach the uppermost put-in, follow Oregon Highway 213 east from Interstate 205. Continue along OR 213 to Oregon Highway 211, turning left on OR 211 (also called Union Mills Road) and taking it past Colton and Elwood to Clear Creek and the upper put-in. Watch for Upper Highland Road as a cue to slow down; it connects with OR 211 about 1 mile before you cross Clear Creek.

Overview: Clear Creek is an enjoyable run when the Clackamas and other rivers are running at high flows. The creek is surprisingly lush and green, offering the feel of seclusion even though it is relatively close to civilization. The creekbed meanders around many sharp bends. Look for nice Metzler Park in the upper stretch for a lunch break; the scenery is spectacular. Numerous huge trees have fallen across the river at several places in the upper 6 miles, but passage under them is easy. Private property lines much of the banks, so be careful and respectful when taking a break or portaging.

The lower creek meanders peacefully to Carver Boat Ramp, with the exception of Sidewinder. The creek rarely gets too high to run.

Going with the flow
Section 1: Oregon Highway 211 Bridge to Redland Road Bridge

Class: II+ to III	**Recommended flow:** 250 to 1,000 cfs	**Miles:** 8

Look at the Clear Creek water level before you launch to decide if there is sufficient flow. Flows of 5,000 to 8,000 cubic feet per second on the Clackamas River are often an indication of enough water. Just below the steep put-in bridge at OR 211, the creek starts off by pushing Class II+ water around a number of sharp corners with brushy overgrown banks. Class II water continues to Metzler Park, a good break spot or put-in. The upper half of the creek is steeper than what comes downstream, but not far below the park are two Class III drops that zigzag down the middle with visible routes. A newer cut along the right bank is visible farther downstream near some debris. Large trees span the creek in two or three places, creating dramatic scenery with easy passage beneath.

Section 2: Redland Road Bridge to Clackamas River at Carver

Class: II (IV)	**Recommended flow:** 250 to 1,000 cfs	**Miles:** 12

The remainder of Clear Creek is mostly Class II water, with the exception of the Class IV- rapid called Sidewinder, just below the Redland Road bridge. Here, a Class III rapid leads into an S-turn that pillows off logs on the outsides of both bends, creating particularly dangerous conditions. The rapid can be scouted or portaged on river right up the steep bank along an old abandoned road. Scout the S-turn before committing to the Class III lead-in, since you have little chance of stopping once you're into the rapid. Listen for the rapid and scout or portage it before rounding a left bend in the river. Below Sidewinder the river winds its way peacefully to Carver.

Deer Crossing

While paddling this creek in the spring of 1995, paddling buddy Jeff Jacob and I spooked a deer from above the creek. It ran down the bank toward where we sat on the water. Having ample momentum, it was unable to stop its descent and instead jumped over us as we floated by. Both of us reached for our cameras to get a shot, but the deer was gone before we could capture it on film. All we could do was smile at each other, wide-eyed at the scene we had just witnessed.

▓14▓ Collawash River
Upper Reaches to Clackamas River

Character: A clearwater river through a remote, forested canyon.

Location: East of Salem, a tributary of the Upper Clackamas River.

Class: III and IV (P), pool-drop.

Skill level: Upper intermediate to expert.

Craft: Kayaks and canoes.

LOWER
WILLAMETTE
BASIN

SEE MAP PAGE **430**

Recommended flow
700 to 1,500 cfs.

Optimal flow
1,000 cfs.

Water source
Rain.

Average gradient
70 ft/mi.

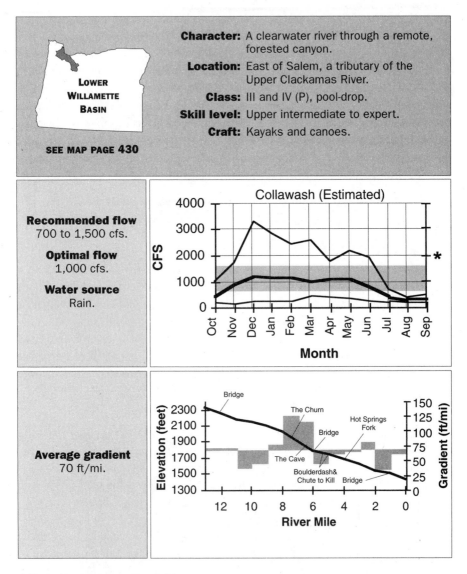

Collawash (Estimated)

*

* *No depth measurement available.*

Hazards: The entire upper Collawash River is a hazard; give yourself plenty of time to get down it safely. The upper canyon is very remote, so even if you hike to the road you will still be in the middle of nowhere. The difficulty of the Collawash rapids makes the upper run an experts-only affair. DO NOT consider this a leisurely afternoon trip, but rather a mini-expedition. The lower run has more Class III water, with a couple of long and difficult Class IV sections. Scout **Chute to Kill** and **Boulderdash** on the drive up.

Access: From Interstate 5 near Salem follow Oregon Highway 22 (the North Santiam Highway) 49 miles east to Detroit Reservoir. Turn left onto Forest Road 46 and follow it along the Breitenbush River for about 39 miles to Forest Road 63. Turn here and being looking for Two Rivers Campground, a good take-out for the lower section.

To reach the upstream put-in or take-outs, continue up FS 63 as desired. Scout Chute to Kill and Boulderdash 3.5 to 4 miles above Two Rivers Campground. The upper section can be viewed in places by hiking down the steep bank. Alternate access is along Oregon Highway 224 beyond Estacada and the Ripplebrook Ranger Station to Forest Road 46. FR 46 may be blocked at times in 1997 due to road reconstruction.

Overview: The upper reaches of the Collawash River may be the most obscure and infrequently paddled section of river in Oregon. This is bound to change. This is a river with two distinct faces: one is calm and serene, allowing paddlers to revel in the canyon's awesome beauty while floating in crystalline green pools; the other is a romping, stomping maelstrom of big, pushy whitewater complete with huge ledge-drops, sloping falls, and tight, technical Class V rapids. Even though the road follows high on river right, the entire Collawash is extremely remote. Its banks are very steep and composed of crumbling basalt covered by thick growth. Hiking out would be no fun.

The river's big drops show up in the second half of the upper run. These are obstacles to be dealt with cautiously. Wear good shoes to scout or portage, since there are no neatly groomed trails. Despite its hazards, the Collawash remains a premier run in a fairly accessible area. The section below Chute to Kill is Class III water that makes a good warm-up for the run downstream along the main Clackamas River. Boaters with above average skill can safely negotiate much of the lower river, and can scout the rapids from the road. **Only expert boaters should consider the upper reaches,** and only after paddling Class V water for some time.

If you're looking for an adventure that packs a punch, the Collawash may be for you. This is where the big dogs go to play.

Going with the flow
Section 1: Forest Road to Five-and-a-Half Mile Bridge

Class: V (P)	Recommended flow: 300 to 1,000 cfs	Miles: 8.5

The put-in at the FR 63 bridge allows plenty of warm-up in amazingly clear water. The Collawash's deep emerald pools look like green glass shattering with each paddle stroke. Riverbanks here are covered in dense old-growth forest, a reminder of what the entire area once looked like. Paddlers may spot otter lazily wallowing in the aquatic environment.

The river meanders for several miles with an occasional riffle to spice things up. One horizon line seems to confront paddlers, but on closer inspection it becomes a small drop of little consequence. Check for debris just to make sure. About 4 miles into the run is the largest log jam I have ever seen. This by itself is enough to discourage all but the most diehard paddler. Portage on the left, with a hike that takes 20 to 30 minutes to complete. Stay close to the tree line and don't get lost.

Once past the log jam from hell, get ready—the next 3 miles take off like an angry bull. Directly below the log jam on a bend to the right is a Class IV drop. In the pool below this drop, eddy out on the right and park your boats for a scout. The walk is long and arduous, but make sure you look at the entire drop ahead of you. Upon inspection, all but the most serious of boaters will opt to portage. This is hard Class V! I have only seen one brave soul run this drop, cleaning it perfectly. I was inspired to run only the bottom portion.

Below this rapid the river drops away. Take it slow and easy, since around the next bend is another big Class V drop, **The Churn,** which culminates in a tight, shallow ledge-drop. The lead-in to this rapid is tricky and must be run in order to scout or portage the crux move at the bottom. Portaging the lead-in rapid might prove to be difficult. The Churn has been run successfully, but pick your route carefully. The portage is on the left.

Downstream, paddlers encounter an almost constant barrage of Class IV to IV+ rapids. This is boating paradise. Almost all of these drops could be boat-scouted, but use extreme caution since the river changes from year to year. After about 1 mile of eddy-hopping through beautiful rapids, paddlers encounter a blind drop that looks menacing from above. A large boulder on the right with a chute on the left marks the spot. Get out on the little beach on the right bank and scout. Most of the water flowing down the left chute smashes into a monster undercut known as **The Cave.** There is only the thinnest of lines to take one clear of this mess; seriously consider the sneak route down the right. After clearing The Cave you can rejoice, because the take-out bridge follows a short paddle with a few more fun drops.

—Andrew Wulfers

Section 2: Lower Bridge to Clackamas River

Class: IV	**Recommended flow:** 800 to 2,000 cfs	**Miles:** 5.5

The lower Collawash River is not for the squeamish! Boulderdash is a long, technical rapid that merits a scout before putting on. Chute to Kill is a hazardous rapid in which staying upright is imperative. Scout to make sure the final drop is free of debris, since any blockage here could be fatal. Pull off the road about 3.5 miles above Two Rivers Campground and scramble to the river to look at the rapids. Paddlers have had to make at least one log-jam portage in the lower section in years past, usually in the less turbulent and less frequently scouted section above Boulderdash.

After the steep put-in at the lower bridge, a short Class II warm-up leads to Boulderdash. Because there are so many moves to try and remember, paddlers inevitably end up picking a path while on the river. Eddy-hopping and boat-scouting continue for over 0.25 mile of technical chutes and boulder gardens. Most routes are center to left at moderate flows, though some boulders have moved around since the recent floods. Wood often is present, but clean routes are usually available throughout.

Below Boulderdash, a 1.5-mile Class II section leads to Chute to Kill. Here a house-sized boulder juts out from the right bank on a right bend in the river. Stop upstream of the boulder and scout your route; this is also a good photographic vantage point. The rapid turns sharply to the right around the boulder, then moves back toward river center and a turbulent ramp containing several holes. Make

Chris Funk lines up for Chute to Kill rapid on Section 2 of the Collawash.

sure you are upright after this stretch, because there is only a short recovery stretch before the crux move to the left. A boulder at the bottom of the recovery separates the river into two chutes. The right chute ends in a deadly boulder sieve, and the left drops 6 feet into a narrow passage. The drop is more turbulent than it looks, but a calm recovery pool follows.

The Hot Springs fork of the Collawash enters 0.25 mile below this final Class IV rapid, bringing up the flow. Class II water follows for more than a mile before reaching a set of Class III pool-drop rapids. The rapids in this area are easier and less consequential than the earlier Class IVs. Boaters can scout from the river in most cases, and several rapids are visible from the road on the drive up. The last Class III rapid, **Up Against the Wall,** is not as difficult as the previous Class III drops. The lower rapids are evenly distributed along a 1.5-mile stretch that contains some great holes and waves for play.

Relaxing Class II water provides a nice cool-down for the last mile to the take-out at Two Rivers Campground. Paddlers may wish to continue along the Clackamas River for more Class II, III, and IV water.

▐15▌ Coquille River, South Fork
Upper South Fork Bridge to Middle fork

SOUTH COAST BASIN

SEE MAP PAGE **446**

Character: A rural run through scenic gorges and forests.

Location: Southern Oregon coast, near Coquille.

Class: I (II) to IV (V), pool-drop and continuous.

Skill level: Beginner to expert.

Craft: Kayaks and canoes.

Recommended flow
400 to 3,000 cfs.

Optimal flow
1,000 cfs.

Water source
Rain.

Average gradient
24 ft/mi.

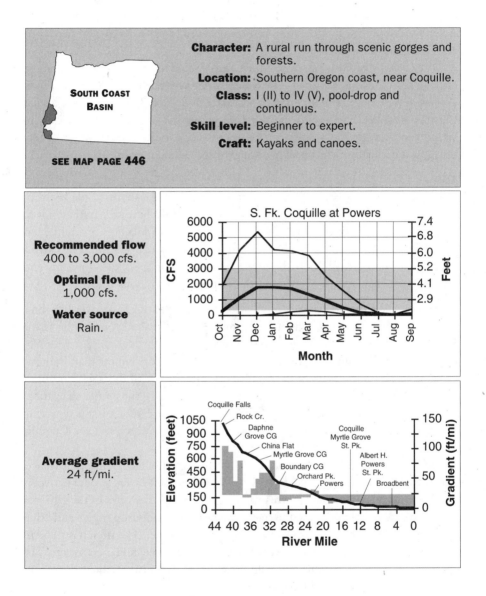

S. Fk. Coquille at Powers

Hazards: The South Fork Coquille River contains Class III and IV whitewater, with optional Class V rapids above the described sections. **Roadside Narrows** and **Hole-in-the-Wall** rapids demand respect and scouting from both the road and the river. **Powers Gorge** contains a Class III to IV drop. Portage the gorge on the right. A fish weir above the gorge should be portaged on the right. Keep alert for debris and logs along all stretches.

The Class IV rapids upstream of the Class V rapid in Section 4 are much more difficult than those in Section 3. The water can be very pushy at levels higher than 2.5 feet at the bridge. **Do not attempt Section 1 or Section 3 unless you are a solid Class IV kayaker.** The rapids are not continuous but are far too numerous to attempt to portage, and a swim can be ugly. Rolling in the shallow water of Section 1 automatically means bashing against rocks along the bottom.

Access: Take U.S. Highway 101 south of Coos Bay to Oregon Highway 42 (the Coos Bay–Roseburg Highway). Turn and follow OR 42 south to the town of Coquille and the Coquille River. Continue along OR 42 beyond Myrtle Point to cross the Middle Fork Coquille River. Just across the Middle Fork Coquille, Oregon Highway 242 branches right and leads to Powers and upstream access areas. It becomes Forest Road 33 at the forest boundary. For specifics on put-ins and take-outs for each stretch of river, see the sectional descriptions below.

Overview: The Coquille River offers a wide range of boating. The river has three main forks, but the most consistent, scenic, and best overall for boating is the South Fork. The most challenging stretch of water runs through the Siskiyou National Forest upstream of Powers, a little logging town more remote than Remote, Oregon. The upper section of the South Fork offers some of the finest and most scenic, technical water in southwestern Oregon. Class V+ runs other than those described include portions or Rock Creek and the South Fork Coquille upstream of the Upper South Fork Bridge (Sixteen-Mile Bridge). Watch out for **Coquille Falls** and portions of Rock Creek.

The entire South Fork Coquille is a scenic and worthwhile boating experience. The area is underlain by sandstone, with more resistant layers producing spectacular waterfalls on tributary streams. Once the South Fork leaves the national forest, the gradient lessens and the river switches from pool-drop rapids and boulder gardens to meandering gravel-bed Class I and II water. The stretch is punctuated by a low head dam near Powers and a Class III+ hole in Powers Gorge. The scenery also changes, moving from old-growth forest to pastures and private timberland in various stages of management.

The Middle Fork and North Fork of the Coquille are run infrequently (even the upper South Fork is run only a few times each year), so little is known about boating these portions of river. These rivers are relatively flat until becoming creeklike. Running through actively managed timberland and highly erodible bedrock, they lack the scenery and water quality for which the South Fork is known. Both the North and Middle forks require higher flows to run their whitewater stretches, and the water is usually turbid at runnable flows. These stretches of the river will likely remain obscure, due to a lack of boaters in the nearby population and the presence of more aesthetic runs in the Coos Bay area. Oregon Highway 42 parallels the Middle Fork along most of its length, detracting from the scenery but providing abundant access.

The upstream limit of tidal influence on the Coquille River is at the main river's confluence with the North Fork Coquille near Myrtle Point. Paddlers can canoe or sea kayak this section of river throughout the summer as it meanders through pastures to the river mouth at Bandon. Occasional debris hazards do exist on these lower flatwater reaches, particularly at low flows, but these typically can be negotiated or portaged. Water in the lower, flatwater portions of river (including the last few miles of the South Fork) can be very silty. Water quality and aesthetic values are greater upstream, along the South Fork above Coquille Myrtle Grove State Park.

Note: Gage and river levels for the Coquille are not available by phone. To check water levels, look for the markings on right-hand pier of the Upper South Fork Bridge. Run the stretches downstream of the forest boundary at much lower flows than areas upstream.

Going with the flow

Section 1: Upper South Fork (Sixteen-Mile) Bridge to Sucker Creek

Class: III and IV	**Recommended flow:** 400 to 2,000 cfs	**Miles:** 3.6

This demanding section of the river is a nearly continuous mixture of Class III and IV boulder gardens and closely spaced pool-drop rapids with 0.25 mile of flatwater near Daphne Grove Campground. The river is not easy to scout from the road. Watch for sweepers and logs. An 8-foot drop into a large pool is located on river right 0.5 mile downstream of the bridge at Daphne Grove Campground. Scout this drop from the trail beginning at the roadside pullout about 0.5 mile downstream of the bridge. The put-ins for this run are 100 yards upstream of the bridge near milepost 48 on the right, or immediately downstream of the bridge. Beware of rebar. Paddlers have encountered it immediately upstream of the bridge in past years, though none has been seen recently.

Section 2: Sucker Creek to Myrtle Grove Campground

Class: II (III)	**Recommended flow:** 400 to 2,000 cfs	**Miles:** 3.5

This stretch of river is straightforward Class II water with a Class III rapid just above the take-out. Sucker Creek is on river left, but put in on the right. The rough trail to the put-in begins at the downstream end of a paved turnout with two large fir trees; look between mileposts 51 and 52. An alternate put-in is located at the bridge across the river at China Flat Campground (River Mile 37).

Section 3: Myrtle Grove Campground to Coal Creek

Class: III (IV)   **Recommended flow:** 400 to 2,000 cfs   **Miles:** 3.1

Section 3 is similar to Section 1 in difficulty, with pool-drops predominant. The water is also deeper along this section, allowing runs at lower flows. The upper mile is not easy to scout from the road, but the remaining river can be scouted on the drive up.

Whitewater begins about 0.25 mile downstream of Myrtle Grove Campground with a Class IV rapid that initiates a 1-mile stretch of Class III and IV rapids. The rapids are closely spaced along the first 0.5 mile, gradually spreading out until the river eases to Class II for about another mile. Class II rapids abruptly end at Roadside Narrows, a 0.25-mile Class IV pool-drop that culminates at Hole-in-the-Wall rapid. This is the most difficult area within this section; scout it from the road (at milepost 57) before putting on the river. Hole-in-the-Wall is located after a sharp left turn in the road heading upstream. Horizontal marks from drilling and blasting are obvious in the rock slope above the road. The rapid is named after a person-sized hole on river left beneath an undercut boulder large as a Volkswagen, upstream of a 5-foot drop. At lower flows (less than 2 feet at the Upper South Fork Bridge) a significant amount of water goes through the hole, creating a hazard for anyone out of their boat—you might be sucked in. The hole is not obvious from the road and it is best observed from the pool at the bottom of the drop. It was filled in by the 1996-1997 storms, but could return at any time. Scout or portage on either side of the river.

Class III and IV pool-drop rapids with much longer spacing extend for 0.5 mile to Elk Creek. The next 0.5 mile between Elk Creek and Coal Creek is Class II water. Take out at Coal Creek (RM 31.4), the largest tributary stream, where the road crosses a double culvert.

Inspecting the outlet at Hole-in-the-Wall rapid. RON SONNEVIL PHOTO

Section 4: Coal Creek to National Forest Boundary

Class: IV (V)   **Recommended flow:** 400 to 2,000 cfs   **Miles:** 1.4

Ready for ratios? Section 4 is to Section 3 what Section 3 is to Section 1— similar, but with larger boulders, more water, and more difficult rapids. The road stays high above the river along this stretch, allowing only glimpses of the rapids. Just downstream of Coal Creek, the water becomes continuous Class IV for 0.25 mile, then turns into a Class V rapid that begins at a large boulder midstream at a left bend in the canyon. Scout or portage the Class V rapid on the right. Paddlers typically run the rapid along the right. Scout before putting on from a rough trail leading from a pullout 0.9 mile upstream of the national forest boundary sign, across the road from the junction with Forest Road 594. A shorter, steeper trail a few hundred feet downstream also leads downslope to the rapid.

Though the next 0.5 mile contains Class IV pool-drop rapids, the final 0.25 mile of this section is flat. The take-out is located on a small gravel bar with trail access from a pullout about 100 yards upriver from the national forest boundary sign next to the road. Walk the trail before putting on the river in order to recognize the take-out.

Section 5: National Forest Boundary to Middle Fork Coquille

Class: I and II (IV)   **Recommended flow:** 400 to 1,500 cfs   **Miles:** 22

The river channel widens and the gradient lessens at the forest boundary. This is due in part to the bedrock, which changes from relatively hard, layered sandstone to less resistant shale. The water is rated Class I and II except for a fish weir and a larger Class III+ to VI- drop in Powers Gorge.

The fish weir is located 0.25 mile above the bridge on the downstream edge of Powers. Scout or portage on the right. A low head dam is visible from the bridge; paddlers can access it from the road on river right just downstream of the bridge.

The 8- to 10-foot Class III+ to IV- drop locally referred to as **The Falls** is typically run or portaged on the right. The drop is located in Powers Gorge, about 1 mile downstream of the town of Powers. A long Class II+ to III- rapid provides a 0.25-mile lead-in to the drop. Scout both The Falls and the lead-in rapid from the top of a large rock at a pullout in the road 0.8 mile downstream of the first bridge in Powers.

Drift boats often run from Orchard Park, 1.8 miles upstream of Powers, to the fish weir. They also go downstream of Powers Gorge, putting in at the mouth of Baker Creek just upstream of Baker Creek Road bridge.

The next take-out for all craft is about 6 miles downstream at Coquille Myrtle Grove State Park. About halfway between the state park and Broadbent, the scenery becomes less appealing as the riverbanks shorten and erode. At low water watch for numerous obstacles, including trees and debris, along the lower river. The last take-out is at an old bridge site 0.8 mile upstream of the Broadbent Store, farther downstream. Other take-outs may be possible between Coquille Myrtle Grove State Park and Broadbent at various gravel pits.

—Ron Sonnevil

16 Crabtree Creek

South Fork Bridge to South Santiam River

Character: A stream that meanders from remote forest to an open rural area.

Location: Northwest Oregon near Albany.

Class: II to III+, continuous and pool-drop.

Skill level: Beginner to upper intermediate.

Craft: Kayaks and canoes.

MIDDLE
WILLAMETTE
BASIN

SEE MAP PAGE **436**

Recommended flow
500 to 2,000 cfs.

Optimal flow
1,000 cfs.

Water source
Rain.

Flows generally follow those on neighboring Thomas Creek. The creek is generally run from late fall through the spring.

Average gradient
37 ft/mi.

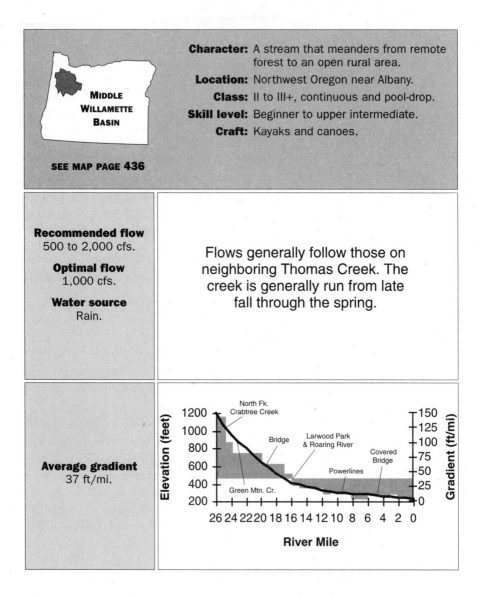

Hazards: Logs are the main concern on Crabtree Creek, particularly on the upper section. The upper 5 miles of Section 1 contain numerous difficult Class III+ pool-drop rapids. Beware of brushy banks and a fence on the lower section.

Access: From Interstate 5 near Albany take U.S. Highway 20 east to Oregon Highway 226. In just under 5 miles, OR 226 takes a 90-degree turn to the north where Fish Hatchery Road branches east. Follow Fish Hatchery Road for roughly 6.5 miles to the intersection with Meridian Road. Stay left on Fish Hatchery Road and continue to Larwood Park and the put-in/take-out there in under 3 miles.

To reach the upper put-in, cross the covered bridge near the park and follow Meridian Road south to the second intersection, where it meets Island Inn Drive. Follow Island Inn Drive east, then make a right turn before crossing the creek. A left turn follows quickly on a road marked as a private logging road. Continue along the logging road past a large parking area in just over 5 miles and turn right at an intersection, heading toward the creek. The road crosses the North Fork Crabtree Creek in about a mile, and the South Fork put-in less than a mile more.

Overview: A good-sized creek, Crabtree Creek flows for more than 25 miles between the North and South Santiam Rivers. The upper creek begins in forest and drops sharply in the first 5 miles, slopes gradually over the next 5 or 6 miles. At Larwood Park, halfway down the run, a beautiful covered bridge crosses the creek and the Roaring River joins in to boost the flow (one of few places where a river flows into a creek.) This forested area has only moderate population with thick vegetation along the banks. In its lower half, the creek finally flattens out to farmland before connecting with the South Santiam River. Paddlers most commonly run the creek during spring and fall rainy seasons, when nearby evergreen and deciduous trees make a colorful presentation.

The rapids on the upper creek can be surprisingly deceptive. Debris and rocks seem to be placed in the most unexpected places. Currents can be pushier than they look. The upper creek is almost solidly lined with downed trees from the 1996 floods; this drainage was one of the hardest hit areas. Paddlers should be extra cautious, watching for strainers and submerged logs. In many places water has gouged out the banks, uplifting large gravel bars and repositioning them in several places. Some of the gravel bars look as if they were dug into the creek by heavy machinery to divert the flow. They certainly do not look natural.

Going with the flow
Section 1: South Fork Bridge to Larwood Park

Class: III+	Recommended flow: 500 to 2,000 cfs	Miles: 10

When starting your run down Crabtree Creek, make sure you put in at the second (South Fork) bridge, since a Class V rapid lies just above and under the North Fork Bridge. The South Fork starts out with a little less water than the North Fork, but within a mile they join forces. The South Fork can be rocky at low volume.

Within the upper 5 miles of creek lies most of the serious action. The first half-dozen pool-drop rapids are steep and technical. Most are short drops requiring a move somewhere in the middle to avoid a rock, tree root, log, or converging current. At low water the upper 5 miles are technical and often shallow. With more current rocks get covered better, but the drops are deceptively pushy. Smaller boats can get unexpectedly rear-ended or pushed into unexpected places.

At the first major horizon line, **Standing Ovation** funnels toward the river left side. Here, a pushier-than-expected hole tends to tail-stand boats. The second major drop below the put-in, **Roller Coaster,** rear-ended several boats (mine included) and vertically pinned them against the river left wall until they slid off and boaters rolled up. The deceptions continued as we made our way down the creek.

In the next 3 miles several Class III rapids are separated by calmer Class I and II water. These pool-drop rapids can usually be boat-scouted, since they have straightforward routes. Beware of logs and tree roots, especially in the narrow passages around these obstacles. After passing a bridge, paddlers will find the lower 5 miles of Section 1 to be less dramatic, with easier Class II+ to III- rapids and frequent play spots.

Section 2: Larwood Park to South Santiam River

Class: I to II	Recommended flow: 700 to 2,000 cfs	Miles: 15.5

Lower Crabtree Creek starts off with Class II water that is fairly continuous, leading to Class I water in the first few miles. Boaters can put-in or take-out at bridges along Richardson Gap Road, Oregon Highway 226, Hungry Hill Road, Gilkey Road, or along the South Santiam or main Santiam Rivers. The stretch of creek below Larwood Bridge is much slower than the upper creek. A run of more than 10 miles could mean a long day or even hiking out before making the take-out. Beaver Creek enters on the left a couple of miles below the OR 226 bridge.

The last half of the creek is flatwater, but current and brushy banks can cause beginning boaters some trouble. Paddlers have reported seeing a barbed-wire fence in the lower creek below the OR 226 bridge. I did not observe a fence in this location recently, but it may lie underwater. This fence could be a serious hazard, so all who boat this stretch should watch for it below the bridge. Perhaps a better option is to take out at the bridge rather than continue to the South Santiam River or other take-out options.

17 Crooked River, Lower
Lone Pine Bridge to Lake Billy Chinook

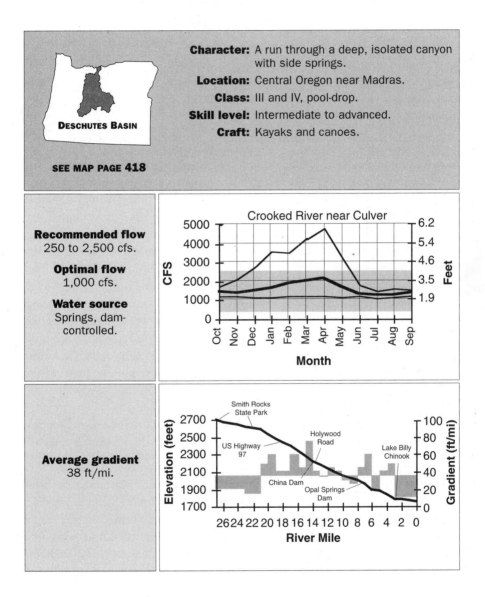

DESCHUTES BASIN

SEE MAP PAGE **418**

Character: A run through a deep, isolated canyon with side springs.
Location: Central Oregon near Madras.
Class: III and IV, pool-drop.
Skill level: Intermediate to advanced.
Craft: Kayaks and canoes.

Recommended flow
250 to 2,500 cfs.

Optimal flow
1,000 cfs.

Water source
Springs, dam-controlled.

Average gradient
38 ft/mi.

Crooked River near Culver

	CFS	Feet
	5000	6.2
	4000	5.4
	3000	4.6
	2000	3.5
	1000	1.9
	0	

Month: Oct Nov Dec Jan Feb Mar Apr May Jun Jul Aug Sep

Elevation (feet): 2700 2500 2300 2100 1900 1700
Gradient (ft/mi): 100 80 60 40 20 0

Smith Rocks State Park
US Highway 97
Holywood Road
China Dam
Opal Springs Dam
Lake Billy Chinook

River Mile: 26 24 22 20 18 16 14 12 10 8 6 4 2 0

Hazards: The upper river contains several Class IV rapids between Smith Rocks State Park and Hollywood Road. Pool-drop Class III rapids dot the river between Hollywood Road and Lake Billy Chinook, with one more difficult rapid called **The Wave.** Another technical Class IV rapid appears at the base of Lake Billy Chinook.

The steep canyon confines below Smith Rocks State Park allow a steep hike out in only two places: Hollywood Road near the Crooked River Ranch and a road at Opal Springs Dam. Paddlers without proper gear, skills, or preparation can easily find themselves trapped in the steep, inaccessible canyon without the possibility of aid. The view of the canyon from Peter Skene Ogden State Scenic Wayside north of Terrebonne reveals the obvious: climbing out is not practical.

Access: From Madras, U.S. Highway 97 leads south to Peter Skene Ogden State Wayside, just across the Crooked River. Here paddlers can get a view of the steep river canyon. Continue south to Terrebonne and Smith Rock, and follow Market Road as it leads east to Lambert Road, heading north. In less than 0.5 mile Lambert Road makes a sharp turn east beyond Smith Rock State Park to a road leading north to the Crooked River at a gaging station near Lone Pine Bridge. Paddlers may put in here, or alternately may put in east of Smith Rock State Park near an aqueduct.

To reach the access point at Hollywood Road for put-in or take-out, turn west between the Peter Skene Ogden State Wayside and Terrebonne at a sign indicating the Crooked River Ranch. Follow the signs to the ranch, passing hat-shaped sand traps in the golf course and following the roadway left past rental units. Park near the gate and carry your craft and gear to or from the river.

Lake Billy Chinook marks the lower take-out. To reach the lake, follow the Culver Highway south from Madras beyond the town of Metolius, then turn west on Gem Lane. Follow Gem Lane to Peck Road, which leads to Lake Billy Chinook Boat Ramp and the take-out bridge beyond it to the south. Make sure to purchase a day permit if you park within the park boundary.

Overview: I first viewed the Crooked River on a rock-climbing trip to the infamous Smith Rocks State Park, a climbing mecca, while still in high school. As a novice free-climber in a group known as the Cliffhangers, I took out my trusty Kodak 110 and shot a photo of the river from atop the cliff wall. Little did I know what lay beyond the placid waters of the stretch near the climbing park. It was not until after college that I began kayaking and felt the true wonders of the river canyon stir my blood.

The spectacular depth of the Crooked River canyon will cause the least claustrophobic paddler to feel perilously confined. The feeling isn't relieved until after one passes the Class IV rapids and the necessity of running the river subsides. Only then can paddlers begin to appreciate breathtaking views and enjoyable water within this mini-Grand Canyon of Oregon. Water gushes from midwall springs, adding flow and scenic beauty to the spectacular journey. Fallen ladders, irrigation lines, and a dilapidated cable bridge on the lower section show historic signs of early habitation.

Both the upper and lower river rapids are technical at lower flows, becoming pushier with larger holes at high flows. Most lower river rapids are pool-drops that can be boat-scouted or easily portaged if you can see no clear route from your boat. The upper section is more continuous. Scout frequently on your first trip down the upper section to determine the best routes and scouting vantages. Above all, have fun, but take special precautions in this long, isolated canyon.

Going with the flow
Section 1: Lone Pine Bridge to Hollywood Road

Class: IV	Recommended flow: 800 to 2,500 cfs	Miles: 16 to 18

From the upper put-in bridge at Lone Pine Bridge above Smith Rocks State Park, the Crooked River is only moderately challenging for a couple of miles to an alternate access at a canal flume about 3 miles above the park. The river then picks up the pace, but eases to Class I water near the park's main climbing area, allowing paddlers to take a gander up the right wall to see the climbers above them.

Below the park and around a right bend in the river the pace picks up again at **Number One,** a steep boulder garden with numerous holes to negotiate around a central boulder. Scout right for a clean line through. The next named Class IV rapid, **Number Two,** should be scouted from the left bank. This second rapid is split by a central lava rock island. Routes in both rapids become tighter at lower flows, but less pushy with more manageable hydraulics. Beyond them, the river eases to Class III+ for about 3 miles.

Kayakers watch a colleague shoot Wap-Te-Doodle on Section 1 of the Lower Crooked River. Jason Bates photo

Next come the Class IV rapids. Big, open waves known as **The Bumps** lead into **Wap-Te-Doodle,** where more technical and dynamic routes flow to a large hole at the bottom. Punch it with speed. Scout on the left to pick your route, since the rapid changes with flow; higher water means bigger holes to punch or avoid. Routes become tighter at low flows, and pinning is a concern.

Technical Class III water below the rapids leads to a broken dam constriction known as **China Dam.** Not much is left of the old dam, placed where boulders constrict the river to narrow passages. Paddlers can take out up the steep, rocky bank to Hollywood Road before running the constriction, or make an easier take-out up a 0.25 mile climb along the road beyond China Dam. Paddlers continuing along Section 2 should make sure they have ample time to complete the section. Otherwise, plan on camping along the river. One of the only good campsites along the river is less than a mile below China Dam at an old cable bridge crossing. There, a deck made from bridge remains provides one of the only feasible campsites along the river's brushy, steep banks.

Section 2: Hollywood Road to Lake Billy Chinook

Class: III (IV)	**Recommended flow:** 250 to 2,500 cfs	**Miles:** 9

Paddlers will have to drag their boats down steep Hollywood Road to reach the river at the start of Section 2. A bulldozer-sized boulder blocks the road about halfway down, having forced a locked gate at the top. You'll need wheels or a buddy to help you carrying unless you wish to shave your boat to a lighter model on the rocky roadbed. Once near the river, put in above or below China Dam rapid, depending on flow. Do not be discouraged by minimum-looking flows at the put-in, since many springs add sufficient water to paddle the section most of the year.

All of the rapids below the China Dam put-in are Class III pool-drops, often with horizon line boat-scouts. The most difficult rapids in the section are near the top and bottom of the stretch. The Wave occurs about 0.5 mile below an old cable bridge and campsite on the right. This significant drop often has logs or debris caught somewhere within it. Scout or portage on the left. At higher water paddlers have more options (center and right), but at lower water only the left looks runnable. A low water run on the left could easily result in a pin near the bottom left channel, so portage at lower flows.

Below The Wave, many fun rapids keep paddlers from gazing too long up at the canyon walls or down through the clear blue water at huge underwater boulders. One 3-foot drop followed by a large eddy is a good ender spot. The next major obstacle, **Opal Springs Dam,** is obvious. You'll have to make a 0.5-mile portage on the right, following the road and a line of fruit trees to a put-in beyond the dam. Most water is directed into a large tube on the left, from which it is dropped into the generator below. The area is private property, so pass through respectfully. The steep road that leads out of the canyon on the right is a private road that is not available for shuttle. Opal Springs enters on the right near the dam. (Another Opal Springs resides on the Deschutes River, one canyon west.)

Once around the dam, paddlers find more Class III rapids separated by calm water. A climactic Class III rapid begins on the left and flows over and around large boulders to a pool at the bottom. While scouting this rapid for the first time, we realized that we had reached Lake Billy Chinook, since a power boat was anchored nearby. Once the rapid is behind you, you face a grueling 3-mile paddle to the take-out bridge. Watch for power boats and pace yourselves. Park shuttle vehicles on the western side of the lake if you can handle the long traverse, since you'll need a day permit to park along the eastern shore. Check park rules before you drop off your vehicle, since permits may soon be needed for western shore parking, too.

18 Deschutes River, Upper
Wickiup Reservoir to Bend

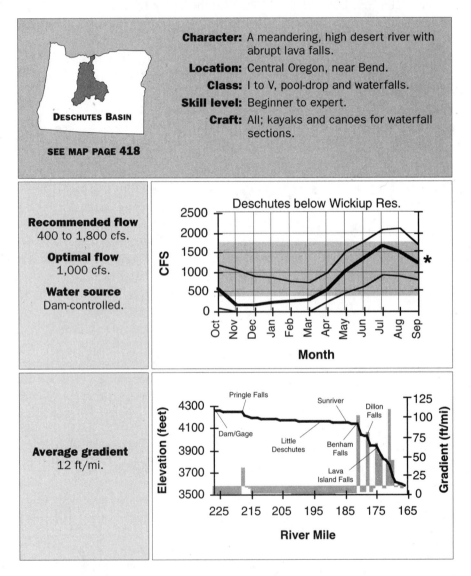

DESCHUTES BASIN

SEE MAP PAGE **418**

Character: A meandering, high desert river with abrupt lava falls.

Location: Central Oregon, near Bend.

Class: I to V, pool-drop and waterfalls.

Skill level: Beginner to expert.

Craft: All; kayaks and canoes for waterfall sections.

Recommended flow
400 to 1,800 cfs.

Optimal flow
1,000 cfs.

Water source
Dam-controlled.

Average gradient
12 ft/mi.

Deschutes below Wickiup Res.

No depth measurement available.

Hazards: Section 1 is mostly moving flatwater with portages at **Pringle Falls** and **Tetherow Log Jam.** At all times boaters should watch for fallen trees in the river channel.

Waterfalls comprise most of the hazards along Section 2, which is divided into 6 parts. Some log hazards exist, one corner jam in particular requiring scouting. Rocks are numerous and sharp. **Upper Benham Falls** is a series of Class IV to V drops leading to a Class V+ waterfall; scouting is required. **Dillon Falls** is a 15-foot drop into a nasty recirculating hole, followed by a Class IV canyon containing a second respectable hole toward the bottom right. **Lava Falls** is the last of the three falls, cascading down 25 vertical feet in 50 yards. It is followed by an additional log-choked, Class V drop.

Access: Drop a shuttle vehicle at Bachelor Village in Bend before heading upstream if you plan to take out there. To access the upper river, drive south of Bend along Century Drive (the Cascade Lakes Highway) toward Mount Bachelor. Turn left onto Forest Road 3933 to reach Meadow Camp Picnic Area, a possible put-in. Alternately, continue along Century Drive and turn left onto Forest Road 41; it's the first left after the Inn of the Seventh Mountain, 0.5 mile beyond the Meadow Camp turnoff. From FR 41, Forest Road 4120 leads left toward the river with access to Lava Island Falls and campground or Aspen Camp. Dillon Falls, Slough Camp, and Benham Falls are easier to reach farther along FR 41 by turning left at the Dillon Falls sign onto Forest Road 100, then going straight or right at the next intersection depending upon your destination. Continuing to Slough Camp is another option. To do so, turn left where indicated and park next to the river, or continue to the Benham Falls access.

Continuing southwest from FR 41, follow signs to Sunriver for a launch or take-out at the boat ramp. Reach Camp Besson by turning left onto Forest Road 200 from FR 41. Forest Road 40 intersects FR 41 just beyond the FR 200 crossing. Here, a left turn leads to Harpor Bridge access and U.S. Highway 97.

Farther along FR 40, a left turn onto Forest Road 4220 leads to Forest Road 42. Turning east here gives access to Big River Campground and bridge. To reach Wyeth Campground, Bull Bend Campground, and Wickiup Reservoir continue west on FR 42, turning south on Forest Road 4350. Cross Forest Road 43 and turn onto Forest Road 4370, which leads to these destinations. At the reservoir, cross the river heading south and turn downstream to Tenino Campground and Boat Launch for the uppermost put-in.

Overview: The Deschutes River has many faces, ranging from a warm smile of flatwater to an angry, snarling glare of whitewater and waterfalls, paired with a hot, sweaty brow marked by its lower desert canyons. The Upper Deschutes offers a wide variety in itself. We have divided the upper river into two distinct sections, allowing either flatwater or whitewater runs. If you're looking for a leisurely float or a place to improve your basic skills, Section 1 will fit the bill. If you want a place to exercise advanced to expert techniques, the whitewater in Section 2 will keep your heart pumping while giving you time to reflect and relax between jolts of excitement.

The Upper Deschutes is always a reliable destination, offering steady flows and fair weather. Porous lava rock drains groundwater into the Deschutes at a steady rate. Even in dry years the upper river has ample flow throughout the summer. Downstream, from Bend to Lake Billy Chinook, the water is diverted for irrigation most of the year, restricting the boating season to winter and early spring. The Cascade Range catches most of the rain as storms cross the state, so fairweather boaters can consider the Upper Deschutes a good bet, even if rain is forecast for coastal areas.

Central Oregon was isolated from its fertile past by the rise of the Cascade Range during the last ice age. The eruption of Mount Mazama to the south later blanketed the valley with a thick layer of volcanic ash, leaving Crater Lake as evidence of this explosive event. The profile of the Deschutes River has continued to change in more recent geologic times. Lava flows from Newberry Volcano dumped lava into the river in five locations. At Lava Island Falls, such flows backed up the river for several miles. Later flows collapsed the volcano dome, forming Lake Paulina. Benham Falls was created by lava flows from more recent Lava Butte, a cinder cone that flanks the former Newberry Volcano site to the north. Dillon Falls was not born in the same fashion. Here a fault line split the rock, which dropped on one side or rose on the other to form the falls.

Families will find plenty to entertain them on the Upper Deschutes, whether fishing for trout, hiking, mountain biking, or floating one of the sections of river. Campsites and access along the upper river are numerous, and much of Section 1 lies within the Deschutes National Forest boundary.

Going with the flow
Section 1: Wickiup Reservoir to Benham Falls

Class: I to II	Recommended flow: 500 to 1,800 cfs	Miles: 44

From Tenino Campground (River Mile 226) or Bull Bend Campground (RM 220), the river is moving flatwater with a very low gradient. Take out at Wyeth Campground (RM 218) to avoid Pringle Falls, since private lands limit downstream escapes above the hazardous falls. Class II water below Wyeth Campground leads under a bridge to the Class IV drop. Logs may jam in this area, so scout carefully; only advanced paddlers should attempt to run the drop.

Access below Pringle Falls is available at Pringle Falls Campground on river left. From here, Class I water continues to **Tetherow Log Jam** in 3.5 miles. Portage the log jam on the right and carry your craft and gear 150 yards around it and back to the river. Paddlers wishing to avoid the portage can put in at a boat ramp access on the right below the jam. Below the log jam, the river continues as a Class I float for the next 32 miles. The river corridor passes through pine forests that become more sparse near LaPine State Recreation Area (RM 206). As the area's population increases, so does the percentage of private land. Respect locals by practicing proper river etiquette.

Paddlers can find diversion loops along the river within LaPine State Recreation Area and near a ranch at RM 195. Relax while watching for osprey that fish along the meandering river. Houses dot the banks below Big River Campground (RM 199). The Little Deschutes River enters from the right 6.5 miles below the campground, contributing to the flow. The Spring River makes its offering from the left in another 2 miles. These and other spring-fed tributaries drain groundwater at a steady rate year-round.

Sunriver Resort (RM 187 to 185) lines the shore a few miles above Benham Falls (RM 181). During World War II, the resort was home to ten thousand soldiers who trained at Camp Abbot. Today the resort offers a full menu of activities and recreation. Arrange for housing and facility privileges within the Sunriver complex by calling (541) 593-1222 for information. The shore is private along the resort, but access is available at the boat ramp on the right.

Take out at Benham Falls Overlook (RM 182) on the left to avoid Class IV and V+ drops! Advanced and expert paddlers may wish to explore the falls and continue on to whitewater in Section 2.

Section 2: Benham Falls to Mount Bachelor Village

Class: I to V+	Recommended flow: 400 to 1,800 cfs	Miles: 14

For 0.5 mile above Benham Falls, the Upper Deschutes is calm. Scout the entire falls section before getting in the water here. The first drop is a large hole with a small tongue on the left at high water. The river then bends right at the second drop, a pourover formed by sharp lava rock. Stay right, then move center and back to the right before the next few drops above the main falls. In the last few drops, it is crucial that you stay on your line. You must get to the extreme left side of the river to eddy-out above the falls to portage or scout at the overlook. This area is very dangerous; any swim upstream of the falls is a life-threatening situation.

For Benham Falls you're on your own. Believe me, it's a lot bigger and pushier than it looks. This rates a serious Class V even at low water. The big hole in the center of the rapid is known as **Discovery**; there, I "discovered" what space shuttle astronauts feel like, looking straight up at blue sky while accelerating many miles-per-hour with absolutely no control. This hole can screw up the best of lines. If you decide to run it, may the River Gods be with you! Take out at the base of the falls or continue through the lower section of rapids to Slough Camp.

Avoid the upper falls by putting-in at the base. Before you do so, thoroughly scout **Lower Benham** rapids, which require a number of quick Class III+ moves. At the bottom of the rapids, look for a good play spot on the right before relaxing into a short Class II stretch. After a calm area, the river bends right. Scout on the left here, checking for logs on river right within the next rapid. Pick your line, then relax. The water stays calm to the take-out at Slough Camp.

But don't relax too much before Dillon Falls, just 1.5 miles away. Many regretful canoeists have missed the boat ramp above the drop. Dillon Falls is a 15-foot drop into a nasty recirculating hole. A Class IV canyon follows, with another nasty hole on the bottom right. Portage on the left. Below these jolts, flatwater leads to Aspen Camp and an optional access.

The next whitewater stretch is known as the Big Eddy Run. From Aspen Camp, flatwater leads to Class I and II rapids in about a mile. Around the corner is **Big Eddy,** with its three named parts: **Maytag, The Notch,** and **Souse Hole.** This is the site of the Big Eddy Rodeo and the 1998 Nike Masters Games. At the top of Big Eddy is a great surfing wave, but be ready to get "Maytaged" in the next hole, which will blow you out toward river right. The Notch is next in the rapid series. It often flips kayaks in the lateral wave that forms from the right side. This is also the best ender spot of the stretch, with two point cartwheels available for those willing to pay the price of a possible roll against the wall or in the Batcave. Souse Hole is the spin, surf, cartwheel, and retendo spot used for the Big Eddy Rodeo. At appropriate water levels this hole will allow it all. Between 1,800 to 2,000 cubic feet per second the hole washes out, but above and below these flows it offers great play. Below the three-part Big Eddy, a Class III rapid known as **Old Stogie** leads into a series of Class II surf waves. Catch 'em while you can, because they mark the last whitewater above the Lava Island Falls Shelter take-out.

Lava Island Falls were first run by Loren Hall, Linda Heisserman, and Morgan Smith in 1988, then again by Morgan Smith at high water in 1989. The usual run begins by paddling across the calm river at the top of the falls and climbing down the irrigation canal walkway to the bottom. The action starts immediately, with no warm-up. The first Class IV rapid is known as **Cut Up,** due to the sharp lava rock that lines its holes and waves, which differ depending on water level. The current is swift, so eddy-hop your way down, keeping alert for new logs in the channel. There are some good play spots along this stretch, but look downstream before you play too aggressively.

A long pool signals the next difficult stretch. The river constricts to a small, narrow chute between canyon walls. A scout is mandatory here; climb above the river on the right to scout the Class V ledge-drop known as **Barry's Back-Ender.** About 100 feet downstream on the left is a big eddy; directly below it are two small eddies on either side. There are logs on both sides of the drop, which you will not be able to see at high water. The logs wedge between the large rock in the center and the right shore. Do not go right! If you run the drop, stay left over the 5-foot pourover where you are likely to understand the reason behind its name. Start left below and thread the needle in the center before a ski-jump over the rocks. If you go too far right, you will end up in **Loren's Lunch Spot** under some wood! A portage here is an ugly undertaking, but a swim is much worse.

High Five is a great play hole just below this drop, visible from the scout. At high water the hole is BIG! Beware of a river-wide strainer just downstream on the right. It, too, is visible from the scout and should be run on the left. Just below, another river-wide strainer contains two submerged trees, one on top of the other; run this one on the right. Farther downstream, a log jam on the right pulls water through it and threatens to pull paddlers underneath. Stay left over one last drop, then it's smooth sailing to the take-out. One last large rock has a small ender spot for practicing pirouettes. Take out on the left at Meadow Camp Picnic Area or continue to Mount Bachelor Village in an additional 5 miles.

A mile of flatwater starts the run below Meadow Camp. After passing a house on the left, paddlers see action. A great play hole waits just past two log homes, followed by another, smaller play spot. Around the corner the river presents its first Class IV rapid, known as **Play Time.** A continuous eddy-hop through great play spots, it leads to the side-surfing hole known as **Rollodex,** toward the middle of the rapid. Paddlers with an appetite for an upstream lean will not leave hungry.

Other ender and play spots dot the river for the next 0.25 mile. In calm water at a diversion dam, get out and scout the next rapid, **Dam It,** on the right. Continue scouting past the first drop to a lateral wave below—it's a real flipper. At most water levels this drop is run center, but at higher flows it can be run left at the top, moving to center below. Take time to appreciate the impressive view from the bottom of the rapid, looking back upstream.

The next scout is at a stream gage on the right. Walk all the way around the next corner, since there is no good eddy within the next big drop. It's called **Amazing,** because it is truly amazing at high water. (It's also amazing that you can make it through the maze of rocks at low water.) A log at bottom right of this drop calls for extra caution. **Frank's Fun Hole** below the rapid rewards paddlers with one of the best play holes below Meadow Camp. Stay awhile and play.

Downstream, keep an eye out for a log jam that looks as if it totally blocks the river. Scout on the right and go right. There are a series of holes along this stretch. At the bottom, hang onto your helmet in the rompin', stompin', rodeo hole called **Ride 'Em Roy.** Below it, the river continues past fallen trees used for fish habitat. When the water ahead of you drops out of sight, scout the last big drop of the run. Do not try to play in the big hole at the bottom known as **100 Percent**—it's 100 percent guaranteed that you will hit a gnarly rock if you flip!

Continue to the Bachelor Village pump house on river left. Take out and carry to your shuttle vehicle.

—Morgan Smith

19 Deschutes River, Central
Bend to Lake Billy Chinook

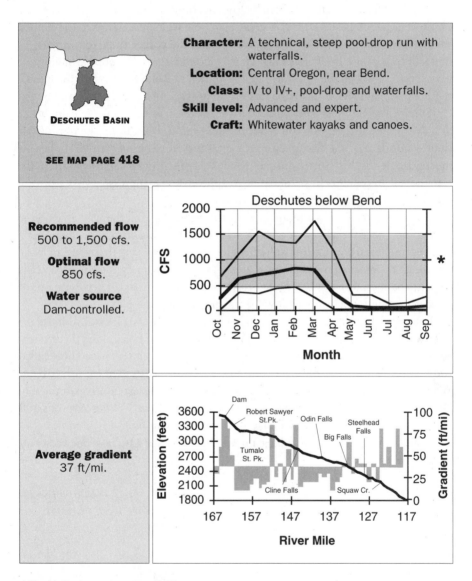

DESCHUTES BASIN

SEE MAP PAGE **418**

Character: A technical, steep pool-drop run with waterfalls.

Location: Central Oregon, near Bend.

Class: IV to IV+, pool-drop and waterfalls.

Skill level: Advanced and expert.

Craft: Whitewater kayaks and canoes.

Recommended flow
500 to 1,500 cfs.

Optimal flow
850 cfs.

Water source
Dam-controlled.

Deschutes below Bend

CFS vs. Month

Average gradient
37 ft/mi.

Elevation (feet) / Gradient (ft/mi) vs. River Mile

Dam, Robert Sawyer St.Pk., Odin Falls, Steelhead Falls, Big Falls, Tumalo St. Pk., Cline Falls, Squaw Cr.

* No depth measurement available.

90

Hazards: Steep, technical rapids pool-drop their way between stretches of Class II and III water on the Central Deschutes River. **Steelhead Falls** deserves a scout before you decide whether or not to run it. If you run the upper stretch above Steelhead, portaging **Big Falls** is necessary. The upper portion of Section 1 contains narrow chutes and rocky drops that can pin a boat. The lower section contains many horizon line pool-drop rapids with keeper holes.

Access: To paddle the upper stretch of the Central Deschutes, put in at Bend, at either Robert Sawyer State Park or the River House Motel. The take-out is north of Bend off of U.S. Highway 20. From the town of Tumalo, follow the Tumalo–Deschutes Highway south to Tumalo State Park and the river.

To access the lower run, follow U.S. Highway 97 to Madras, then take the Culver Highway southwest through Metolius and turn west on Gem Lane. Follow Gem Lane to Peck Road and Cove Palisades State Park. After winding down the steep road to the park, continue across the bridge over the reservoir to a parking area on the left. This is the take-out. Permits may soon be required to use this parking area; obtain them at the state park.

To reach the lower run put-in, return to US 97 and head south over the Crooked River at Peter Skene Ogden Scenic Wayside to Lower Bridge Road above the town of Terrebonne. The road leads to a bridge and put-in above Big Falls. For a shorter run, paddlers may follow signs to Crooked River Ranch, taking a dirt road west to a campground and put-in that avoids the Big Falls portage and makes a shorter run.

Overview: Most of the Central Deschutes River gets diverted for irrigation at Bend and below. Only during winter and early spring is the flow adequate for paddlers. We divide the river into two separate sections, both Class IV: the upper, Class IV stretch begins near Bend, while the lower run drops into the deep canyon gorge leading to Lake Billy Chinook. Many Bend area paddlers enjoy the upper stretch after work on a nice winter afternoon. The river winds through sharp, hard rock before easing toward Tumalo Park.

The lower or Steelhead Falls stretch of the Deschutes drops below Big Falls into a deep, impressive canyon gorge. Steelhead Falls was featured in *Paddler Magazine* as one of the nation's top runnable falls. The falls drop roughly 20 feet into a huge pool. Those who wish to take photos can follow a trail below the falls along the river's right bank.

Going with the flow
Section 1: Sawyer Park to Tumalo State Park (Lava Canyon Run)

Class: IV to IV+	Recommended flow: 500 to 1,500 cfs	Miles: 5

Section 1 begins at the River House Motel in Bend, where a Class II warm-up leads to a short stretch of Class I water. Sawyer Park lines both sides of the river, which is sandwiched between residential and business areas. The first Class III+ rapids begin near one of Bend's mansions. The third drop in the series is known as the **Wright Stuff.** This ledge-drop becomes tricky at low flows and is generally run along the right of a midstream boulder.

Scout the next rapid, the Class IV **Flumes of Doom,** from an island just downstream. Pinning potential is high along either long, narrow chute. The chutes become tighter at lower flows. A nice ender spot rewards those who make it to the bottom.

The river maintains a steep descent (though maps do not indicate this), contributing several technical Class III to III+ rapids. The series of rapids becomes more technical toward the bottom, where a long rapid known as **T-Rex** forms a river-wide hole at higher flows. The rapid is generally run along the right. More blind drops twist to **Ogre** rapid in less than a mile. Scout this rapid on the right, since a huge boulder complicates routes over the drop and ledges beyond it make a swim dangerous. Below Ogre, the action eases to the take-out at Tumalo State Park, with various entertaining play spots.

Section 2: Big Falls to Lake Billy Chinook (Steelhead Falls)

Class: IV (V)   **Recommended flow:** 500 to 1,000 cfs   **Miles:** 14.2

In Section 2, known as the Steelhead Falls section of the Deschutes River, paddlers may put-in above or below Big Falls for more Class III action. Big Falls is a mandatory portage. To avoid it and make a shorter day, I have put-in downstream at the campground just over a mile above Steelhead Falls.

Below Big Falls, fun and fast Class III water leads around an abrupt left-to-right bend in the river to Steelhead Falls. The water is swift in the narrow channel, so watch carefully for the horizon line and quickly move to the left bank to scout. Most paddlers opt for the arduous portage along the left bank rather than run the falls. The falls are generally run near the center with speed, but at shallow water levels it is easy to scrape over the lip and drop into the maul at the bottom. Some paddlers have ended up behind the falls before getting flushed out.

Beyond the deep pool at the waterfall's base, easy Class I water leads for 1.5 miles to the next horizon line drop. Most of the drops rate Class III+ to -IV with routes that wind past large holes and midstream boulders. The drops are spread out at first, becoming more closely spaced toward the end.

At the entrance of Squaw Creek, on the left, paddlers face the long, difficult Class IV **Squaw Creek** rapid. The rapid winds through a maze of boulders and holes. More horizon line drops follow. Those running the river for the first time should scout the drops from either bank. One drop contains two nasty holes in quick succession. Punch the first, then move quickly to the right to avoid a keeper hole on left, just beyond.

Below the whitewater fun, a 2-mile paddle awaits along Lake Billy Chinook. Take out on the left up the bank near the bridge. A cement wall lines the right bank before plunging over the falls.

20 Deschutes River, Lower
U.S. HIghway 26 Bridge to Columbia River

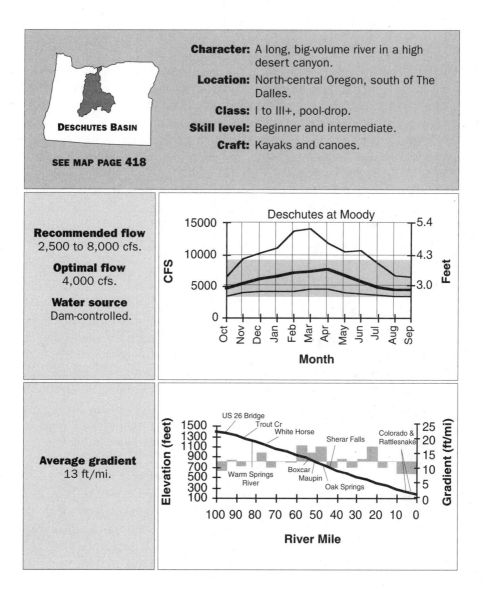

DESCHUTES BASIN

SEE MAP PAGE **418**

Character: A long, big-volume river in a high desert canyon.

Location: North-central Oregon, south of The Dalles.

Class: I to III+, pool-drop.

Skill level: Beginner and intermediate.

Craft: Kayaks and canoes.

Recommended flow
2,500 to 8,000 cfs.

Optimal flow
4,000 cfs.

Water source
Dam-controlled.

Average gradient
13 ft/mi.

Deschutes at Moody

US 26 Bridge
Trout Cr
White Horse
Sherar Falls
Colorado & Rattlesnake
Warm Springs River
Boxcar
Maupin
Oak Springs

Hazards: **Whitehorse, Boxcar** (Lower Wapinitia rapid), and **Oak Springs** rapid present the most difficult Class III to IV- water on the Lower Deschutes River. In Section 1, Whitehorse is a long rapid that may result in a long swim before getting to shore or gathering gear. Higher flows wash out smaller rapids, but increase the speed of the flow.

Sherar Falls, in Section 2, is a Class VI drop and mandatory portage below Maupin. It is now illegal to run the stretch just above the falls where a take-out near the road on the left was formerly used; the lowest take-out above Sherar Falls is now Sandy Beach, on the right. Paddlers need a permit to run Section 2; purchase yours at the Maupin store.

Few hazards exist in upper Section 1 and lower Section 3, other than occasional Class II to III rapids. Only the very upper and lower parts of Section 3 contain Class III rapids of any concern; the section's central 30+ miles contain mostly Class I to I+ water. Most novice boaters can float Sections 1 and 3 without much difficulty, since routes are wide with calm stretches below the difficult drops.

Watch for motorboats in the spring and summer on Section 3. Strong winds often blow upstream along the lower river. Take extra time and precautions in open, unprotected areas.

Access: Reach the upper sections of the Lower Deschutes River by following Oregon Highway 197 from Maupin to U.S. Highway 26, then taking US 26 northwest to the Deschutes. Alternately, reach the river via Oregon Highway 216 by following US 26 between Madras to the south and Portland to the northwest. The uppermost put-in is above the US 26 bridge on river right. For a shorter trip, look for access areas above and below Trout Creek, such as Gateway Recreation Area, 9 miles below the US 26 bridge, or the access points 1.5 miles downstream of Trout Creek.

Access Section 2 by following a paved and dirt road from Maupin south to various put-in locations along the river. More access can be found in Maupin and along OR 197 to the north. It is now illegal to float the last 1.5 miles above Sherar Falls. Take out at Sandy Beach on the right above **Osborne** rapid.

To reach Section 3 and the lower take-out, take Interstate 84 east of The Dalles and look for a boat ramp just up the Deschutes River near its confluence with the Columbia River on the western shore. To reach upstream access areas, follow OR 197 south from The Dalles to OR 216 at Tygh Valley. OR 216 leads east to Sherars Bridge over the Deschutes, and then to a 12-mile-long paved and dirt road that heads north, offering campground access in several places. OR 197 leads south across Sherar Bridge to Maupin and a paved and dirt road south along the river for access to Section 2.

Overview: The Deschutes River is one of Oregon's most popular rivers due to its regular year-round flows, commercial trips, nearby rental shops, and abundant fair weather. Located in north-central Oregon, the lower Deschutes runs through high desert with little rainfall and lots of sun. Make sure to pack your sunscreen even if rain is forecast for coastal areas. Water flows into the lower river from its upper reaches and from several side streams fed by springs, snowmelt, and rain from Mount Hood and the Cascade Range, providing reliable year-round flows. Farms and ranches dot the riverbanks between populated areas. Section 3 is more isolated, with a few ranches and cattle herds but only remnants of farms or settlements. Trains pass along the river daily, and hikers follow an old roadbed on the lower river's right-hand bank to reach the Columbia River.

The lower Deschutes offers moderate action, with Class II to III+ rapids and long, open, isolated stretches of river for multiday trips. If you like to see people and be seen yourself, Section 2 is the place for you. Day trips are common in that section, where most of the whitewater exists. By contrast, Sections 1 and 3 allow boaters to get away from it all and relax along secluded, quiet, easier stretches of water for longer trips. In general, the river's rapids pack a punch but are fun and tame enough for most novice boaters. Long stretches of flatwater give boaters time to regroup and relax before the next exciting plunge.

Campsites are plentiful along the river above and below Maupin, but on busy weekends competition for these sites can be fierce. Camping fees have recently increased to help pay for upkeep and patrol of the river. Boating numbers have increased dramatically along the Lower Deschutes in recent years, creating the need to police the river corridor for rowdy behavior, drunkenness, and unsafe boating practices. The inconsiderate behavior of a few is costing all of us the right

Dennis Schultz paddles his faithful "cat" down the Lower Deschutes.

to boat and enjoy this popular area. Though it is easy to overindulge in this big-water funhouse, play it safe and keep the volume, trash, and violence to a minimum.

Warm Springs Indian Reservation lines the left bank of the river in Section 1, from the Warm Springs River confluence below the upper put-in to Two Springs Ranch (at River Mile 69), less than 5 miles above Dant. The reservation is private, and paddlers are prohibited from setting foot on land along the left (western) shore within its boundaries. All camping should be done along the right (eastern) shore near the reservation.

Many campsites along the river provide toilets, but boaters should be prepared to pack out all waste at undesignated camping areas. Paddlers need permits to float Section 2 above Maupin to the take-out above Sherar Falls; purchase them at the store in Maupin. Upper Section 1 and lower Section 3 do not require permits. Watch for motorboats in Section 3 during spring and summer.

Going with the flow
Section 1: U.S. Highway 26 Bridge to Wapinitia Creek and Rapids

Class: II (III)	**Recommended flow:** 4,000 to 8,000 cfs	**Miles:** 41

To begin your trip down Section 1 of the lower Deschutes, put in above the US 26 bridge, on the right. The easy gradient produces long stretches of Class I water. The current increases with volume. In 9 miles, the Class I stretch leads to Class II+ **Trout Creek** rapids (RM 87). Enjoy the break in pace, since the next 12 miles ease back to Class I for relaxed scenic viewing.

The Warm Springs River enters on the left 3.8 miles below Trout Creek, marking the start of the Warm Springs Indian Reservation. Setting foot on Indian land is strictly prohibited for the next 14.8 miles; the reservation boundary stretches to Two Springs Ranch, about 4 miles below a railroad bridge. Stop for camping or break spots along the right shore, avoiding private property.

After passing homes along the right bank, paddlers see the river canyon narrow and steepen. **Whitehorse** rapid (RM 76) follows in roughly 3 miles. Scout the rapid on the right where it begins at a right bend in the river. The rapid contains many holes and waves with much maneuvering required. Rafts have a tough time negotiating the minefield of rocks that threaten to snag boats. The rapid is most difficult at the top and extends for nearly a mile. A swim in this stretch could be long and cold. Most rafters and paddlers will enjoy the whitewater action.

Once successfully through this long stretch, paddlers find easier Class I and II water leading to take-out areas on the right. Many islands and Class II rapids dot the river for the next 3 miles. After passing under a railroad bridge, relax and enjoy the ride and scenery. The Warm Springs Indian Reservation ends 3 miles below the bridge near Two Springs Ranch. From here boaters are allowed on the left shore, but the railroad closely follows the left bank to the Columbia River. **Buckskin Mary** rapid (RM 64) is 8.5 miles below the railroad crossing. Large waves lead down the middle for a roller-coaster ride. This Class II+ rapid is followed by Class II+ **Four Chutes** rapid and smaller Class I and II water above the take-out area and Section 2.

Many access areas exist below the locked gate along the east shore road. Boaters may take out above or below the more challenging rapids of Section 2.

Section 2: Wapinitia Creek to Sherar Falls

Class: III (III+)   **Recommended flow:** 3,000 to 8,000 cfs   **Miles:** 11

This section is the most famous on the Deschutes River. More people float this stretch of river than any other in Oregon. If you're looking for a place to meet fellow boaters, find an easy shuttle, rent boats and gear, or take a guided trip down exciting whitewater, Section 2 will fit the bill. Folks looking for solitude and a casual float will be disappointed here, however, and should consider less popular Sections 1 and 3.

Dramatic and scenic, the lower Deschutes is a common gathering place for hordes of boaters of all skill levels looking for a thrill. Most visitors can negotiate the challenging big-water rapids here, but novice boaters are bound to take a swim at **Boxcar** or **Oak Springs**. Unskilled rafters often bumble down the river without injury or incident, but the potential for harm does exist. In the past, excessive indulgence on and off the river has been a problem. On busy weekends the river can seem more like a fraternity party than a Wild and Scenic River float. Though many folks appreciate the camaraderie and uninhibited atmosphere, problems on the river have caused concern and forced legal changes. Today boaters may be subject to fines for boating while intoxicated or possessing open containers. Day permits are required along this section of river and can be obtained at the local store in Maupin. The fees pay for upkeep and regulation of the river access areas.

The uppermost access for this stretch of river is near the locked gate on the riverside road north of Maupin. **Upper Wapinitia** rapid is just downstream, with Class -III big waves. Paddlers must maneuver well to avoid boulders in the central river at this spot. In less than a mile, around a bend to the right, a train once wrecked and lost one of its cars in the river. Near the spot, **Boxcar** (**Lower Wapinitia** rapid) contains narrow, turbulent passages within basalt rock. A large hole resides against a boulder to the left, with big waves and swirly water leading into the drop. Many boaters take a spill here and recover gear in the pool and calmer water below. Run, scout, or portage on the right. If you do not plan to run this challenging drop, it is more practical to put in below it initially. Look at it on the drive to the put-in to make your decision.

Various Class II rapids and surfing spots dot the river to Maupin. Paddlers have plenty of time to look at the scenery and reminisce about individual runs through the upper rapids before reaching town. Look for a take-out site at a grassy access area and park on the right below the bridge over the river in roughly 3 miles. Camping or parking fees are required here.

Below Maupin the river contains Class I and II water bending around rocky outcroppings along the right shore. Occasional surf waves and rocks keep the trip busy, but flat areas allow breaks to float, catch eddies, and admire the view. About 4 miles beyond Maupin Surf City (RM 48) provides great surfing for paddlers at moderate flows. At higher water it can be a lot of work to paddle back up to surf the waves once you've blown by, so catch a wave while you can.

The waves are a good indicator of upcoming **Oak Springs** rapid in about a 0.5 mile. At higher water, the main drop can be avoided by taking the left-hand channel where the river divides in two. At lower water, only the main right and central channels have ample water for rafts. Scout or portage on the right up the steep, rocky bank to the road. Rafters cannot easily portage the rapid, but boaters may scout or line the rapid on the right. This is the most dangerous rapid on the Lower Deschutes due to the sharp lava rock that channels the river. A large boulder rests on the right at the drop next to a large hole that often flips rafts. Run the right channel near the center, since the right side contains a large hole. Swimmers at the base of the drop often float for some distance before getting safely to shore or being rescued by rafts. Shallow areas of river can cut or bang-up swimmers, so all rescue attempts should be expeditious. Boaters attempting the more difficult right channel should wear helmets.

Below Oak Springs, Class II to II+ water narrows in places to the confluence with the White River. In one spot, swirly water requires good balance for paddlers. A large eddy circles near the left bank just below a railroad bridge over the White River, allowing boaters to reach a popular sand beach. Class II+ rapids lead into the strong eddy. Just below the eddy is upper **Elevator** rapid, with its large wave train that boaters often swim through with just a life jacket. Remember to breathe before or after the next big wave! A river right eddy leads back to the top for additional surfs. Be prepared to wait your turn to surf the waves here, since this is a popular surfing location.

Boating beyond Elevator is now off-limits. You must take out at Sandy Beach along the right shore just beyond the drop. The river continues in Class II form to the former take-out above Osborne rapid. This Class II rapid is the last rapid before Sherar Falls. Take a look at Sherar Falls from the road along the river right shore before crossing the river. This turbulent Class VI drop has claimed several lives. Fishing structures erected over the 15-foot falls during the season are used by local Indian tribes.

Section 3: Sherar Falls to Columbia River

Class: I to II (III)	**Recommended flow:** 3,000 to 8,000 cfs	**Miles:** 44

Below Sherar Falls, cross the Deschutes River and take the paved road leading to the right. The road soon changes to gravel, following the river for 12 miles before it is blocked to traffic. The remaining roadbed has been converted from a train route to a hiking trail that continues to the Columbia River. Abandoned due to competition from the still-active rail lines on the left (west) bank, the east bank rail "trail" provides a place for hikers to wander. Fees are required for camping or parking; pay at drop boxes near the entrance to the sites.

On river right, campsites along the road for the first 12 miles below Sherar Falls provide toilets for boaters on the lower stretch. Beyond the blocked road, 12 miles beyond the bridge, there are a few facilities. Shade and protection from upstream winds are scarce in this section. Boaters looking for a campsite should opt for a sure thing rather than hope for something better downstream. Use firepans at all times and pack out waste from locations where toilets are not available.

The lower Deschutes River is a perfect place to begin rafting or paddling whitewater. Long, leisurely floats allow boaters to scan the barren rolling hills for wildlife. Fishing is good; obtain a license before dipping a line. Multiday trips provide a few Class II and III rapids before the confluence with the Columbia River. The rapids are wide and easily negotiated by most craft. Open whitewater canoes could swamp in the big waves of the lower 10 miles, but most open boaters will enjoy the excitement and change of pace.

Within the first 2 miles below Sherar Falls, there are a couple Class III rapids known as **Upper Bridge** and **Lower Bridge** rapids, plus some great surfing spots. The rapids are visible from the paved section of road above the river on the right. Rafts have a hard launch below the falls at the parking area near the bridge, since the rock bank there is steep. Most rafters put in at one of the campground and boat launch areas below these first rapids instead.

Since the floods of 1996 a great surf area has been created along the upper portion of this stretch at **Trestle Hole.** Cleaned out during the floods, this large wave has been transformed into a nice play spot at moderate flows. The wave is large enough to support several paddlers at a time and makes a wonderful start to the lower stretch of river.

The next 30 miles contain Class I water with a few Class II areas that can be avoided. Plan to spend time watching the banks, which are home to white-tailed deer and antelope. All types of birds also fly up the river corridor. Practicing eddy-turns and maneuvering helps entertain boaters along this flat stretch. Campsites below the right bank roadblock are rare, since the open terrain provides few suitable places with shade and wood. Prepare for strong evening winds as the temperature drops. Later in the evening winds generally subside unless a stormfront is moving in.

A new rapid, **Washout** (RM 8), was created in July 1995. The rapid can be scouted on the left, but is easily run center to right through large standing waves. Avoid the large hole on the left. Two miles below Washout, Class II+ **Gordon Ridge** rapid presents a ledge-drop with big waves above and below. **Colorado** rapid follows in about 1.5 miles where the river presents large standing waves; avoid the hole on the left by following the central wave train. **Rattlesnake** is just a mile downstream. This Class III rapid drops over a ledge, creating large holes on the right and left at higher flows with a large wave-filled passage that is sure to dampen passengers. Open boaters may find these lower rapids more difficult due to large waves that can swamp loaded canoes. All rapids can be portaged along the right shore, but generally come up so quickly after long floats that shore scouting is rarely done. The river is large enough to allow boat-scouting.

At higher flows, watch for a rapid just before Heritage Landing on the right, your take-out site. Watch for power boats below the lower rapids. In summer and spring, power boats are sometimes seen along the upper stretches of river, but measures are being taken to limit them to the last few miles above the Columbia.

21 Donner Und Blitzen River

Bllitzen Crossing to Page Springs Campground

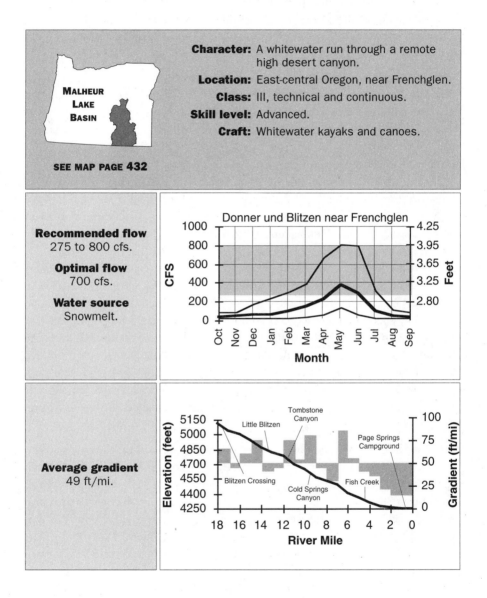

MALHEUR LAKE BASIN

SEE MAP PAGE **432**

Character: A whitewater run through a remote high desert canyon.

Location: East-central Oregon, near Frenchglen.

Class: III, technical and continuous.

Skill level: Advanced.

Craft: Whitewater kayaks and canoes.

Recommended flow
275 to 800 cfs.

Optimal flow
700 cfs.

Water source
Snowmelt.

Donner und Blitzen near Frenchglen

CFS: 1000, 800, 600, 400, 200, 0
Feet: 4.25, 3.95, 3.65, 3.25, 2.80
Month: Oct, Nov, Dec, Jan, Feb, Mar, Apr, May, Jun, Jul, Aug, Sep

Average gradient
49 ft/mi.

Elevation (feet): 5150, 5000, 4850, 4700, 4550, 4400, 4250
Gradient (ft/mi): 100, 75, 50, 25, 0
River Mile: 18, 16, 14, 12, 10, 8, 6, 4, 2, 0

Little Blitzen, Tombstone Canyon, Page Springs Campground, Blitzen Crossing, Cold Springs Canyon, Fish Creek

Hazards: The Donner und Blitzen River is long and remote, making rescue or assistance in case of injury or equipment failure difficult. Brush crowds the narrow first mile below the put-in, a nuisance if not a hazard. The most difficult rapid is a Class III+ ledge-drop (River Mile 14.9) 2.6 miles below the put-in. A fence is suspended over the river just upstream from the take-out at Page Springs Campground.

Access: From Burns, along U.S. Highway 20 in east-central Oregon, take Oregon Highway 78 east for 2 miles. Turn right (south) on Oregon Highway 205 and go about 55 miles to the tiny community of Frenchglen. Just south of town, OR 205 proceeds steeply uphill to the right and a gravel road angles off to Steens Mountain on the left. Follow the gravel road for 3 miles to the Bureau of Land Management's Page Springs Campground, the take-out.

To reach the put-in, continue south on OR 205 from Frenchglen for about 10 miles to Steens Mountain Loop Road. Turn left onto this gravel road and continue 16 miles to Blitzen Crossing, a steel bridge where Steens Mountain Loop Road crosses the South Fork Donner und Blitzen River. Blitzen Crossing is the put-in point. Primitive camping is possible in the small field just east of the bridge.

There are four gates on Steens Mountain Loop Road. Gate 4, the South Gate, is opened by the BLM in May and provides access to the South Fork at Blitzen Crossing. Gate 3 is just east of Blitzen Crossing and is opened later, depending on snowpack. This does not help boaters, however, since there is no public access to the river via the Riddle Brothers Ranch, at the confluence of the Little Blitzen and the South Fork. Check with the BLM District Office in Hines, (541) 573-5241, for gage readings and to determine that Gate 4 is open. (Another source of gage readings is the USGS in Portland.) In Frenchglen, paddlers can arrange for a shuttle from Page Springs Campground to Blitzen Crossing or the nearby Steens Mountain Resort.

Overview: The Donner und Blitzen River, often referred to as the Blitzen, is a Wild and Scenic River and a superb fly-fishing stream. The mountain river flows through a parched southeast Oregon setting with no outlet beyond Malheur Lake. It drains magnificent Steens Mountain, a 50-mile uplift fault block in the Basin and Range Province. The John Scharff Section of the Desert Trail crosses the river at RM 5.5. Malheur National Wildlife Refuge, Diamond Craters, Alvord Desert, and Hart Mountain National Antelope Refuge are nearby. Hart Mountain also boasts natural hot springs with small rock pools.

Located in a region of exceptional biological diversity, the Donner und Blitzen is boated infrequently. The run described here is 17.2 miles long and drops more than 800 feet from Blitzen Crossing to Page Springs Campground through a deep, remote basalt canyon. Major tributaries are Indian Creek, the Little Blitzen River, and Fish Creek, all flowing out of high glacier-carved gorges on the west side of Steens Mountain. Paddling time, including occasional scouting of rapids, is about six hours. For those with a little more time to spend on the river, the run makes an attractive two-day trip.

Going with the flow

Class: III (III+)	Recommended flow: 550 to 800 cfs	Miles: 17.2

The run down the Donner und Blitzen River has three distinct sections: the South Fork from Indian Creek to the confluence with the Little Blitzen; the main Donner und Blitzen from the Little Blitzen River to about 1.5 miles above Fish Creek; and from there to Page Springs Campground. Because there is no access to the lower two sections, paddlers must undertake all three parts, a total of 17.2 miles.

The first 3.8-mile section on the Blitzen has an average gradient of 57 feet per mile. Put in just upstream of the bridge at Blitzen Crossing (RM 17.5). The river is a narrow stream here, crowded by brush from both banks, particularly in the first mile. Downstream it begins to open up, providing more room to maneuver. After 2.6 miles (RM 14.9) the canyon narrows and the river makes a steep, sharp, nearly blind bend to the left. At the very end of the bend is a 4- to 5-foot Class III+ broken ledge-drop, beginning a 1-mile section with a gradient of 75 feet per mile. The Little Blitzen River (RM 13.7) enters on the right in less than 0.5 mile. The confluence has a broad, grassy delta with an old jeep trail leading down from the Riddle Brothers Ranch. At this point the canyon walls rise 100 to 150 feet.

From the Little Blitzen to about 1.5 miles above Fish Creek, the river presents 7.9 miles of Class III water with an average gradient of 56 feet per mile. The Little Blitzen increases the flow of the South Fork by about 60 percent, widening the river substantially. Two steeper sections of 70 to 75 feet per mile are each roughly 1 mile in length. They begin 2 and 4 miles respectively (RM 11.7 & RM 9.7) downstream from the Little Blitzen. Tombstone Canyon (RM 11.7) enters from the left, followed by Cold Spring Canyon (RM 9.5) just over 2 miles beyond. The canyon walls in this section rise 200 to 300 feet above the river. The steep side canyons offer interesting hikes to the canyon rim.

About 1.5 miles above Fish Creek, the bottomland begins to open up on either side of the river, and the gradient decreases. From there to Page Springs Campground the river is Class II- over 5.5 miles, with a gradient of 31 feet per mile. The Desert Trail and an old jeep trail cross the river near Big Springs (RM 5.5), on the right. Fish Creek (RM 4.3) enters from the right 1.2 miles later. The Page Springs Gaging Station is located on the left just upstream from a 5-foot dam (RM 1.4) that can be run. Just upstream, almost within sight of the Page Springs Campground, a fence is suspended over the river. With care, paddlers can make it through gaps in this fence. Take out on the right at Page Springs Campground (RM 0.3).

—*Steve Cramer*

22 Drift Creek, the Alsea River Drainage

Meadow Creek to Alsea Bay

MID COAST
BASIN

SEE MAP PAGE **434**

Character: A wilderness trip through lush coastal rain forest.

Location: Central Oregon coast, south of Newport.

Class: II (III), continuous.

Skill level: Beginner to intermediate.

Craft: Kayaks and canoes.

Recommended flow
200 to 500 cfs.

Optimal flow
400 cfs.

Water source
Rain.

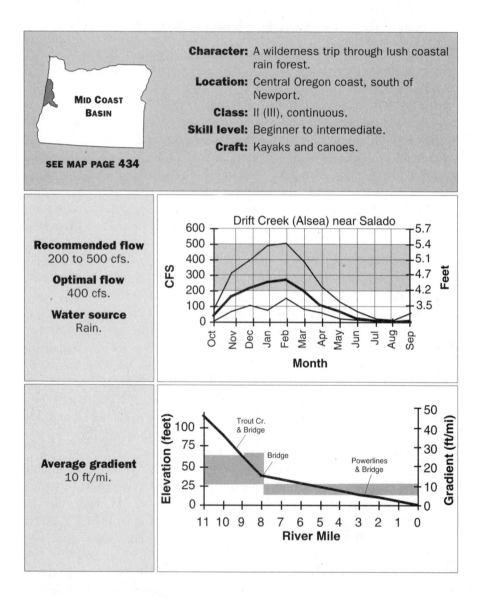

Drift Creek (Alsea) near Salado

Average gradient
10 ft/mi.

Hazards: Logs are always present in Drift Creek, forcing limbos in two locations. Portaging is not a problem except for brushy banks. The Drift Creek Wilderness Area is remote, with no roads and only one hiking traill crossing.

Access: From U.S. Highway 101 along the central Oregon coast south of Newport, turn east on County Road 701 just north of Alsea Bay. Turn right onto Forest Road 51 (County Road 702) in about 2 miles. At the second road to the south (County Road 202), various take-outs are available. Alternately, paddlers may take out on the south shore of Alsea Bay. Take US 101 south across the bay and follow Oregon Highway 34 east to boat launches across from Drift Creek.

To reach the put-in, continue along FR 51, staying right at the intersection onto Forest Road 50 to the east. Wind along FR 50 until you reach a three-way intersection; one of the roads is Forest Road 31. Take a hard right along FR 31 and stay left at the first two intersections, taking the third right and following it along Meadow Creek to its confluence with Drift Creek. Optional put-ins are available at bridges upstream when the water level is sufficient.

Overview: Drift Creek is a tributary of Alsea Bay that runs through the Drift Creek Wilderness Area of the Siuslaw National Forest. The creek is a pleasant Class II float for most of its length, containing one Class III rapid near the wilderness area

Drift Creek rapids spill over one of the tougher Class II spots. JEFF JACOB PHOTO

boundary. Many small side creeks boost the flow along the way. Lush, brushy banks and numerous deciduous trees line most of the route. During rainy seasons in fall and spring, the area resembles a rain forest. The undergrowth is thick and spongy with lots of ferns, moss, and mushrooms. Slugs, salamanders, frogs are prevalent in this damp environment.

Take good ground cover and a well-sealed tent, even if you are just planning a day trip. Few open campsites look inviting, and lighting a fire with the water-saturated wood here is nearly impossible. Except for a couple of houses before entering the wilderness, there are no roads, powerlines, or trails along the creek. One hiking trail crosses the creek just over halfway through the wilderness area. Other than this one spot, where a campground can be found high on the left, hiking out of the dense undergrowth would be very difficult. Because the run is long and slow at lower flows, make sure to start early.

Going with the flow

Class: II (III)	Recommended flow: 200 to 500 cfs	Miles: 20

Flows in this small creek can change quickly. Frequent rains during the rainy season may bring the water level up more than a foot during a trip. At first, paddlers float down a shallow, winding creek past a residence that sees few people navigating the waters. Within the next few miles several tributaries boost the flow to a more manageable level before the creek reaches the Drift Creek Wilderness boundary.

The rocky creekbed is lined with thick vegetation that would make walking out difficult. The creek itself frequently meanders around sharp bends. Rocks dot the way, keeping your attention. In places, shorter pool-drop slides of Class II water require rock-dodging. At very high flows the creek takes on a higher classification, and the continuous gradient creates a quick Class II+ ride.

Before reaching the wilderness area boundary, one Class III pool-drop rapid presents large waves at high water; it's a more technical zigzag down the middle at lower water. Intermediate paddlers will not find this rapid particularly difficult, but it could easily swamp an open boat. A recovery pool and calm water lie below.

Downstream from the wilderness area, the creek slows and begins to meander through open, grassy areas where grazing cattle may join paddlers in the creek. The landowners here do not allow access or stopping along the bank. Small public areas exists on national forest lands next to the road at bends in the river. Use a Siuslaw National Forest map to locate the areas accurately. Otherwise, continue along the creek to one of the bridges for a take-out, or continue to the Alsea River and Alsea Bay, where boat launch take-outs are available.

23 Drift Creek, Siletz River Drainage
North Creek Camp to Siletz Bay

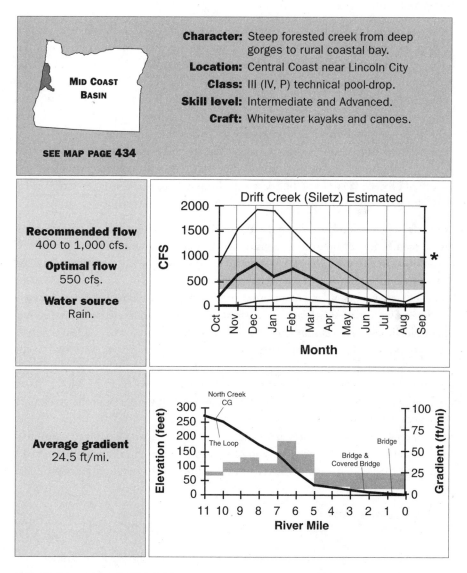

MID COAST BASIN

SEE MAP PAGE **434**

Character: Steep forested creek from deep gorges to rural coastal bay.

Location: Central Coast near Lincoln City

Class: III (IV, P) technical pool-drop.

Skill level: Intermediate and Advanced.

Craft: Whitewater kayaks and canoes.

Recommended flow
400 to 1,000 cfs.

Optimal flow
550 cfs.

Water source
Rain.

Drift Creek (Siletz) Estimated

CFS vs. Month (Oct, Nov, Dec, Jan, Feb, Mar, Apr, May, Jun, Jul, Aug, Sep)

*

Average gradient
24.5 ft/mi.

Elevation (feet) / Gradient (ft/mi) vs. River Mile

North Creek CG

The Loop

Bridge

Bridge & Covered Bridge

* *No depth measurement available.*

Hazards: Watch along the upper creek for log jams and logs that completely span the creek, creating lethal strainers. The creek contains two Class IV boulder gardens that narrow toward the bottom. Paddlers should be alert for wood in any drop and scout any uncertain routes.

Access: To put in, head east on Drift Creek Road (County Route 109), which begins just south of Cutler City, before crossing the creek. Stay right at the intersection with Forest Road 17 and continue to Forest Road 19, farther south. Head east along FR 19, keeping toward the south at intersections, following signs that point to North Creek Camp. A pullout just before the bridge to the private camp makes a good parking and launch site, but scout for logs immediately below this put-in. If logs get in the way, you may want to ask at North Creek Camp (farther up the road) for permission to park and launch downstream at the far western edge of the camp. The normal take-out is near U.S. Highway 101 at Siletz Bay, south of Lincoln City along the coast. An alternative is near the old covered bridge site along the drive. A parking area is northeast of the bridge.

Overview: Drift Creek is a steep tributary of Siletz River Bay and offers a wonderfully scenic ride through a steep mountain gorge, forested with evergreen and deciduous trees. Moss hangs from branches and carpets large boulders, making for spectacular photos.

The upper creek is heavily forested with two gorges containing huge boulders and narrow passages. In some short stretches, the gradient rises to over 100 feet per mile, but the highest gradient for any complete mile is roughly 75 feet per mile. Always be alert for log hazards; they may block any narrow route within the steeper gorge areas.

The lower creek meanders through Class I water to the bay. Much of the surrounding forest has been clear-cut, but cuts are not visible from the creek until you get near the bay.

Lincoln City is a major tourist location, complete with taffy shops, motels, restaurants, and good beaches. If you're a seafood lover, this is a good place to get hungry. If you'd rather watch than eat the marine life, the overlooks along US 101 offer good observation points.

Going with the Flow:

Class: III (IV, P)	**Recommended flow:** 400 to 1,000 cfs	**Miles:** 9 to 11

The upper creek begins with an easy stretch of Class I to II water for 2 miles, then reaches an area of steeper drops and pools within the gorge. You may be forced to portage where logs span the creek near Drift Creek Camp. These obstacles occur the first 1.5 miles below the upper bridge. Once you've passed them, the mountain gorge narrows and steepens for about 2 miles. Class III pool-and-drop rapids dot the creek until you reach a longer, steeper boulder garden with steeper drops in the middle and at the end. A couple more Class III drops follow, after which the creek mellows to Class II for about a mile or more.

A second set of Class III horizon-line drops occurs as the gorge narrows a second time. A longer Class IV- boudler garden ends with a slide toward the lower left against a sharp rock wall. The slide can be avoided by staying just left of the large boulder at the bottom of the boulder garden. Beyond this steeper rapids area are a few more Class III pool-drop rapids that can be scouted from your boat before reaching a water plant along the left shore. The plant is a good break spot and signals the end of the whitewater.

The last 2.5 miles to a take-out at the bridge is a leisurely paddle. You can also opt to continue along tidal water to Siletz Bay and the US 101 bridge, south of Lincoln City.

24 Eagle Creek

Fish Hatchery to Clackamas River

LOWER WILLAMETTE BASIN

SEE MAP PAGE **430**

Character: A rocky, clearwater creek with waterfalls and boulder gardens.

Location: Southeast of Portland, near Estacada.

Class: III (IV-, V, P), pool-drop.

Skill level: Intermediate.

Craft: Kayaks and canoes.

Recommended flow
300 to 1,200 cfs.

Optimal flow
800 cfs.

Water source
Rain.

Average gradient
64 ft/mi.

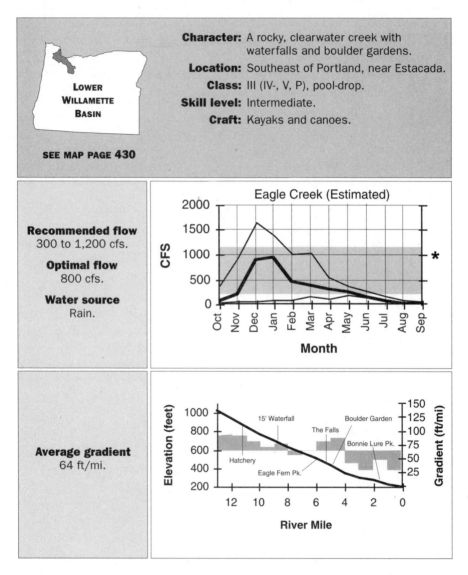

* No depth measurement available.

Hazards: Eagle Creek is home to many logs, and requires one or more portage along either section. A 15-foot runnable waterfall occurs 3.2 miles from the fish hatchery. There is a low head dam, dropping 2 feet, near Eagle Fern County Park. The Falls is a Class V+ drop that appears after a long Class III rapid below Eagle Fern Park. This rapid and the steep boulder garden that follows it are the most significant hazards. Watch for anglers and fishing line. Scout the Class III+ boulder garden from a roadside pullout before you run it.

Access: To reach the creek from either Interstate 84 or Interstate 5, follow Interstate 205 to Oregon Highway 212 and then to Oregon Highway 224, which follows the Clackamas River. Follow OR 224 until you are a few miles past Barton, then turn east on Wildcat Mountain Drive and head toward Eagle Fern County Park. This is the take-out for Section 1. Scout as desired from this road, using trails to the river. To reach Bonnie Lure Park, follow the road to the west at the BP station between Barton and Wildcat Mountain Drive. Take Donity Road to a bridge over the creek and park at the park on the far side.

To reach the put-ins, keep right at intersections to Eagle Creek Road, following this to the park. Beyond the park, follow George Road at the next intersection. Turn left at the fish hatchery sign after about 4 or 5 miles, and follow Rainbow Road to the bridge after about 2 miles and put in near the fence at the hatchery.

Overview: Eagle Creek is a tight, technical creek with many pool-drop rapids and two significant waterfalls that require a portage. Scouting can often be done from your boat, but make sure that you do not run any drop blind, since logs often jam in the chutes on this stream and can shift from year to year. Most of the rapids have straightforward routes weaving down the middle, but paddlers should only attempt them in smaller, rugged craft since many passages are narrow and rocky.

Vegetation is heavy along the creek's often steep banks. The water is clear and blue above a rock and gravel bottom; it is also cold, so don't forget your dry-top. During periods of fair weather and low water, Eagle Creek is a popular hangout for people of all ages seeking a swimming hole and sunning spot. Eagle Creek Road offers numerous places to park, with trails leading down to the creek. These trails provide alternate put-in or take-out options along the way, allowing paddlers to choose the type of run desired. Just make sure you know the location of the major falls and portages. A popular run is the lower section below The Falls to Barton Park on the Clackamas River.

Anglers are almost always present during the fishing season, so respect them when passing. You may want to carry a knife on your vest here, since you may encounter snagged, lost, and abandoned fishing line.

Going with the flow
Section 1: Hatchery to Eagle Fern County Park

Class: III (V, P)	**Recommended flow:** 300 to 1,200 cfs	**Miles:** 6

From the put-in, Eagle Creek is a succession of pool-drops and boulder gardens, with a 15-foot waterfall about 3.2 miles below the fish hatchery. Most boaters

Ron Killen negotiates a boulder garden on Eagle Creek.

choose to portage this drop on the right near a cement fish ladder, watching for the cement dividers on the right and taking out above them. Scout this runnable falls from below the fish ladder to make your decision.

About a mile below the falls, paddlers pass a youth camp. Beyond it is a long boulder garden ending with a right-to-left S-turn in the river, which increases in difficulty toward the end. A low head dam drops about 2 feet at River Mile 6.5, but can be run easily down the center ramp.

Shortly after passing under a bridge, the North Fork Eagle Creek enters on the left. This signals that The Falls, a Class V+ hazard, is only 0.5 mile away. Eagle Fern County Park makes a good take-out for the upper portion of the creek, avoiding the more difficult stretch and falls below.

Section 2: Eagle Fern County Park to Bonnie Lure Park

Class: III (IV, P)	Recommended flow: 300 to 1,200 cfs	Miles: 8

Below Eagle Fern County Park, the river makes a long turn to the left and then back to the right. Work toward the right bank and watch for various small eddies before you reach the fish ladder at The Falls. This is a mandatory portage, so don't miss it. Scout the lower portions of The Falls along a trail at a yellow steel gate along Wildcat Road. Carry around the main drop to a steep put-in off the trail. Alternately, you may run down the fish ladder at the bottom of the upper portion. If you do so, be aware of the strong current at the bottom of The Falls, which pushes into the far right bank. Below the main drop is a long, difficult Class IV rapid with drops and boulder gardens, frequent log jams, and a steep gradient. It would be difficult to aid a swimmer in this section, since the steep banks force a run down the rapids past terrain that would make an almost impossible portage. Scout the entire area by hiking down trails along Wildcat Road prior to running the section. Several logs currently require portaging, and these will undoubtedly move around with fluctuations in flow. The remains of an old Cadillac have been in the river for several years. There are also other car remains along the upper creek.

Past the most difficult sections, a few more fun Class III rapids drop between flat stretches. There are some good surfing spots along eroding banks where chunks of earth have dropped into the creek. The last couple of miles meander at a lesser gradient, but wood collects here, often requiring a portage above Bonnie Lure Park. At the park, take out just past the bridge on river left or continue to the Clackamas River, where a longer float leads one to Barton Park in roughly 2 miles.

25 Elk River

Blackberry Creek to Pacific Ocean

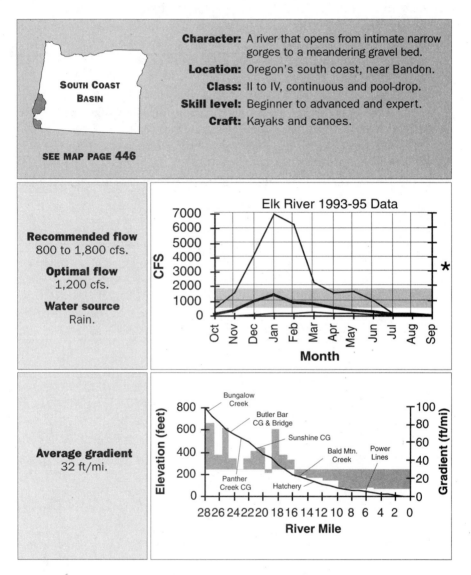

SOUTH COAST BASIN

SEE MAP PAGE 446

Character: A river that opens from intimate narrow gorges to a meandering gravel bed.

Location: Oregon's south coast, near Bandon.

Class: II to IV, continuous and pool-drop.

Skill level: Beginner to advanced and expert.

Craft: Kayaks and canoes.

Recommended flow
800 to 1,800 cfs.

Optimal flow
1,200 cfs.

Water source
Rain.

Average gradient
32 ft/mi.

Elk River 1993-95 Data

CFS

Month

Elevation (feet)

Gradient (ft/mi)

Bungalow Creek

Butler Bar CG & Bridge

Sunshine CG

Bald Mtn. Creek

Power Lines

Panther Creek CG

Hatchery

River Mile

*

* No depth measurement available.

Hazards: Though logs are not generally a hazard along the old-growth areas of the upper Elk River, paddlers should scout the narrow Class IV gorges from the road before putting in. Strainers caught in the gorge could have deadly consequences. Potential for pins in **The Sluice** increases as flows decrease. In addition, **Slides** rapid demands respect, and novice paddlers should avoid the Class II+ rapid below the fish hatchery.

Access: South of the U.S. Highway 101 bridge across the Elk River, Elk River Road follows the river upstream to the Elk River Fish Hatchery. Continue east along this county road, which becomes Forest Road 5325 just beyond the hatchery and follows the river for the length of the run. Overnight campers can find campgrounds at and below Panther Creek before reaching Forest Road 5201, with an additional campsite along FR 5201 at Butlar Creek. Another campground can be found at Laird Lake, 2.5 miles beyond Blackberry Creek.

Put in or take out at desired locations along the Elk River, parking along either FR 5325, FR 5201 at Butlar Bar, or Elk River Road. The only Elk River take-out downstream of U.S. Highway 101 is the beach at the river's confluence with the Pacific, which requires a 1- to 2-mile carry to Paradise Point State Park along Paradise Point Road, or to Cape Blanco State Park along the Cape Blanco Highway. Windy conditions are likely to complicate the carry along the beach, since gale force north winds typically prevail during spring and summer—this is the windiest beach on the Oregon Coast. The only easy public take-out between US 101 and the Elk River Fish Hatchery is located just over 0.5 mile above the US 101 bridge.

Overview: The Elk River is a small, coastal river renowned for its salmon and steelhead fisheries and its exceptional water clarity. Since November 1996, water turbidity has been relatively high, even after small storms. The floods of that month marked the Elk River's largest discharge on record. Turbidity should decrease over time as the numerous landslide scars heal and the streambed cleans itself. The Elk River responds quickly to intense winter storms. Stormfronts producing more than a couple of inches of rain raise the river to levels too high to run comfortably. The river drops quickly, however, and the Elk commonly returns to a comfortable level in only a few days.

The Elk River Fish Hatchery divides the river into two sections. Downstream of the hatchery the river is a meandering gravel bed of Class I and II water. The whitewater section above the hatchery is best described as intimate; its narrow channel is confined within a bedrock gorge. The whitewater season here begins in November after the first good rains and can extend into May depending on weather. More often than not, the river above the hatchery is considered too high or too low to be comfortably run by average kayakers. Small paddle rafts can enjoy the whitewater section beginning at Slate Creek at flows higher than 5.5 feet at the hatchery.

Towering old-growth fir, red cedar, and hardwood trees dominate the scenery wherever the banks are not 30- to 50-foot bare rock walls. Above Slate Creek the river resembles a creek. Below Slate Creek it takes on the character of a small, steep river. Whitewater paddlers most commonly run between Slate Creek and the hatchery, enjoying Class II and III pool-drop sections between the section's two Class IV gorges. The essence of the Elk River is contained in these two spectacular bedrock gorges, where the river channel narrows to 25 feet

FR 5325 closely parallels the Elk River, allowing paddlers to access the river in several locations. Wood hazards above the hatchery are uncommon, but the potential for obstacles exists due to the narrow channel and surrounding old-growth forest. A log caught in the narrow portions of either gorge could result in a deadly situation. For this reason, paddlers must scout the two gorges from the road before putting on the river. Check the upper gorge closely, since it is difficult to portage within its confines.

Going with the flow
Section 1: Blackberry Creek to Panther Creek

Class: II (III+)	Recommended flow: 800 to 1,800 cfs	Miles: 5.6

Section 1 of the Elk River is continuous Class II water except for a Class III+ slot located 0.5 mile downstream of Butlar Creek. The slot can be scouted or portaged from the left bank. Submerged wood in the middle of the slot could pose a hazard at flows lower than 5 feet at the hatchery. Butlar Bar Campground provides an excellent take-out for Class II boaters along this stretch.

Section 2: Panther Creek to Slate Creek

Class: I to II (IV+)	Recommended flow: 800 to 1,800 cfs	Miles: 3.5

Section 2 starts as a Class II run, but picks up speed 0.25 mile downstream of Panther Creek at **Slides,** a Class IV+ combination boulder garden and pool-drop rapid. The rapid is easily recognized by the two large landslides flanking both sides of the river. Scout or portage on the left; only the lower part of this rapid is visible from the road. A series of closely spaced Class III and IV- rapids takes up the next 0.75 mile. Beyond these rapids the river is Class I and II to Slate Creek.

Section 3: Slate Creek to the Elk River Fish Hatchery

Class: II (III+)	Recommended flow: 800 to 1,800 cfs	Miles: 6.7

The action picks up downstream of Slate Creek, where the river bedrock changes from sandstone and shale to granite. A series of closely spaced Class III and IV- rapids begins 0.25 mile downstream. Beyond them is the upper gorge. The gorge includes **The Sluice,** a Class IV rapid with a long Class III+ lead-in. Scout it from the road, since once you enter the gorge it is nearly impossible to climb out. A portage along the road is possible, but long; it requires taking out above the lead-in rapid and putting in far below The Sluice due to a lack of river access. Kayaks have been pinned in The Sluice at low flows. At moderate flows it is typically run tight against the right bank. A series of Class III to IV drops follow, culminating in a 5-foot drop at a 90-degree turn in the river.

The gorge opens and disappears where the bedrock changes from granite back to softer sandstone and shale. Here the river eases to Class II for 2 miles, then rates Class II to III for an additional 1.5 miles. Paddlers who wish to run the lower Class II to III stretch typically put in off the rocks just downstream of a parking spot 5 miles upstream of the fish hatchery. The usual take-out for a Class III trip is located immediately upstream of the bridge at the mouth of Bald Mountain Creek.

The Class IV lower gorge begins with a 4-foot drop at a right bend in the channel where the bedrock changes again, this time to a more resistant conglomerate. Note the various fist-sized cobbles exposed in the rock on the canyon walls as you eddy-hop through this spectacular gorge. The lower gorge must be scouted and portaged along the road. A portage within the gorge is impractical, since paddlers cannot descend to the river until about 0.25 mile upstream of the take-out. The lower gorge is typically run tight against the right bank at moderate flows. The river is Class IV pool-drop for 0.25 mile, becoming Class II for the remaining 0.75 mile to the hatchery.

Starting in March or April, hatchery staff place a trap for sampling migrating juvenile salmonids 0.25 mile upstream of the hatchery. If the water is sufficiently low, paddlers must portage the trap, which is one of the few in the entire state that has not been vandalized. Take out at the gravel bar boat ramp just beyond the hatchery gates and cable car crossing, or continue a few hundred yards downstream and take out below a Class II+ rapid that forms a low dam for the hatchery.

Section 4: Elk River Fish Hatchery to Pacific Ocean

Class: I to II	**Recommended flow:** 800 to 1,800 cfs	**Miles:** 13

Downstream of the fish hatchery, the river meanders in its gravel bed with Class I and II water. Much of this section passes through private property. The upper stretch is forested, with houses located high on the banks. The lower river meanders through a wide floodplain of grazing land. This portion of the Elk River is popular among drift boats during the salmon and steelhead runs, November to March. Canoes or inflatable kayaks may run it into the summer months, but paddlers should take care around the Class II+ rapid at the hatchery. It is easy to put in downstream of this rapid; novice paddlers should consider this option.

The take-out is located among willows on the left bank, identified from the road by a large, gravel parking area 0.7 mile above US 101. For a fee, paddlers may take out at the RV park 1 mile upstream. Steep access trails exist off the county road near mileposts 5 and 7.

Paddlers also may float the river to its mouth on the ocean beach 3 miles south of Cape Blanco. The water is rated Class I below the coast highway, with Class II areas created by wood debris. The take-out at the beach requires a 2-mile carry most of the year, though access may be possible along the beach with a four-wheel drive during winter from Cape Blanco State Park. Strong northerly winds in spring and summer can make the lower reaches miserable, particularly along the beach.

Note: River levels at the hatchery, (541) 332-7025, are given during salmon and steelhead season and occasionally in spring.

The stage on the USGS staff plate does not correlate with the reading at the hatchery. Optimum flow is 1,200 cubic feet per second. Comfortable boating ranges from 800 to 1,800 cfs, which roughly correlates to the hatchery gage at 4.2 to 6 feet. The discharge data for upper sections refers to discharge level at the hatchery; discharges of 1,800 cfs in Section 1 would make it very difficult to run.

—Ron Sonnevil

26 Fall Creek

Bedrock Campground to Fall Creek Reservoir

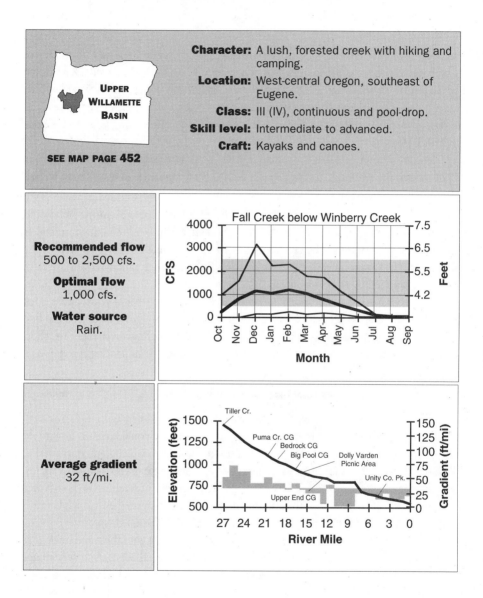

UPPER WILLAMETTE BASIN

SEE MAP PAGE **452**

Character: A lush, forested creek with hiking and camping.

Location: West-central Oregon, southeast of Eugene.

Class: III (IV), continuous and pool-drop.

Skill level: Intermediate to advanced.

Craft: Kayaks and canoes.

Recommended flow
500 to 2,500 cfs.

Optimal flow
1,000 cfs.

Water source
Rain.

Fall Creek below Winberry Creek

CFS — Feet — Month
(Oct, Nov, Dec, Jan, Feb, Mar, Apr, May, Jun, Jul, Aug, Sep)

Average gradient
32 ft/mi.

Elevation (feet) — Gradient (ft/mi) — River Mile

Tiller Cr.
Puma Cr. CG
Bedrock CG
Big Pool CG
Dolly Varden Picnic Area
Upper End CG
Unity Co. Pk.

Hazards: Like most Oregon Cascade rivers and creeks, Fall Creek has logs. The last time I ran it, I had to portage or duck under logs in a couple of places. **Fish Ramp** rapid is tougher than it looks and is by far the most difficult rapid on the run. The rapid can be portaged by novice boaters who scout it before they put on the river and decide on a place to eddy out at its top.

Access: From the Eugene area, drive southeast along Oregon Highway 58 to Dexter Reservoir. Cross the covered bridge on the reservoir and head to Lowell. Drive north through Lowell, following signs to Unity. Turn right onto Big Fall Creek Road, which stays north of the reservoir. Follow this road to the reservoir bridge; before you reach it, pick a take-out spot along the shore that fits your liking. Alternately, you can take out at Fish Ramp.

To get to the put-in, drive upstream about 7 miles to Bedrock Campground. The only road to the river that you will see on your drive up is the short access road to Fish Ramp, allowing a scout or take-out.

Overview: The area surrounding Fall Creek is beautiful, with several campgrounds and picnic sites. Dense green forest lines the creek, and on its south side a hiking trail makes for a fun shuttle option. The creek has lots of Class II and III rapids as well as the infamous Fish Ramp, plus some nice play spots. In between the many rapids are calm pools surrounded by lush vegetation.

Fall Creek has been a favorite of Eugene paddlers for a number of years, and is often thought to be a good introductory run for winter paddlers. This was one of the first Class III runs I practiced on. While you're in the area, you might want to make the short jaunt to nearby Winnberry Creek (Class IV-) as the next step in your paddling progression.

Going with the flow

Class: III (IV)	Recommended flow: 500 to 2,500 cfs	Miles: 7

At the Fall Creek put-in, a rock shelf has provided many paddlers with their first seal-launch. Do your warm-ups in the pool at Bedrock, because you'll have no time to do them as you head downstream. First up is a tricky rapid with a turbulent, narrow slot. Below it, the river has a lot of Class II rapids and a sprinkling of Class II+ and III rapids. Many have sneaky ledge-drops. One deceptive drop comes just below the first bridge over the creek. If you can't see the line, get out and take a look on the left. Just below a second bridge, the whitewater picks up with a couple of Class II+ drops.

Below these the river makes a sharp right bend and starts into the rapid known as Fish Ramp. You can run the first little piece and eddy out on the left just before things start to get serious. Scout this rapid during your shuttle so that you will recognize it and not enter by accident. Take out at the ramp on river left at the end of the rapids or continue to the reservoir.

Below Fish Ramp, the creek continues in similar fashion to the bridge at the head of the reservoir. Just above this last bridge, watch for a major rapid on a left turn. A small pool under the bridge is followed by a sharp drop to the right. This bridge rapid can be seen from the road and is the second most difficult rapid of the run.

—Jason Bates

27 Fifteenmile Creek

Petersburg Bridge to the Columbia River

Character: A weir-infested creek through farmland.

Location: In the Columbia Gorge, south of The Dalles.

Class: IV+ to V (P), pool-drop.

Skill level: Upper advanced to expert near the Columbia River.

Craft: Whitewater and inflatable kayaks.

HOOD BASIN

SEE MAP PAGE 424

Recommended flow
300 to 800 cfs.

Optimal flow
500 cfs.

Water source
Rain.

Adequate flows follow heavy rains from late fall through the spring.

Average gradient
67 ft/mi.

(lower 3.5 miles).

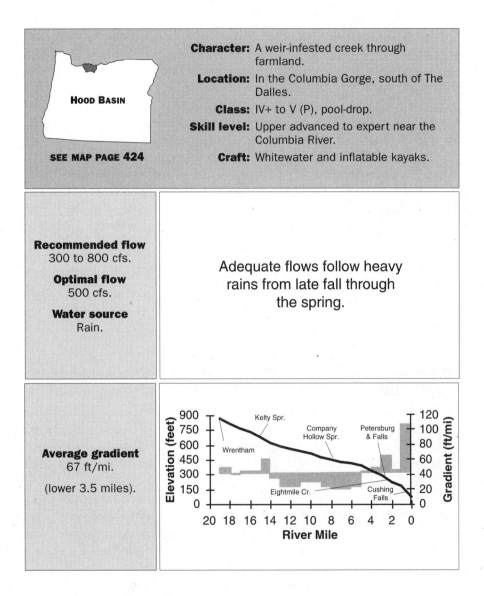

Hazards: Watch out for old weirs, farm equipment, and trash in the river. Scout all drops! Beware of boating restrictions along the Columbia River below the Fifteenmile Creek confluence. The water below The Dalles dam can be very turbulent, so floating there is not recommended (or allowed).

Access: From Interstate 84 near The Dalles, take the Bend exit. Turn right, crossing over railroad tracks, then turn right again. At Big Jim's Hamburgers, take a sharp right heading east. Follow the road that angles off to the left across from The Dalles Motel. Leave your shuttle car at the bridge that crosses Fifteenmile Creek.

To reach the put-in, return to The Dalles Motel and continue along the main road to Petersburg School. Put in upstream of the bridge there.

Overview: Fifteenmile Creek enters the Columbia River just below The Dalles. The area gets little rain, but lots of wind. A dry climate makes the creek home to lizards and snakes. Summers can be scorching hot, as the barren landscape attests. The Columbia Gorge has a special beauty with its steep, rolling hills along both banks of the massive Columbia.

During the summer months, most water users take to sailboards here. During the rainy seasons of winter and spring, kayakers and canoeists come out since Fifteenmile Creek generally has enough flow. Be aware that high flows can increase the ratings drastically. Look carefully at the creek to judge the water volume.

Going with the flow

Class: IV and V	Recommended flow: 300 to 800 cfs	Miles: 3.5

Most of the major drops on Fifteenmile Creek can be scouted along the east bank while you do your shuttle. The majority of the drops are located near I-84—in fact, I first decided that this creek had possibilities when I viewed it from the highway. Although there is ample room for parking near the take-out and put-in sites, once you leave the paved road you are on private property. Though these are usual parking sites, be aware they are on private land.

The put-in is below the bridge just above Petersburg School, Fifteenmile Creek starts off with a few Class III+ drops that are pretty straightforward. Scout from the left bank if you are in the water, or from the school parking lot onshore. After these drops you will see Eightmile Creek enter from the right. Here the channel splits; take the left-hand fork, since it has the most water.

The creek keeps paddlers busy as it passes several residences. Pieces of several diversion dams remain in the water, though all of the old dams have been breached and are runnable. There were no fences across the creek as of this writing, but there may be in the future. Keep an eye on what's ahead of you.

Cushing Falls, a Class V drop and recommended portage, marks the start of the descent to the Columbia River. This rapid is the only ledge-drop you cannot see from the road. Scout and portage on river left. If you mess up on this one, you're in for a nasty swim. Watch out for an old bridge abutment just downstream.

The next drop is an old dam that has breached. It has a stopper rock right in the middle. Sneak this one on the right side of the rock. From this point downstream, be very careful. The many old weirs here can be deadly! I have portaged the next drop because a swim could throw a paddler into the fish ladder at **Inhaler** rapid. Run Class IV+ Inhaler on river right; the deadly fish ladder is on the left side.

The next rapid of note occurs under the I-84 freeway bridge. The right channel on this one is easier. When you get through it and reach the backwater of the Columbia River, take out. The Columbia is closed to all boating traffic in this area.

—*Val G. Shaull*

28 Grande Ronde River

Above Starkey to Snake River

Character: A run meandering through mountain forests, fields and desert.

Location: Northeast Oregon, near La Grande.

Class: I to III, pool-drop and continuous.

Skill level: Beginner to intermediate.

Craft: All in most sections

GRANDE
RONDE
BASIN

SEE MAP PAGE 422

Recommended flow
500 to 10,000 cfs.

Optimal flow
3,500 cfs.

Water source
Rain and snowmelt.

Average gradient
15 ft/mi.

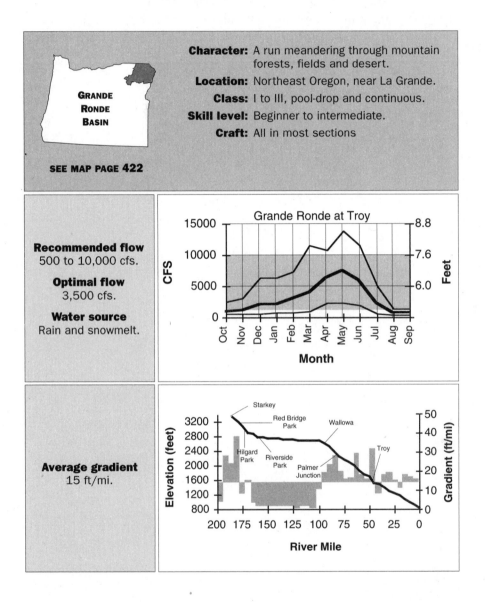

Hazards: Watch for logs and barbed-wire fences above Red Bridge Park. Beware potential log hazards and the firing range below Red Bridge. At some bridges, pillars extend into the river; boats could wrap on these. **Riverside** rapid is the most difficult on the upper section. View it from the Riverside Park take-out in La Grande. **Minam Roller,** below the Wallowa River put-in, increases in size with water volume. **The Narrows,** 10 miles from the Snake River confluence, is a difficult Class III+ rapid at higher water. The lower river is remote and the water often cold.

Access: To reach the upper stretches of the Grande Ronde River from Hilgard State Park, Starkey or Tony Vey Meadows, follow Interstate 84 west of LaGrande to Exit 252. Hilgard Park is just beyond the exit before the bridge over the river. Continue along Oregon Highway 244 to reach Redbridge State Park, the bridge near Starkey, or points beyond.

Access the Riverside Park put-in/take-out by taking Exit 261 off I-84, turning southwest toward La Grande. Take a right at a five-way intersection (with traffic light), and go 1 block to Spruce Street. Turn right on Spruce and follow it roughly 1 mile to where it crosses the river. Take out near the bridge here to avoid Riverside rapid (Baum's Swimmin' Hole), or continue to Riverside Park on the right just beyond the bridge.

Between La Grande and Palmer Junction there are endless possibilities for access along intersecting roads. The most common access options are Riverside

A view of the Grande Ronde at Troy.

Park in La Grande; the Oregon Highway 82 bridge north of Elgin; and the Palmer Junction Boat Ramp at Looking Glass Creek. From La Grande, OR 82 leads to the Elgin Bridge take-out in 23 miles. From Elgin, follow Palmer Junction Road north to Moses Creek Lane. Turn east to reach the lower take-out.

Paddlers may continue to the Grande Ronde's confluence with the Wallowa River, but those who take out must do so at the bridge since private property holders in Rondowa do not permit access. Boaters may float along the designated Wild and Scenic River to Troy or beyond, but plan on taking three to four days to complete the trip at lower water levels. Consult a Wallowa–Whitman National Forest map or a copy of Delorme's *Oregon Atlas & Gazetteer* to locate other road access locations for the central river section.

To reach Minam on the Wallowa River, follow OR 82 from Elgin to Minam in 14 miles. To reach take-outs at or near Troy, continue east on OR 82 for 14 miles to Wallowa. Then turn onto Forest Road 500 (known as the Powwatka Road or Troy Road), which travels east, then turns north to reach Troy in roughly 32 miles. The road is very steep to the river. Look for boat access bridges at Wildcat Creek and Mud Creek before you reach Troy.

To reach the access at Boggan's Oasis, continue along OR 82 to Enterprise and take Oregon Highway 3 north across the Oregon–Washington border where the road becomes Washington Highway 129. Continue up the few steep, twisting miles of Rattlesnake Summit to the store and cafe at Boggan's Oasis.

To reach the take-out at Heller Bar on the Snake River, continue along WA 129 to Montgomery Ridge Road, heading east. Follow Snake River signs along Montgomery Ridge Road and upriver (south) to Heller Bar boat ramp, roughly 31 miles from WA 129.

Paddlers can reach access areas near Troy by turning onto Lost Prairie Road, which heads west from the turn 34 miles north of Enterprise at Flora. Watch for an intersection after the road begins to head north. Take the road to the left here, which leads down a steep, winding route to Troy. Alternately, you can reach other take-outs listed above by heading north of Troy after crossing the river, following a road that leads to WA 129 in 17 miles.

Overview: The Grande Ronde River begins in the Elkhorn Mountains and flows more than 185 miles to the Snake River. It begins as a mountain stream and ends by making a large-volume contribution to the Snake in southeastern Washington. Most of the Grande Ronde is lazy Class I and II water, passing through isolated areas. Scenery changes from forested hills with jagged basalt and thick undergrowth to the open Grande Ronde Valley. The river then flows into a steep-walled canyon through stepped foothills of the Wallowa Mountains and ends in a desert.

The river's upper reaches are frequented by few paddlers—overall, more innertubes than boats make their way down the upper Grande Ronde. Above Redbridge State Park only anglers regularly notice the river. Most boaters float the sections below Minam, which are designated Wild and Scenic. This section of river offers good camping, wildlife viewing, and seclusion for multiday trips. Boaters with average skill can negotiate its rapids, and the river offers plenty of time to recover boats and gear for those who need to do so. Most accidents here are due to lack of proper gear or faulty use. Higher water in spring can swell the river to intimidating levels, however, and its waves and holes become more formidable. Trip time is greatly reduced at high flows. Always wear a life jacket, and take plenty of dry clothes since a swim here can be long and cold.

The Grande Ronde Valley was named by French trappers for its large, round configuration. Surrounded on all sides by steep mountains, it is still relatively isolated. It is not uncommon for both passes to be snowed in, trapping trucks and residents while crews work around the clock to keep the roads open. Weather can be unpredictable here through spring and early fall, so boaters should prepare for the worst.

In historic times, many members of the Nez Perce tribe were massacred by newly arriving settlers along the lower Grande Ronde River. Chief Joseph of the Nez Perce led a fierce battle and retreat from the U.S. military before he offered his tribe's final surrender, laying down arms and stating, "I will fight no more forever." The Nez Perce were strong, peaceful, and ingenious people. Hunting and gathering roots for sustenance, they built strong pit shelters. They were also good at catching fish. After their surrender to army forces, tribe members were relocated to a reservation and taught to farm. The dramatic change in lifeways killed many; they died of starvation the first winter. Though Nez Perce descendants live in the West today, many tribe members died from smallpox or other diseases. A memorial to Chief Joseph stands at the foot of Wallowa Lake, just south of Joseph, commemorating their history.

Going with the flow
Section 1: Starkey to La Grande

Class: II (III)	Recommended flow: 500 to 2,500 cfs	Miles: 25

Above Redbridge State Park, the Grande Ronde River gets little attention. Intermediate paddlers will find more action and seclusion here at higher flows. Four-wheel drives are common sights, since Starkey hosts local four-wheel-drive races in the spring. River races were held between Hilgard Park and Riverside Park until insurance costs forced their discontinuation. Boaters competed for most unusual craft and fastest downriver time in various categories. Folks took all kinds of craft down this stretch, and a few even swam it using boogie boards, wetsuits, and fins. Awards were presented at a post-run party at Riverside. Many people hope these races will be continued in the future.

The upper Grande Ronde is low in summer, when wading is more popular than floating. Adequate to raging flows occur in spring and fall. Some boaters venture to Tony Vey Meadows for Class III water at higher flows. Watch for logs and possible fences on the entire upper river. Several campgrounds line the banks above Starkey. A shooting range just downriver of Redbridge Park may present a hazard for those boating past; make your presence known! Bear and cougar reside

127

in the surrounding countryside, but are rarely seen. Though deer and elk roam above Hilgard Park, sightings are rare from the water and the road.

Below Hilgard Park, the river is mostly Class II water with more difficult rapids near bridge crossings before LaGrande. Just beyond a bridge before Riverside Park, watch for Riverside rapid (Baum's Swimmin' Hole) on the right. Scout it from the bridge while dropping off your take-out vehicle. The hole can be avoided by staying left, where only a wave train usually exists. This is the most difficult rapid on the river below Starkey to the confluence with the Minam River.

Take out at the park on river left or continue along sedate Section 2.

Section 2: LaGrande to Rondowa

Class: I (III)	**Recommended flow:** 1,500 to 8,000 cfs	**Miles:** 32

This stretch of the Grande Ronde River is the least boated, since the river is slow and the gradient very low. Farming and grazing lands flank the river for many miles as it meanders through the Grande Ronde Valley floodplain. Be alert for fences, since landowners do not expect many paddlers on this stretch. Birding is good along this section, but the banks are often high, making viewing difficult. Stop along your route to check out migrating birds. You'll find river access in many locations, but no campsites due to the privately held surroundings. Take an open canoe for a leisurely float along this meandering stretch.

Below Riverside Park, the river moves west at Island City, then continues west where it is joined by several sloughs over the next 6 miles. In another 4 to 5 miles, the flow is increased by Catherine and Mills creeks. The river then heads northeast and loops its way toward Imbler between Mount Emily to the west and Mount Harris to the east.

Past Imbler, the river straightens out and drops more quickly to Elgin. The Union Pacific Railroad and Oregon Highway 82 closely follow the river, high on river left, between Imbler and Elgin. Both tracks and road are far enough above the river to keep from intruding. Take in the spacious scenery and distant mountains. Before long, the mountains close in as the river drops into a narrow canyon between Imbler and Elgin. Grazing land and cattle are prevalent here, so don't drink the water.

The pace picks up from Elgin to Palmer Junction with one Class III drop known as **Andy's** rapid about 4 miles outside Elgin. Scout or portage on river left. The normal route through the rapid sticks to the right. Class II water continues to Palmer Junction and a boat launch/take-out on river right. The rim of the Blue Mountains climbs high on the left along this stretch, paralleled by the Union Pacific Railroad and OR 82. Boaters can no longer take out on private property at Rondowa without permission, so most take out at a campground below Palmer Junction on river right near Looking Glass Creek.

Section 3: Minam to Snake River

| **Class:** II to III | **Recommended flow:** 1,500 to 10,000 cfs | **Miles:** 94 |

This popular river section includes wonderful scenery and great camping opportunities. Most groups take several days to do the run from Minam to Troy, Boggan's Oasis, or Heller Bar on the Snake River. The river traffic decreases as boaters move farther downstream. In early spring and late fall, higher flows mean more demanding current, waves, and rapids. Summer flows are more sedate and relaxing, but below 2,000 cubic feet per second the river is rocky and requires maneuvering for rafts or drift boats. The water is always cold here, since it melts off glaciers high in the Wallowa Mountains; the Minam and Wallowa rivers contribute roughly half of the summer flow. Current speed and running time change dramatically with volume. Spring and fall runs may take half the time in any section. At lower levels, boaters should plan on making less than 15 miles on any given day.

The 10-mile float along the Wallowa River has a similar character to the Grande Ronde, but contains Minam Roller rapid near the top. Avoid this rapid completely at lower flows by staying right on the inside of a right bend in the river just 1.5 miles from the put-in. At moderate flows the rapid forms a fun surf/play hole; at high flows, it increases in difficulty and stretches completely across the river. Minam State Recreation Area, at the end of a short dirt road that follows the Wallowa, allows a look at the rapid or alternate put-in below it. This is a good place to camp

A peaceful camp spot along the Grande Ronde.

if you are planning a next-day launch. The folks at the motel in Minam can provide accommodations and shuttle service; call (541) 437-4475 for details.

Vincent Falls (Blind Falls) follows Minam Roller in 3.5 miles. Here, a drop following a rock garden presents a Class II to III rapid that is more difficult at high water. At low flows it is an easy rock dodge. More Class II water continues to the Wallowa's confluence with the Grande Ronde River in 5 miles.

The Wallowa River enters the Grande Ronde (River Mile 90) near two bridge crossings at Rondowa. Boaters can find several nice campsites along the river between the Wallowa confluence and Troy. One in particular, not far downstream on the left, has a large grassy field and an old cabin just a short hike up a hill. Geese and their droppings are common here in the spring. Eagles, bear, elk, and deer are common in the Umatilla National Forest; unfortunately, so are rattlesnakes. Take a snakebite kit and know how to use it. Snakes become more prevalent as the river moves through the forested canyon into the desert. Paddlers may also encounter scorpions along the lower river.

Below Rondowa, the river becomes a Wild and Scenic waterway until it reaches Washington State. The only rapid in 11 miles is at Sheep Creek, 1.5 miles below the Wallowa confluence. **Sheep Creek** rapid presents a Class II to II+ wave train that can become rocky at lower flows. Great camping along this stretch makes it the most popular section of the Grande Ronde. Holiday weekends can get congested, and competition for prime campsites can be fierce.

Martin's Misery, a long Class II+ rapid that builds from a Class II lead-in, begins about 0.5 mile below Alder Creek. Watch for it where the river bends right then back sharply to the left. Below Martin's Misery, the river eases to Class I and II water that lasts to the take-outs near Troy and at Boggan's Oasis. On the way, cacti replace trees and signs of reduced rainfall become apparent. Several creeks enter, increasing flow as the river begins to meander. Cliffs line the left bank along much of the lower river, and islands divide the stream in a couple of places.

The Narrows presents the biggest difficulty on the lower river. Paddlers can avoid it by taking out at Boggan's Oasis. Luckily, the rapid is only 2.5 miles above the take-out at Heller Bar, so losing gear here is not as serious as it might be. The rapid begins after the river bends from right to left. Scout left to see how the water constricts into a narrow passage, creating a large wave. This wave, as well as the entry waves, gets bigger as flows increase. At high flows it can flip a raft, raising the difficulty from Class III to IV. A Class II rapid follows near a bridge and possible take-out. Those who wish to do so can continue 0.5 mile below the Grande Ronde's confluence with the Snake River, taking out at Heller Bar on the left.

29 Grave Creek

Daisy Cutoff to Rogue River

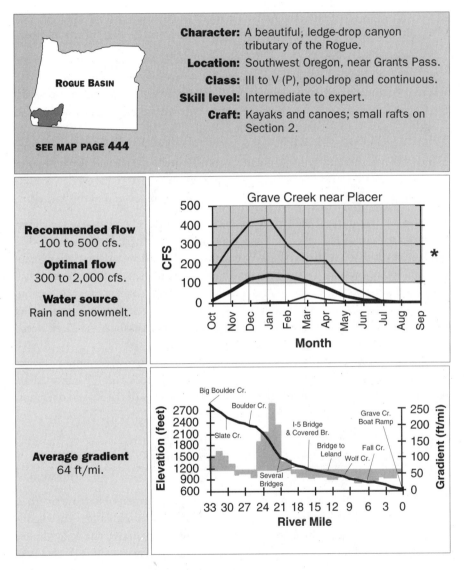

Character: A beautiful, ledge-drop canyon tributary of the Rogue.

Location: Southwest Oregon, near Grants Pass.

Class: III to V (P), pool-drop and continuous.

Skill level: Intermediate to expert.

Craft: Kayaks and canoes; small rafts on Section 2.

ROGUE BASIN

SEE MAP PAGE **444**

Recommended flow
100 to 500 cfs.

Optimal flow
300 to 2,000 cfs.

Water source
Rain and snowmelt.

Grave Creek near Placer

*

Average gradient
64 ft/mi.

* No depth measurement available.

Hazards: Upper Grave Creek is for experts only! Several Class V rapids mix with Class IV and IV+ water. Undercuts, sticky holes, long stretches of difficult rapids, continuous scouting, and log hazards make the 3.5 river miles above McCoy Creek Road bridge an option for only the best paddlers. Intermediate paddlers will marvel at the canyon scenery and fun Class III water in the 12 miles between McCoy Creek Bridge and the Rogue River. Take your camera and be alert for wood debris.

Access: From Interstate 5 at Sunny Valley, take Exit 71 and head east along Leland Road. The main road west of Leland intersects with Lower Wolf Creek Road where it becomes Grave Creek Road, leading southwest to the intersection with the Rogue River at Grave Creek Boat Ramp, the lower take-out. The lower put-in is at the Trestle Bridge near the town of Leland.

Expert paddlers can reach the upper creek by following Placer Road east from Sunny Valley to the Daisy Mine Road Cutoff, following this road farther east to McCoy Creek Road Bridge. This is the upper put-in.

Note: A few miles between Sections 1 and 2 are not covered in this write-up.

Overview: A tributary of the Rogue River, Grave Creek is fast becoming a classic creek run for paddlers headed to the Rogue or other southern Oregon rivers. The creek offers both Class III and Class V sections with boulder gardens, tight maneuvers, and blind corners. Eddies are small. As with many small streambeds, brush and wood are constant concerns. Tall firs line steep banks where numerous tributaries empty into the creek. Paddlers usually run the creek in winter and spring when rain and snowmelt supply enough flow. In other seasons, the creek needs several days of rain to rise to an adequate level.

The upper creek is for experts only. It contains steep, narrow, continuous drops. Section 2, on the other hand, makes a good Class III creek run for intermediate paddlers. If you've got time before running bigger waters of the Rogue or Illinois rivers, take your creek boat and pray for rain!

Going with the flow
Section 1: Daisy Cutoff to McCoy Creek Road Bridge

Class: IV to V	**Recommended flow:** 200 to 600 cfs	**Miles:** 3.5

The upper stretch of Grave Creek is short but steep. It contains a narrow riverbed with shallow boulder-filled drops, making a terrific creek run for experienced paddlers. You'll keep busy through plenty of narrow drops, powerful ledge holes, tight turns, and blind corners. Although most of the creek rates Class IV and IV+, there are four Class V drops to contend with. The Class IV stretches are blind and contain many small eddies at creekside. Scout or portage from either side of the creek.

Brush-filled Class III rapids fill the first mile. As the creek steepens, the brush is replaced with rock. Soon the banks lead you into three Class IV ledge-drops. The first Class V rapid, known as **Tunnel Vision** (or **TV**), is not far below the third ledge-drop in the series. Here the creek makes a sharp left turn before disappearing over a big ledge. Catch one of the small eddies on the left to scout or portage. Tunnel Vision is a series of three 5-foot ledge-drops with a shallow ledge hole at the bottom. The last two drops are very narrow and contain turbulent holes. Most paddlers will be happy just to watch "TV" rather than run this one.

Continuous Class IV+ rapids follow for roughly 0.5 mile before the next major drop. Scout or portage **Off the Wall,** the next Class V drop, along the left. The drop starts on the right down a steep, shallow rapid, colliding into the right wall before turning sharply into the left wall and back again to the right with ledge-drops at the bottom.

After you've pinballed your way through that one, **Terminal Velocity (TV 2)** follows in 0.5 mile. Scout or portage along the left. This is a steep and demanding Class V stretch that continues for about 0.5 mile. The rapids start with a 6-foot boof over a big midstream boulder to avoid the undercut rock on the left, where most of the water is directed. After landing in a small eddy, follow the line down the left, past the undercut and down a steep, 10-foot slide with strong lateral waves on both sides. The rapid immediately pours over a 7-foot ledge as it crashes downstream. The river narrows into a tight passage with lateral waves that pummel paddlers from both sides before ending in a rockslide into a sticky ledge-hole. Watch out for the undercut rock 10 feet downstream on the right. Catch an eddy and your breath!

Once past Terminal Velocity, run everything down the right channel over fun ledges and big rock boofs. Scout or portage along river right. It is all Class IV+ water down to the McCoy Creek Road bridge take-out. This section of Graves Creek was run in 1996 by Kale Frieze, Dustin Knapp, and Brandon Knapp. Good flows are indicated when the Rogue River is flowing 10,000 cubic feet per second at the gage in Grants Pass.

Section 2: Trestle Bridge to Rogue River

Class: III	Recommended flow: 800 to 5,000 cfs	Miles: 12

The lower stretch of Grave Creek is a great technical stream at low water and fun and playful at higher flows. The streambed is larger on the lower creek, so higher flows fit comfortably between the banks. This section of creek is very scenic as it winds through two different canyons that are not visible from the road. A variety of Class III rapids entertain paddlers to the take-out. With enough water, the section can be run in a small raft! The creek was run in 1983 by Jim Frieze.

—Kale Frieze

30 Hills Creek
Landes Creek to Hills Creek Reservoir

Character: A lush gorge with waterfalls and technical drops.

Location: West-central Oregon, southeast of Eugene.

Class: IV+ to V-, technical pool-drop.

Skill level: Upper advanced to expert.

Craft: Kayaks and canoes.

UPPER
WILLAMETTE
BASIN

SEE MAP PAGE 452

Recommended flow
500 to 1,500 cfs.

Optimal flow
800 cfs.

Water source
Rain.

Average gradient
80+ ft/mi.

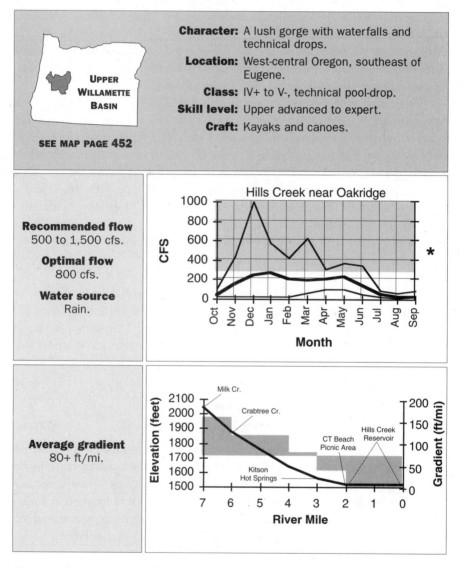

* *No depth measurement available.*

Hazards: The entire Hills Creek run is fairly challenging, with more rapids than there are pages in this book. There are two big waterfalls just above the upper bridge. Be sure to scout them before you put in, since they have been jammed with logs in the past. Logs are sprinkled elsewhere on the run, the majority appearing below the clearcut towards the end. The lower gorge has a wad of roots jammed between the walls. At low water, paddlers may float under this hazard, but it is often obscured from sight by another rapid just above. Scout the lower gorge before you run it.

The road is always nearby, allowing emergency bailout.

Access: From Eugene, take Oregon Highway 58 southeast to Oakridge and turn onto Kitison Springs Road just south of town. Follow signs to Hills Creek Dam, then continue along the north side of the reservoir to CT Beach Boat Launch; this is the lower take-out. When the lake is high, paddlers can continue upstream a short distance to a bridge for a good take-out that eliminates the flatwater paddle.

To reach the put-ins, stay on Kitison Springs Road for another 4 miles, crossing Hills Creek. This crossing can be used as a put-in for those who don't want to run the two waterfalls just upstream. Those who seek the big-air experience should drive upstream until they notice a distinct change in gradient, which lasts about 0.5 mile. Where the road levels out, there is a big grass flat on your right. Park here and carry your craft and gear down to the creek.

Overview: Near the small town of Oakridge, Hills Creek flows into Hills Creek Reservoir. The run starts about 2,000 feet above sea level, as a small creek flowing over a gravel bar in a relatively open canyon. Just below the put-in, the creek's character changes dramatically. The waterway enters a beautiful, deep canyon, curving around a big wall and dropping off the face of the earth in two spectacular and runnable falls. The stream then flows through numerous Class III and IV boulder gardens and a couple of gorges. The gorges are lush, with moss and ferns hanging off the walls plus countless small waterfalls cascading into the river.

Toward the end of the trip, Hills Creek runs through a corner of a massive clearcut. Here the paradise setting disappears. The creek consoles saddened kayakers with a fine section of whitewater at its very end, where it dumps through the mud walls of Hills Creek Reservoir.

Going with the flow

Class: IV+ to V- (P)	Recommended flow: 500 to 1,500 cfs	Miles: 5

Do your stretching and warm-ups at the put-in because just downstream you will encounter the biggest drops on the whole Hills Creek run. The view coming around the first corner is intimidating—the river disappears from sight completely as it pours over a 20-foot runnable falls. After a short pool, the water drops over another 12-foot falls. These waterfalls may become unrunnable at higher flows. I strongly suggest hiking down to look at them before putting in by bushwhacking

Michael Primeau runs a waterfall on Hills Creek. JASON BATES PHOTO

to creekside just below Landes Creek (watch for the steep grade in the road as an indicator).

After its intense beginning, Hills Creek flows under a bridge and through several long Class IV rock gardens. This upper bridge can be used as a put-in for those who want to start below the two waterfalls. Downstream, the river enters the upper gorge. This section holds a few Class IV drops as well as the most technical, tricky Class IV rapid on the run. This rapid is visible from the road, although paddlers cannot scout the Class IV drop that is just out of sight.

Around the corner from the upper gorge is the lower gorge. Though not as difficult, it does have a major hazard in the form of a nasty root wad jammed into a 5-foot-wide slot. This could be a disaster if you are unprepared, because it is only visible once you have committed to running the slot. Backtrack from the upper gorge's big rapid, visible from the road, to scout.

Below this mossy, low-walled gorge, the creek offers a nice mix of fun drops all the way to the reservoir. Sometimes the lake actually covers some of the good rapids at the run's very end, especially in spring.

—Jason Bates

31 Hood River

East and West Hood Confluence to Columbia River

Character: A large river with islands, gravel beds, and rock gardens.

Location: Northern Oregon, east of Portland.

Class: III (III+), pool-drop and continuous.

Skill level: Intermediate to advanced.

Craft: Kayaks and canoes.

HOOD BASIN

SEE MAP PAGE **424**

Recommended flow
700 to 3,000 cfs.

Optimal flow
1,500 cfs.

Water source
Rain and snowmelt.

Average gradient
60 ft/mi.

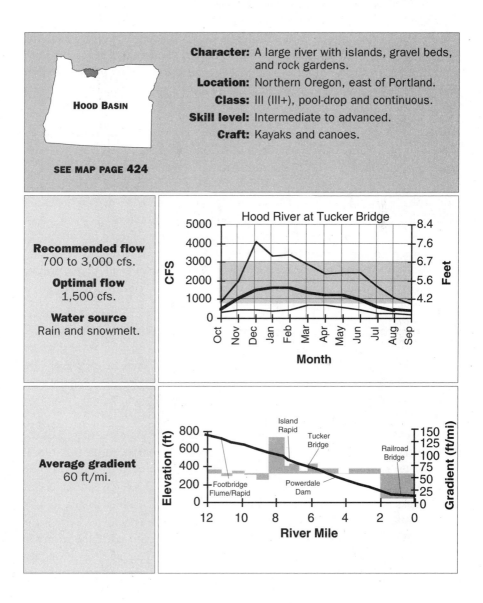

Hazards: Logs are a hazard on the Hood River, more so on the lower run than on the upper tributaries since they tend to get washed downstream and pile up at the numerous islands. The lower Hood also has numerous Class III rapids, evenly distributed along most of the river. Two rapids are more demanding than most. The first occurs just above Tucker Bridge at an island; scout or portage from the island itself. The second is located just below **Powerdale Dam.** Other rapids in this stretch contain a variety of S-turns, boulder gardens, and powerful holes at moderate to higher water levels. Powerdale Dam must be portaged on river left, up a steep bank.

Access: From Portland, head east on Interstate 84 to the town of Hood River. Take Exit 64 to reach the riverside marina, one possible take-out. From here, follow Oregon Highway 35 past Pine Grove and several orchards to Ehrck Hill Road. Turn right and follow Ehrck Hill Road past a left-to-right jog to its intersection with the Odell Highway, leading north. Turn here and continue to the Hood River Highway and Tucker Bridge, on the right. Tucker Bridge is a popular access site where folks can often hook-up with others for boating companions or shuttle.

To reach the upper river, follow the Hood River Highway southwest to Dee, along the lower East Fork of the Hood River. For Punchbowl Falls access, follow Lost Lake Road to the right off the Hood River Highway near Dee and take a second right onto Punchbowl Falls Road.

Overview: The Hood River is one of the few main rivers that originate as runoff from Mount Hood. Snowmelt and rainfall feed the river, making it particularly popular during winter and spring. Still, for many boaters, these prime seasons are too cold, so the Hood sees few problems with congestion. Orchards line the various roads to the river. In spring, paddlers may see smudge or heating pots that keep the fruit trees from freezing.

The town of Hood River lines the banks of both the Columbia River and the lower Hood River. The town is a welcome sight for boaters who dream of local microbrews at the end of a hard day's paddle. The town is also a windsurfing mecca, famed for its proximity to the windy Columbia River gorge. Watch for cars, trucks, or vans mounted with racks that hold both sailboards and kayaks here. The idea is this: if you don't have wind, you can always paddle.

The Hood River offers fast-paced, intermediate to advanced action from top to bottom. The river character changes from forest to rolling hills and a run past residential areas, but the rapids continue nonstop in pool-drop fashion. Banks are steep, with basalt rock and brush or grass in places.

Going with the flow

Class: III (III+, P)	Recommended flow: 700 to 3,000 cfs	Miles: 12.5

Rapids on the main Hood River are mostly Class III with continuous Class II water in between. There are two notable exceptions: the rapids at an island before Tucker Bridge, and the rapid below Powerdale Dam. The former occurs just above

Tucker Bridge, a popular access. Run these long rapids, known as **Island** rapids, down the right side of the island. Scout or portage on the island itself, making note of holes along the way. The river has been diverted toward the bank since the 1996 floods, and small trees waited in the river on the right entry to the rapid in spring 1996. A good deal of debris is still piled on this and many islands along the way, so make sure that routes are clear before running any drop.

After running a handful of Class III evenly spaced drops, paddlers will see **Powerdale Dam** come into view. Portage the dam on river left, up the steep dirt and grass bank. The portage is arduous, requiring a short hike around the dam. The second fearsome rapid occurs just downstream of the dam. It has a nasty hole along center-right (where most of the current goes).

Many drops have changed in the lower river since the 1996 floods. Some of the harder rapids have become easier, and vice-versa. A rapid at the railroad bridge over the river has widened and is less difficult than in the past. Still, at higher water this sharp S-turn can push boaters into the right wall, so be careful. Below the railroad bridge, the river eases up to Class II to II+ water before reaching the Columbia River and the take-out at the marina just upstream along the Columbia River.

32 Hood River, East Fork
Upper Bridge to Lower Bridge

Character: A steep run through fruit orchards and forest.

Location: Northern Oregon, near the town of Hood River.

Class: IV to V at medium water, V (V+) at high water; technical and continuous.

Skill level: Expert.

Craft: Whitewater kayaks.

HOOD BASIN

SEE MAP PAGE 424

Recommended flow
300 to 600 cfs.

Optimal flow
450 cfs.

Water source
Rain and snowmelt.

Like the West Fork, gage readings for the main Hood at Tucker Bridge should be 5.5' to 7.0'. If flows look too high, the West Fork is usually good.

Average gradient
130 ft/mi.

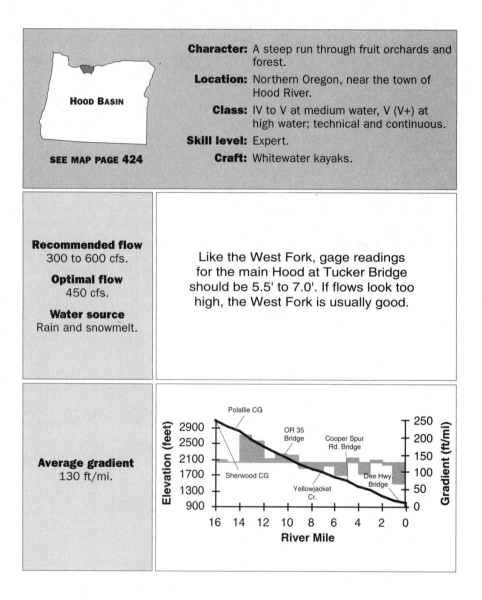

Hazards: A few of the East Fork Hood River's many rapids stand out, but the rest blend together like a stampede of white horses. At low water (at or below 4 feet on the Hood River gage), the river is very rocky; eddies are everywhere, with greater definition between pool-drops. At flows approaching 10 feet, the run becomes very difficult. Large, powerful holes are backed up by larger, more powerful holes; eddies surge, if they exist at all. Wood is always present on this run, with river-wide logs in dangerous places, changing from year to year.

Access: From Interstate 84, take the Hood River exit and turn onto Oregon Highway 35. The put-in is above the community of Hood River, about 2 miles after OR 35 crosses to river right. Watch for a roadside pullout that makes an easy put-in. Take out where the river begins to calm at the second bridge.

Overview: The East Fork Hood River winds through fruit orchards above the town of Hood River. Majestic Mount Hood rises sharply in the distance, allowing paddlers to view its snowpack. Because they are fed by runoff from Mount Hood, both the East and West forks of the Hood River are generally paddled during late winter and spring, or during the rains of late fall. Boaters who wish to camp can find sites farther up the road above the put-in and along the lower Hood River. Most metropolitan area paddlers make day trips here, but staying overnight makes for an easy two-day boating fest that includes both forks. If you opt to make both runs, use the West Fork (River 38) as a warm-up for the more difficult East Fork.

At higher flows, the East Fork Hood River is Oregon's version of the famous North Fork Payette River in Idaho. For those who can handle it, it is one of the best winter runs around. When your other steep favorites are running too high, expect the upper East Fork Hood to be just about perfect.

Going with the flow

Class: V (V+)	Recommended flow: 300 to 600 cfs	Miles: 6

Below the East Fork Hood River put-in, paddlers get a few warm-up drops before reaching **The Ramp.** This 10-foot sloping waterfall drops into a large reversal that sent one friend swimming all the way to the bridge on a chilly winter afternoon. If you are not having fun at this point, get out at the bridge; things only get harder downstream.

Around the corner from the bridge, boaters must portage around a log or two. Be careful here, since the logs can sneak up quickly. Beyond these interruptions, enjoy the float for 0.25 mile before the river drops through **The Worm.** This is perhaps the most notorious drop on the run. Give The Worm a close inspection before committing; a very good boater was dangerously pinned here. The rapid gets its name from a giant culvert that has rolled into the river and now presents a dangerous obstacle. The usual line is down the far right through some large holes.

After The Worm, get ready because the river starts to drop away through a maze of boulders, holes, and ledges. Keep your eyes peeled for wood and catch every eddy. I strongly recommend staying upright. The river is shallow here and its underlying rock is very sharp. Boaters who run out of control through these drops are at great risk.

The river gradually mellows as it approaches the take-out bridge.

—Andrew Wulfers

33 Hood River, West Fork
White Bridge to Hood River

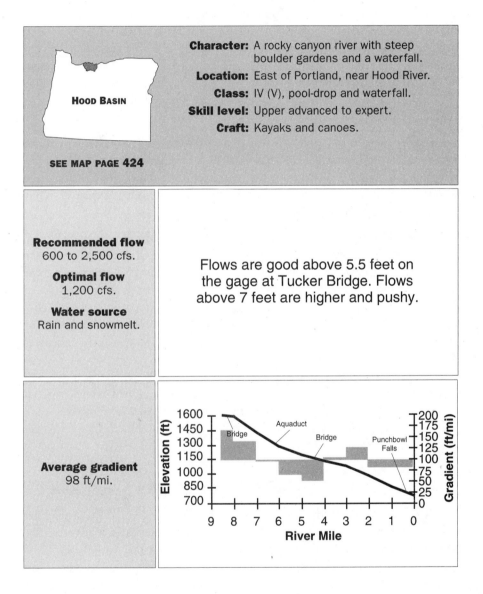

Character: A rocky canyon river with steep boulder gardens and a waterfall.

Location: East of Portland, near Hood River.

Class: IV (V), pool-drop and waterfall.

Skill level: Upper advanced to expert.

Craft: Kayaks and canoes.

HOOD BASIN

SEE MAP PAGE 424

Recommended flow
600 to 2,500 cfs.

Optimal flow
1,200 cfs.

Water source
Rain and snowmelt.

Flows are good above 5.5 feet on the gage at Tucker Bridge. Flows above 7 feet are higher and pushy.

Average gradient
98 ft/mi.

Hazards: New downed logs are always possible in this narrow mountain river. The West Fork Hood River's water, from snowmelt, is cold. About a mile into the run, cables sometimes hold a fish trap in the river. Watch for rebar embedded in cast-off concrete slabs near the old bridge footing in this area. To avoid it, stay in the deep channel. About 2 miles into the run, watch for a river-wide fish ladder; portage on the left. **Boulder Drop** (Class IV) is one of the longer and most congested drops in this section. The drops in the last third of the run tend to be steeper and more congested than those in the upper half. **Punchbowl Falls** (Class V), at the end of the run, is an 8-foot waterfall that creates a powerful hydraulic. Scout or portage on the right.

Access: See the main Hood River write-up for directions to Punchbowl Falls or take-outs farther downstream. To reach the West Fork Hood put-in, follow directions for the main Hood River to Dee and Lost Lake Road. Follow Lost Lake Road about 6.5 miles northeast, crossing two bridges, to a left turn at White Bridge Park and the put-in bridge.

Overview: The West Fork Hood River is a beautiful, clear river running through dense mountain forest. Although the river is never more than 0.3 mile from the road, it has an isolated feel. Though the rapids are distinctly pool-drop, they come one after another to make a fast-paced run. Most of the drops are fairly straightforward, though types are numerous and varied: bedrock ledges; short and congested boulder gardens ending in forgiving pools, and an 8-foot waterfall at the end of the run. Many rapids in the run's last third are steep, making end pools difficult to see from above.

Paddlers usually run the West Fork Hood during late winter and spring runoff. The take-out on river right at Punchbowl Falls is a bit long and fairly steep, but boaters can avoid it by extending their run to the confluence with the East Fork Hood River, or paddling an additional 6 miles on the main Hood River to Tucker Bridge.

Going with the flow

Class: IV (V)	Recommended flow: 600 to 2,500 cfs	Miles: 6.5

Before you put in, check the stream gage on the West Fork Hood River, river left just above Punchbowl Falls. Though most boaters judge water levels from the gage at Tucker Bridge on the main Hood River, contributions from the East and West forks vary enough to make readings from Tucker Bridge less accurate. Usually a river height of 4.2 feet at Tucker Bridge indicates a low-water run on the West Fork. River heights between 5 and 6 feet at Tucker Bridge usually indicate some pushiness. Paddlers have gone down the West Fork at a gage reading of more than 7 feet at Tucker Bridge, but it's a wild ride down fast, turbulent water full of nasty holes.

The West Fork run begins at the confluence with the Lake Branch of the Hood River. The first drop is a shallow, cluttered rock garden. The river soon descends into a series of short ledge-drops cut into basalt bedrock. The run is narrow with relatively low volume at first, and feels intimate. But the numerous creeks that feed the West Fork continually add to the volume as the run progresses.

About a mile downstream, boaters may encounter a fish trap hung in the river near the base of an old bridge. In the past it has been on river right; watch for a warning sign that usually is posted upstream. A mile later, you will need to make a mandatory portage around a fish ladder, which creates regular hydraulics. Carry or line boats down the left bank.

Not far below the fish ladder, Boulder Drop (Class IV) begins on a gentle right bend. This 75-yard boulder garden gets steeper at the bottom before the river crashes into a pool. The next drops follows as a short, turbulent chute.

The gradient eases for a fairly short section in the middle of the run, but soon picks up again. The second half of the run has many short, boulder gardens that drop into relatively calm pools. Most rapids here start with a wide entry into routes that converge before dropping sharply into the recovery pools. About 5 miles into the run, Green Point Creek enters on river left, sometimes increasing the volume by a third or more. The remaining drops tend to be steeper and pushier than the earlier rapids.

Brent Mahan aims his Sleek over Punchbowl Falls.

Downstream of a bridge over the river, Punchbowl Falls (Class V) punctuates the run. The river narrows to a deep channel between steep walls of columnar basalt before it takes an 8-foot plunge. Many good boaters choose to skip this drop because of its turbulent terminal hydraulic. Paddlers should pull out well upstream of the falls on river right to scout or portage along the steep, jagged bank. There is a fish ladder encased in concrete on river left next to the falls. At low flows, brave boaters can eddy out next to the concrete slab, but at medium to higher flows this eddy disappears. Paddlers shooting the falls usually run far left where the hydraulic is weakest, landing next to an eddy by the lower gate of the fish ladder. Boof into the eddy at speed.

Boaters who wish to avoid the falls can take out by scrambling up the embankment on river right. The steep trail joins an old road leading to a pullout on the main road. Some boaters prefer to take out at the base of the bridge upstream. Those who continue past the falls will face a couple of additional drops before reaching the confluence with the East Fork Hood. A trail uphill on river right leads back to the take-out at Punchbowl Falls. For a longer day, continue to Tucker Bridge on the main Hood River beyond **Island** rapids above Tucker Bridge. Take out up the ladder below the bridge.

—*Richard Frenzel*

34 Illinois River

Miami Bar to Lower Oak Flat

ROGUE BASIN

SEE MAP PAGE **444**

Character: A wilderness trip through a steep canyon with clear green-blue water.

Location: Extreme southwest Oregon, near Agness.

Class: IV (V), pool-drop and continuous.

Skill level: Advanced to expert.

Craft: Whitewater rafts, kayaks, and canoes.

Recommended flow
500 to 3,500 cfs.

Optimal flow
1,800 cfs.

Water source
Rain and snowmelt.

Average gradient
24 ft/mi.

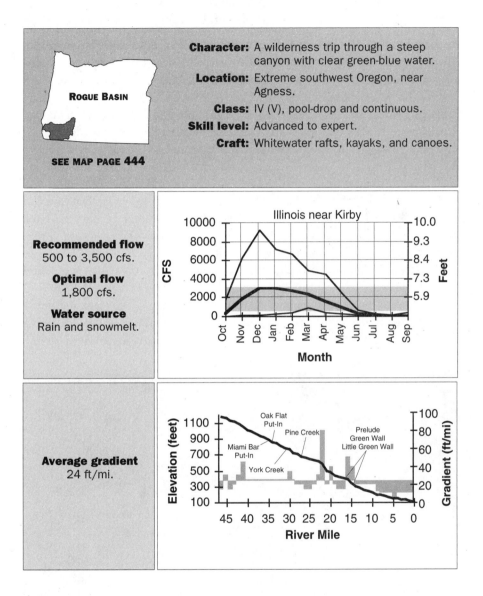

Hazards: Several of the Illinois River's rapids warrant mandatory scouts. Green Wall (Class V) is the most notable of these. In addition, the area is remote, with no access roads. Water levels can rise suddenly, leaving boaters stranded over their heads in difficulty, or necessitating a hike out. Portages are not always viable.

Access: To reach the take-out at Agness, follow U.S. Highway 101 to Gold Beach on the southern Oregon coast. Turn east on Jerrys Flat Road just south of the Rogue River. At Forest Road 33 (the Agness Road), continue 26 miles to reach Agness. Look for boat ramps below Agness across a bridge to the north on river right, or above Agness on river left. To reach Lower Oak Flat, turn south on Oak Flat Road (FR 450) and follow it roughly 4 miles to the access. Paddlers may choose to float to Gold Beach, taking out on either side of the Rogue River below US 101.

To reach the put-ins, return to Gold Beach and follow US 101 south into California to US Highway 199. Follow US 199 northeast to Selma, then turn east on Forest Road 4103 (the Illinois River Road) and follow it for 16 miles to Miami Bar; this is the put-in. If traveling west from Grants Pass and Interstate 5, turn southwest onto US 199 and follow it to Selma in roughly 26 miles. The Illinois River Road can become difficult, especially when wet, so travel in a four-wheel drive if you can.

The shuttle between take-out and put-in on the Illinois is long. One alternative would be to arrange shuttle from the many services available in Galice, Merlin, or Grants Pass. Contact the USDA Forest Service for listings at (541) 471-6500.

Rafters shoot the Green Wall rapid on the Illinois. MATT REA PHOTO

Brent Mahan and Witt Anderson tackle the Illinois in tandem. MATT REA PHOTO

Though some paddlers follow other routes to the put-in, such roads often are blocked by snow in winter and spring.

Overview: A jewel of western rivers, the Illinois River gained protection under the National Wild and Scenic Rivers Act in 1984. Its crystal-clear water, exotic scenery, wilderness setting, and challenging whitewater truly make it a special two- to four-day trip. To really enjoy the experience, take plenty of time. Paddlers can run the 32 miles in two days, but to do so you must spend so much time focusing on the exciting (and occasionally nerve-racking) whitewater that you miss many of the run's aesthetic qualities.

The Illinois drainage rarely accumulates high levels of snowpack due its location in the relatively low coastal mountains. Thus the river's boatable season usually occurs during the rainy months from November to May. Most boaters run the Illinois in spring, from early March to late May, when warmer weather and longer daylight hours are more conducive to a pleasant trip. More so than on most rivers, weather plays a critical role on any Illinois run. The river's steep watershed means that frequent Pacific storms produce widely fluctuating flows. A flow increase of just 1,000 to 2,000 cubic feet per second can turn this hard Class IV run into a thundering Class V nail-biter. Overnight increases of several thousand cubic feet per second are common during the boating season. Many boaters have put on under sunny skies then become stranded midrun due to heavy rain and high water. Limited trail access makes walking out problematic or impossible, and poison oak is prevalent.

Since the chance of miserable weather here is good, prepare for the worst and hope for the best. If you happen to catch a few days of warm, sunny weather, the Illinois is paradise. To ensure a reasonable trip under any conditions, keep your schedule flexible. Have your boat ready, gear packed, and meals planned, then be ready to hit the road as soon as flows are right and weather looks stable.

Keep in mind that the nearest river gage, at Kirby, is 15 miles upstream of the put-in at Miami Bar. Even during stable flows, discharge in the lower river is two or more times greater than the Kirby gage reading due to numerous tributaries. Below 800 cubic feet per second the river becomes rocky and technical, though some self-supported canoe parties have run it as low as 300 cfs. At flows greater than 2,000 cfs, the Illinois is very big and pushy. Groups have run the river as high as 12,000 cfs, but not by choice.

The Illinois is a pool-drop river with most of its rapids formed by natural landslides. In general, the first half of the run is somewhat easier than the last half; the infamous **Green Wall** (Class V) at River Mile 18 is the dividing point. The river provides a gentle warm-up for the first 2 to 3 miles. After that, the action starts and doesn't let up until the gradual wind-down just above the take-out.

Going with the flow

Class: IV (V)	Recommended flow: 500 to 3,500 cfs	Miles: 34

From Miami Bar, the Illinois River is characterized by several Class III and IV rapids with a Class V at Green Wall rapid. Paddlers encounter **York Creek** rapid (Class IV) at mile 5. The rapid crops up below York Creek (on river right), where the river splits at a rock island with most flow going left against a wall. Scout left to see a line over a boulder-drop, after which paddlers must move right to avoid a large hole. With sufficient water, a good route goes right of the rock island; scout it from the right, but watch out for sharp rocks protruding from the gravel bar as the water plunges steeply to the pool below.

About 8 miles from the put-in, the river canyon opens somewhat at Pine Flat. As the water bends left below Pine Creek (on the right), watch for another Class IV drop. This should be scouted. Most flow passes right of a large rock creating a raft-flipping hole after a steep entry chute. A sneak route is possible left of the rock. Pine Flat provides several campsites, rare things on the Illinois. Another good site is located on a series of small, timbered benches at Klondike Creek, 10 miles downstream on the left bank.

The approach to Green Wall is signaled by **Prelude (Fawn Falls)** at RM 17.5. The Prelude begins as the river bends right in a steep boulder drop. Scout left to check out the macho route between the high and rocky left bank and a boulder. The downstream pool entices many boaters to try this narrow slot and accompanying hydraulic. Several technical lines through boulders can be found on river right. The short section of flatwater immediately below Prelude is the last you'll see for a while.

Witt Anderson plays in a wave on the Illinois. MARK MINTERN PHOTO

As the river turns left below this pool, paddlers must seize the opportunity to land left and scout the Green Wall (Class V) from above the challenging entry rapid. There is a small eddy adjacent and upstream of some large boulders on the left; catching this eddy can be an unnerving challenge at most flows, due to fast current and guard rocks above it. The preferred line for Green Wall depends on the type of boat you are in. The standard approach is to leave the eddy and stay left while maneuvering over a river-wide boulder-drop (center-left at higher flows) before passing to the center through huge waves at the lower end of Green Wall. Avoid the right side at the start of the wall section or risk flushing through a boulder slot against the wall (at lower flows) or encountering a massive hole (at higher flows). If it looks too tough, make the extremely difficult portage along the left bank.

You'll see lots more action over the remaining 14 miles. **Little Green Wall** (Class IV) is followed by several Class III and IV rapids prior to **Submarine Hole** (Class IV), 21 miles from the put-in. Scout right on the high, rocky bank to choose a line avoiding the hole. Stay left to miss the hole and the rock point on river right. Although you've passed the most significant drops at this point, there's more whitewater and big waves in the remaining 10 miles. The Lower Oak Flat take-out is 32 miles from the start of the trip. Alternately, paddlers may continue for 4 miles to reach Agness or go 30 miles downstream to Gold Beach along the Rogue River.

—Brent Mahan and *Witt Anderson*

35 Imnaha River

Indian Crossing Campground to Snake River

Character: A steep, isolated gorge run from scenic campgrounds to Snake River.

Location: Extreme northeast Oregon, near Hells Canyon National Recreation.

Class: III (IV), pool-drop and continuous.

Skill level: Upper intermediate to advanced.

Craft: Kayaks and canoes.

GRANDE
RONDE
BASIN

SEE MAP PAGE **422**

Recommended flow
900 to 2,000 cfs.

Optimal flow
1,250 cfs.

Water source
Rain.

Average gradient
65 ft/mi.

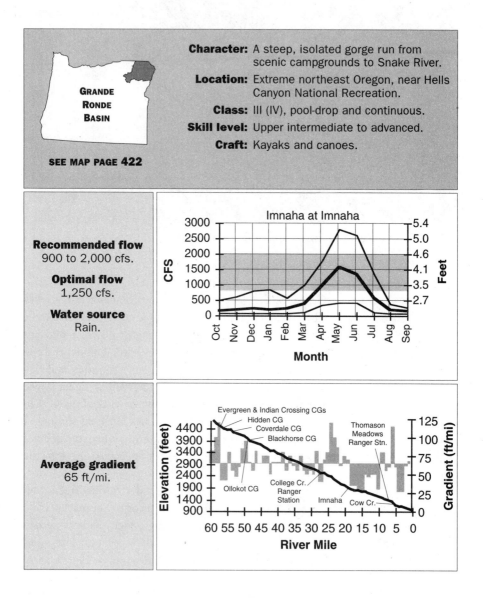

Hazards: Below the town of Imnaha, the Imnaha River presents continuous Class III rapids with Class IV sections along its lower gorge. The river is remote, with little access. Paddlers should be prepared for potentially long swims in cold water with numerous log hazards. Expert paddlers should consider the upper river exploratory and expect log hazards, portages, long scouts, and difficult road access. Roadside campgrounds provide access along the upper river, where the gradient is spiked with steeper stretches. The gradient, 65 feet per mile overall, can jump to 125 feet per mile in steeper segments.

Rattlesnakes, cacti, and poison oak all reside along the river. Boaters must carry water at least as far as Cook Creek on the Snake River, since the Imnaha has high levels of mercury (1 milligram per liter; the accepted limit is 0.12 milligram per liter). Since the river and its lower tributaries flow through rangeland, they also are contaminated with cow and sheep feces. Do not drink the water above Cook Creek, which is 8.2 miles below the Snake–Imnaha confluence.

Access: Hiking and taking-out on the isolated Imnaha can inspire unusual alternatives. Paddlers may arrange for a jet boat shuttle, make the long hike to Cow Creek, or shuttle all the way from Heller Bar on the Snake River. To reach possible access points from Interstate 84 near La Grande, follow Oregon Highway 82 east along the Grande Ronde River to the town of Joseph just north of Wallowa Lake. Turn onto County Route 350 (the Little Sheep Creek Highway), which leads northeast from Joseph to Imnaha. Beyond town, the road heads north along the Imnaha River to Fence Creek before becoming a dirt road. The unimproved Dug Bar Road follows the river to the take-out at Cow Creek before crossing the Cactus Mountains to access the Snake River.

Above Imnaha, dirt Forest Road 3955 follows the Imnaha River to the upper campgrounds and access areas. Alternate routes to the upper river are available from I-5 near Baker along Oregon Highway 86, which leads to Oxbow Dam on the Snake River. East of Halfway, Forest Road 39 leads north before reaching the Imnaha River near Ollokot Campground. Forest Road 3960 also leads to the upper Imnaha River and campgrounds, and FR 3955 (the Imnaha River Road) continues downstream from Gumboot Creek to the town of Imnaha.

Overview: The Imnaha River was named after a Nez Perce subchief, Imna. The "ha" ending refers to the territory—thus, Imnaha meant "the territory of Imna." Explorers Meriwether Lewis and William Clark referred to the river as the Innahar, but it was not explored by Europeans until Captain Benjamin Bonneville mapped the area in 1834.

The Imnaha flows from a glacial tarn about 7,000 feet above sea level on the flank of Eagle Cap peak (9,675 feet) in the Wallowa Mountains. The river valley drops as low as 3,000 feet at the Imnaha's confluence with the Snake River. The river's forested upper section contains logs, some of which have been "installed" by the Forest Service to create better fish habitat. In the section of river from FR 3955 to the town of Imnaha, a good dirt road parallels the river for about 15 miles.

The lower Imnaha River, stretching 25 miles below the town of Imnaha, is the section most worth boating. It lies in a rain shadow formed by the Columbia Plateau and the Imnaha–Snake Divide, both of which rise to 4,000 feet above sea level. From town, a paved road follows the river right bank for 7 miles to Fence Creek, where it crosses to the opposite bank and turns to rough dirt, hugging the mountainside for about 15 miles. Paddlers can glimpse the river in places from the road, but cannot see into the first gorge, about 15 miles above the confluence with the Snake. The road crosses the river again at Cow Creek, where there is a fancy pit toilet and some shade, but no obvious water despite the name. Cow Creek Crossing is at the head of the second gorge. A well-maintained trail with profuse poison oak follows the left bank of the river all the way to Eureka Bar on the left bank of the Snake River, the site of an old mill and mines.

The Imnaha was once renowned for its salmon runs, but major dams along the Columbia River have caused a dramatic drop in the number of salmon returning here. Efforts to plant hatchery-reared salmon have helped the fishing, but the large runs of chinook and steelhead are events of the past. Trout fishing is popular in the summer and early fall, since the heavily stocked river also has a good native rainbow trout population.

Going with the flow
Section 1: Indian Crossing to Imnaha

Class: III to IV	Recommended flow: 600 to 1,500 cfs	Miles: 38

Recent floods may have opened the upper Imnaha River for more serious consideration. Access is good, since several campgrounds line the river's upper reaches: Indian Creek (River Mile 57), Evergreen (RM 56.6), Hidden (RM 56), Ollokot (RM 48.7), and Blackhorse (RM 48.4). For a reasonable trip from one of these upper campgrounds, paddlers could run as far as the lower campgrounds. Alternately, boaters could put in at the lower campgrounds and run to one of the bridges downstream. The town of Imnaha is more than 28 miles below Blackhorse Campground, making it impractical as a take-out due to distance and challenging river conditions.

Because the Imnaha contains many log hazards, rafting is not recommended. Only expert canoeists or kayakers should attempt this run or the lower section due to its remoteness and unpredictable conditions. The floods of 1996 removed several houses from their foundations, sending them crashing into bridges downstream. All kinds of debris hazards are bound to exist in these areas, shifting over time. Scout the river before you put on where you can, getting along the road, and keep on top of river conditions, flow, and access information. Be aware that some stretches contain steep gradients of up to 125 feet per mile.

Expert paddlers who wish to explore the Imnaha's first gorge may find it to be either a boater's paradise or an unnavigable nightmare. Take all precautions in this remote, untraveled area. Recent reports indicate a good Class IV run here.

—Robb Keller

A view of the rugged Lower Gorge along the Imnaha River. Thomas Bell Photo

Section 2: Imnaha to Snake River

Class: II to III (IV)   **Recommended flow:** 800 to 2,000 cfs   **Miles:** 20

The lower Imnaha's gradient is a steady 60 to 65 feet per mile. From the town of Imnaha to Fence Creek, the gradient is about 60 feet per mile. Some bridge pilings require easy maneuvers. At a gage height of 4 feet (about 1,400 cubic feet per second), we drifted the first 7 miles in just 40 minutes. The gage is in town, facing the river. To read it, ask at the general store how to get permission to cross the cattle lot downstream of the school, on the left bank. This stream gage sends data to Portland.

For the first 10 miles below the town of Imnaha, the river is continuous Class II with a couple of easy Class III rapids that have clear routes. The canyon widens into a valley, but the gradient keeps things busy. The river stays almost continuously Class II and III. The few farms along this stretch of river provide some access to spur roads. The gradient lessens just above Cow Creek Crossing, where a cable holding a fish trap is strung across the river. Though this section of river is not especially difficult, paddlers should take it seriously; the current is fast, with no pools and only a few eddies and few points of access.

Cow Creek marks the head of the challenging second gorge, which funnels the Imnaha into the Snake River at mile 191.7 of the latter. The gradient lessens over the first 2 miles, but the river becomes more difficult because it is constricted by rocks that have fallen from the vertical wall on the right. A trail follows the left bank just above the river, but the right bank is essentially a 4-mile-long wall. Paddling the first 2 miles should take about 20 minutes without mishaps.

The gradient steepens to more than 115 feet per mile for roughly a mile above the faster, erosive Snake River. Keep your eyes peeled for a landmark that warns you of this section's first Class IV drop—a subtle rock pinnacle 30 feet up the right wall. Scout the steep rapids ahead for debris and route. The turbulent water lasts 30 to 50 yards.

Expect to find a second Class IV rapid in another 100 yards. This rapid contains a river-wide irregular ledge with a strong backwash, and is followed by 1.5 miles of intense, continuous Class III to III+ rapids that are not easy to read and full of large holes. At the end of the stretch, one last Class IV rapid requires extra vigilance. A fairly direct route left of center leads down the steep drop, then more continuous Class III rapids bring you to the confluence with the Snake River. Paddlers can take out anywhere along the well-maintained trail that follows the left bank of the river between Cow Creek and the Snake River. Be aware that the trail contains profuse patches of poison oak. Take self-contained gear in case daylight fades while you are hiking.

Just below the Imnaha–Snake confluence, **Imnaha** rapids provide Class II to III big water fun. Many more Class II rapids dot the way to Heller Bar along the Snake River, though many of these rapids wash out during high flows. Eureka Bar just below the confluence with the Snake is a good campsite, though you'll have to bring your own water. Those who have come this far can take out at Eureka Bar and hike the 5 miles back to Cow Creek; contract for a jet boat ride to Dug Bar (up the Snake River) then catch a shuttle back to Imnaha; or take out at Heller Bar near the confluence with the Grande Ronde River for a longer shuttle. Contact the USDA Forest Service at (541) 426-4978 for shuttle listings.

—Thomas Bell

36 John Day River

Kimberly to Cottonwood Bridge

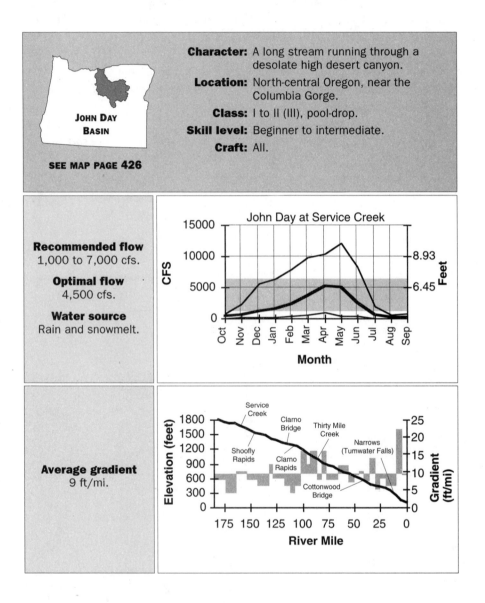

JOHN DAY BASIN

SEE MAP PAGE **426**

Character: A long stream running through a desolate high desert canyon.

Location: North-central Oregon, near the Columbia Gorge.

Class: I to II (III), pool-drop.

Skill level: Beginner to intermediate.

Craft: All.

Recommended flow
1,000 to 7,000 cfs.

Optimal flow
4,500 cfs.

Water source
Rain and snowmelt.

John Day at Service Creek

Average gradient
9 ft/mi.

Hazards: The main stem of the John Day River offers few significant hazards. The main difficulty on this stretch is Clarno Rapid at River Mile 104. Attentive boaters can avoid some Class I and II rapids in addition to islands and rocks.

Access: From Interstate 84, travel south on either Oregon Highway 19 (from Arlington) or U.S. Highway 97 (from Biggs Junction) to Oregon Highway 206. To reach the take-out at Cottonwood Bridge, follow OR 206 to the eastern shore of the John Day River.

To reach the upper access options, follow OR 206 to Condon where it intersects OR 19. Follow OR 19 south from Condon for 20 miles to Fossil. From Fossil take Oregon Highway 218 east to Clarno, continue along OR 19 to Service Creek in 10 miles, or to Kimberly for upper access.

Twickenham Bridge is an alternate access. Access it by taking Oregon Highway 207 south from Service Creek to Girds Creek Road, then following this road northwest to the bridge at Twickenham. OR 207 and US 97 can both be accessed from U.S. Highway 26 to the south as well as from I-84 to the north.

Overview: If you're looking for a peaceful place to get away from it all, the John Day River is a perfect choice. This relaxing river meanders over 280 uninterrupted miles from its sources in the Blue Mountains to its confluence with the Columbia River, making it the longest undammed river west of the Rockies. The river is

Wildflowers grace a hillside above the John Day River in the spring.

protected by State of Oregon Scenic Waterway and National Wild and Scenic River designations, ensuring that it remains free flowing and undeveloped.

Rounded hills covered with sagebrush and juniper create recurring scenes down this sometimes-deep basalt canyon. In places, columnar basalt reaches as high as 2,000 feet above the river. Look for interesting patterns and swirls in the rocky canyon walls. In spring, mushrooms and wildflowers grow from the many cow pies. Occasional camping oases of ponderosa pine and cottonwood trees provide shade from the sun, but they are few and far between. Take sunscreen even in cooler weather.

Volcanic ash once covered this entire area, trapping and preserving plants and animals whose fossilized remains have since been discovered. The John Day Fossil Beds National Monument is located at the intersection of OR 19 and US 26 near the Painted Hills just southwest of Twickenham; other fossil beds are east of Clarno. Revealing the climate and life of the past, the many layers of ash take on colors ranging from buff, green, or rust.

In more recent times, salmon filled the John Day River and its North Fork during spawning migrations after making their way hundreds of miles from the Pacific Ocean. The annual salmon runs have been much reduced since the construction of mega-dams on the Columbia River, which continue to be controversial factors in terms of fish habitat. The John Day is still one of the best small-mouth bass rivers in spring and summer, with good annual catches of cutthroat trout, too. Don't forget your fishing pole, bait, and license—but bring enough to eat on multiday trips, regardless of your intended catch.

The historic Oregon Trail crossed the John Day River at Scotts Ford along Rock Creek, where pioneers floated their wagons to the other side. Several ranches still operate along the John Day River in an otherwise desolate area. Paddlers will see evidence of failed endeavors in many locations. The controversial Bhagwan Rajneesh once set up a commune along the southern shore of the river near Muddy Creek; Rajneeshpuram now supports more cattle than followers. Only near Service Creek, Twickenham, and Clarno is there any visible population. Powerlines and jeep trails are the only (infrequent) signs of human presence between sparsely populated ranches or towns.

Private property lines much of the river above Service Creek, so be careful camping in the area. The Bureau of Land Management has purchased much of the land on both sides of the John Day below Clarno; camping is allowed anywhere in that stretch, except at a few ranch locations. Be careful with campfires since wind can spread fire quickly on the open range. Use firepans (required), carry out your ashes, and keep water handy in case of an emergency. You may not be able to find firewood easily along the river. Waste carry-out is recommended, not required (not surprising, given the cow pies); bury your waste if you do not pack it out.

In spring, high runoff can speed the John Day's current and muddy its water. Bring plenty of water for a multiday trip, or let river water settle overnight before filtering. Filtering is always necessary, due to the many cattle that wander the shoreline. Upstream winds can be particularly strong here at times, especially on the lower river. Give yourself plenty of time to make the trip, even with a headwind. The sections from Service Creek to Clarno, and Clarno to Cottonwood Bridge, often take up to four days each to complete. Though the mileage is less on the upper river, the river there is slower.

Going with the flow
Section 1: Kimberly to Service Creek

Class: I to II	**Recommended flow:** 1,000 to 7,000 cfs	**Miles:** 23

The stretch of the John Day River from Kimberly to Service Creek is less popular than lower stretches due to the number of ranches in the area, plus a major road that runs along the river right side. Though fishing is good, scenery is less dramatic here. Still, Section 1 is a good choice for a day trip, since paddlers can cover its 23 miles in a long day. (Some boaters make a shorter trip of about 14 miles from Kimberly to a boat landing below the Spray Bridge.) Other than a few small Class II sections and some riffles, this section causes little difficulty. At high flows during spring runoff, swift currents can catch inexperienced paddlers off-guard.

Section 2: Service Creek to Clarno

Class: I to II	**Recommended flow:** 1,000 to 7,000 cfs	**Miles:** 47

Many anglers float the first 13 miles of Section 2, from Service Creek to Twickenham, as a day trip. The drift is slow, but boaters usually cover the distance. A road that runs from Cherry Creek to Twickenham offers alternate access options. Avoid camping between Service Creek and Twickenham and in the last 8 or 9 miles before Clarno, since private property and ranches line much of the river here. Access down Rattlesnake Canyon is possible, but roads are rough.

Shoofly rapid (also called **Russo** rapid) at River Mile 150, **Fossil** rapid (also called **Wreck** rapid) at RM 138, and **Burnt Ranch** rapid (also called **Schuss**) at RM 134 are the only named rapids of Class II difficulty. The rest of the river is flatwater with a few Class I riffles. You'll focus most of your attention on the scenery, fishing, or companions, since the river requires little maneuvering except to change the direction of your view. The canyon makes many twisting bends in this section, but is not as deep as in Section 3.

Beginning boaters can shave 13 miles off the section by putting in at Twickenham Bridge. The area is private property, but the landowners allow parking and boat access. Respect the property to keep access open. No camping is allowed, so plan to drop a shuttle vehicle here after camping in either the Umatilla National Forest to the north, or Ochoco National Forest to the south.

Section 3: Clarno to Cottonwood Bridge

Class: I and II (III)	**Recommended flow:** 1,000 to 7,000 cfs	**Miles:** 69

The lower John Day River from Clarno to Cottonwood Bridge is slightly more difficult than the upper section, due to steeper gradient, higher water volume, and an early rapids section. After a 4.5-mile drift, boaters encounter a long stretch of the most difficult water on the river. Clarno Rapid starts with a Class II lead-in to a big-water Class III- section. Boaters can opt for excitement or take more conservative lines without having to bail any water in the end. Some holes could flip a raft, but in most cases they only provide a good splash of water. Open boaters will have a harder time canoeing this rapid without proper gear; all open boats should have flotation bags, and all boaters should wear life jackets. Kayakers and canoeists should also wear helmets, since this rapid could present more of a challenge than some beginners are willing (or ready) to handle.

Beyond this long rapid, a short Class I stretch gives boaters a breather before Class II **Basalt** rapid. This easier rapid has a good surf wave near the bottom. It's only waves, with a couple of smaller holes that boaters can easily miss. After this fun rapid, the river eases to flatwater with some occasional Class I riffles. Kick back and enjoy the scenery, quiet, wildlife, and solitude.

As mentioned in the section above, firepans are required on the John Day and paddlers are asked to remove human waste. Be particularly careful with campfires in this dry, windy, grassy area. Upcanyon winds can be strong in morning and evening. Rowing against the strong winds can slow progress downstream. Boaters should plan on a minimum of three to four days to complete the 69 miles unless they have arranged take-out options in private areas such as Thirty-Mile Creek.

37 John Day River, North Fork
North Fork Campground to Monument

JOHN DAY BASIN

SEE MAP PAGE 426

Character: A multiday trip from secluded forest to high desert, best in spring.

Location: Eastern Oregon, south of Pendleton.

Class: II+ to III (upper), pool-drop and continuous.

Skill level: Advanced beginner to expert.

Craft: Whitewater kayaks, canoes, and rafts.

Recommended flow
500 to 4,000 cfs.

Optimal flow
2,000 cfs.

Water source
Snowmelt.

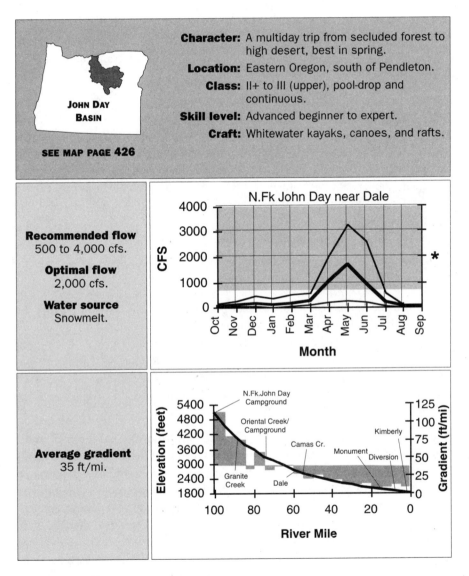

Average gradient
35 ft/mi.

* No depth measurement available.

Hazards: Various Class II to II+ rapids dot the North Fork John Day River. The upper river contains one Class V rapid below the confluence with Granite Creek, plus several longer Class III+ areas. The most demanding rapids of Section 2 occur along the upper portion below the town of Dale.

Log hazards are common along the upper reaches. This secluded river requires special care and preparation, since help is far away. Only skilled, prepared, advanced paddlers should run its upper portions. Paddlers generally plan multiday trips that last from two to four days.

Access: Reach the upper North Fork John Day River (Section 1) from Interstate 84 by taking Exit 252 at Hilgard Park, turning onto Oregon Highway 244, which follows the upper Grande Ronde River. Beyond Redbridge State Park, Forest Road 51 leads south to North Fork John Day Campground and Forest Road 73. FR 73 continues south, meeting Granite Creek and Forest Road 10. FR 10 continues along Granite Creek to become Forest Road 1035. Stay left at the intersection to reach unimproved Forest Road 3016 and Forest Road 3033, both leading to the North Fork John Day. Paddlers may also find river access at Oriental Campground by taking Soap Hill Road south from OR 244. Forest Road 55 leads east from Soap Hill Road to Forest Road 5506 and Oriental Campground.

The lower North Fork John Day is best reached via U.S. Highway 395 (the Pendleton–John Day Highway), which connects I-84 on the north with U.S. Highway 26 to the south. The highway passes through the town of Dale along the North Fork John Day River. To reach the take-out at Monument, drive the Kimberly–Long Creek Highway west of Long Creek on US 395 (the Pendleton–John Day Highway). The road continues to Kimberly for take-out, or to alternate sites along the main John Day River at Spray, Service Creek, and beyond. Section 2 paddlers can put in near the town of Dale, at town access sites, Tollgate Campground, or along the road below Camas Creek.

Overview: The North Fork John Day River drops from forested foothills of the Blue Mountains to the high desert plateau of central Oregon. The transition is dramatic beyond a river confine where basalt walls squeeze the river to a narrow passage. The canyon widens to farm and grazing land. Lodgepole and ponderosa pines thin toward the river's confluence with the main John Day River. Grasses, sagebrush, and juniper thrive here, specked by cow pies. The area is desolate, with small, widely separated farming and ranching communities.

The North Fork John Day is a designated Wild and Scenic River above Dale, but few paddlers explore this rough water through an old placer mining area. Consider upper river runs to be exploratory, since they have not been run recently by anyone that I could find. Advanced paddlers only on the upper reaches!

The lower river is easy and enjoyable for advanced beginning paddlers, and a good place for beginning whitewater rafters. Below Monument, diversion dams force passage down the middle at times. The stretch between Monument and Kimberly is less interesting than other parts of the river due to flatwater and its proximity to farmlands and a nearby road. Look for the new BLM boat ramp near Kimberly beyond the bridge. Paddlers who want a long expedition may float the entire North Fork and continue along the main John Day River to Cottonwood Bridge. Camping is allowed along the river corridor on BLM land or on private lands held by gracious owners. Respect private property along the middle river.

The boating season is short on this long stretch of river. Fed by snowmelt, the river generally reaches a runnable level in early April, peaks in early May, then drops quickly to a rock-scraping level by early June. At higher flows the river moves quickly, but rapids tend to wash out.

Going with the flow
Section 1: North Fork Campground to Dale

Class: III+ to V	**Recommended flow:** 300 to 1,500 cfs	**Miles:** 41

Though I have traveled the area often (La Grande is my hometown), I have not yet had the opportunity to run the upper reaches of the North Fork John Day River. I searched high and low for information about this section of river, but was unable to find anyone who had run it recently. T. R. Torgersen reported that some eastern Oregon paddlers ran this section and Granite Creek many years ago during higher spring flows. Strong, skilled paddlers who are interested in a multiday trip along a remote, Wild and Scenic stretch may wish to consider a spring trip here.

Placer mining has left evidence along the upper North Fork John Day, leaving mine tailings that stretch over several miles above Oriental Creek and Campground (River Mile 73.1). Granite Creek nearly doubles the flow on the North Fork John Day at RM 87.4. Below this confluence is a Class V rapid; scout it before running, since log hazards are common on the upper river. The North Fork Campground, at RM 101, is easily accessed along FR 51, south of OR 244. It offers a possible launch site for an upper run. Consider the entire upper river above Dale exploratory, and take with all proper precautions in this remote area.

Section 2: Dale to Main John Day River

Class: II to II+	**Recommended flow:** 800 to 4,000 cfs	**Miles:** 60

Tollgate Campground (RM 60.5), less than a mile above the small ranching and farming community of Dale (RM 59.7), makes a good put-in for Section 2. Below Dale, the North Fork John Day flows serenely through pine forest. A road follows the river's northern bank for several miles below town, with many roadside pull-outs that allow a variety of launch points. Traffic is light along the seldom-traveled road. Many boaters put in below Camas Creek and OR 395 (RM 57). Boaters can access campsites in this stretch from river and road.

Basalt cliffs line the river's south bank, exposing interesting columnar basalt formations in places. Rapids early in the trip are Class II+ in nature, beginning with **Grandstand**, about 6 miles below Dale. **Surprise** rapid (Class II+) follows in less than 2 miles with a similar pool-drop. Both rapids contain strong eddies on either side and large standing waves down the middle. Long **Chainsaw** rapid presents more Class II action in another 1.5 miles. **Zipper,** one of this section's more demanding Class II+ rapids, requires an S-turn with large waves down the middle. Once you're through it, you've zipped up the stretch's more difficult rapids; there are only a handful of Class II to II- rapids between here and the take-out. Above and below the bridge at RM 43.4 are the only named rapids that follow: **Upper Bridge** and **Lower Bridge** rapids, both Class II-.

Below Mallory Creek (RM 42.9), there are no commonly traveled roads along the river until it reaches the town of Monument. The muddy Middle Fork John Day River (RM 32.4) enters roughly 4 miles below the next bridge, adding 25 percent to river volume. Campsites are plentiful below the Middle Fork. Dave Baum ran the Middle Fork John Day River some years ago, but was unable to provide an update for this book. The 9-mile roadless stretch of river is reported to contain Class II and III water. Road signs near here lead to Ritter and a hot springs for a soak.

Rafters seldom run the stretch of the North Fork John Day between Monument and Kimberly, since surrounding grazing lands and fewer rapids provide less excitement. Anglers commonly launch drift boats below Monument in the slow water backed up above diversion dams. Boaters can find passage down the middle river at the dam sites during spring flows. If you plan a lower river float, take your fishing pole and try your skill at some of the best bass fishing around. Take out in Kimberly at the new boat ramp near the bridge, or continue along the main John Day River.

—Robb Keller and *Jeff Jacob*

38 Jordan Creek
Fork Bridge to Wilson River

Character: A narrow, technical creek along a wooded dirt road.

Location: Northwest Oregon, near Tillamook.

Class: III, pool-drop and continuous.

Skill level: Intermediate.

Craft: Kayaks and canoes.

NORTH COAST BASIN

SEE MAP PAGE **438**

Recommended flow
350 to 1,200 cfs.

Optimal flow
700 cfs.

Water source
Rain.

Good flows are above 7 feet on the Wilson River Gage. Flows above 10 feet can be fast and pushy.

Average gradient
120 ft/mi.

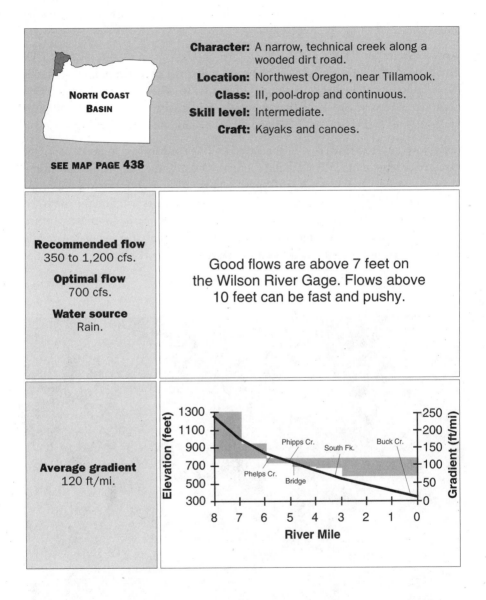

Hazards: Logs are always a concern on Jordan Creek, as on so many other Oregon streams. Creek-spanning logs required two portages when we ran it; one, in a bad spot, was particularly difficult. Scout the creek on the drive up for logs and to check the Class III technical pool-drops that dot the run. Currents get swift at flows above 7 feet on the Wilson River.

Access: From the Pacific Coast, follow Oregon Highway 6 east to Jordan Creek Road, heading south. The road is about 13 miles east of Tillamook or 3.5 miles west of the Jones Creek take-out/put-in on the Wilson River. Follow Jordan Creek Road to put-ins at either the first or second bridge; the upper bridge is about 5 miles up the road. The remote dirt road can be muddy during the rainy season.

Overview: Eager to reach the Wilson River, I always overlooked Jordan Creek. But the creek merits more interest than I thought. Quite picturesque within a forested canyon, it offers frequent Class III rapids. Most are straightforward pool-drops evenly spaced between Class II water. Intermediate boaters will find the run to be busy, interesting, and reasonable, and the road is always nearby for those who are in over their heads. For boaters who want more action than they get on the middle Wilson River, but not so much as on the Devil's Lake Fork, Jordan Creek is the ticket.

Jarod Andre maneuvers his inflatable kayak down Jordan Creek.

Going with the flow

Class: III   **Recommended flow:** 350 to 1,200 cfs   **Miles:** 7

Rapids start just downstream of Jordan Creek's upper bridge, around a sharp right bend in the creek. It is easy to scout these drops, and boaters should do so to check for debris. The first rapid is about as difficult as they come on the creek, but there are many more like it. Often the creek closes in under a tree canopy. In places the rock walls squeeze in, but many nice beach pullouts line the creek for a break.

Toward the middle of the run, one rapid has a double drop and a passage along the right bank that is sharp and tight. It would be easy to wedge a boat here, so boaters should stay left in the wider channel. Below this rapid is a calm stretch with a good break spot on the right.

Rapids from here to the Wilson River are more continuous, but keep their pool-drop character. One last Class III rapid finishes the run to the Wilson River where a good play/wave-hole awaits. Below the wave-hole, look for an eddy and recovery pool on the left with a flat, rocky bank. Take out at the creek's confluence with the Wilson River or continue along the Wilson for a longer trip.

For more action, drive up stream to the next bridge for more fun Class III+ drops.

39 Kalama River, Washington
Upper Kalama Falls to Columbia River

Character: A river dropping from a forested canyon to rural view.

Location: Southwest Washington, near Kalama and the Columbia.

Class: II to III (IV), pool-drop and continuous.

Skill level: Intermediate.

Craft: Whitewater kayaks and canoes.

SOUTHWEST WASHINGTON BASIN

SEE MAP PAGE **448**

Recommended flow
800 to 2,000 cfs.

Optimal flow
1,500 cfs.

Water source
Rain and snowmelt.

Average gradient
34 ft/mi.

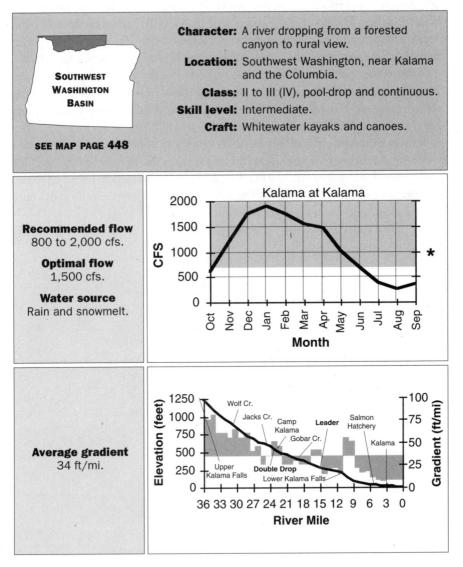

Kalama at Kalama

* *No depth measurement available.*

No data available for high or low flows.

Hazards: Watch for logs, which have been present in bad locations in years past. Visually inspect the river on the drive upstream. Scout the two Class IV rapids, **Double Drop** and **Leader,** on the way to the put-in to scout for debris and to determine if you wish to run them.

Access: From Portland, follow Interstate 5 north into Washington. North of Vancouver, Exit 32 leads east along Kalama River Road and Forest Road 6000 to reach all access locations. Heading upriver, common access points are as follows: the store above the town of Kalama; below Lower Kalama Falls (River Mile 10.7) at a pullout between guardrails; a bridge above Gobar Creek (RM 19.5); a bridge at Jacks Creek (RM 24.6); a bridge at Wolf Creek (RM 31.2); a bridge 2 miles above Wolf Creek (RM 31.2); and the gage and bridge below Upper Kalama Falls (RM 36.4). The falls are 0.3 mile above the bridge. In addition to these locations, paddlers can use several roadside pullouts to avoid the Class IV rapids or determine alternate run lengths. Avoid any private property near homes along the river.

Overview: The Kalama River provides Portland-area boaters with good intermediate and advanced water with lots of good play waves, pool-drop rapids, isolated scenery, and some challenging Class IV drops. Paddlers have ample access to the river, allowing them to decide the character of run desired. Most of the river can be viewed on the drive upstream. Scout for debris and make decisions regarding the Class IV rapids before you put in.

From the town of Kalama, Washington, just off I 5, paddlers can see the cooling tower of the Trojan Nuclear Power Plant looming in the distance. Fear not, since the water that flows down the Kalama River is not connected in any way to this inactive nuclear power plant. Beyond the town of Kalama, the access road and river rise gradually to the Kalama Fish Hatchery. From the hatchery, the road leads along steeper stretches of river as it enters the river canyon and forested area. Some nice residences line the right side of the lower river; one has a spectacular view of a cascading waterfall flowing in from the left. Respect private property along this popular and beautiful stretch.

Going with the flow
Section 1: Upper Kalama Falls to Lower Kalama Falls

Class: III (IV)	Recommended flow: 800 to 2,500 cfs	Miles: 25.7

The upper Kalama River contains more continuous, closely spaced, Class III rapids, with three sharp headwalls before reaching Wolf Creek Bridge. Large holes develop at higher flows. Most of the river above Lower Kalama Falls contains widely spaced Class III pool-drop rapids with Class II water and surf waves between. Exceptions are two Class IV rapids spaced far apart: the first, **Double Drop,** is located 1.5 miles below the bridge at Jacks Creek (RM 24.6) and just above private Camp Kalama (RM 23). The rapid drops over a ledge into a river-wide hole, followed by a second ledge hole along the right. Move quickly left after punching the first hole to miss the meatiest part of the second hole.

A calm before the storm on the Kalama.

The second Class IV rapid, known as **Leader,** is 8 miles downstream. Here the river narrows after some boulders at the top. Most of the current then banks against the left wall, with a scrapy ledge on the right. At higher flows current rushes over the second ledge, allowing an easier ride past the left wall. In years past, a log was wedged against the left wall, leaving little room for error. The log has since washed out—but scout this one on the way up just to make sure.

The upper river contains lots of play holes and waves at moderate to high flows. Scenery is more rural along the upper river, where few homes line the banks. Several Class III pool-drop boulder gardens punctuate the river, but they are generally easy to read and run. Gobar Creek (RM 19.5) has been the dividing line for shorter runs. Good access is at a bridge less than 1 mile above the creek. Below the bridge the river contains mostly Class II water with Class III pool-drop ledges. Watch for an interesting cave along the right rock wall not far below the bridge.

The gradient eases from Gobar Creek to Lower Kalama Falls, with rapids spaced farther apart. Though there are still good play spots along this stretch, they are fewer and farther between. About 0.25 mile below Knowlton Creek, which enters on the left, is **What's That Falls.** This Class III to III+ ledge-drop is just above a bridge. Take out at the bridge to avoid Leader rapid, which follows in just 1.5 miles.

Below Leader the river tapers off to mostly Class II water until it reaches the take-out at the fish hatchery. After homes begin to appear along the right bank, keep an eye out for the spectacular waterfall that drops into the river from the left bank. Do not miss the take-out at the hatchery, since Lower Kalama Falls are extremely hazardous.

Section 2: Italian Creek to the Columbia River

Class: II (II+)   **Recommended flow:** 800 to 2,500 cfs   **Miles:** 10

Below Lower Kalama Falls the river contains several Class III to IV rapids, but access is difficult. The lower river is generally Class II, with some Class II+ areas at higher flows. Most paddlers opt to put in near Italian Creek, running to either Modrow Bridge or beyond it on 3 miles of Class I flatwater to reach the Columbia River. Access roads lead to the Kalama and the Columbia from the I-5 exit above the town of Kalama.

40 Kilchis River

North Fork to Tillamook Bay

NORTH COAST BASIN

SEE MAP PAGE **438**

Character: A lush, mossy, rock-lined coastal river.
Location: Oregon's north coast, near Tillamook.
Class: II to III+, pool-drop.
Skill level: Beginner to advanced.
Craft: Kayaks and canoes.

Recommended flow
250 to 2,000 cfs.

Optimal flow
1,000 cfs.

Water source
Rain.

Flows above 7.5 feet on the
Wilson River Gage are adequate.
Flows above 10 feet become pushy
and increase the difficulty of
rapids along the upper river.

Average gradient
42 ft/mi.

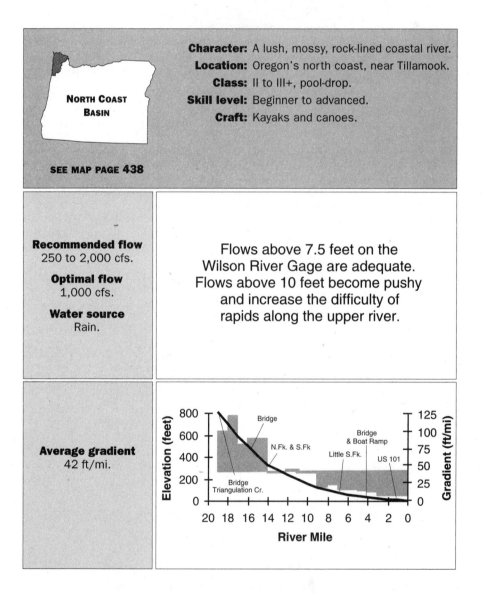

Hazards: The North Fork Kilchis River offers continuous Class III to IV whitewater. Below the South Fork Kilchis confluence, rapids become pool-drop but retain a Class III to III+ rating, depending on flow conditions, to the Little South Fork confluence near River Mile 7. Logs are the primary, unpredictable concern. Keep a watchful eye and you will have no problems. Below the Little South Fork there are few hazards, but current can be swift at high water.

Access: From Tillamook on the northern Oregon coast, follow U.S. Highway 101 north beyond the Tillamook Cheese headquarters to Kilchis River Road, which heads east. Follow this road to Parks Landing, a possible take-out, on the left before you cross the river. A second take-out for the lower river is a couple of miles farther, just across another bridge across the river, near an intersection beyond Murphy Creek.

The usual take-out for the upper river is at a washed-out park near the confluence with the Little South Fork Kilchis River. To reach it, follow Sam Downs Road on river left after crossing above Murphy Creek to what was once a park near the confluence with the Little South Fork. Paddlers can reach another take-out at a nicer park on river right by staying on Kilchis River Road. However, this option entails a longer shuttle if you planning an upper river run.

Upper river put-in options are along Sam Downs Road near the confluence of the North and South forks, or a couple of miles farther along the North Fork at

Leaning subtly to opposite sides of their canoe, these paddlers ferry aggressively across Section 1 of the Kilchis.

bridges and pull-outs. The South Fork looks good for paddling here, but the only access is a mile upstream.

Overview: The Kilchis is a small river located north of Tillamook on the northern Oregon coast. It passes into Tillamook State Forest between its upper forks and Little South Fork. Below the forest boundary much of the land is private, so paddlers must use designated take-out areas. Like many small coastal rivers, it has a short runoff period and an equally short length, flowing a total of only 20 miles. Paddlers often choose to run the Kilchis when water levels are high. Good flows are indicated when the stream gage at the Wilson River is between 7 and 12 feet.

Regardless of flow, the Kilchis is always clear compared to other streams at high flows. This magical place transports paddlers on a carpet of clear green water over a rocky riverbed. Abundant moss grows on everything: long beards hang from trees and pad the rocks. Brush, trees, and thick undergrowth line the banks above an often steep, rocky shore. The river is narrow above the upper forks where the water is almost completely white between complex ledge-drops. Small, rocky beaches along the middle river make great break spots to reflect on the upper rapids and enjoy the scenery. As the river approaches Tillamook Bay, its banks stick closer to river level and slowly open as the river gains in flow.

Don't forget your camera. On a rare sunny day with ample flows, take an extra roll of film.

Going with the flow
Section 1: North Fork to Little South Fork

Class: III to IV	Recommended flow: 250 to 1,500 cfs	Miles: 7 to 13

Paddlers can access the upper North Fork Kilchis River as high as RM 19 at a bridge, but there is a good put-in 2 miles above where the North and South forks split, near the first bridge over the North Fork. From either location, the water is challenging and continuous to the South Fork confluence. Though the North Fork is rated mostly Class III to III+, it earns a Class IV at high water. Most of the rapids along the upper river are winding ledge-drops, closely spaced.

Beyond the confluence with the South Fork, the Kilchis rapids begin to spread out. They maintain their ledge-drop character while easing to Class III water. The most difficult rapid, **The Gutter,** drops midway between the South Fork and Little South Fork. This ledge-drop has a turbulent passage that finishes with a diagonal hole at high flows. Scout or portage along the rock ledge from the eddy on the left. Beware of a log just downstream on the left in case of a swim.

More rapids follow, and the river narrows and passes beneath a large, river-spanning log. From here on, Section 1 paddlers face only the challenge of catching a few surf waves or play holes. Take out near the Little South Fork or float along Section 2 for a longer day.

The author finds a calm eddy among moss-covered trees on the Kilchis River.
JEFF JACOBS PHOTO

Section 2: Little South Fork to Tillamook Bay

Class: I to II   **Recommended flow:** 250 to 2,000 cfs   **Miles:** 5 to 7

From the Little South Fork to Tillamook Bay, the Kilchis River relaxes to Class I and II water, with most of the rapid water near the top of the stretch. Banks open toward the bottom, revealing farmlands and fields between the trees. The road is always close by, but it does not intrude since traffic is sparse. Bridges mark the best take-out areas and are usually visible well in advance.

Fishing for salmon, steelhead, and sea-run cutthroat trout is good in winter, best along the lower river at lower flows. When the water is high, go for the whitewater; at low flows, take your pole. The drift is swift and the river is short, so plan on anchoring if you wish to make a day of it. Take out near any of the bridges. The last is the bridge on US 101. Don't miss this one, since access is difficult once you reach the bay.

41 Klamath River

J. C. Boyle Powerhouse to Copco Reservoir

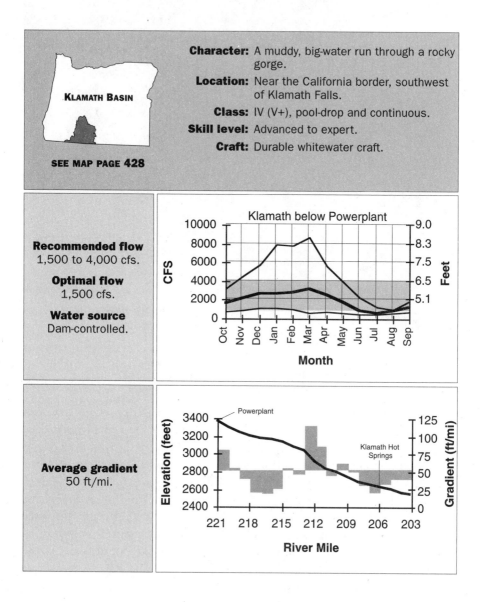

KLAMATH BASIN

SEE MAP PAGE 428

Character: A muddy, big-water run through a rocky gorge.

Location: Near the California border, southwest of Klamath Falls.

Class: IV (V+), pool-drop and continuous.

Skill level: Advanced to expert.

Craft: Durable whitewater craft.

Recommended flow
1,500 to 4,000 cfs.

Optimal flow
1,500 cfs.

Water source
Dam-controlled.

Average gradient
50 ft/mi.

Klamath below Powerplant

Powerplant

Klamath Hot Springs

Hazards: Brown water and phosphate suds make underwater rocks difficult to spot on the Klamath River. The bedrock, formed by lava flows, is unusually sharp and abrasive, threatening both boats and swimmers. Four rapids in the middle of the run are especially long and turbulent. On the plus side, there are few undercut rocks in this stretch.

Access: To reach take-outs on the Klamath River just upstream of Copco Reservoir, drive south into Northern California to where Interstate 5 descends to cross the Klamath and take the Henley–Hornbrook exit. Drive east about 2.5 miles, then turn south and cross the river on Ager Road. In about 3.5 miles, turn east onto Ager–Beswick Road. After another 15 miles, you will pass Copco Reservoir. Proceed to the river and park near Fishing Access 1.

To reach the put-in, drive back to Copco Reservoir, crossing on a bridge to the north shore. Continue another 5 miles, then turn north onto Copco–Pinehurst Road, following this dirt road 10 miles north to Oregon Highway 66. Turn east on OR 66. Just before OR 66 crosses the Klamath River (6 miles west of Keno), turn south onto an unmarked dirt road. This leads to the J. C. Boyle Powerhouse. The put-in is about 0.2 mile past the powerhouse and involves a very wide left turn onto a rough road leading down to the river.

Overview: Between Keno and Copco Reservoir, the Klamath River crosses a plateau formed by volcanic rock that flowed northward from the Mount Shasta area. The river has not yet had time to form a deep canyon in the relatively recent lava flows, or to smooth out rocks along its bed. In many places on this run, rocks just seem to be in just the wrong spot, presenting interesting technical challenges.

Although the Klamath can be run year-round, late summer is its prime season—blackberries are ripening then, and few other rivers are flowing. The run crosses wilderness and ranchland, with abundant birds, wildlife, and potentially good fishing. There are good campsites along the river's upper section, though most people do the run in one day. It may be difficult to navigate the steepest 4 miles with loaded boats.

The upper Klamath has been called the Hell's Corner run. It rates a Class III at the beginning, then Class IV with a gradient of 75 feet per mile for 4 miles, then Class II to III to the end. Commercial outfitter Dean Munroe named most of the rapids on this section, using satanic imagery. This description employs his unfortunate names.

When one turbine is operating at the powerhouse, the flow is about 1,500 cubic feet per second. When two turbines are operating (in winter and spring), the flow is a stomping 2,700 cfs. Rain and snowmelt can cause these flows to increase.

179

Going with the flow

Class: IV (IV+)　　**Recommended flow:** 1,500 to 3,000 cfs　　**Miles:** 15

The run down the Klamath River starts off in Class II rapids, with some respite after 0.25 mile. More Class II rapids follow, beyond which a large island splits the river. Most of the current goes left into Class III **Osprey** rapid. Paddlers can find good campsites here on the right.

Below Osprey, the busyness of the river diminishes. After 1.5 miles, boaters face a Class II+ rapid. Look for the Bureau of Land Management campsite on the right in another 0.5 mile. About 1.5 miles below the campsite, a Class II rapid follows; a pair of Class II rapids occur 1 mile later. About 0.5 mile below these drops, Frain Ranch sits on the left side of the river. The ranch makes an interesting side excursion and includes some good campsites.

The river next turns 90 degrees right, then left, announcing that **Caldera** rapid is just ahead. Scout this Class IV+ rapid from either the left or right bank. Rafters often choose routes on the left, while kayakers choose routes on the right. Caldera is almost 0.3 mile long and very turbulent at first. With rocks and holes everywhere, it's a bad place for a swim. Portaging is less strenuous on the right.

After Caldera come three Class III rapids, then a Class III+ rapid named **Branding Iron,** then a Class II+ rapid, all in quick succession. About 7 miles below the put-in, the river then bends right and pours into Class IV **Satan's Gate.** This rapid often requires that you keep to the inside (right) of the turn. Immediately below, eddy out on the left to scout the next rapid, **Hell's Corner,** which is the hardest on this run aside from Caldera. At high water it is easier to eddy out on the right, but this makes scouting difficult. Hell's Corner holds 0.5 mile of Class IV to IV+ water. Fortunately, it's not as steep as Caldera, but it's still full of rocks and maneuvering.

The river bends left, curves left, bends right, then left again at **Dragon's Teeth** where two underwater fangs grab your boat. Beyond them is a short pool, followed by an easier exit rapid. The action continues as the river curves right into Class III **Jackass,** then bends left into Class III **Scarface.** Shortly after this drop, the river splits around some islands, picks up speed, and turns right into **Ambush,** a Class IV rapid where large rocks block the center and left channels; be careful that you do not wrap your boat. A large Class III+ hole named **Bushwhacker** waits below the last island.

Two Class II rapids with a pool between announce Salt Cave on the left bank. This opening in the cliff is visible from across the river. Please do not enter the cave, since it is home to rare species of bats. The beach below it makes a good lunch stop.

A long stretch of Class II water follows, then Class III **Pony Express.** A long pool below this rapid leads to Class III **Captain Jack,** immediately followed by Class III **Roughshod.** The last tough rapid, Class III+ **Snag Island Falls,** is just ahead where the river divides around an island. Stay right, since the left channel becomes an unrunnable boulder pile. The bottom of the right channel contains a submerged boulder midstream, but you can easily avoid this if you see it.

You are now 10 miles below the put-in. From here, the gradient eases as rapids are spaced farther and farther apart. Watch for Class III **Wells Fargo** rapid in about 0.5 mile, then Class III **State Line Falls** where the river curves left in another 0.7 mile. After this are some steep drops over old diversion dams, but nothing very tricky.

In August, ripe blackberries line the river, but the swift current makes it hard to pick them. Most of the land along the lower river is privately owned, so camping is not allowed. Watch for an old logging chute that is still visible on the right bank about 3 miles from State Line Falls. The take-out comes in another 2.5 miles. It's a nice one, covered with grass and offering a variety of sun and shade for boat drying and relaxation.

—Bill Tuthill

42 Klickitat River, Washington

Yakima Indian Reservation to Old Icehouse

SOUTHWEST WASHINGTON BASIN

SEE MAP PAGE **448**

Character: A meandering, brushy river lined with steep, basalt cliffs.

Location: South-central Washington, north of The Dalles.

Class: II+ to III+, pool-drop and continuous.

Skill level: Advanced beginner to intermediate.

Craft: Whitewater kayaks and canoes.

Recommended flow
500 to 2,000 cfs.

Optimal flow
1,200 cfs.

Water source
Rain and snowmelt.

Average gradient
39 ft/mi.

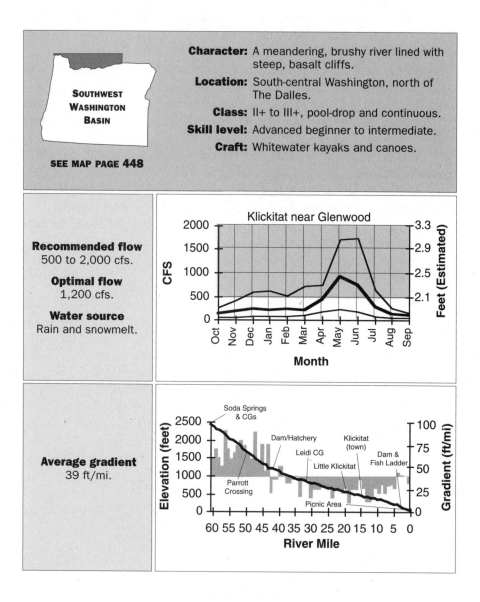

Hazards: The upper Klickitat River is steep, with continuous rapids. The impressive columnar basalt cliffs are continually shedding columns of rock into the river. Watch for wood hazards at all times on the entire river, being especially cautious at every blind bend. Scout, negotiate, or portage as needed.

Below the fish hatchery and dam, the river calms to an easier run for advanced beginners and intermediates. Brush is overgrown in places, allowing only narrow passages. The lower rapids are less continuous and technical than those upstream, but become more difficult with higher flows. Several miles beyond the icehouse that marks the end of this section is a Class VI waterfall. Make sure to take out above this difficult drop.

Access: Interstate 84 follows the Oregon side of the Columbia River between Portland and The Dalles. Cross the river at The Dalles or Hood River and take Washington Highway 14, which follows the same stretch. Reach access points on the upper Klickitat by taking Washington Highway 141 north along the White Salmon River to Trout Lake, roughly 23 miles. At Trout Lake, follow Glenwood Road east to Glenwood, then continue east about 0.5 mile and turn onto a gravel road heading left (north) for upper put-in access. Stay left at all intersections to reach Road K1400 in about 4.5 miles.

If you plan on going the distance to the Yakima Indian Reservation, continue along the main gravel road to reach a steep river access site below the reservation sign. Easier access can be had by driving east along Road K1400 and turning on Road K1410 in 0.75 mile. Follow Road K1410 to the right and go about 1.5 miles, then turn left on a dirt road that leads to the river and a small campsite.

To reach the Klickitat Fish Hatchery, continue east about 3.5 miles from Glenwood to the hatchery sign; follow the gravel road left to the hatchery access. The Leidl Campground access is farther south along Glenwood Road at a bridge across the river. Paddlers can also reach Leidl Campground by taking Washington Highway 142 to Goldendale, then following Glenwood Road north.

The lower take-out is along WA 142 at an old icehouse near Klickitat Springs, east of the town of Klickitat and west of Goldendale. Paddlers are advised to take a good look at the river at this public access site, since difficult road access leads to the dam and the violent lower river gorge.

Overview: South-central Washington's Klickitat River boasts dramatic scenery. Steep columnar basalt cliffs line the upper river in many places, and chunks of basalt have fallen into the river from the walls. Wildflowers grow everywhere from spring through midsummer. Brush and deciduous trees line the entire length of river, presenting difficult hazards. Keep to river center to avoid getting tangled in debris, and hug the inside bends to check for logs.

Despite its hazards, the Klickitat is a great place for advanced beginner or intermediate paddlers. The upper river contains continuous Class III whitewater with some easier stretches to the Klickitat Fish Hatchery. Below the hatchery the river is less demanding, with continuous Class II water and a few Class II+ pool-drops above the icehouse. Though the normal season is spring and early summer, paddlers have run the lower river as late as August in years with good snowpack. Rafters frequent the entire river, and several outfitters from White Salmon, Washington, run commercial trips here.

Going with the flow
Section 1: Yakima Indian Reservation to Leidl Campground

Class: III+	Recommended flow: 500 to 2,000 cfs	Miles: 21

Near the Yakima Indian Reservation, the upper Klickitat River is steep and continuous. At higher flows paddlers should consider this stretch to be Class III+ to IV-. Access sites are steep below the reservation, so most paddlers opt for easier access at the small, unofficial campsite near the river. From either location the river starts with a bang as Class II+ to III+ whitewater winds its way downstream at a steady rate. The floods of 1996 and 1997 cleared much of the gravel from the upper river, leaving more pool-drops here than in years past.

Take out at the Klickitat Fish Hatchery for a good day of boating, or continue to Leidl Campground for a very long day or self-contained venture. Below the hatchery the river eases to continuous Class II+ water with similar scenery to Leidl Campground.

Section 2: Leidl Campground to Old Icehouse Access

Class: II+	Recommended flow: 500 to 2,500 cfs	Miles: 17+

This long stretch of the Klickitat River is difficult to make in a short day, though it's a good choice for a self-contained two-day trip. In late spring or early summer, the mosquitoes can be deadly here. Camp on higher ground away from muddy, marshy areas.

The lower Klickitat gains more pool-drops toward the end, with continuous Class I and II rapids below Leidl Campground. The river has carved channels around gravel bars in places with low-hanging deciduous trees and brush. Paddlers can usually find routes around obstacles, but keep an eye out for wood.

Below the Little Klickitat River much of the river is lined with private property; camp upstream to ensure that you are within public lands. Plan on packing out waste or burying it far from the river. Completely extinguish all fires in this dry area. Take out at the old icehouse, where dry ice was once produced from natural wells. Stay out of the dilapidated building, which is unsafe to explore.

The river can be paddled for roughly 11 miles beyond the icehouse to either a pullout along the road or to Pitt Bridge for a longer Class II+ trip. Paddlers should refer to *Soggy Sneakers* or Jeff Bennett's *Whitewater Rivers of Washington* for details. Anyone traveling beyond the icehouse should familiarize themselves with the Class VI waterfall a few miles downstream of Pitt Bridge. Treacherous Class V+ water lies beyond to the confluence with the Columbia River.

43 Lake Creek
Triangle Lake to Siuslaw River

MID COAST
BASIN

SEE MAP PAGE 434

Character: A popular surf destination on a high-volume creek.

Location: Western Oregon, between Eugene and the coast.

Class: II to V, pool-drop and continuous.

Skill level: Intermediate to expert.

Craft: All, but mostly kayaks and canoes.

Recommended flow
1,000 to 3,500 cfs.

Optimal flow
2,000 cfs.

Water source
Rain.

Average gradient
30 ft/mi.

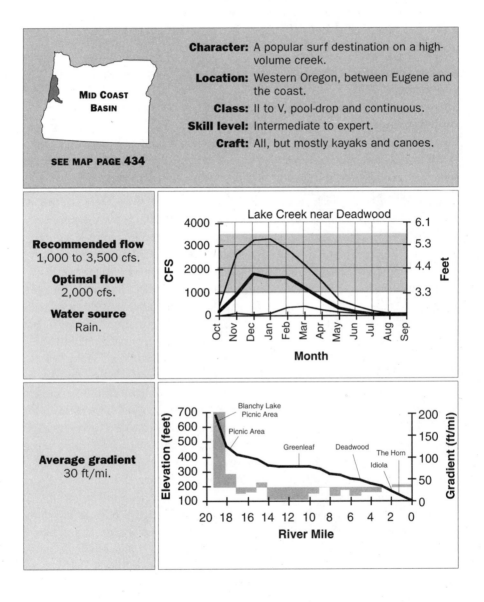

Hazards: The upper 2 miles of Lake Creek contain dramatic Class V rapids and drops. Avoid this area at high water especially; we don't recommend it at any flow. Logs and brush along the banks are present all along the creek, but logs are more concentrated along the upper creek before reaching Deadwood. **The Horn** rapid and **The Ledges** below it are the most significant hazards. They crop up 1 mile above the creek's confluence with the Siuslaw River.

Access: From Eugene, follow Oregon Highway 126 east toward the coast. OR 126 intersects with Oregon Highway 36 at Mapleton. Turn right onto OR 36 after crossing the Siuslaw River, and follow it to the desired put-in or take-out.

If traveling south toward Eugene on Interstate 5, take Exit 209 and head west along Diamond Hill Drive to Harrisburg. Oregon Highway 99 East continues south from Harrisburg; follow it through Junction City to OR 36. Turn west on OR 36 to reach Triangle Lake and sites beyond along Lake Creek.

Overview: The Lake Creek area is a lush, forested region nestled between mountain ridges. Triangle Lake drains into the creek about 20 miles above the confluence with the Siuslaw River, but paddlers run only the last 5 miles of creek regularly, since these hold the best play spots and whitewater.

Only the most extreme boaters will wish to venture in the water below Triangle Lake, since the mile below the picnic area access there is a very turbulent, steep, waterfall- and log-infested onslaught. The 15 miles between this hard stuff and the surf mecca is flatter, narrow, and brushy. The water rates a Class II, but paddlers should watch for strainers in a few places. Put in at Greenleaf for a warm-up above the surf section, or to enjoy a more relaxed float to Deadwood.

Lower Lake Creek is the surf capital of Oregon. No other creek or river has as many great play waves and holes. Many of the waves extend almost completely across the creek, which has a river's volume. Take time to look downstream for debris before catching the next wave, since it is easy to get into surf mode and forget about looking for what lies below. Don't worry if you miss one good wave; you'll have the chance to catch plenty more. Save some energy for the end of the trip, since some of the best play spots (including **The Horn** and **The Ledges**) are near the end of the normal run.

Flows commonly range in the thousands of cubic feet per second during winter and spring. Higher water means bigger waves, but also faster current and bigger holes. Paddlers from the Eugene area who run the creek frequently have rarely seen flows too high to paddle. They prefer flows at or near 2,000 cubic feet per second for surfing.

Going with the flow
Section 1: Blanchy Lake Picnic Area to Greenleaf

Class: V to VI	Recommended flow: None	Miles: 1.5

I don't recommend running the dangerous water below Triangle Lake. Paddlers have run this Section 1 at lower water, but you're on your own if you decide to do so. Scout whatever hazards you can see from the road and make your own decisions. The section between the hairy stuff and Greenleaf is more tame, but still contains strainers and very brushy banks. Most paddlers opt to put in at Greenleaf or below.

Section 2: Greenleaf to Deadwood

Class: II to II+   **Recommended flow:** 1,000 to 2,500 cfs   **Miles:** 4

Below Greenleaf, Lake Creek offers Class II water that makes a good float for less-skilled paddlers. Stay alert for logs and other debris, however. Since most of the creek can be seen from the road on the drive up, paddlers should check the water often to see that the route is clear. There are a few good surf spots along this section, but they are few and far between at higher flows. At flows below 1,000 cubic feet per second, Section 2 may be too low to paddle easily.

Section 3: Deadwood to Siuslaw River

Class: III (IV)   **Recommended flow:** 1,000 to 3,000 cfs   **Miles:** 5+

Lake Creek's Section 3 is Oregon's premier whitewater surf section. There are more waves to catch here than you can count. Save your energy for a few nice play spots above and below The Horn. Keep a watchful eye on paddlers within your group, since it is easy to miss or catch a wave and get separated from your paddling buddies. Eddies are generally small and can be tough to catch at high water.

Brent Mahan waves from a wave at Red Hill Rapid.

The only Class IV hazard in this section is **The Horn.** Scout it from a pullout along OR 36 just over a mile up the road from Swisshome. Here, Class II+ to III water leads around an S-turn (sometimes called **Little Horn**) into a constricted drop where Grand Canyon-sized waves crash and curl upon boaters. If you have a solid roll, just hang out until you get through the big stuff. If you don't have a good roll, you're better off making the difficult portage up the steep bank on the right to the road. Avoid this area if you aren't comfortable with what you see.

Two potentially keeper ledge-holes develop at higher flows just around the next right bend in the river. These are known as **The Ledges.** Scout from the eddy on the left and scramble over the rocks to get a good view. Proficient play boaters may wish to try the surf above or see how grabby the holes really are. The easy route is on the far right of the first wave (known as **Golf Hole**), missing the lower ledge known as **Bus Stop.** The stretch below The Ledges is affectionately known as the **Golf Course,** according to Eric Brown, who reported hitting eighteen retentive holes here. One of these holes is a good play spot on the left with a return eddy. This large but usually friendly hole is known as **Lawn Hole** for the view of a nice lawn across the river.

Take out at Swisshome on the right bank, or continue (as most paddlers do) to Tide on the Siuslaw River. Lake Creek enters the Siuslaw River at Swisshome. Not far below the confluence are some fantastic surf waves. **Mill Wave** is near an old mill, and **Red Hill** rapid (sometimes known as **The Blob**) is not far below on the left. Large and friendly, The Blob has a difficult turbulent entry from a left eddy at higher flows. Paddlers generally stay awhile, since the ride is worth the effort. More waves continue to Tide and the take-out on the right.

44 Laying Creek
Rujada Campground to Row River

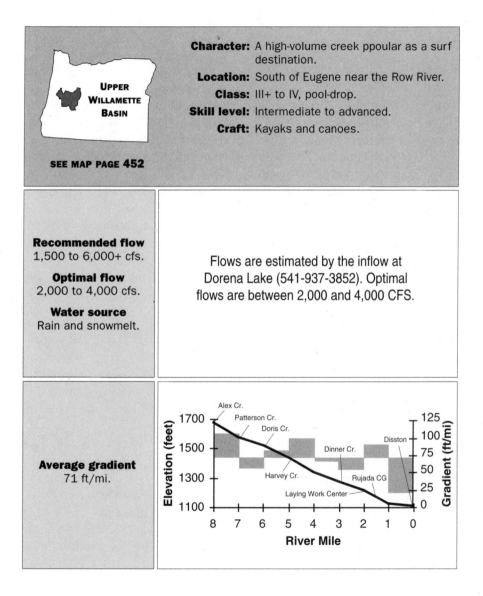

UPPER WILLAMETTE BASIN

SEE MAP PAGE **452**

Character: A high-volume creek ppoular as a surf destination.

Location: South of Eugene near the Row River.

Class: III+ to IV, pool-drop.

Skill level: Intermediate to advanced.

Craft: Kayaks and canoes.

Recommended flow
1,500 to 6,000+ cfs.

Optimal flow
2,000 to 4,000 cfs.

Water source
Rain and snowmelt.

Flows are estimated by the inflow at Dorena Lake (541-937-3852). Optimal flows are between 2,000 and 4,000 CFS.

Average gradient
71 ft/mi.

Hazards: The Plunger on Laying Creek can be very dangerous at high flows, so be sure to scout it. It is located about 1 mile upstream from the bridge at the Brice Creek confluence. Portage **Wildwood Falls;** you can view them from the road on the north side of the river. A set of Class IV rapids just above the covered bridge have been mislocated in past guidebooks—the rapids are just upstream of the bridge. Logs can be a problem.

Access: From Interstate 5 south of Eugene, take Exit 174 into Cottage Grove. Turn left at the stoplight and follow signs to Dorena Reservoir, taking Row River Road east. Continue along the southern shore of the reservoir. Beyond the lake you will cross the Row River, where a covered bridge is visible just upstream. To reach either put-in, continue upstream past the Sharps Creek Road turnoff, where the Sharps Creek confluence is visible. At the next fork you can go either way, but the put-in at Wildwood to the right offers easier access.

For a lower take-out on the Row River, take the right fork and continue a short distance to a small park on the left. Turn into the park and drive to the river.

The base of Wildwood Falls provides a nice put-in for running the Row. To reach Wildwood Falls, take the left fork at the intersection mentioned above and drive until you see Laying Creek. Park in the picnic area just above the falls for the take-out. To get to the put-in, keep driving upstream until you come to a stop sign, turn left (upstream), and drive another 1.5 miles to the put-in at Rujada Campground.

Overview: At Rujada, a pleasant little campground, Laying Creek is fairly small. Its flow increases dramatically after 1.5 miles, however, when Brice Creek enters from the left. Downstream are numerous Class III rapids (Class IV at high water) and many surf waves for play. The scenery is pleasant, but not striking. A thin layer of trees separates the river and the road, which leads to numerous farmhouses and cow pastures.

Spectacular Wildwood Falls is the dividing line for Laying Creek and Row River runs. Officially, the creek becomes the Row River below the falls at the Sharps Creek confluence. From here down, the river is an excellent novice run with tons of Class II+ rapids at low flows, and some great surfing at high flows. Whitewater boating ends abruptly at the head of Dorena Reservoir.

Laying Creek makes a nice little run close to Eugene, but it receives little traffic due to more popular and more difficult Brice Creek, which is just a stone's throw away. At high flows, Laying Creek has some great surfing and is well worth paddling.

Going with the flow

Class: III+ to IV	Recommended flow: 1,500 to 6,000+ cfs	Miles: 5

Put in on river left at the bridge to Rujada Campground, and warm-up on the small waves just below. Not far beyond the put-in, and visible from the road, is **Rujada Falls,** a steep ledge dropping about 4 feet. About 0.5 mile below the put-in is the toughest rapid on the run, **The Plunger.** Scout this rapid before you put in, since it gets dangerous at high flows. Some paddlers will want to put in below it.

Brice Creek enters on river left at the first bridge, increasing the flow substantially. Just around the corner is a fun drop, which is quickly followed by **Corner** rapids, a long rapid with big waves and holes at high flows. This rapid, like most of the main rapids, is visible from the road.

The run from Brice Creek to Wildwood Falls provides the most action, with lots of waves and holes for play and a sprinkling of Class III rapids. At very high water this run rates Class IV, with lots of big holes and nearly continuous waves. Kayakers who run it when the water is high should have a good roll and be proficient at identifying holes. It makes a good introductory Class IV run for those who are looking for a new challenge.

Take out on river right at Wildwood Falls or portage the falls and continue along the Row River (River 69).

—Jason Bates

45 Lewis River, East Fork, Washington
Green Fork to Paradise Point

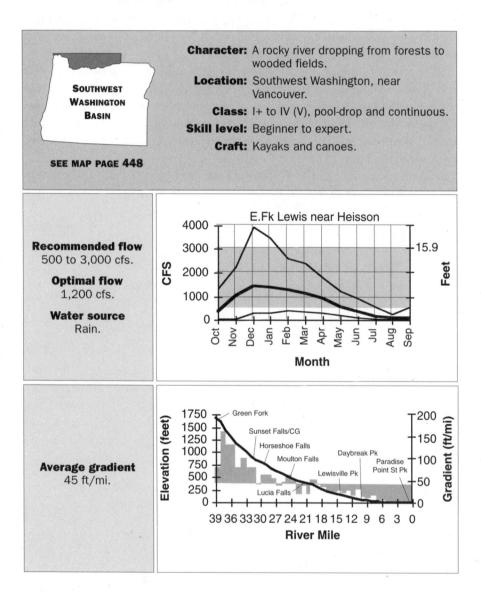

SOUTHWEST WASHINGTON BASIN

SEE MAP PAGE **448**

Character: A rocky river dropping from forests to wooded fields.

Location: Southwest Washington, near Vancouver.

Class: I+ to IV (V), pool-drop and continuous.

Skill level: Beginner to expert.

Craft: Kayaks and canoes.

Recommended flow
500 to 3,000 cfs.

Optimal flow
1,200 cfs.

Water source
Rain.

Average gradient
45 ft/mi.

E.Fk Lewis near Heisson

Month

River Mile

Green Fork
Sunset Falls/CG
Horseshoe Falls
Moulton Falls
Daybreak Pk
Paradise Point St Pk
Lewisville Pk
Lucia Falls

Hazards: Wood hazards exist along the entire East Fork Lewis River. Two very proficient paddlers have been killed on the upper river after being pinned by submerged logs. Various Class IV to IV+ rapids and Class V to VI waterfalls demand expert boat control and common sense. Scout all horizon line drops for routes and debris. Avoid private property as much as possible after the river leaves Gifford Pinchot National Forest below Sunset Falls.

Below Lewisville Park, the river has little challenging whitewater but provides more leisurely floats for beginners to either Daybreak Park or Paradise Point State Park. Log hazards, brushy banks, and sharp bends can catch novice paddlers off-guard. Always be alert for possible trouble spots.

Access: For more challenging upriver locations, take Interstate 5 into Washington and take the Washington Highway 502 exit. Follow WA 502 west to Washington Highway 503, which heads north before Battle Ground. After you cross the East Fork Lewis River, turn on County Road 12, which branches south then west along the river's north bank. All upriver access areas are along this road or at bridge intersections. Once you reach Gifford Pinchot National Forest, the road becomes Forest Road 42 and continues to the bridge across the Green Fork and the upper access.

For lower river access, follow I-5 farther into Washington. Take Exit 16 and go west along Pekin Ferry Road to Paradise Park Road in a short distance. Follow Paradise Park Road north to Paradise Point State Park for the lowest take-out before the river combines with the main Lewis River.

To reach Daybreak Park, backtrack to 11th Avenue and turn right (south) to either 279th Street or 264th Street, then turn right (west) to intersect 10th Street. Turn left (south) on 10th and turn right (west) on 259th Street. Continue along 259th Street to 82nd Street, turning left (north) and to reach Daybreak Park. Access is available above or below the bridge and Class I+ rapid upstream.

To reach Lewisville Park, continue south on 10th Street, past 259th Street, to reach WA 502. Follow WA 502 west beyond Battle Ground, then follow signs to Lewisville Park, to the north.

Overview: The East Fork Lewis River has developed a nasty reputation over the years—several good paddlers and a few anglers have drowned in its treacherous waters. Resistant basalt rock has formed ledges and waterfalls in many locations along the upper river. Old-growth cedar and other evergreen trees line the banks, creating serious log hazards. The rural surroundings are spotted with houses below Sunset Falls and the Gifford Pinchot National Forest boundary, but these do not intrude on the river experience.

Like the upper stretches of many Washington rivers, the East Fork Lewis flows through a rugged, steep canyon with challenging whitewater. Only advanced and expert paddlers should attempt the upper stretches. It's not always possible to hike out in case of an emergency. Submerged logs and undercut rock can lead to pinning in many locations. Scout what you cannot see and portage all uncertain drops.

The East Fork, as it is commonly known among area boaters, gradually eases in difficulty as it winds downstream. Beyond Lewisville Park the once-Class IV to V onslaught is replaced by more relaxing Class II water. Below Daybreak Park the river meanders to the main Lewis River with only a few Class I riffles. Intermediate paddlers may wish to look to the Kalama or other area rivers for more challenging runs.

Going with the flow
Section 1: Green Fork to Sunset Falls

Class: IV+	Recommended flow: 400 to 800 cfs	Miles: 5.5

The upper East Fork Lewis River is for advanced and expert paddlers only. Those who run it should be comfortable with Class IV+ drops. The stretch begins with easier Class II+ water for about a mile below the put-in bridge (River Mile 38). The river then presents a 5- to 6-foot horizon line initiation drop. A short distance beyond the first horizon line, **Double Drop** drops 14 feet in two steps. Scout or portage on the right. About 50 yards later, **Tombstone Falls** drops 8 feet with a subsurface rock just downstream to complicate matters. Scout or portage on the right.

Below Tombstone, easier water contains good surf and play as the water level rises with additions from tributary streams such as McKinley Creek. A 17-foot plunge, **Sunset Falls** (RM 32.5) marks the final drop of the section. Scout or avoid on the right, or view on the way to the put-in. Sunset is most commonly run left of center or off the left bank.

Paddlers take out above or below the falls on the right at Sunset Falls Recreation Area.

Section 2: Sunset Falls to Roadside Pullout (Waterfall Run)

Class: IV+ (V)	Recommended flow: 400 to 2,000 cfs	Miles: 4.5

Section 2 is commonly known as the Waterfall Run by local paddlers, since it contains several large Class IV+ drops and one large waterfall: Horseshoe Falls. Competent boat handling is a must on this demanding advanced-to-expert run.

Put in at Sunset Falls Recreation Area, scouting the falls to decide whether or not to run it. It does make a great photo opportunity. Below the falls, Class II to III water leads to **Hippie John's Boulder-Drop.** Here, a Class III+ to IV drop skirts brush along the left and boulders in the middle. Scout the left and middle channels, since the right one has severe pinning potential. Class IV **Back Stabber** is next, with a left-to-right diagonal pourover into a hole. Run left to right to avoid the left wall.

In 50 yards **Sky Pilot** follows with a ramp that drops 5 feet into an ender hole, giving paddlers a skyward view. A second narrow ramp known as the **Green Tongue** follows more Class III turns. Below the Tongue is **Screaming Left Turn.** Catch a small eddy on the left to scout or portage this narrow slot; the left bank is undercut with pinning potential. We recommend portaging since the rapid requires a do-or-die move from left to right.

Once you are safely below the drop, immediately eddy-out on the left above **Dragon's Back,** a 7-foot diagonal drop that moves from left to right. Hug the right bank, angling left as you punch the drop, but stay right at the bottom. You'll need to make a fast recovery in order to avoid a limbo log 200 yards downstream. The log is wedged diagonally, running underwater on the right to about 8 feet up the left wall. Run left under the log as the river narrows into a 15-foot-wide canyon. Debris tends to get trapped under the log. Beyond it lies a deep, calm pool.

About 200 yards of calm water follow, pooling in a deeply carved canyon where paddlers have a chance to admire the clear blue water before their next major drop. A horizon line marks **John's Swimmin' Hole,** where a 5-foot ledge drops into a sticky hole. Run the ledge on the extreme left or right. The preferred right side drops into an eddy, while the left banks 90 degrees off the tall cliff 15 feet beyond the drop. There is potential for splatting against the left wall without a strong ferry back to the right (or a quick roll).

A slab of rock marks the entrance of Copper Creek on the left, which boosts the flow by 25 to 33 percent. Easier ledge-drops and play waves lead to **Mr. Twister,** a dynamic S-turn. The road is 200 feet up the canyon on the right in this section. Watch for debris from the eroded roadcut that has dropped into the canyon.

Small ledges and waves cover the next mile to **Horseshoe Falls.** Several openings lead over the horseshoe-shaped falls; they are referred to as Doors 1 through 6. Most of the water flows right, where the drop is considered Class VI. From the right to left, the doors are as follows:

Door 1:	Known as **No Way,** this door leads over the Class VI route to the right with much of the flow. It contains an undercut and splat rock at the bottom.
Door 2:	Taking this door means making a required hard left to miss a trench on bottom right.
Door 3:	A sweet spot where a cattle-sized, 3-foot-wide chute leads into the pool. There's also a 16-foot rolling ramp into the pool. A slight forward lean is recommended.
Door 4:	Not recommended. It's loaded with pinning potential.
Door 5:	Not recommended due to pinning potential. At high flows, paddlers have run the extreme left of the channel. Boat-scout before running.
Door 6:	Yes! This is the recommended route at high flows. Take the far left channel if you can.

Below Horseshoe, Class III rapids and surf waves lead to a take-out accessed from a pullout along the road about 1 mile above the Dole Valley Bridge. **Rainbow Falls** are located less than a mile downstream. These falls require a mandatory

Mike Olsen pops an ender on the East Fork of the Lewis River in Washington.
MILAN CHUCKOVICH PHOTO

scout or portage along private property. To avoid landowner disputes, forget this last drop and take out at the roadside pullout.

Section 3: Dole Valley Bridge to Lucia Falls

Class: IV+ to V   **Recommended flow:** 400 to 2,000 cfs   **Miles:** 5.6

Below the put-in at/under the Dole Valley Bridge, Class III+ boulder gardens lead to the Rock Creek confluence in less than a mile. More Class III+ boulder gardens lead to Class V **Naked Falls** about 1.5 miles below Rock Creek. Scout on the left bank or boat-scout on right, if you dare. Stay left as you boof the edge of a V-grooved waterfall. In another 25 feet angle left to right into a large pool. Across the 100-foot pool, stay right of center as you slide down a 7-foot slide. Avoid the hole on the left.

About 0.5 mile of easy water leads to **Moulton Falls.** Stop at the parking area on the right above the falls for a scout, portage, or take-out. Class III water then leads into a turbulent Class V+ to VI chute split by a column of rock, pouring into a turbulent pool below. Another mile of Class II and III rapids lead to Class IV **Lalond's Drop.** At Lalond's, a large ramp leads into a series of holes and waves followed by a turbulent stretch.

About 1.5 miles of easier water follow as you continue toward **Lucia Falls.** At Steelhead Lane bridge, the river banks off a headwall and enters a steep, rock-walled gorge. Keep up your speed to punch the boils at the foot of the bridge. You'll see houses along the left bank before you reach the falls. Portage around this tough Class V drop at newly constructed Lucia Falls Park on the left or right; left is better. Take out at the park above or below the falls on the right, or continue along Section 4.

Section 4: Lucia Falls to Lewisville Park

Class: III to IV   **Recommended flow:** 500 to 2,500 cfs   **Miles:** 7.4

Put in below **Lucia Falls** at the new Lucia Falls Park, on the right. About 60 feet below the falls, a rapid named **Drowning Machine** presents a potentially keeper hole. The hole was named after a fisherman drowned here. Below it for 2.5 miles, Class III rapids dot the river among continuous Class II water. The gradient increases above the one-lane concrete Heisson Bridge, which is a good place to gage flow and scout the rapids below. A Class IV+ boulder garden is next, followed by a narrow gorge with a calm pool.

Below the pool, the river resumes its Class III+ character, which dwindles to Class II before reaching Lewisville Park.

—Mike Olsen

Section 5: Lewisville Park to Paradise Point State Park

Class: I to II	Recommended flow: 500 to 3,000 cfs	Miles: 13

Class I and II water flows from Lewisville Park to Paradise Point State Park, allowing more casual floats by beginning whitewater boaters. Logs are present in the river in places, so paddlers should stay alert. The run can be divided at Daybreak Park, where Class I water follows a Class I+ rapid near the park bridge. Put in above or below the riffle.

The river meanders through open fields and near residential areas beyond Daybreak Park to the take-out at Paradise Point. The take-out is up a dirt road on the right.

46 Little Klickitat River, Washington
Olson Road to Klickitat River

Character: A technical run on a small, steep creek.

Location: Southern Washington, north of The Dalles.

Class: IV to V, pool-drop and continuous.

Skill level: Upper advanced to expert.

Craft: Kayaks and canoes.

SOUTHWEST WASHINGTON BASIN

SEE MAP PAGE **448**

Recommended flow
200 to 300 cfs.

Optimal flow
250 cfs.

Water source
Rain and snowmelt.

A visual gage is marked near the take-out , but levels are difficult to estimate. Good flows are estimated between 200 and 300 CFS.

Average gradient
90 ft/mi.

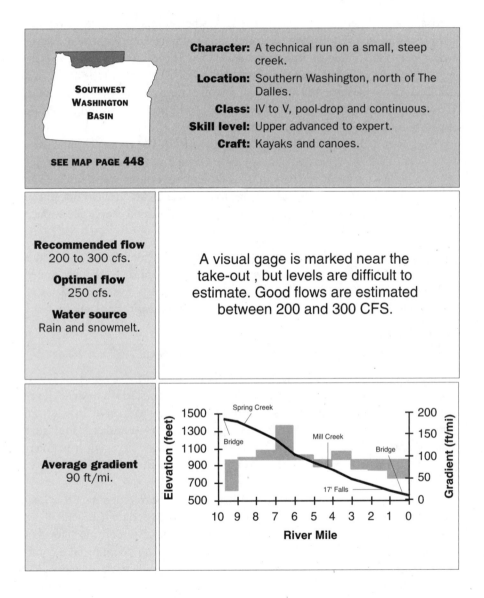

Hazards: Take all precautions when running this advanced river. The Little Klickitat contains numerous boulder gardens, ledges, boulder sieves, and brushy banks. Riverside property is private, so show respect.

Access: Follow Interstate 84 east of The Dalles beyond the Deschutes River and take U.S. Highway 97 north. After crossing the Columbia River, jog west on Washington Highway 14 then continue north on US 97. At the intersection with Washington Highway 142 at Goldendale, turn left (west). The take-out is at the WA 142 Bridge over the Little Klickitat River, 5.6 miles north of the town of Klickitat, Washington (near mile marker 19). Take out under the bridge on river right. Please respect private property at this access point.

The put-in is along Olson Road, which turns off WA 142 about 6.7 miles from the WA 142/US 97 intersection. Turn south on Olson Road and drive to the bridge over the Little Klickitat River. Park at one of the small turnouts north of the river, and put in beneath the bridge on the upstream river right side. **Do not put in anywhere else.** This is private property, owned by kind-hearted people. Show these local landowners respect!

Overview: The Little Klickitat River was first explored by Ron Reynier and friends in the early 1990s. Since then, the river has grown in popularity, though limited parking at the put-in and tough-to-catch water levels keep most paddlers away. Those who do run the Little Klickitat exit the river with ear-to-ear smiles.

Going with the flow

Class: IV to V	Recommended flow: 500 to 900 cfs	Miles: 9.7

Below the put-in, the Little Klickitat River is a tiny, brushy stream that winds across a broad valley past open pastures. The river quickly starts to descend, however, dropping through small Class II to III stairstep rapids as it carves its way into a ponderosa-lined basalt canyon. The first significant drop—a broken 4-foot ledge that hides around a gradual right bend—contains a killer sieve. Most paddlers portage this rapid, though at higher flows many go for the sneak route on river right. Don't blow the move!

Below this first rapid, the river tilts downward and starts running into a long series of boulder gardens. Most of the boulder gardens contain beachball- to Volkswagen-sized boulders and offer lots of different routes. Some are much tougher to run than others. After the first few boulder gardens lull you into false confidence, bigger, beefier Class IV to V boulder gardens slap you back to reality.

After the boulder gardens ebb, the riverbed consolidates and becomes more ledgy. The first notable ledge stands 5 feet tall and runs the width of the river. Look for the easy route near the left bank, which avoids the meat of this rapid. Downstream, a sloping 10-foot ledge and a towering 17-foot ledge form the biggest vertical drops on the trip. You can pick all sorts of lines down either drop, provided you scout them first. The 17-footer follows a well-defined island, which makes it easier to spot ahead of time. Stay right of the island, and scout from the left bank.

Although a fun series of Class III to III+ chutes, ledges, and boulder gardens fill the mile of river below the 17-foot waterfall, the Little Klickitat gradually loses its punch the closer it gets to the main Klickitat River. In fact, the last mile above the confluence can be shallow, flat, and uneventful at low to medium water levels. Check this run out in early spring when rain and snowmelt combine to create high water in the Klickitat drainage. Treat every trip like a first descent, bring a camera, and have fun!

—Jeff Bennett

47 Little White Salmon River, Washington
Above Willard to Drano Lake

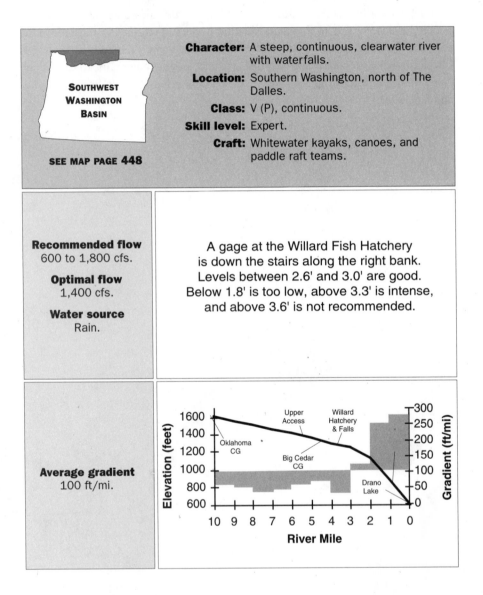

SOUTHWEST WASHINGTON BASIN

SEE MAP PAGE **448**

Character: A steep, continuous, clearwater river with waterfalls.

Location: Southern Washington, north of The Dalles.

Class: V (P), continuous.

Skill level: Expert.

Craft: Whitewater kayaks, canoes, and paddle raft teams.

Recommended flow
600 to 1,800 cfs.

Optimal flow
1,400 cfs.

Water source
Rain.

A gage at the Willard Fish Hatchery is down the stairs along the right bank. Levels between 2.6' and 3.0' are good. Below 1.8' is too low, above 3.3' is intense, and above 3.6' is not recommended.

Average gradient
100 ft/mi.

Hazards: The entire Little White Salmon River is hazardous. The water is cold and the rapids are difficult. Continuous, they also contain constantly shifting wood. If you're an expert paddler—honestly—this run is the best! If you're not, don't dishonor the river or yourself by trying to run it.

Access: Get to the take-out at Drano Lake by driving 10 miles west of the town of White Salmon, Washington, along Washington Highway 14. On the west side of Drano Lake, turn onto the access road that leads to the Little White Salmon Fish Hatchery. Park in front of the hatchery gates in an appropriate spot.

To reach the put-ins, return to WA 14, turn right (west), and take the first right to Cook–Underwood Road. Follow this road to the Willard Fish Hatchery; the bridge here is the put-in for the lower section. Seek out the stream gage, which is just upstream by the hatchery buildings on river right.

If you're planning an upper run, or a run that covers both upper and lower sections, return to the first street in Willard (Willard Road), turn right (the only turn possible), and drive through town. Continue north out of town on Oklahoma Road, driving about 0.5 mile to where the river and road meet. Find a parking spot and put in here.

Overview: The Little White Salmon River flows through a basalt gorge that combines crystal-clear water with a riotous mix of steep boulder gardens, ledges, and waterfalls. The spring-fed water is always cold. For expert paddlers only, this river has few peers in the Pacific Northwest. The run is a continuous experience of boat- and bank-scouting along the river's entire length. Be prepared for long scouts your first time down and always be on the lookout for logs.

The bridge over the river below the Willard Fish Hatchery divides the river into two sections. Paddlers reasonably run the upper section (Section 1) at a much narrower range of water levels than they do the lower, primary section (Section 2). A stream gage is located on the right bank of the river down steps near the Willard Fish Hatchery. Run the upper section at readings of 3 to 3.6 feet (1,000 to 1,500 cubic feet per second); run the lower section between 1.8 and 3.6 feet. Levels above 3.3 feet are intense, requiring paddlers to have prior knowledge of the lines through the rapids. Below 2.5 feet on the gage, the river is bony and full of rocks. Levels between 2.6 to 3 feet are ideal for a first-time experience on the lower river. **Note:** Flood events have altered the flow of the river, so gage readings may not correlate with historic flows. Talk to local paddlers to get reliable information about river level and wood sightings on the river.

Going with the flow
Section 1: Above Willard to Willard Fish Hatchery

Class: V	**Recommended flow:** 1,000 to 1,500 cfs	**Miles:** 2

From the bridge below the Willard Fish Hatchery, look upstream to scout Willard Falls. Walk along the right bank at the hatchery to scout **Simon Says,** a boulder garden that leads to the waterfall drop. This is the most difficult and enjoyable part of the upper section. If you don't like what you see, don't put on the upper river and reconsider putting on the lower section. If you do like what you see, drive to the put-in above Willard.

The river is a quiet and meandering stream at the put-in, but 0.25 mile downstream the action starts with a 0.5-mile warm-up of Class III and IV ledges and boulder gardens. Below the bridge at Willard Road, the excitement level picks up considerably. Numerous drops require scouting to locate wood hazards. Scout whatever you cannot see.

Several ledge-drops occur next, after the river constricts. The second drop is a good ender spot. The next three drops are steeper, higher, and less visible. The following distinctive drop has a diagonal wave hole created by a ledge running almost parallel with the river. Scout on the left. **Shroom Tripper** lies ahead, recognized by a large midstream boulder pourover. Scout on the left and run over the top of the boulder or slightly right of center. Collect in the pool below to scout the next 150 yards of excitement. A pool empties on river left, but stay tight right to avoid being pushed too far left, staying in the middle of the flow. Both far left and right have serious pinning potential as you exit the pool. Hang on and enjoy the roller coaster, but eddy-out to regroup.

The next mile is a sweet Class IV and V boulder garden known as Simon Says. Boat-scout and enjoy! A fish weir runs halfway across the river at the end of this section. Boof its center section. Catch your breath in the nearest eddy, though, since up ahead is the steepest stretch of boulder garden on the river, culminating in **Willard Falls.** Scout on the right. There are nice lines staying primarily right, but lines exist both center and left for adrenaline junkies. Paddlers will want to end up on river right to run Willard Falls. The farther left you go, the bigger the hole out of which you will have to claw.

Pass the river gage on the right and float under the bridge at Cook–Underwood Road. This bridge is the take-out for the upper section. Because the upper section is short, paddlers usually run it in combination with Section 2. Keep in mind that at higher flows the lower section can be formidable.

Section 2: Willard Fish Hatchery to Drano Lake

Class: V (P)	Recommended flow: 700 to 1,000 cfs	Miles: 3.5

When the stream gage at Willard Fish Hatchery reads higher than 3 feet, only paddlers who are familiar with the river should run Section 2. This is the primary section run on the Little White Salmon, and it has been paddled every month of the year (though only during droughty winters). The lower section starts with a short Class III warm-up before the gradient increases. Welcome to **Get Busy,** 0.5 mile of continuous Class IV and V boulder gardens punctuated by several blind drops. Scout these if you are unfamiliar with the lines. There are many pitches in this section, so it is easy to get out of control if you do not stay focused. At higher flows, prior knowledge of routes is crucial for safe, fun passage. Constantly shifting wood is always a hazard.

The boulder garden section ends with **Boulder Sluice.** Scout left to observe the main flow plunging center and right down an 8-foot drop into a large boulder. Stay in the left channel and boof the diagonal ledge to reach the pool below. Next, a couple of Class IV pitches precede a short section of calm water above a boulder-strewn segment known as **Thread the Needle.** Run the first pitch on the left, then immediately ferry right and paddle through one of two narrow slots. Continue down right-to-center over several pitches.

Ahead, **Island Drop** guards the downstream side of an island. Paddlers generally run the left channel, but getting there depends on the arrangement of wood. You'll have to run several pitches before you reach the island. Scout on the right to see where the holes are before you run. Collect your wits in the pool at the bottom of this steep boulder garden.

Enjoy the next 0.25 mile of fun Class IV water leading to **Sacriledge,** an 8-foot ledge-drop. When you see a horizon line, scout right. Run left with the tongue, but avoid being pushed left or you will end up in **Dave's Cave** at the bottom, a submerged cave in the left basalt wall. **Double Drop** follows closely downstream. Scout right and note that many have gone swimming in the first hole. Then relax and enjoy **Typewriter** as a diagonal wave takes you for a ride!

The next 0.75 mile contains two Class IV boulder gardens separated by a calm stretch. At the end of the second boulder garden, a horizon line marks **S-Turn Falls.** This is a 10-foot ledge followed by a second pitch with turbulent water. Scout right, boof left, and run the second pitch on the left as well. **Lunch Spot** follows, with two pitches leading to a 6-foot ledge-drop. Run tight right unless you want to go deep with the main flow. This is a great ender spot at lower flows.

Pay attention when you get to the next extended Class IV boulder garden, since it ends with the **Bowey Hotel,** a hole/cave combination that checks in unsuspecting guests. The hole is on the left, so get far right as the boulder garden approaches a horizon line; if you do it right, you'll end up in a calm pool. Immediately below this pool are the spectacularly scenic **Wishbone Falls,** followed by **The Gorge.** Take out in the nearest micro-eddy on the left and prepare for a long scout or portage along a slight trail. The falls are 20 feet of pure fun. Run the left channel as far left as the water allows. You'll land in a basalt chamber that exits into The Gorge.

Scout on the left before you run the next three pitches. **Horseshoe,** a pitch named by its shape, follows. Run tight right or prepare to swim after a scoring a ringer. **Stovepipe,** a 12-foot drop, immediately follows this waterfall. Scout on the left. At low flows you can portage on the left, but at higher flows a huge log blocks the necessary ferry after the portage, forcing a run over the drop. The line is a narrow slot on the right, which takes paddlers over an 8-foot drop first, then down a fast chute that continues to another basalt bowl.

Paddle out of the bowl through calm water to reach 300 yards of Class IV rapids known as **Humpty Dumpty.** The next horizon line and plumes of mist signal **Spirit Falls,** a 30-foot pourover waterfall leading into a spectacular basin

Ron Blanchette takes the plunge at Spirit Falls on the Little White Salmon. ANDREW WULFERS PHOTO

cathedral. No description can do this drop justice. Scout or portage on the left down either the rock face or the dirt face farther downstream. Throw ropes are useful here. Paddlers have run the main pourover, and the lines are obvious for those willing and able to do so.

Below the cathedral pool lies **Chaos,** a 6-foot river-wide ledge-drop punctuated by a basalt outcropping just right of center. The hole on the right is retentive, so avoid it by staying left. Another 100 yards of Class IV rapids lead to a calm pool followed by the last Class IV to V rapid, known as **Master Blaster.** Scout right and run on the left, staying with the flow through the gut of a huge hole. You'll go over two fish weirs before ending in Drano Lake with ducks and geese in front of you, salmon below you, and a sweet smile on your face.

—*Jens Mullen*

48 Lobster Creek
Bark Shanty Bridge to Rogue River

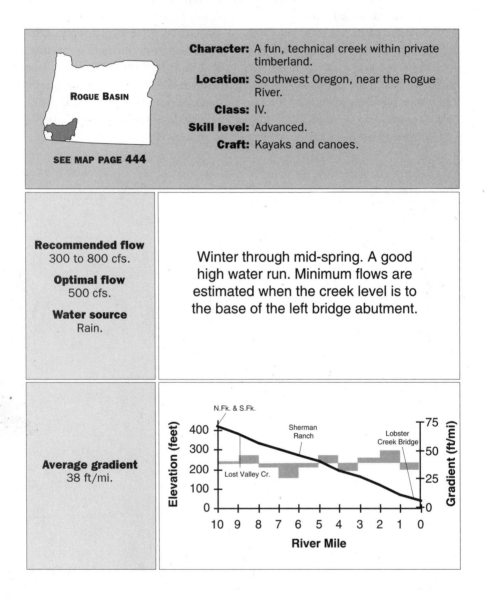

ROGUE BASIN

SEE MAP PAGE **444**

Character: A fun, technical creek within private timberland.

Location: Southwest Oregon, near the Rogue River.

Class: IV.

Skill level: Advanced.

Craft: Kayaks and canoes.

Recommended flow
300 to 800 cfs.

Optimal flow
500 cfs.

Water source
Rain.

Winter through mid-spring. A good high water run. Minimum flows are estimated when the creek level is to the base of the left bridge abutment.

Average gradient
38 ft/mi.

Hazards: Lobster Creek is a remote, technical run that Class IV boaters will enjoy. It's not exceptionally steep, and has none of the Class V rapids typical of many classic creek runs. Still, the creek does contain the shallow water, numerous boulder gardens, and many wood hazards that paddlers might expect. There were no log jams or channel-spanning logs on the creek in spring 1997, but there were smaller alder and other mobile hardwood logs measuring 1 to 2 feet in diameter.

Access: At the Rogue River along U.S. Highway 101 on Oregon's south coast, travel northeast along the North Bank Rogue River Road. Stay right at the intersection with Edson Creek Road in roughly 4 miles. Stay right again at the intersection with Squaw Valley Road and continue to the bridge across Lobster Creek. Drop a shuttle vehicle near the bridge on river left.

To reach the put-in, continue east another 0.2 mile and take the next left at a gravel road. If you cross the Rogue River, you've gone too far. The gravel road passes through private timberlands but provides public national forest access. Continue up this road for roughly 5 miles, passing several gated turnoffs. Turn left toward the creek about 4 miles in from the paved road. You will come to a locked gate in about 0.25 mile. Park so as not to block the gate and carry your boat 200 yards to a bridge. Put in just upstream of this bridge on river left. Please note that walk-in access to this area is a privilege. Do not abuse it!

An alternate take-out is at the Lobster Creek Campground and Boat Ramp on the south side of the Rogue River opposite the mouth of Lobster Creek. Reach it via the South Bank Rogue River Road.

Overview: Near the Rogue River and Gold Beach on the southern Oregon coast, Lobster Creek provides a vibrant whitewater experience during high water in winter and early spring. If other area runs are too high, paddlers who need their whitewater fix can opt for this enjoyable run.

The creek is runnable during winter and early to mid-spring. though it does get pretty bony if it hasn't rained for a week or two. If water comes to the base of the bridge abutment on river left at the take-out, it's a good sign of minimum flow. The creek never gets too high but can become very pushy, developing a couple of river-wide holes, especially at **Shotgun.** At high water, a significant backwater effect from the Rogue River makes it difficult to tell just how high the creek is running at the take-out.

The lower Lobster Creek watershed is private timberland actively managed by The Campbell Group, a partner of the Hancock Timber Resource Group. Until a few years ago, the area exemplified the typical cut-and-run policy of logging coastal lands. Since the 1960s, the slopes had become a mess of overgrown alder and other hardwoods that took over after old-growth fir and redcedar had been hauled to the mills. The land was left to heal itself, revegetating with alder. In recent times, much of the alder has been removed to help accelerate conifer reintroduction on the slopes above Lobster Creek. Removal of these hardwoods all the way to the creek channel is not a violation of the 100-foot buffer zone required by the Oregon Department of Forestry, but is instead a mitigation measure requested by the Oregon Department of Fish and Wildlife. Most of the mature conifer trees along the creek are not destined for the mill, but are meant to provide future shade and habitat diversity along the aquatic system.

The scenery from the creek is picturesque and overgrown with myrtle, maple, and alder. The drive to the put-in offers a stark contrast, since it crosses many hardwood clearcuts. In several places the logging extends to the creek, but you won't notice, the intense whitewater demands your full attention.

Going with the flow

Class: IV	Recommended flow: 300 to 800 cfs	Miles: 5

The first 0.5 mile down Lobster Creek is relaxing Class II water. After this warm-up the rapids change to pool-drop Class IIIs, followed by the first Class IV rapid, known as **Ignition**. Scout or portage on the left. You'll recognize the start of the rapid by a large log located on the left side of the channel, followed by a boulder in the middle of the channel immediately downstream.

Class III pool-drop rapids continue to a second Class IV drop, **Shish-Ka-Bob**, midway into the run. This boulder garden typically contains one or more vertical logs extending out of the water. A portage here is not easy, but may be attempted on the left.

A mix of Class III boulder garden and pool-drop rapids follows. Then a 0.25-mile stretch of Class II water leads to the last Class IV rapid, known as Shotgun. Look for the rapid near a recent landslide along the left bank. Scout from either bank, but portage on the right. Shotgun contains a 4- to 5-foot drop into a boulder garden. Unfriendly holes at the bottom of the drop demand respect. Immediately downstream you'll get another 200 yards of Class III+ boulder gardens.

Within 0.25 mile of the last Class IV rapid, Lobster Creek eases to Class II water and continues at that level to the take-out. Take out on the left just upstream of the bridge along North Bank Rogue River Road, or continue to Lobster Creek Campground and Boat Ramp on the left side of the Rogue River.

—Ron Sonnevil

49 McKenzie River
Sahalie Falls to Willamette River

Character: A long river dropping from lava beds and forest to an urban area.

Location: West-central Oregon, near the Eugene/Springfield metro area.

Class: I to V, continuous and pool-drop.

Skill level: Beginner to expert.

Craft: All; kayaks and canoes on Section 1.

UPPER
WILLAMETTE
BASIN

SEE MAP PAGE 452

Recommended flow
500 to 2,500 cfs.

Optimal flow
2,000 cfs.

Water source
Rain, springs, and snowmelt.

Average gradient
27 ft/mi.

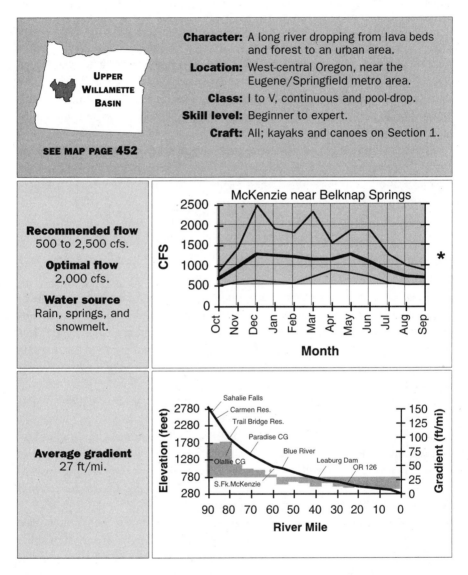

McKenzie near Belknap Springs

CFS

Month

Elevation (feet)

Sahalie Falls
Carmen Res.
Trail Bridge Res.
Paradise CG
Blue River
Olallie CG
Leaburg Dam
OR 126
S.Fk.McKenzie

Gradient (ft/mi)

River Mile

*

No depth measurement available.

211

Hazards: The upper sections of the McKenzie River require mandatory portages around waterfalls. The lower sections are usually trouble-free except at **Fishladder** rapid (Class III+), which demands technical moves in a boulder garden- and hole-laden stretch. **Brown's Hole** and **Martin's** rapids also deserve respect. Avoid Brown's Hole on river right. Martin's rapid has rocks at the top, with big waves through a narrow stretch of river.

Access: Oregon Highway 126 crosses the McKenzie River at Hendricks Bridge State Park, just east of the Eugene/Springfield metropolitan area, and follows the river to its source at Clear Lake Campground, past numerous boat-launching sites. Above Olallie Campground the river is small; only advanced boaters should attempt runs here.

Below Hendricks Bridge State Wayside, both Bellinger Landing and Hayden Bridge sites make good put-in/take-out locations. Reach them by taking Marcola Road off OR 126 in Springfield, then turning onto Camp Creek Road, heading east just after the McKenzie River crossing.

Armitage State Park Boat Ramp is downstream on river left just before the Interstate 5 bridge. This is a common take-out and the last public access on the McKenzie before it merges with the Willamette River. Follow Interstate 5 north of Springfield to the park.

Overview: The McKenzie River cuts through the Cascade Range from its origin at Clear Lake between Mounts Washington and Jefferson, dropping to the city of Springfield. The headwaters, which spring from underground sources at Clear Lake, are supplemented by springs along the river. Hot springs are frequent along the river corridor, with popular soaking spots at Belknap on the main McKenzie and Cougar Hot Springs on the South Fork. Cougar Hot Springs is an undeveloped site where clothing is optional. It has been closed to nighttime use due to past violence in the area. Other sites provide soaks at the river's edge.

The wooded Cascades provide good shade on hot summer days and collect ample snow for year-round boating. Watch for campgrounds about every 5 miles along OR 126 above Blue River; many of these offer river access. Holiday weekends are usually the only times that campsites are filled. Olallie and Paradise campgrounds are popular sites providing upper river access.

The McKenzie River area provides great entertainment for the whole family. Its heavily forested hills hold lodges, Tokatee Golf Course, and popular fishing and hiking spots along the river. Horseback riding and backpacking are popular along the upper South Fork McKenzie. Cougar Reservoir on the South Fork allows motorboats and jet skis.

Trout and salmon fishing attract anglers along the lower river, which is home to chinook salmon and native redside rainbows in addition to hatchery trout. Anglers should check regulations to make sure they have appropriate gear and know catch limits. The lower river is best accessed by boat, since private property lines its banks except at boat launch areas. Rafters love the upper McKenzie, where several outfitters run commercial day trips. Check with local fishing supply stores or the Willamette National Forest office for commercial listings, (541) 822-3381.

Though the McKenzie is a long, scenic river, few paddlers run self-contained trips here since private property flanks the lower river. Most people run one or more sections and car camp in the area. Many small communities dot the river on its passage from Eugene to Sisters, providing gas and supplies. One popular stop is Mom's Pie House, where fresh-baked pies reward boaters who have completed a trip along the river or one of its tributaries.

Going with the flow
Section 1: Sahalie Falls to Trail Bridge Reservoir

Class: V	Recommended flow: 250 to 600 cfs	Miles: 0.4 and 2

The upper McKenzie River between Carmen Reservoir/Sahalie Falls and Trail Bridge Reservoir is an experts-only run due to extreme hazards: steep waterfalls, gradient with continuous rapids, logs and logjams, etc. A nice hike along the uppermost river begins near **Sahalie Falls** at a parking area. The waterfalls are an excellent subject for photography, and the hike downriver is exercise enough for many people. Scout the river from the trail and decide if it is worth running.

Just below Sahalie Falls, the river heads over a 10-foot drop where a log juts from the left bank. Most of the water pushes toward the log, and the hydraulics at the base of the drop can be tricky. Boaters should work hard to remain in their boats since another 8-foot drop follows in only 25 yards. This second drop is a rocky slide into a small pool below.

Class IV technical rapids continue to **Koosah Falls,** just 0.4 mile downstream of Sahalie Falls, with a couple of breaks of calmer water between them. In late summer 1996 a huge logjam gathered at the base of Koosah Falls, making this drop a death-trap. If you want to run the exciting section below Sahalie, make sure you take out along the trail up the steep bank well before Koosah Falls. Don't miss this portage! You may want to have a rescue person downstream in case someone is forced to swim, since life and gear could easily be lost in the Koosah Falls log jam.

Below Koosah Falls rapids continue to Carmen Reservoir. Keep alert for logs in this stretch. Below the reservoir, water leads through lava beds to **Tamolitch Falls.** From here, the river continues to the take-out at Trail Bridge Reservoir in about 2 miles. I couldn't find anyone who had boated this section. Let me know what you find if you decide to explore it.

Section 2: Olallie Campground to Leaburg Dam

Class: II and III	Recommended flow: 700 to 3,000 cfs	Miles: 42

Popular with rafters, Section 2 of the McKenzie can be rocky and shallow at lower flows. There is normally enough water throughout the summer. Several tributaries add to the flow below Olallie Campground. There's also a nice hot spring on river right 0.25 mile into the run, near a bridge crossing. Continuous Class II water with some pool-drop Class II+ rapids and good surfing waves characterize most of this section, but boaters will find tougher Class III rapids at intervals along the way.

Roughly 3 miles below Olallie, the most difficult rapid on this section enters on a left bend in the river. Scout Fishladder rapid from a dirt road along the right bank. Here the river flows through a long, technical boulder garden with narrow chutes in places. At higher flows, holes develop and the water becomes pushier (but easier for rafts to negotiate). Rafters will find Fishladder to be technical. Unless you are quick to line up your craft as you pinball your way down, you risk a wrap on one of the various boulders.

Past Fishladder, the river eases to more continuous Class II water with a couple of short Class III drops. About 5 miles below your put-in at Olallie Campground, Belknap Hot Springs (River Mile 74) provides a nice break spot. Just above the springs, Class III **Belknap** rapid follows a right bend in the river; below it, the river makes a 90-degree turn left to change its course from south to west. Between the bends, Belknap Rapid has big waves and some smaller holes that can easily catch beginning and intermediate boaters off-guard. An eddy at the bottom provides a stopping place to view the hot springs that are piped across the river to Belknap Resort. A soak in the pool at this resort is well worth the small fee and steep climb up the bank.

Below Belknap the river continues to entertain boaters, reaching Paradise Campground (RM 71.5) in 2.5 miles. This is a popular access, a nice midpoint on day trips between Olallie Campground and Leaburg Dam. Below Paradise Campground, the river rolls along at a Class II level. A beautiful covered bridge crosses the road 1 mile below Harris Wayside State Park (RM 68). The South Fork McKenzie River enters on the left just 4 miles downstream of a covered bridge known as Rainbow Bridge. The Blue River (RM 57) enters 2.5 miles downstream on the right. Massive floods took out the road here and left a large log jam on the Blue River farther upstream.

The river maintains its continuous Class II character with some good surf waves and larger pool-drop sections along private property until it reaches **Brown's Hole** (RM 47). Here the river is fairly sedate except for the potentially hazardous hole on the left. Boaters can easily miss the hole by staying right at the horizon line. I have been window-shaded here at lower water after bumping an inflatable kayak out of the hole and sticking myself sideways. Brown's Hole is not particularly bad at lower water levels. It can be a good place for play-boating, using an eddy on the left to work your way back. Novice or intermediate boaters on relaxing float trips should avoid it, however, since the hole can be deceptively difficult.

Martin's rapid follows in less than a mile. The rapid is Class III to III+, depending on water level and craft. Big waves follow some boulders at the top; a recovery stretch follows the wave train. Rafters have a technical entry at the top, where a wrap on one of the large guard boulders can spill gear and boaters down the wave train. Stay right at the top and move toward the center of the drop after clearing the boulders. Some good surf waves follow to the take-out at Helfrich Boat Landing, on the right in less than 1 mile. Boaters may wish to continue down another 3 miles of easy water to a boat ramp on river right just above Leaburg Dam.

Section 3: Leaburg Dam to Willamette River

Class: I to II	**Recommended flow:** 700 to 3,000 cfs	**Miles:** 39

Most paddlers divide Section 3 into several day trips of varying lengths. The most common access locations are Leaburg Dam, Hendricks Bridge State Wayside, Hayden Bridge, and Armitage State Park. Short trips in this slow section can take a long time, since the gradient is low. Plan accordingly.

This easier stretch of water is a good place to start testing your paddling strokes. Long calm stretches with occasional riffles and sharp bends provide a warm-up for some Class II rapids later on. The many islands in this section may have changed shape in recent floods, so keep boats pointed toward the inside of river bends and be prepared to portage on any blind channel. Though the gradient is low, current can funnel and speed up around islands.

A Class II rapid will entertain boaters with some rock-dodging and waves about 0.5 mile above Hendricks Bridge. Below the bridge the river continues in similar character for another 15 miles to Hayden Bridge. There are good surf spots with eddies here at some water levels. Logs and brushy banks can cause problems for swimmers.

Hayden Bridge rapid is the most difficult rapid below Leaburg Dam. Watch for it below the Weyerhaeuser Paper Mill near Hayden Bridge State Wayside. Here paddlers can practice catching small eddies, surfing, or just staying upright in standing waves. Stay left to avoid the worst part of the rapid, which is at the bottom where the current cuts left.

From Hayden Bridge the river eases up, flowing around several islands. There are few hazards between Hayden Bridge Rapid and the Willamette River. Innertubers frequent this stretch on hot days. A popular float is from Hayden Bridge to Armitage State Park, or to the Willamette River and one of the take-outs at or before Harrisburg. This classic Class I float trip passes through both agricultural and residential areas, with views of the rounded Coburg Hills.

50 Metolius River
Headwaters to Lake Billy Chinook

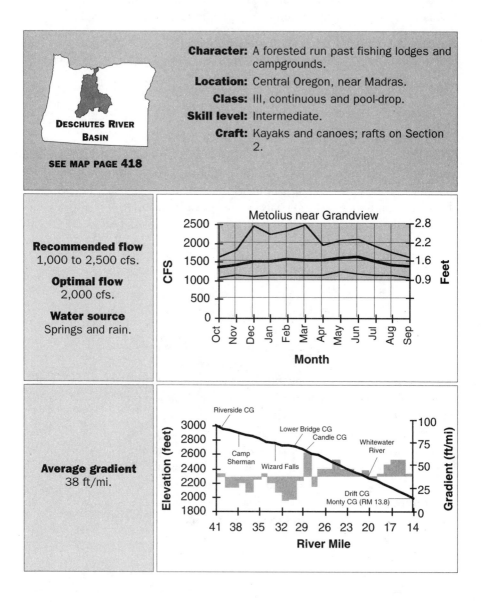

DESCHUTES RIVER BASIN

SEE MAP PAGE **418**

Character: A forested run past fishing lodges and campgrounds.

Location: Central Oregon, near Madras.

Class: III, continuous and pool-drop.

Skill level: Intermediate.

Craft: Kayaks and canoes; rafts on Section 2.

Recommended flow
1,000 to 2,500 cfs.

Optimal flow
2,000 cfs.

Water source
Springs and rain.

Metolius near Grandview

Average gradient
38 ft/mi.

Hazards: Like many Oregon rivers, the Metolius contains log hazards. Brushy banks line most of the river, giving swimmers a hard time. Watch out for several low bridges in the upper section. Class III to III+ rapids are present in both sections. The lower section is remote.

Access: From Portland and northern Oregon, follow Oregon Highway 26 (the Mount Hood Scenic Highway) southeast of Mount Hood to Forest Road 63 on the west side of Madras. Turn here and follow signs to Lake Billy Chinook. You will cross the lake about 1 mile past the boat launch. After climbing a hill, turn north at an intersection with Forest Road 64. Turn west here and go to a second intersection. Stay on FR 63 here and continue for roughly 20 miles to Camp Monty. This is the preferred take-out, the last above the lake.

Paddlers can reach alternate take-outs by following the rough gravel road that continues along the south bank of the river to the Whitewater River on the opposite shore. Several take-out or camping options are available there, but you may need four-wheel drive to reach them.

To reach the put-ins upstream, backtrack along FR 63 for 7.4 miles to an intersection with Forest Road 1170. FR 1170 becomes Forest Road 1180 at an intersection; follow it to a second four-way intersection 8.6 miles from FR 63. From this intersection, go straight on Forest Road 1140 for 1.4 miles to reach Forest Road 1490, marked by its red lava dirt and gravel. Follow this narrow road 16.1 miles to Forest Road 14 and Lower Bridge Campground. This is the put-in

Mount Jefferson can be seen from the headwaters of the Metolius River.

for the lower section. FR 14 continues upstream to Camp Sherman, **Wizard Falls,** and the headwaters of the Metolius.

Paddlers can also reach the Metolius River by taking either Oregon Highway 20 east of Eugene, or Oregon Highway 22 east of Salem. These roads intersect before reaching FR 14, which heads north to the put-ins.

Overview: The designated Wild and Scenic Metolius River originates from head-water springs. Filtering through lava rock, the clear blue water flows to where it meets the Whitewater River, clouded by glacial silt, snowmelt, and mud during summer months. Spring colors are brilliant here, and the light-colored trunks of ponderosa pine add to the dazzling scenery. Redcedar, lodgepole, and ponderosa grow tall and straight close to the river, attesting to low rainfall in the area. Despite the low precipitation, the Metolius flows at consistent levels year-round.

Private property lines both banks of the upper Metolius, but public camp-grounds allow breaks or alternate access points. Camp Sherman and various private resorts provide lodging and supplies. The Warm Springs Indian Reservation lines river left (the north shore) along most of the lower section, from Candle Creek to Lake Billy Chinook. Paddlers may not set foot on the reservation, but they can use campsites on the opposite bank. Anglers flock to the Metolius for outstanding trout fishing. Though the river has been heavily stocked in past years, wild trout are common. Check for the presence of an adipose fin before taking fish, since only the stocked trout, which have this fin clipped, are legal to keep. Kokanee salmon migrate upriver to spawn. These land-locked salmon find their way to the headwaters in large numbers in the fall.

The sections described here are long, but the water is swift. Kayakers have run both the upper 13 miles and lower 17 miles in less than 3 hours—and we were usually paddling upstream to catch surf waves and holes. The water is always cold, so bring hand protection and wear wetsuits or other coldwater gear. Hypo-thermia is a danger, since the cold water could easily flush a swimmer a long way before he or she reaches a safe spot on dry ground.

Going with the flow
Section 1: Headwaters to Lower Bridge

Class: II to III	Recommended flow: 300 to 1,000 cfs	Miles: 13

Putting in at the headwaters of the Metolius River is not practical, but paddlers should stop to see the springs and view Mount Jefferson. Just below the springs the river is small, though it soon gains flow from underground springs above Camp Sherman. An easier put-in is just downstream at the Camp Sherman Bridge.

Take kayaks or canoes on this shallow, slower section, since many low bridges cross the river in the upper 7 miles; rafting would require multiple portages on private property. Anglers are more prevalent on the upper river, since it is shallow enough to wade. Respect them when passing.

Boaters encounter the river's first Class III rapid about 2 miles below Camp Sherman. Typical of other rapids on the river, it contains large waves spotted with smaller holes. The next major rapids occur just after a narrow gorge below a river left campground. A sign alerts boaters about upcoming rapids over the next 4 miles. In the gorge just before the rapids begin, springs flow from river right, beautifully marking the transition from casual float to action-packed adventure.

After rounding a left-hand bend, the river drops and continues its wave and hole action for several miles, occasionally letting up between tougher sections. In the last mile or two of rapids, the river channels into narrow chutes in the bedrock. Stay in the sometimes turbulent channels for the best route. Wizard Falls, the only named rapid on the river, ends the rapids section with a small drop into a Class III chute. It is a bit disappointing as falls go, and is easier than some of the upstream rapids. Keep your head down under the low bridge! Scout the drop by taking a short road north to Wizard Falls on the shuttle drive along FS 14.

The remainder of the run to the Lower Bridge is peaceful. Soak up the scenery and relax until you reach the take-out.

Section 2: Lower Bridge to Lake Billy Chinook

Class: III	Recommended flow: 1,000 to 3,000 cfs	Miles: 17+

The lower section of the Metolius is the most popular, since rafters and boaters alike enjoy a portage-free trip. Kayakers and canoeists will find fun surf waves and fast, nonstop action to the end. The river has more volume here and is still very cold. Boaters should prepare for unexpected, long swims and cold, big-water conditions.

Paddlers encounter the first rapid of the stretch about 0.5 mile from the put-in at Lower Bridge. This first rapid resembles those to come, but contains a submerged log on river right. Look for the log sticking out from the right bank and move left, since the log juts out to the middle of the river.

Most of the river is a fast Class II run, but Class III drops dot the way down. One more difficult Class III drop occurs 0.5 mile below the confluence with the Whitewater River, which enters on river left. The Whitewater is often cloudy due to glacial silt and snowmelt, clouding the Metolius from here to Lake Billy Chinook.

Within 2 miles of passing the Whitewater River, log jams line the river. Root systems are visible cues, though some logs have been cut out of the river to allow passage for rafts. Since the water here is fast, boaters must move quickly to avoid getting caught in or on the logs. The Warm Springs Indian tribe has attempted to close the river due to the log hazards, but the obstacles here are no more significant than on other rivers where logs are a concern. Rafts are more likely to have trouble, but at press time passage along the river is uninhibited for skilled rafters with Class III ability.

Campsites are sparse but present along the river right bank. Most of the river left shore is off-limits, since the land there is part of the Warm Springs Indian Reservation. Respect the Indians' land and stay off. Camp Monty is a good place to take out. The river slows there, and Lake Billy Chinook reaches up the canyon to just below the campground. Boaters wishing for a longer trip may continue to the lake or the campground above it for a soothing finale to a fast, continuous trip.

51 Mill Creek

Triple Drop to South Yamhill River

Character: A log-infested creek flowing from forest to farmland.

Location: Northwest Oregon, west of Salem.

Class: II to IV, continuous and pool-drop.

Skill level: Beginner to advanced.

Craft: Kayaks and canoes.

MIDDLE
WILLAMETTE
BASIN

SEE MAP PAGE **436**

Recommended flow
300 to 800 cfs.

Optimal flow
800 cfs.

Water source
Rain.

Average gradient
50 ft/mi.

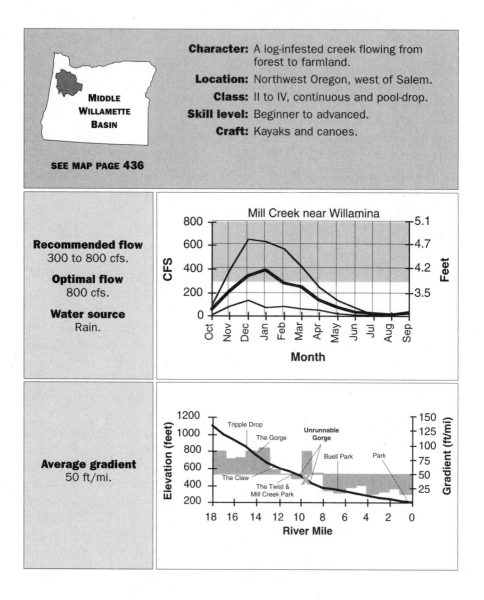

Hazards: Upper Mill Creek contains numerous logs, since recent logging operations have dropped several trees into the creek. Watch for mandatory portages in Section 1. An unrunnable gorge follows Mill River Recreation Area, so don't miss the take-out at the park! Watch for brushy banks, tight bends, and occasional logs in Section 2.

Access: From the Portland area, head west on Oregon Highway 18 toward the coast. Continue past Sheridan to Harmony Road, on the left. The park on the right just under the OR 18 bridge makes a good take-out. Alternately, paddlers may continue down the South Yamhill River to make a longer run; in that case, take out in Sheridan. To reach the lower put-in at Buell Park, follow Harmony Road to Oregon Highway 22. Turn left and follow OR 22 to Buell Park. The park gate is often closed in winter, but it's a short walk to an easy put-in here.

To access the upper section, turn right onto Mill Creek Road just before you reach Buell Park from OR 22. Follow Mill Creek Road 2.5 miles to Mill Creek Recreation Area, the mandatory take-out on this stretch. On you way there, take a look at the unrunnable gorge that lies downstream. Below the park, there's only a short Class II stretch before the deadly gorge. Continue up Mill Creek Road to the put-in, about 6 miles. Scout **The Gorge** on the way up and watch for wood in the creek!

Overview: Mill Creek is a great run to try after it has been raining cats and dogs for several days. When the South Yamhill River is at or near flood stage, Mill Creek usually has the right amount of water to make a fun run. The creek is divided into two sections due to an unrunnable gorge in the upper half of the creek. The top portion invites advanced boaters looking for Class III to IV technical water, while the lower creek offers steady Class II water with several large surfing waves. Beware of sharp bends with brushy banks that can cause trouble in Section 2.

Logging has completely decimated the eastern slope of the mountains along the upper stretch of this creek, and clearcuts now replace the once-scenic slopes. Luckily the cuts do not extend to Mill Creek Recreation Area, where the banks once again are lined with unlogged forest. The lower creek passes through wooded farmland, rolling hills, and open fields. Runoff muddies the creek and can wash droppings from nearby livestock into the water.

Going with the flow
Section 1: Triple Drop to Mill Creek Recreation Area

Class: IV	Recommended flow: 400 to 1,000 cfs	Miles: 5

Scout Mill Creek carefully on the drive up. Before you drop your shuttle vehicle, take a look at the severe hazard downstream of the Mill River Recreation Area. As you peek at the terror that lies ahead for those who miss the mandatory take-out, keep off private property and stay away from the steep bank. From the recreation area, scout the run's final Class III rapid, **The Twist**. On the drive to the put-in, watch the river for logs. In January 1996, strainers forced portages at three locations;

two of these were difficult. The put-in area was cut short that year due to a river-wide strainer just upstream.

A roadside pullout near **Triple Drop** rapid allows for an easy put-in where the action starts. Class IV Triple Drop is the most difficult drop on the creek, but not necessarily the most dangerous. It drops in three steep steps with good hydraulics at the bottom of each one. Calmer water follows for recovery.

The Gorge occurs after a short calm stretch just around a sharp left bend. Scout it by scrambling down the bank above and below to check for hazards and get a view of the rapid's final plunge into a pool over a turbulent 4-foot drop. Look over the rock side from the top to see the narrow center of the gorge, where another sharp drop plunges into turbulent water. Portage on the right if in doubt before entering The Gorge.

Below here, the river keeps the action coming with continuous Class II technical water and wood. In two places, paddlers may have to portage in fast water around strainers that span the creek. One is just after **The Claw**, a Class III drop that can ender a boat in the hole at the bottom. At higher water routes are not too clawlike, but a strainer just downstream is deceptive since much of it is underwater. A route on the river's far left just scrapes over it.

Beyond a bridge and before the take-out, a third log spans the creek, forcing another portage. One final drop awaits; The Twist follows a sharp bend in the

Kayakers steer clear of the banks of Mill Creek in high water.

creek and drops 4 feet into turbulent water. Take out at Mill Creek Recreation Area on the left. If you plan to continue down the lower section, shuttle the 2.5 miles around the deadly gorge below. Put in again at Buell Park.

Special note: Logs have undoubtedly shifted since the floods of '96 and '97.

Section 2: Buell Park to South Yamhill River

Class: II	Recommended flow: 400 to 2,000 cfs	Miles: 7

The lower section runs from Buell Park to Mill Creek's confluence with the South Yamhill. The creek offers continuous Class II water here, with many great surf waves in the upper portion and a few eddies at higher flows. Its banks are lined with brush in several places, making a portage difficult. Always watch for logs. Look carefully, since one nice-looking surf spot in this section turned out to be a submerged log when we ran this section. Most boaters will find the rapids on lower Mill Creek easy enough to handle, but many sharp bends do require boat-scouting. Boaters should be comfortable scouting in fast current while looking for probable debris.

This run is similar to boating the South Yamhill River, but faster and tighter. Smaller islands appear in the lower portions of the creek. Even though the gradient picks up before the confluence with the South Yamhill, the trip here is a relaxing float. The South Yamhill below the confluence is flatwater to Sheridan.

Farmland and cattle line the banks of both Mill Creek and the upper South Yamhill. Livestock waste can enter the waterway, especially during high flows and rainy conditions. I was unfortunate enough to contract giardiasis after roll practice on lower Mill Creek and the South Yamhill at the end of an early 1996 run.

52 Minam River

Red's Horse Ranch to Minam River Recreation Area

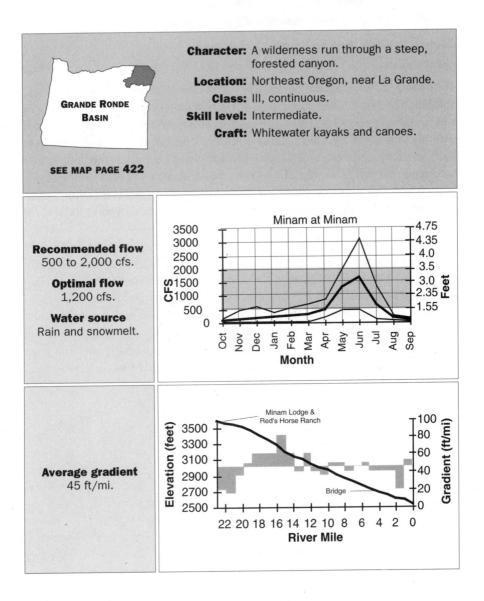

GRANDE RONDE BASIN

SEE MAP PAGE **422**

Character: A wilderness run through a steep, forested canyon.

Location: Northeast Oregon, near La Grande.

Class: III, continuous.

Skill level: Intermediate.

Craft: Whitewater kayaks and canoes.

Recommended flow
500 to 2,000 cfs.

Optimal flow
1,200 cfs.

Water source
Rain and snowmelt.

Minam at Minam

Average gradient
45 ft/mi.

Hazards: The Minam River is remote, with only trail access between Minam Lodge and the Minam River Recreation Area. Logistics (flying boats in, or packing in on horseback) limit recreational floating along the river. Boaters should remain alert for log hazards. Swims could be long in the continuous upper stretches.

Access: Reach the take-out by following Oregon Highway 82 east from La Grande toward Enterprise. The Minam River Recreation Area is midway between La Grande and Enterprise along OR 82.

To reach the put-in, you'll need to arrange a plane shuttle. It is possible to ride horses to Red's Horse Ranch along the trail on river right, but hauling boats presents an unusual difficulty. Most paddlers who run this river fly gear into either the ranch or Minam Lodge.

Overview: The Minam makes for unusual boating since it requires an expensive and difficult flight to put-ins at Red's Horse Ranch or Minam Lodge. Only small planes can land at the ranch's rough airstrip, so groups of paddlers will need to make several flights. Despite these unusual concerns, the river is spectacular. It originates high in the Wallowa Mountains and the Eagle Cap Wilderness, at Minam Lake (I've been there). The area is rugged and filled with wildlife. Deer sightings are common and fishing is good. Pine trees line the banks of the river as it slopes fairly evenly to its confluence with the Wallowa River.

Going with the flow

Class: III	Recommended flow: 500 to 2,000 cfs	Miles: 22

Paddlers will wish to spend time at Minam Lodge before paddling out. The 22 miles downriver make a long trip; most paddlers go self-contained and camp along the way. You can do the trip in one long day if you're skilled enough, since the water moves along at a fast pace.

The first 2 miles are a good Class II to II+ warm-up for the more continuous Class III water below. The Class III action continues for more than 8 miles before calming down. There are few signs of civilization below the ranch. A trail follows the right bank for the entire length of the river. Boaters may occasionally see hikers, but cold weather deters most hikers until later in the summer, when the river is more suitable for wading than floating.

The take-out is above the confluence with the Wallowa River, on the left.

53 Molalla River

Copper Creek to Willamette River

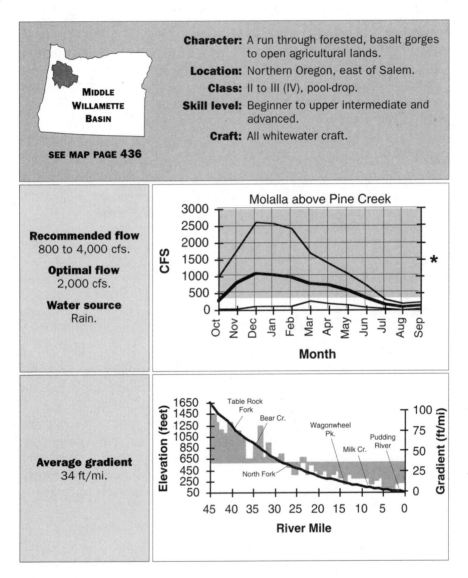

MIDDLE WILLAMETTE BASIN

SEE MAP PAGE **436**

Character: A run through forested, basalt gorges to open agricultural lands.

Location: Northern Oregon, east of Salem.

Class: II to III (IV), pool-drop.

Skill level: Beginner to upper intermediate and advanced.

Craft: All whitewater craft.

Recommended flow
800 to 4,000 cfs.

Optimal flow
2,000 cfs.

Water source
Rain.

Molalla above Pine Creek

Average gradient
34 ft/mi.

* No depth measurement available.

Hazards: Technical pool-drop rapids, narrow canyon gorges, and logs are present along the upper and middle portions of the Molalla River. Scout **Lightning Lonnie** and **The Three Bears** rapids on the drive to the put-in. Gravel bars, islands with debris piles, and wide meandering stretches comprise the lower river.

Access: From Interstate 5 north of Salem take the Woodburn exit (Exit 271) to Oregon Highway 214, heading east. At the east end of Woodburn, stay right on Oregon Highway 211. At its intersection with Oregon Highway 213, turn left (north) on OR 213 to reach the take-out at a bridge over the Molalla River in a short distance, or continue toward the town of Molalla to reach the OR 211 bridge, another possible take-out.

To reach put-ins, drive through the town of Molalla to Feyer Park Road, heading south. The road leads to Feyer Park, where a gage on the bridge pillar was formerly used to judge the flow. This park is a good put-in for the Class II section below, or a take-out for the Class II+ section above. For other access points, go across the bridge from the park and take Dickey Prairie Road right (south). Continue along this road to Glen Avon Bridge. Just beyond the bridge on river right is a pullout that makes a good put-in. If it's not what you're looking for, cross the bridge and continue south along Molalla River Road to choose from several pullouts and begin your trip. Various pullouts allow views of **Baby, Mama,** and **Papa Bear** rapids and Lightning Lonnie. **Note:** Due to a washout, the road to section 1 may be closed at times for reconstruction in 1998.

There are wonderful break spots above Goldilocks rapid on Section 2 of the Molalla River.

Overview: Paddlers often overlook the free-flowing Molalla River, since there is no active gage to judge the flow. The gage on the bridge at Feyer Park once gave boaters a good idea of water level, but since the 1996 floods the gage reads higher than in past years. Today, a good flow for the upper river is 5 to 6 feet at this gage. (In the past, only 3.5 feet were required.) The gage height may continue to change over time, since the large gravel bar restricting flow above it is unstable. If there is ample water at the put-in, there is usually enough for a trip downstream. When the Clackamas River is running above 3,000 cubic feet per second, the Molalla is usually high enough to boat. At higher flows the river becomes pushy, with big water. Large surf waves develop on the upper river, and rapids increase in difficulty with huge holes and hydraulics.

The Molalla is smaller and more technical than the neighboring Clackamas River, but it offers similar variety for kayakers and canoeists. Rafters can put in below Turner Bridge at higher flows, but access is steep along the banks. The upper river is heavily wooded with moss-covered deciduous trees. Its banks are brushy with technical basalt ledges, tight gorges, and occasional rocky beaches. The road follows the river, allowing boaters to car-scout many rapids. One exception is **Goldilocks**, above Glen Avon Bridge. Paddlers commonly boat the lower river to the OR 213 bridge. Below this take-out the river meanders through open agricultural areas, channeling around large gravel bars and islands. The water can be shallow at low flows. Higher flows spread the riverbed over a wide floodplain on private agricultural land.

Going with the flow
Section 1: Copper Creek to Glen Avon Bridge

Class: III+ (IV)	Recommended flow: 800 to 3,000 cfs	Miles: 14.5

This upper section of the Molalla River is more secluded and scenic than areas downstream. It also contains the most demanding whitewater. The Class IV rapid known as Lightning Lonnie follows **Dungeon** (below Dungeon Creek, entering on the right) just 2 miles below the uppermost put-in. Below these rapids the river is Class II water with Class III to III+ pool-drop rapids that can rate Class IV or greater at higher flows.

After a good Class II warm-up, boaters hit the run's first major rapid below Copper Creek. It begins with a boulder garden, followed by an S-turn and small holes. A short, narrow gorge follows, leading to Lightning Lonnie. Here, rapids course into a technical, rocky 5- to 6-foot drop. The best route depends on the flow; scout from the road on the way up. Boaters who wish to avoid this drop can put in below it at a pullout along the road.

Below the initial rapids, the river is Class II with Class III water in a couple of places. Trees jut from the bank on the outside corners of two sharp bends. The Table Rock Fork of the Molalla enters just before paddlers reach the first bridge across the river. About 1.5 miles below the bridge, a Class III lead-in narrows into a tight Class III+ gorge with turbulent waves that bounce off the walls. A solid brace comes in handy here, but there's calm water at the bottom. From here to the second bridge, known as Turner Bridge, the water calms to Class II and II+, with a couple of good surf waves toward the end. Take out at Turner Bridge or continue along the river toward The Three Bears rapids.

The next portion of river is known as the Three Bears run, since paddlers encounter three Class III to IV rapids near Bear Creek, which enters on river right. About 0.5 mile below Turner Bridge, the first major drop is called Papa Bear. A midstream rock protrusion divides the current here. The left channel requires a sharp turn around the rock in turbulent water; the easier right side is threatened by an undercut wall as the current rushes toward the protrusion and banks off the right. Paddlers should head toward river left after passing the midstream obstacle.

Mama Bear follows in about 0.5 mile, after paddlers round a sharp right bend. The river narrows into a chute down the middle between a jutting left ledge and two large boulders on the right. The lead-in contains waves and holes at higher flows. Before the recent floods, this rapid dropped into a large hole that had to be punched, but it now flushes into the eddy on the right. Below Mama Bear, paddlers push through a narrow, turbulent gorge known as "The Narrows." The natural gorge walls contain beautiful basalt swirls; the water below contains the ugly remains of a compact car dumped into the river years ago.

About 1 mile downriver, Baby Bear sits in the middle of another right-to-left bend. The far right side of the rapid has been gouged out by floods, but most of the current sweeps left between the rocky left bank and a large island. A turbulent

Paddlers attempt to free a wrapped canoe from a rock in the Molalla River.

diagonal wave hole can flip even the best paddlers. Make sure you can roll, since another ledge-drop follows just a few yards around the bend to the left.

Once you're past The Three Bears, relax and enjoy the scenery for a couple of miles. Roadside pullouts have trails to the river, allowing boaters to opt for a shorter trip. Flag your take-out with signal tape or some recognizable feature, since much of the bank here looks the same from the river. At Goldilocks rapid, the current narrows and sweeps to the right off the left undercut bank. Debris tends to collect along the channel, so scout carefully from your boat or the large gravel bar island on the right. The rapid was completely clean as of March 1997. Just beyond Goldilocks, **Porridge Pot** once rewarded paddlers with a good play hole at moderate flows, dropping over a river-wide ledge. A large eddy followed the ledge for recovery and a river right return for more play. The hole has filled in since the recent floods, but it may be back in the future.

Easier Class II water continues to Glen Avon Bridge. There are some nice break spots on the river, at ledges with good scenery on sunny days. Take out before the bridge on the right or continue along Section 2.

Section 2: Glen Avon Bridge to OR 213 Bridge

Class: II	Recommended flow: 1,000 to 4,000 cfs	Miles: 12

Section 2 is mostly Class I water, with a couple of more difficult Class II+ spots that include holes and a ledge-drop. It's a suitable run for beginning boaters who have been practicing their roll and who have tried easier stretches of river first. Practice bracing, eddy turns, negotiating rapids, and avoiding holes before you come here. Calm water follows the more difficult parts, allowing for recovery.

Paddlers can miss one hole about a mile below Glen Avon Bridge by keeping left at the rapid. It is difficult for many beginning boaters to see, but paddlers will flush out for a roll if they happen to hit it. More skilled paddlers may wish to play here. A short distance downstream is a Class II rapid that could become more difficult at high water. Large waves lead down and to the left.

The rest of the river is Class I+ water with smaller waves and several new gravel bars since the recent floods. Debris collects on the bars and at corners, so keep aware at all times and stay to the inside of river bends. Always paddle in groups to ensure that rescue is available, especially if you are new to the river or the sport. Take out just after the bridge at Feyer Park, or continue downstream for more Class I and II water.

Beyond Feyer Park the river slowly flattens, but at higher water some Class II spots are still present. The river has greater volume on this lower stretch and is much wider than the technical upper river. About 2 miles below Feyer Park, the OR 211 bridge is a possible take-out spot. Below it, the banks open as the river enters grazing areas and a floodplain area. The OR 213 bridge is about 4 miles farther; many paddlers continue along Class I and I+ water beyond OR 213 bridge. The Pudding River joins the lower river before reaching the Willamette River confluence. A take-out is available at Molalla River State Park along the right bank near the confluence with the Willamette.

54 Nehalem River
Timber Road to Nehalem Bay

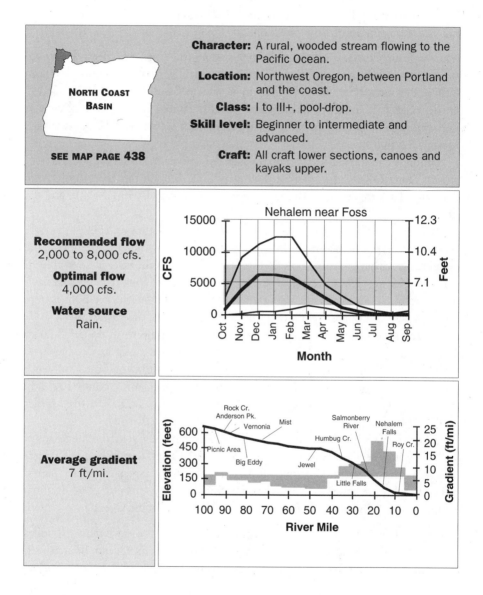

Character: A rural, wooded stream flowing to the Pacific Ocean.

Location: Northwest Oregon, between Portland and the coast.

Class: I to III+, pool-drop.

Skill level: Beginner to intermediate and advanced.

Craft: All craft lower sections, canoes and kayaks upper.

NORTH COAST BASIN

SEE MAP PAGE 438

Recommended flow
2,000 to 8,000 cfs.

Optimal flow
4,000 cfs.

Water source
Rain.

Average gradient
7 ft/mi.

Nehalem near Foss

River Mile

Hazards: Sections 1 and 3 of the Nehalem River are mostly Class I water, although there are islands, sharp bends, fast currents at high water, and some wood hazards to negotiate. Section 2 contains Class III to III+ pool-drop rapids, including **Little Falls, Salmonberry Drop,** and **Nehalem Falls.** Lower Section 3 is tidal, requiring tide charts to determine flow direction.

Access: From Portland follow U.S. Highway 26 (the Sunset Highway) west toward the coast. Oregon Highway 47 (the Nehalem Highway) leads north less than 8 miles beyond where Oregon Highway 6 splits off to the west. Follow OR 47 north roughly 12 miles to its intersection with Timber Road, heading west at Treharne. To reach the upper access bridge, continue west along Timber Road for roughly 2.5 miles.

Paddlers can also access the upper Nehalem River from many places downstream along OR 47 and Oregon Highway 202. Among the access points are Anderson Park in Vernonia (River Mile 90.7); Big Eddy Park (RM 89); and the bridge at Mist (RM 72.2).

Between the OR 47/202 intersection and Jewell Junction on US 26, the river has few developed access areas. In Clatsop County below the OR 202 bridge, the Nehalem is within Clatsop State Forest. OR 202 crosses the river at several locations here for possible access; the road follows the river to Vinemaple before deviating southeast. Paddlers can also get to the river at Pope–Meeker Boat Ramp, which is west of Pope Corner along OR 202 just north of Jewell Junction.

To reach access areas below Jewell Junction, continue west along US 26 to Lower Nehalem Road at Elsie. There are several bridges along Lower Nehalem Road for possible access, with even more access sites just beyond the confluence with Humbug Creek (RM 34.7) and at Spruce Creek Campground (RM 30); Nehalem Falls Campground (RM 15.5); Beaver Slide Boat Ramp (RM 14); Mohler Sand and Gravel (RM 9.8); and Roy Creek County Park (RM 8).

Below Roy Creek County Park, paddlers can reach the river from the towns of Nehalem or Wheeler by continuing west to Oregon Highway 53 and U.S. Highway 101. Nehalem is north along US 101 just across the river; Wheeler is south. Paddlers who are interested in exploring Nehalem Bay can put in at Brighten Moorage and Jetti Fishery before the river reaches the Pacific Ocean.

Overview: The Nehalem River is a rural stream flowing for more than 100 miles between Oregon's northern coastal mountains and the Pacific Ocean. Boaters usually run the upper river during the rainy season, from late fall to early spring. Ample flows or tidal waters are available year-round in the lower stretches. The low-elevation coastal mountains receive less snow than inland ranges, tending to drain during winter and early spring. Temperatures can be cold during the boating season, so gear up for weather even on sunny days.

The Nehalem flows through Clatsop and Tillamook state forests along much of its length, but private property lines the river in places. Make sure to camp within forest boundaries if you make a multiday trip. Upper river access is limited to parks and bridges. Access along the lower river is available in many places, with the most common sites listed above.

A railroad follows the lower Nehalem River to the Salmonberry River. Trains travel the tracks daily, shipping freight between Tillamook and Portland.

Going with the flow
Section 1: Upper Timber Road Bridge to Jewell

Class: I	Recommended flow: 2,000 to 8,000 cfs	Miles: 53

The upper Nehalem River has a short boating season—only early winter and spring rains supply enough water. In late spring, the river drops to a boat-scraping level. Paddlers should prepare for cold weather, cold water, and fast current at higher flows. The river originates above the Timber Road Bridge, but its flow is divided there between several tributary creeks.

Section 1 is well suited for paddlers with flatwater or Class I experience who yearn to try faster currents and more advanced maneuvers. Few rapids exist along the upper river, but the narrow stream is subject to wood hazards. Be alert for logs as you paddle. You will also want to watch for several sharp bends, gravel bar islands, and occasional Class I riffles between the river's tree-lined banks. Fall leaves are particularly colorful here after heavy rains.

Section 2: Jewell to Roy Creek County Park

Class: I+ to III	Recommended flow: 2,000 to 8,000 cfs	Miles: 39

From Jewell to Humbug Creek, the Nehalem opens wider in a stretch of Class I water. Below the Humbug Creek confluence, the river gradually picks up more Class I+ and II characteristics, with some good surf spots at higher flows. Just below Spruce Run Campground (RM 30), **Little Falls** presents a cascade of small ledges that can be seen from the road. Novice paddlers should scout the drop before running it, but routes are generally easy for intermediate paddlers to see and run.

Several miles of easier Class I with a few Class II rapids follow, leading paddlers to Salmonberry Drop (RM 22.4). The rapid lies beyond the confluence with the Salmonberry River, which enters on the left. Scout the drop at higher flows since a good hole forms at the bottom of the main chute, to the left of a large boulder. The 4- to 6-foot drop can ender boats before flushing them out.

Below Salmonberry, the middle river rapids continue in Class II to III fashion with some good surf waves to Nehalem Falls. The falls are fairly straightforward Class III rapids below Nehalem Falls Park. At lower flows, an exposed fish ladder containing exposed concrete slabs contains most of the river's flow. Scout or portage along rock islands in the central river. The river right is the safest route at any flow. Scout them before running to decide if you wish to take out at the park or continue downstream to try this drop. A bridge follows just downstream of the falls, offering an alternate take-out. Paddlers may also use access points in Batterson, on the right side of the river 2 miles beyond the falls.

Class II water continues below Nehalem Falls to Roy Creek County Park. The river gradient eases before reaching the park, and soon feels the upstream influence of tidal waters. Take out at the park or continue along Section 3.

Section 3: Roy Creek County Park to Nehalem Bay

Class: FW	Recommended flow: Tidal	Miles: 8+

From Roy Creek County Park to Nehalem Bay, the river slows due to tidal flows. Paddlers can purchase tide charts at the kayak shop in Wheeler. You'll need them to determine which way the water is running; fighting currents and occasional upstream winds can make a Section 3 trip longer than expected. With the right timing and weather, however, the float is easy and flat.

Boaters see many shorebirds and blue herons along this stretch. The lower Nehalem's banks are often muddy, lined with trees and thick vegetation. Always be alert for logs in the river, and watch for motorboats along the lower river near the bay. A bayside restaurant in the community of Nehalem makes a nice lunch stop or ending to a day's float.

55 Nestucca River

Rocky Bend Campground to Nestucca Bay

Character: A run from rocky coastal mountains to a rural ocean bay.

Location: Oregon coast, south of Tillamook.

Class: I+ to III (-V to V), pool-drop.

Skill level: Beginner to upper advanced.

Craft: Kayaks and canoes (Section 1); all craft (Section 2).

NORTH COAST BASIN

SEE MAP PAGE 438

Recommended flow
500 to 4,000 cfs.

Optimal flow
1,000 cfs.

Water source
Rain.

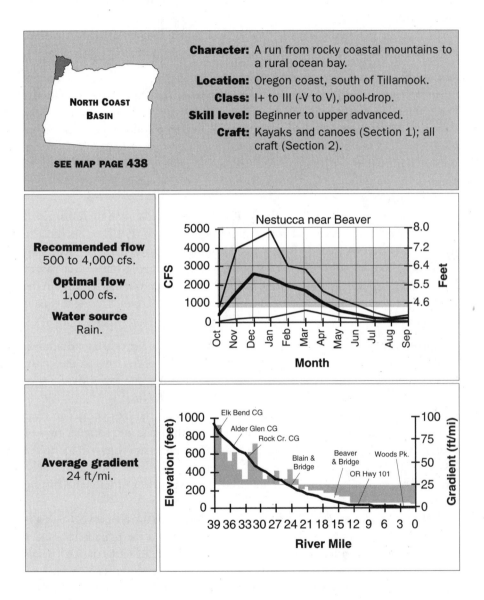

Nestucca near Beaver

Average gradient
24 ft/mi.

Elk Bend CG
Alder Glen CG
Rock Cr. CG
Blain & Bridge
Beaver & Bridge
Woods Pk.
OR Hwy 101

Hazards: The upper Nestucca River is quite technical in places along Section 1. Class IV to V **Silver Falls** and several boulder garden drops known as **Bible Belt** occur 1.5 miles below the put-in at Rocky Bend Campground. Stay below the high water mark as you scout the drops, since the surrounding land is private. Easier Class II and occasional Class III- rapids occur above Blaine. Wood hazards are uncommon, though wood and debris are most likely to collect in constricted areas.

Access: To reach the Nestucca River, take U.S. Highway 101 south from Tillamook or north from Lincoln City crosses along the Oregon coast; the road crosses the lower river. Brooten Road leads west from US 101 to Pacific City, south of the Nestucca. The lower take-out at Fisher Tract Boat Ramp is along the south side of the river here. Paddlers can find other lower river access areas along US 101 to the north: Cloverdale Boat Ramp at Cloverdale; Three Rivers Boat Ramp south of Hebo to the west; Farmer Creek Boat Ramp north of Hebo; and Bixby Boat Ramp south of Beaver.

To reach the upper river, take Blaine Road (County Road 858 or Forest Road 85 within the Siuslaw National Forest) as it leads east from US 101 at Beaver. The road follows the Nestucca to Rocky Bend Campground and all upper access areas. Paddlers commonly put in or take out across from a large white church east of Blaine, or at bridge locations. Beyond Rocky Bend Campground, a left fork in the road leads to several Bureau of Land Management campgrounds along the main Nestucca River.

Overview: The Nestucca River winds through Oregon's lower coastal mountains, nestled along a pleasant, narrow valley that gradually opens toward the coast. Small communities are displayed in quaint settings along the lower river. Dairy farms and grazing land line much of the river between towns.

Anglers have named every rock, bend, and hole in the Nestucca. The river boasts one of the best annual steelhead catches, with spring and summer runs of chinook salmon and stocked cutthroat trout. Drift boats are common along the lower river, particularly along the tidal stretch where fishing restrictions apply. Always be respectful when passing these boats, staying clear of lines and casting areas.

The whitewater manual *Soggy Sneakers* reported an incident involving paddlers arrested for trespass while scouting Silver Falls and the Bible Belt boulder gardens. The issue is still unresolved. Paddlers should remain below the high water mark while scouting on the upper river. Please respect landowners' concerns regarding noise, litter, and vandalism. The resolution of this case could set a precedent for access along other Oregon streams.

Going with the flow
Section 1: Rock Creek Campground to Blaine Church Pullout

Class: III (V)	**Recommended flow:** 400 to 1,500 cfs	**Miles:** 8.3

Below Rocky Bend Campground, the Nestucca River is busy. Paddlers here get continuous waves, boulder-dodging chances, and surf warm-ups before reaching the big stuff. After about 1.5 miles, Silver Falls presents a jumble of boulders with various technical routes. Scout or portage along the right bank for routes and debris, but don't forget to stay below the high water mark! At lower flows routes are less pushy but narrow. The falls earn a Class V rating at higher water, since consequences of a pin or broach are more severe. At lower flows they rate a less stressful Class IV.

A few yards downstream is another Class IV technical boulder garden. I call the rapid Bible Belt, in keeping with tributary names upstream. Routes weave from center to right through megaboulders and rock walls. It is easiest to scout the entire stretch from a rock midstream just into the rapid, but at higher flows you may have difficulty reaching this vantage point safely. Alternately, scout along the steep, sloping rock at the right. Twisting stairstep drops lead into a pool at the bottom.

Below Bible Belt there are several enjoyable smaller Class II+ to III- rapids scattered between Class I and II water. The larger drops spread farther apart as the river widens and the take-out (across from the Blaine church) approaches. At

Jeff Jacob heads over a drop below Silver Falls on the Nestucca.

lower flows the river can scrape hulls near the take-out; if there's ample water here when you drop your shuttle vehicle, there will be plenty of water upstream.

Paddlers can access the Nestucca above Rocky Bend Campground at Alder Glen and Elk Bend campgrounds over 6 miles upstream. The river is steeper in this area, with many braided channels; it has not been explored by any boater I know. The road closely follows the river, though, so if you're in the area you might want to check it out.

Section 2: Blaine Church Pullout to Nestucca Bay

Class: I (I+)	Recommended flow: 1,500 to 4,000 cfs	Miles: 24

Below Blaine the river moves along at a good pace, though it requires more water to cover its wide, shallow bed. Enjoy the small Class I+ wave trains and few good surfing spots. The river is wide enough to avoid most of the larger waves, pourovers, and debris. The pace slowly eases as you approach the town of Beaver. Seven bridges span the river between Blaine and Beaver, providing alternate access points.

The river rates a continuous Class I to I+ for roughly 2.5 miles below Beaver, then it flattens. At the US 101 bridge, the river becomes influenced by tides. Take extra time to paddle the flatwater and changing currents. One possible take-out is Woods County Park, on river left near the bridge above Pacific City. The last take-out above Nehalem Bay is south of Pacific City at Fisher Tract Boat Ramp. Beyond Cloverdale, watch for exposed tidal flats at low water and low tide.

56 Owyhee River

Garat Crossing on the East Fork to Leslie Gulch

OWYHEE BASIN

SEE MAP PAGE **440**

Character: A river in an isolated, scenic desert canyon with hot springs.

Location: Oregon's eastern border, near Jordan Valley.

Class: III to IV (P), pool-drop.

Skill level: Upper intermediate to expert.

Craft: Rafts, kayaks, and canoes.

Recommended flow
500 to 4,000 cfs.

Optimal flow
2,500 cfs.

Water source
Rain and snowmelt.

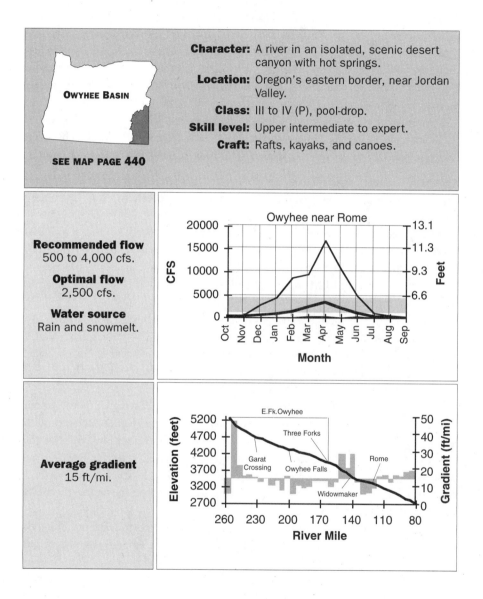

Average gradient
15 ft/mi.

Hazards: Mostly Class I or II at best, the Owyhee River has sections of Class III whitewater and a few significant Class IV to V drops requiring advanced skills and/or arduous portaging. **Owyhee Falls** is a mandatory and difficult portage. Experts commonly run Class V **Widowmaker** rapid, but others should scout and portage from either side. Rafts are often lined down on the right. Several Class IV rapids above Rome deserve a scout and/or portage. Along the lower river, **Whistling Bird** and **Montgomery** rapid are Class III rapids that deserve more attention. **Bullseye** must be run, since it sits in a narrow canyon where water pours into a large hole through narrow slots around a midstream boulder.

Extreme remoteness is the Owyhee's other hazard. Rescue efforts here would be limited by the terrain, and rescuers could be a long time coming. The steep canyon prohibits access in many places. This area is excellent rattlesnake habitat.

Access: The most popular stretch of the lower Owyhee River runs from Rome to either Leslie Gulch on Owyhee Reservoir or Birch Creek Ranch access, just before the reservoir. To reach Rome from most Oregon locations, follow U.S. Highway 20 through central Oregon to Burns. Oregon Highway 78 leads southeast to Burns Junction in 96 miles. At Burns Junction follow U.S. Highway 95 east to Rome and the access upstream just across the bridge over the Owyhee River. No permit system is in effect, but BLM personnel will check to see if you have a fire pan and proper equipment for the trip.

Lower river take-outs are at either Leslie Gulch or Birch Creek Ranch. To reach the take-out at Leslie Gulch continue east along US 95 past Jordan Valley and Sheaville to Leslie Gulch-Succor Creek Byway to the west off of US 95. Leslie Gulch Road intersects Succor Creek Road in about 10 miles and leads to the take-out to the west an additional 14 miles.

Alternate access is available at Birch Creek Ranch by following US 95 to Danner Road to the north before reaching Jordan Valley. Danner Road intersects with Lower Cow Creek Road to the north at the first intersection. Stay right at the intersection to Upper Cow Lake and continue to Blowout Reservoir Road to the west. Blowout Reservoir Road intersects with Birch Creek Road to the north in roughly 12 miles and continues down a steep four-wheel-drive road to the BLM take-out at Birch Creek Ranch.

To reach the access at Three Forks for an upper Owyhee or East Fork Owyhee run follow US 95 west to Sheep Spring Road to the south before reaching Jordan Valley. Follow Sheep Spring Road to JACA Road which converges with Soldier Creek Road. A couple of intersections later, the road branches onto Fenwick Ranch Road to the right. Follow Fenwick Ranch Road to the put-in. A BLM map is recommended and is available from the Boise office. They are also occasionally available from the BLM folks at Rome.

To access the put-in locations at Garat Crossing or the Duck Valley Indian Reservation continue along US 95 east past Jordan Valley to Marsing near the Snake River. Idaho Highway 78 leads southeast beyond Murphy and Grand View to Idaho Highway 51 before reaching Brueau. Follow ID 51 south beyond Grasmere to an unmarked road to the west before reaching the town of Riddle. From here unmarked four-wheel drive roads lead to Garrett Crossing and a pipeline. Take the road that crosses Shoofly Creek and continue west to the river crossing and access. Make sure to have a high-clearance four-wheel-drive if you intend to drive down to the river. After a moderate rain the fine dust on the roads at the put-in and take-out turn into a muck that will easily mire any vehicle.

Access is possible at the Duck Valley Indian Reservation upstream for an extended trip. Gain permission at the reservation before launching. This stretch reportedly contains a difficult Class V gorge, so paddlers should be prepared for more difficult water.

Overview: The East Fork Owyhee River runs through a spectacular, steep-walled canyon cut deep into the Idaho high desert. After joining the main Owyhee, the river continues into Oregon. It can be hard to catch the river at optimum flows because of the short runoff season. Much of the run is lazy Class I+ water with an occasional Class II riffle; but a mandatory portage of Owyhee Falls and a handful of Class III and IV to V rapids interrupt the languid journey.

The extreme remoteness of the East Fork Owyhee canyon gives boaters a feeling of solitude despite the sound of warplanes flying overhead from Mountain Home Air Force Base. The scenery on this river trip is nothing short of stunning. Basalt walls rise abruptly on both sides of the river, often directly from the water's edge. The unending variety of rock formations—columns, spires, needles, and arches—will continually astound even the most jaded river rat. Wildlife is abundant; paddlers often spot golden eagles, prairie falcons, bighorn sheep, otters, white-throated swifts, swallows, and much more. The remnants of a few old cabins and aborted ranching efforts provide historical interest. Scattered campsites with clearwater creeks and springs provide drinking water. A world-class hot spring at Three Forks rewards paddlers who pass through this little-traveled canyon. Contact the BLM Boise District Office for regulations, information, and trip registry (see Appendix B).

The lower Owyhee River is similar to the East Fork but has more volume. Flows are generally reliable through spring and early summer for the main river. Trips are more common along the lower river beginning at Rome. The entire river is one of the loneliest in the Lower 48. Winds can gust in the morning and early evening to tremendous velocities on both sections. Be sure to bring extra tent poles or use aluminum ones that are less likely to break. The desolate surroundings can be cold at night and very hot during the day. Bring lots of sunscreen, even in spring.

Going with the flow
Section 1: East Fork, Garat Crossing to Three Forks

Class: II (IV, P)	**Recommended flow:** 500 to 1,500 cfs	**Miles:** 70+

When driving to the East Fork Owyhee put-in, paddlers see the seemingly endless sagebrush landscape suddenly broken by the abrupt lip of Owyhee Canyon at Pipeline Crossing. A slightly gentler slope descends to the bottom of the canyon just downstream at Garat Crossing. Wary boaters may opt to drag or carry their boats and gear down a fair portion of this slope to avoid damaging or stranding vehicles in this rugged and often slick terrain.

The East Fork run, which usually takes five or more days, begins on slow water just below the narrow and steep whitewater marking the end of Garat Gorge. From the put-in, the narrow river meanders through vertical walls of basalt and eroded tuff. It's a good thing that the river isn't too challenging here, since boaters can't give all their attention to the water. Instead they find themselves looking skyward and gawking at the surrounding cliffs.

The canyon widens in spots, but closes abruptly again at Lambert Gorge, about 28 miles below the put-in. At 31.5 miles below the put-in boaters are confronted with Owyhee Falls, a mandatory portage! At high water this waterfalls is a double drop with huge reversals; at low water, every channel ends in a death siphon. Portage on the left bank along precarious scree slopes with poor footing. At lower flows you can carry over car-sized boulders on river right, but this route deadends along a rock wall and necessitates running the falls' Class III+ runout.

Less than 2.5 miles downstream is **Thread the Needle** (Class IV). This drop has a Class III entry rapid, then pools before a clutter of rockfall across the entire river. A very narrow chute leads through the center of the drop. The chute on the far right ends in a sieve at any water level. At low water, paddlers can lift boats up and over the boulders on the river left without too much difficulty. The Needle is followed by some narrow, twisted, boulder-studded channels.

The next 2 miles bring some easy whitewater. About 40 miles below the put-in is Crutcher's Crossing (an alternate access), marked by an abandoned log cabin and a stone structure with a sod roof. Below this historic site, a flatwater canyon with needles and arches leads to the confluence with the South Fork Owyhee River in 3 miles. High, sheer walls rise on all sides. The East Fork ends here, gently flowing into the face of an immense cliff as it joins the main stem of the Owyhee.

In the 9 miles between the South Fork confluence and the Oregon/Idaho border, paddlers will see two straightforward Class III drops. About 3 miles downstream of the state border on river right is Stateline Cabin, a small, low structure with walls made of stone and chinked with mud. Just downstream, a large rockfall blocks the river at **Cabin** rapids (Class IV). Consider portaging this drop. At very low flows boaters can approach the top of the drop on river right and paddle through a maze of cracks in garage-sized rocks. The runout is a 0.25-mile boulder garden. Below Cabin Rapids you'll get a good 1.5 miles of fun Class III water.

At roughly 15 miles below the confluence with the South Fork, boaters encounter **Cable** rapids (Class IV to V). The drop is marked by a high cable that was hung along the right bank by an early outfitter. Scout and portage on the difficult, boulder-strewn right side. This is a complicated rapid: the boulder-choked left side forces entry on the right, but the middle of the drop is blocked right and center by a powerful sieve. The main current plows into a huge, cracked boulder. Boaters choosing to run Cable must ferry across swift, turbulent water to an eddy on the left, where narrow chutes plunge into a lower pool.

Look for some nice Class II whitewater in the 9 miles down to Five Bar Cabins. This abandoned ranch on river left has several log and stone structures, including a shop built into a cliff face. Old ranching equipment and tack is scattered around the spread. Make sure you don't paddle by the superb warm spring just 2 miles above the take-out. This is the first place you are likely to encounter other people since putting in. A creek of bath-warm water on river left cascades into a series of pools. At river's edge the creek pours over a short rock face, creating endless showers of warm water to soothe weary paddlers.

An alternate put-in at the Duck Valley Indian Reservation adds 23 miles to the upper end of this trip. You'll need permission to use the reservation access. In the added section, the river canyon includes roughly 5 miles of Class III whitewater before the gradient eases. About 1.5 miles above the normal put-in at Garat Crossing, the canyon narrows and steepens into Garat Gorge, creating several Class IV+ to V drops and additional portages.

—Richard Frenzel

Section 2: Three Forks to Rome (Middle Owyhee or Widowmaker Run)

Class: II to IV (V)   **Recommended flow:** 1,000 to 4,000 cfs   Miles: 35

Commonly referred to as either the Middle Owyhee or Widowmaker run, Section 2 makes a good three- to four-day trip. Like the other sections of the Owyhee River, this one contains spectacular scenery, with jagged canyon walls in an often-steep canyon of the dry high desert.

From the rough put-in road, the trip begins with 1.5 miles of flatwater to the first Class IV obstacle, **Ledge** rapids. Scout on the left, picking a route through a wall of guard boulders that allow only narrow passage. Beyond the initial drop you'll have to dodge more huge boulders. Once through this initial rapid, you'll have easy water for almost 9 miles. Along this easy stretch the canyon widens and opens up along the area referred to as Deary Pasture.

The next Class IV rapid, known as **Half-Mile** rapid, begins at an island. Turbulent water leads to a short pool before ending in a boulder garden toward the bottom. Scout the rapid on the right above the island and around the bend to pick a route through the rocks. Easier routes are generally along the far left at the bottom.

Class II to III+ rapids lead in pool-drop fashion over the next 10.5 miles. Less than 0.5 mile downstream lies **Raft Flip**, a Class III drop with a hole at the bottom. At low flows rocks become exposed here, making routes more complex for kayaks and possibly unrunnable for rafts. More Class II+ to III- rapids lead to **Subtle Hole** and **Bombshelter Drop**. Both rapids begin with wider entries into boulder garden rapids that narrow toward the end. A nice stop along the way is the big cave for which Bombshelter was named. Be cautious if you land, since animals, snakes, and birds use the cave as shelter. Easier Class II+ **Shark's Tooth** rapid occurs 2 miles downstream. It can easily wrap unsuspecting boaters.

Widowmaker, the most difficult rapid on the entire river, waits in the lower middle part of this section. Many boaters camp in the good sites near Soldier Creek on the left shore, about 0.5 mile above the rapid, preferring to be well rested when they tackle the Class V drop. Getting an early start at the rapid also ensures you'll have enough time to line or portage the drop as needed. Some boaters prefer to use the upper Class III stretch as a warm-up for Widowmaker, putting the rapid behind them and gaining a more relaxed float to the take-out. The rapid is a long, steep section of river where large boulders have dropped into the water, creating huge holes that require tight maneuvering. A short section of calmer water leads into a second set of boulders and holes. The banks (strewn with car-sized boulders) and steep canyon walls make a run more tempting than long and difficult lining or portaging. Most paddlers line from the right shore, but this may vary depending on water flow.

Below Widowmaker, the rest of the trip is easy Class II water with a couple of Class II+ to III- rapids near the middle. About 3 miles from Rome, the canyon opens from its jagged rhyolite core to more widely spaced walls of layered basalt. The take-out at Rome is along the right shore above the bridge. Boaters wishing to continue beyond Rome should be prepared to take three or four additional days to travel the 50+ miles before reaching a possible take-out.

Section 3: Rome to Leslie Gulch

Class: III (IV)   **Recommended flow:** 1,000 to 4,000 cfs   **Miles:** 60

Section 3 is commonly referred to as the Lower Owyhee, though the river continues downstream of the take-out for more than 55 miles before reaching its confluence with the Snake River. Large reservoirs of still water prevent practical boating beyond Leslie Gulch. Spring temperatures can fluctuate from 100 degrees Fahrenheit during the day to freezing at night. Be prepared for wind along the lower canyon; strong early evening winds gust upstream early in this section. The stiff breeze broke several of our tent poles when we camped in the BLM campground at Rome! Choose your site by seeking protection from the wind. During the day winds normally calm down, subsiding as you move downstream. Inviting open beaches serve as great camps, and hot springs dot the riverbanks.

Below Rome, the Owyhee River provides 12 miles of warm-up Class I riffles and islands in open terrain. As the river canyon narrows and deepens, the gradient rises and creates Class II to II+ rapids. The first is **Upset** rapid, where a large midstream boulder and smaller rocks block the center and right routes. Stay along the left as you bounce your way down the slide to the bottom. At higher flows you can run the right side, but you'll have to punch several holes. Rafts should stay left. **Bullseye** rapid follows Upset in just 0.5 mile with more midstream boulders to dodge. This rapid is constricted at lower flows, requiring technical maneuvering for rafts.

The excitement eases for 9 miles, then revives for the next Class II+ rapid. The canyon then opens for several miles, providing many campsites with sandy beaches. Where the rock walls start to close in again, the Weeping Wall springs trickle down from the left. Boaters often fill bottles here with additional water. About 4 miles from where the canyon starts to narrow again, Class II+ **Artillery** rapid presents a long washboard slide that narrows along the left bank before opening toward the bottom. About 1 mile below this rapid, Rustlers Cabin makes a nice break stop along the right. The cabin has been badly damaged over the last ten years, and only some of the walls remain. Old farm equipment and rock corrals here are impressive historic sights. Look for a hot spring near the river within the marshy area if you crave a warm soak.

Lambert Rocks rise majestically along the left 2 miles beyond Rustlers Cabin. The many good campsites here have sandy beaches and hiking trails up side canyons in the Lambert Rocks area. Colorful layers in eroded Chalk Basin form hoodoos, arches, and all sorts of natural sculptures. One group of spires known as Pruitt's Castle is just downstream.

Whistling Bird is the first Class III rapid on this section. It occurs where the river is diverted toward the right wall and house-sized slabs of rock. At higher flows paddlers should have no trouble negotiating around these slabs to the left at the bottom. More technical maneuvering is required at lower flows. A Class II boulder garden known as **Rock Trap** follows in about a mile. Another mile farther is **Montgomery** rapid, the most difficult rapid below Widowmaker. The canyon narrows dramatically as it makes an S-turn that banks to the left, then back to the right. Water pillows off vertical rhyolite walls around a house-sized midstream boulder. Tight slots drop down either side into a hole that is followed by a pool. At high water this hole can become huge, but it generally flushes out and avoids forming a keeper hydraulic.

The canyon widens beyond Montgomery with more good camping beaches. Beautiful, spring-fed Rinehart Creek cascades down the left bank about 4 miles downstream. A short hike up the creek makes a great stop; paddlers can take a plunge in the pools below a waterfall and refill water jugs. Just downstream of Rinehart Creek is **Morcum Dam** rapid (also known as **Rock Dam** rapid), formed by the remains of an old diversion dam for Hole-in-the-Ground Ranch, 2 miles downstream. This drop is not bad at high water, but it can be rocky and technical at low flows. Hole-in-the-Ground Ranch is still occupied; only emergency access or access with permission is allowed at this private site.

A mile below the ranch, on the left, look for some historic Indian petroglyphs on rock slabs near the river. Respect the area and take only photos. A hot spring is located at a grassy spot on the left just 2 miles below the petroglyphs. This makes a perfect break spot above the take-out at Birch Creek Historic Ranch. Recently purchased by the BLM to provide river access, the ranch allows boaters to take out without having to row or paddle the additional 10 miles of flatwater to Leslie Gulch. Those who choose to continue downstream will find the Leslie Gulch take-out along the right shore of Lake Owyhee.

57 Pine Creek

Upper Forks to Below Oxbow Dam

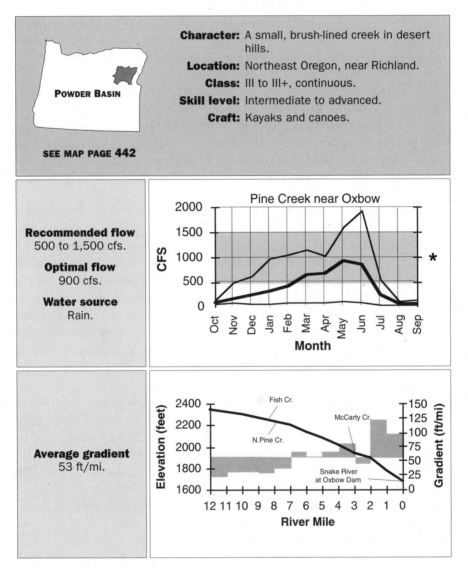

Character: A small, brush-lined creek in desert hills.

Location: Northeast Oregon, near Richland.

Class: III to III+, continuous.

Skill level: Intermediate to advanced.

Craft: Kayaks and canoes.

POWDER BASIN

SEE MAP PAGE 442

Recommended flow
500 to 1,500 cfs.

Optimal flow
900 cfs.

Water source
Rain.

Pine Creek near Oxbow

Average gradient
53 ft/mi.

* No depth measurement available.

Hazards: The continuous Class III water on Pine Creek has few eddies and a steep gradient of more than 125 feet per mile in places. Some banks are heavily vegetated, so a swim could be long and hazardous. Watch for wood, since recent floods may have moved or created log hazards from streamside hardwoods. Steep slopes sometimes hide the road along river left, but the road is always up there if you need it.

Access: From Baker and Interstate 84, follow Oregon Highway 86 east to Richland then north to Halfway before heading northeast to Oxbow Dam. The 70-mile drive from Baker to Oxbow Dam leads up steep hills and around many sharp bends in the road. If you are traveling at night, take extra time on this dangerous twisting route. If traveling by day, scout the creek above Halfway since the road closely follows the water to Oxbow Dam. But don't let your eyes stray too long from the road ahead! Pick a good spot to pull out and hoof it down the bank to the creek.

Overview: Pine Creek makes an unlikely paddling destination, since it is a long drive from populated areas. Located in the barren hills west of the Snake River near Oxbow Dam, it may make a good side trip on longer journeys to the Snake River/Hells Canyon, the Middle Fork Salmon River, the main Salmon River, and the Selway River in Idaho. Paddlers with a little extra time may wish to consider a Pine Creek run before continuing to one of these locations.

Proper flows are difficult to catch on this creek, since there's only a brief window of opportunity in late winter and spring. By late June the creek drops below a runnable level and can only be revived by several days of rain. The creek is long,

Pine Creek has continuous Class III action. THOMAS BELL PHOTO

extending through and beyond the town of Halfway. Branches intersect below Halfway, feeding the creek enough water for a fun, continuous Class III to III+ trip.

Going with the Flow

Class: III to III+	Recommended flow: 250 to 800 cfs	Miles: 8+

Upper Pine Creek rates an easy Class II to III above the confluence with the North Fork Pine Creek and Fish Creek. The creek then picks up in flow and gradient for several miles, changing to more continuous Class III water above McCarty Creek. In this stretch the creek is busy, requiring continuous moves within its narrow banks. About 1 mile above McCarty Creek, which comes in on the left, paddlers will encounter steeper rapids as the gradient picks up.

Below McCarty Creek the pace eases for about a mile before dropping sharply in the last 2 miles to Oxbow Dam. The gradient in this area exceeds 125 feet per mile in places, providing continuous action. At very high flows the creek may earn Class IV rating in this stretch. A stream gage is located about 2 miles above the dam; check flow levels when you drop your shuttle vehicle.

58 Pudding River
OR 214 Bridge to Molalla River

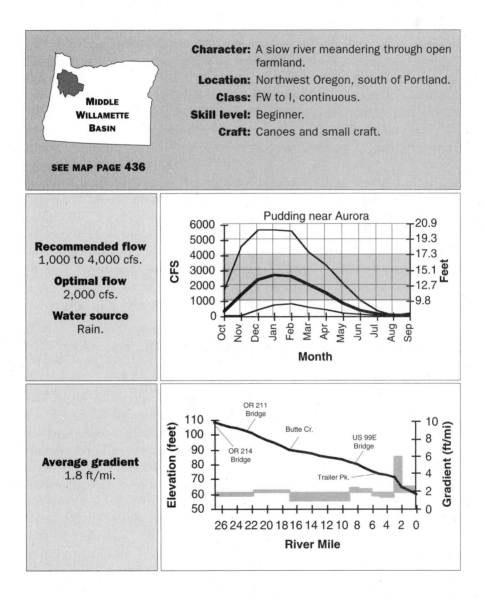

MIDDLE WILLAMETTE BASIN

SEE MAP PAGE **436**

Character: A slow river meandering through open farmland.

Location: Northwest Oregon, south of Portland.

Class: FW to I, continuous.

Skill level: Beginner.

Craft: Canoes and small craft.

Recommended flow
1,000 to 4,000 cfs.

Optimal flow
2,000 cfs.

Water source
Rain.

Pudding near Aurora

Average gradient
1.8 ft/mi.

OR 211 Bridge
Butte Cr.
US 99E Bridge
OR 214 Bridge
Trailer Pk.

249

Hazards: There are no whitewater hazards along the Pudding River, but debris piles, gravel bars, and brushy banks are present along all stretches. The banks are often muddy at the many sharp bends. Drift time is slow, so paddlers should plan to take plenty of time to complete any stretch.

Access: Bridges and roadside pullouts make up the only access sites along the Pudding River. Much of riverside property is private farm and grazing land. Respect the rights of property owners. To get to the river from Interstate 5, take Exit 278 and head east to Canby along Ehlen Road and Oregon Highway 99E. From Canby, follow Holly Street north to Ferry Street and Molalla River State Park. This is the take-out. Paddlers who want a longer run can continue to the boat ramp along the Willamette River just beyond the confluence with the Molalla River.

To reach upstream access areas, continue south along OR 99E to Anderson Road. Turn on Anderson Road and look for roadside pullouts beyond the railroad crossing. Steep access can be had at bridges on various roads off OR 99E. At Hubbard, look for Whiskey Hill Road (crossing at River Mile 18). At Woodburn, Oregon Highway 211 (RM 22.4) and Oregon Highway 214 (RM 26.8) both cross the river. OR 214 crosses the river at Monitor, with alternate access along Elliot Prairie Road where it crosses the river between the two highway bridges (RM 24). OR 99E crosses the river at RM 8.2, where there is a gage upstream.

Overview: The Pudding River is long, slow, meandering river with no rapids. It flows through open fields and farmland before joining the Molalla River just a mile above its confluence with the Willamette River. The river is usually muddy brown, carrying silt from its ever-changing banks.

With little gradient, the river meanders more than most rivers of its size. Paddlers face many sharp (though slow) bends, oxbows, and gravel bars. Banks are brush lined with deep mud and a few deciduous trees. Birds are common here, and paddlers often see blue herons as the river moves toward its confluence with the Molalla. Beaver and muskrat thrive along its banks and in the debris piles along outside bends. Take your bird book and plan on a leisurely float around the Pudding River's seemingly endless bends. Where islands and old river channels appear, stick to deeper water.

Going with the flow

Class: FW (I+)	Recommended flow: 1,000 to 4,000 cfs	Miles: 26.8

The Pudding River is generally small above its confluence with Butte Creek (RM 20.2), below the upper access bridges. Look for a stream gage along the right bank upstream of the OR 99E bridge to estimate flows. The riverbed may have changed in the 1996 and 1997 floods, so take all readings with a grain of salt. If there is enough water to float at the put-in, there will usually be enough to float the lower reaches. At lower water levels you may have to make a few short carries or scrapes to reach deeper water. At very high flows the river begins to spread into the neighboring fields. A virtual lake was created in the area during the floods of 1996 and early 1997.

There is a small Class I+ rapid near the Pudding River's confluence with the Molalla River. Some paddlers enjoy hiking upstream to run the stretch along the Molalla. Within less than a mile, the combined Pudding/Molalla River joins the Willamette at Molalla River State Park. Watch for the boat ramp, which is the final take-out, along the right shore just downstream. Always be alert for power boats along the Willamette and lower Molalla rivers.

59 Quartzville Creek

Bruler Creek Bridge to Green Peter Reservoir

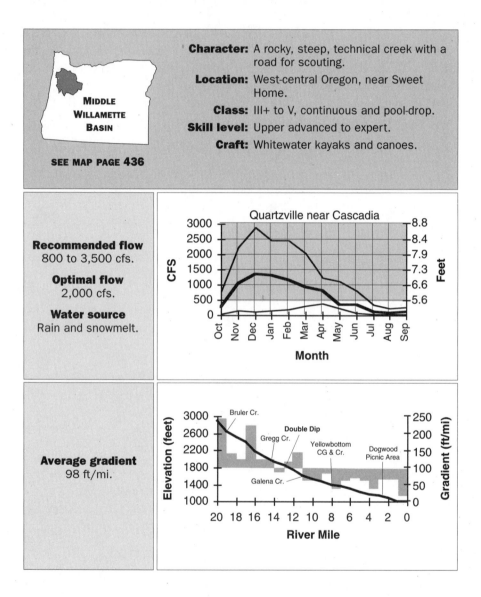

MIDDLE
WILLAMETTE
BASIN

SEE MAP PAGE **436**

Character: A rocky, steep, technical creek with a road for scouting.

Location: West-central Oregon, near Sweet Home.

Class: III+ to V, continuous and pool-drop.

Skill level: Upper advanced to expert.

Craft: Whitewater kayaks and canoes.

Recommended flow
800 to 3,500 cfs.

Optimal flow
2,000 cfs.

Water source
Rain and snowmelt.

Quartzville near Cascadia

Average gradient
98 ft/mi.

Hazards: Scout Quartzville Creek on your drive up; the road closely follows the water for a view of the major rapids. The upper river contains steeper gradient and more continuous whitewater. Take special note of **Double Dip,** a combination of two waterfalls that are separated by only a few yards. You'll need to make a quick recovery. The falls are located about 2 miles above the Galena Creek bridge. Below Galena Creek the river rates a technical Class IV, with more pool-drops overall.

Access: From Interstate 5 near Albany, take Exit 233 and follow U.S. Highway 20 east. Continue along US 20 beyond Sweet Home, then along Foster Reservoir to Quartzville Road, heading north. Turn here and follow Quartzville Road along the reservoir's north shore and the banks of Quartzville Creek. Look for a desirable put-in or take-out along the way. Access locations are at Green Peter Reservoir, Dogwood Picnic Area, the Galena Creek bridge, and a pullout about 2 miles above Gregg Creek.

Overview: Quartzville Creek is a middle Willamette Valley wintertime mainstay, featuring easy access, clear water in all but the most severe floods, and a variety of quality segments at an intermediate to expert level of difficulty. Its only drawbacks are the cold conditions that dominate its runnable season. Snow is common, particularly along the creek's upper reaches; paddlers often find that put-in choices are dictated by a snowdrift across the road. Despite its chilly climate, Quartzville Creek has enough pool-drop action to keep even widely traveled paddlers entertained.

Advanced and expert boaters often paddle the pool-drop Upper Quartzville section (Section 2) from Gregg Creek to Double Dip. Logs are a constant problem, particularly on the steep upper section where crux moves often involve wood. Intermediate to advanced paddlers and advanced rafters will enjoy the Lower Quartzville segment (Section 4) from Yellowbottom Recreation Site to Green Peter Reservoir. This continuous run is spiced up by powerful rapids.

Going with the flow
Section 1: Bruler Creek Bridge to Little Meadows Creek Bridge

Class: V	Recommended flow: 800 to 2,200 cfs	Miles: 2.9

To say that the uppermost portion of Quartzville Creek is enjoyable would be wrong. Potentially lethal wood, unscoutable and unportagable Class V drops, and inescapable box canyons are what this run is all about. If the wood lies in the right places and someone in your party knows the lines, you may get an incredible voyage through some big trees and blissful canyons. But that's the off chance. Since lines and wood shift with every flood, the upper creek stands as a constantly evolving dangerfest. Don't bother to put in here—nobody is ever glad to have done it. This run has been described as "pure hate!"

Section 2: Little Meadows Creek Bridge to Double Dip (Upper Quartzville)

Class: IV+ (P)   **Recommended flow:** 2,200 to 3,000 cfs   **Miles:** 4.2

Twisting 6-foot drops and interactive wood typify this upper, expert section of Quartzville Creek. Expect to see snow at the put-in. You'll quickly forget what season it is in the face of big trees, green water, and short, Disneyland-esque drops. This section, known as Upper Quartzville, has been one of the main training grounds for mid-Willamette Valley boaters working toward Class V runs.

Putting in at the bridge below Little Meadows Creek, paddlers face 0.7 mile of unique Class II ledges and logs as a warm-up. At Gregg Creek the river bends hard right and the fun begins. The rapid known as **Technical Difficulties** features a steep boulder garden leading to an innocent-looking 2-foot drop that can cause serious pins. Boof left. Below the pin spot, the creek flows over an 8-foot sloping drop and slams into the right wall; go left. Following a short pool, the creek splits at a bedrock ledge. This fun drop is called **Grocker**, and is best scouted and run along the left chute.

After some brief Class III boulder-dodging, paddlers may find logs plugging the chutes and drops off another ledgy rapid. Scout it on the right. Downstream, the creek remains playful and rates a Class III+ until the bridge at McQuade Creek. This bridge makes an excellent alternate access for paddlers who are not interested in the steeper upper mile.

Immediately after a portage around a log-jam, paddlers run into the **Wooden Wall**. This rapid demands a strong move down the center chute, avoiding a hidden log that slopes from the right wall at a 45-degree angle. Fun ledges and eddy-hops lead to the next blind drop, **David from Behind,** which is easier but no less fun. Here boaters choose between a 90-degree airplane turn on the right and a tricky boof move on the left. Scout on the right.

Many streams have a rapid named **Corkscrew,** but Quartzville Creek's is better than most. Recognize it by a horizon line near bedrock formations on the right; look for it where the road becomes visible on the right for the first time since the McQuade Creek Bridge. Scout for wood on the right, then enjoy the ride down the 8-foot drop. Prepare for more good stuff that follows, namely **Twist Off** and **Movie Star** rapids, among others.

Most paddlers take out at unmistakable Wrapped Bridge because of a nightmare log-jam just below, called **Pick-Up Sticks.** From Wrapped Bridge, paddle 200 yards to a right bend in the creek and portage around the log-jam on the right. At flows above 3,000 cubic feet per second the move into the portage eddy is difficult, but the price for missing the move is a trip over a 5-foot ledge into the log pile. Take this move seriously. Nobody has become part of the jam yet, but several good boaters have near-miss stories.

After 0.5 mile of continuous Class IV- water, the river briefly flattens then suddenly constricts. This narrowing, where the road is visible on the left, signifies the start of Double Dip. Take out above the rapid and end your run here, or start into the powerful and narrow series of chutes and drops, dumping into a low percentage hole backed by a wall and undercuts. Most people take out above the drop. Those who run Double Dip often find themselves wishing they had called it a day 100 yards earlier.

Note: At flows above the recommend level, Section 2 becomes quite serious with combinations of large holes, wood, and various must-make moves. Become familiar with the run before venturing in when the flows measure more than 3,000 cubic feet per second.

Section 3: Double Dip to Yellowbottom Recreation Area

Class: IV	**Recommended flow:** 2,000 to 3,200 cfs	**Miles:** 3.1

Below **Double Dip** the river opens up, inviting advanced boaters and rafters to play with the many small ledges that typify Section 3. Many folks put in at the bridge above Galena Creek, but the best rapid on the section is above that launching point, only 0.2 mile below Double Dip. From here, the river is constant Class III water with several tricky Class IV drops concentrated in the first and last miles of the run. Above Galena Creek a technical, steep nature prevails. With the addition of water from Galena Creek on the left and Canal Creek on the right (both runnable on their own), Quartzville Creek becomes more like a river. As a result, the water power increases dramatically.

After a relatively calm second mile, the creek creates several small but excellent play spots in its bedrock channel. It then turns left at a horizon line with a large ledge. Scout this drop on the right. It's called **First Ledge,** and the reversal across its base is more powerful than it looks—it has several near-drownings to its credit. The safe route is down the right.

In just 200 yards is another tricky rapid. This one is difficult to scout. Its narrow chutes are all runnable (barring logs), but paddlers must check them prior to committing. Once you are in the eddy midway down on the left, you have no choice but run the drop or wait for summer. At high flows (above 4,000 cubic feet per second) this rapid forms a hideous hydraulic. Avoid it altogether when the water is high. Portage with difficulty through logs at the far right.

Another 0.5-mile section of play leads to **Second Ledge.** This drop is harder to see than First Ledge. Identify it by noting a horizon line broken by a low bedrock island in the center of the creek where the road runs close to the water on the right. Scout right. At recommended flows, run the chute that sits 1 yard right of the island. After continuing through a brief Class III section with several great play holes, take out up a set of steps at Yellowbottom Recreation Area behind a bedrock dike that intrudes from the right.

Note: Because of large hydraulics created by ledges, paddlers should not run Section 3 at high water (above 4,000 cubic feet per second). When water is high, Section 4 makes a safer and more enjoyable day. At normal flows do Section 3 as a bonus run, since it makes an excellent extension to runs above and below, but pales when compared to the same runs directly.

Section 4: Yellowbottom Recreation Area to Green Peter Reservoir (Lower Quartzville)

Class: III+ (IV)   **Recommended flow:** 1,200 to 3,500 cfs   **Miles:** 8

Arguably the best advanced to intermediate run in the middle Willamette Valley, Section 4 of Quartzville Creek is certainly one of the best runs in the state. Known as Lower Quartzville, this segment of creek has a little something for everyone. Surfing waves and holes are plentiful, as are ender or cartwheel spots. On top of the great play areas are semi-continuous Class III rapids with occasional distinct rapids bumping into lower Class IV. Capping it all off is a solid Class IV gorge. Paddlers can easily reach access points above and below the 2-mile gorge, making it perfect for a solid Class IV run or an easy dividing point for groups of paddlers with mixed abilities.

After shoving off from Yellowbottom Recreation Area, boaters meet several warm-up play spots that are almost immediately followed by the first Class III+ section. After several hundred yards spent getting the kinks out, paddlers settle in as the stream does for a while. The creek gains water from Packers Gulch and other side streams that add to the flow.

Soon the action grows more continuous, as play spots and occasional Class IV-rapids hold a steady rhythm. Scout all rapids from here to the lower gorge on the drive upstream. About 0.2 mile below the second bridge is **Bankshot,** a blind right turn along a wall. Follow the left channel and punch through the turbulent holes of this Class IV obstacle. In another 0.2 mile, a significant rapid takes the form of an S-turn. It's called **Tractor Beam** for its ability to catch anything in its massive hydraulic at flood stage. At normal flows, paddlers can identify it by its sweeping 90-degree left turn against the road. Scout from the road and keep a lookout for bad rocks in the second part of the rapid.

Just below a possible take-out at a road construction depot the creek takes another hard left turn, this time creating a sticky hydraulic on the right half of the river; go left. Beyond large waves and more play spots the stream flattens briefly as it passes Dogwood Picnic Area, on the right. This is the take-out for anyone not interested in the Class IV gorge that follows.

Beyond Dogwood, paddlers have 0.3 mile to get pumped for the lower gorge. Be sure to keep one eye on the left bank for Cascade Creek and its spouting 80-foot waterfall, an amazing sight. Cascade Creek also marks the beginning of the first rapid in the gorge. Scout this rapid on the right. Over the next 1.5 miles Quartzville Creek travels through a series of solid Class IV rapids that vary in length from 200 yards to nearly 0.5 mile. The water changes from year to year, so scout it from the road or, if skilled, from your boat.

After passing a large cliff—the road is perched hundreds of feet above—paddlers drift along a brief flat section that leads to a right turn and an extremely wide streambed. Take care to enter this rapid on the far right down a very shallow channel; alternately, tackle it via the faster and more powerful center-right channel. Left is no good, since the left half of the river flows through a huge log-jam.

Downstream, several retentive holes lead another 0.3 mile to one last sleeper Class IV rapid on a right bend. The take-out is up the muddy slope on the right in another 100 yards. In summer, this is the reservoir bottom.

Note: Section 4 can be run at very high flows by experienced teams. At flows of 4,000 to 5,500 cubic feet per second it is big Class IV water overall, with the gorge rating a solid Class IV+. From 6,000 to 7,500 cubic feet per second, Quartzville Creek becomes a classic big-water Class IV+ and V- run. Above 7,500 cfs, it ranks Class V with several serious holes and huge, mobile log-jams. Take a close look at Tractor Beam, which develops an almost river-wide hydraulic with truly evil backup from a bedrock dike that is as much as 80 feet away from the ledge. After a big flood, it's always fun to look for lost boats in Green Peter Reservoir.

—*Eric Brown*

60 Rogue River
Grants Pass to Gold Beach

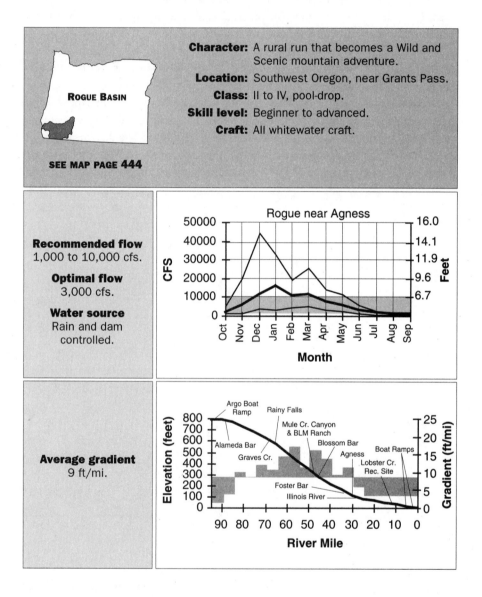

ROGUE BASIN

SEE MAP PAGE **444**

Character: A rural run that becomes a Wild and Scenic mountain adventure.
Location: Southwest Oregon, near Grants Pass.
Class: II to IV, pool-drop.
Skill level: Beginner to advanced.
Craft: All whitewater craft.

Recommended flow
1,000 to 10,000 cfs.

Optimal flow
3,000 cfs.

Water source
Rain and dam controlled.

Rogue near Agness

Average gradient
9 ft/mi.

Hazards: Section 1 of the Rogue River rates Class I and II with few unusual hazards. Whitewater classes and non-permit floats are popular along this stretch, from Grants Pass to Graves Creek Boat Launch. Stay alert for jetboats during summer. Anchoring or blocking passage is prohibited along special areas near the confluence with the Applegate River, **Brushy Chutes,** and **Highway Hole.**

The only major rapids lie within designated Wild and Scenic Section 2. Boaters need permits to travel this wilderness section. All but the most experienced boaters should avoid the main chute at **Rainy Falls.** Several other rapids can be difficult, including **Slim Pickins, Double Drop, The Narrows,** and **Blossom Bar.** Jetboats regularly run up the river below Blossom Bar. When surfing, make your presence known and listen for motors, since jetboats travel at high speeds and create large wakes. Below Foster Bar the river is unregulated and contains Class I and II riffles. Boaters should remain alert for jetboats and treat anglers with respect in the final stretch to Gold Beach.

Access: To reach the upper river put-ins near Grants Pass, take Interstate 5's Exit 55, traveling south to the uppermost boat launch at Pierce Riffle Park. Alternately, taking Exit 58 leads you across the Rogue River along either Sixth or Seventh streets in Grants Pass to Oregon Highway 99. Follow OR 99 east to Chinook Boat Launch. Oregon Highway 199 (the Redwood Highway) leads west to Redwood Avenue and Schroeder Park. The Redwood Highway also crosses the Applegate River, where it intersects with Riverbanks Road. Follow Riverbanks Road right to Griffin Park or Robertson Bridge for access.

Access take-outs for Section 1 by taking Exit 61 off Interstate 5 near Grants Pass. Follow Merlin–Galice Road (Forest Road 2400) south to Robertson Bridge Road (left at an intersection) or Hellgate Bridge. Hog Creek, Indian Mary Park, Galice, Rand, and Argo access areas may also be reached along FR 2400, which crosses the Rogue at Graves Creek.

For access along the lower Rogue, take U.S. Highway 101 along the Oregon coast to Gold Beach. Drive south until you cross the Rogue River, then turn onto Forest Road 595 heading east (upriver). This road becomes Forest Road 33 at the Lobster Creek Bridge and continues along the south bank. Access areas include Lobster Creek Campground and Boat Ramp, Quosatana Campground and Boat Ramp, and Agness Boat Landing. Cross the river at Agness to reach Forest Road 450, which travels the north bank past Illahe Campground to reach Foster Bar Boat Ramp. This is the uppermost put-in below the permits-only section.

Overview: The Rogue River was one of the first national Wild and Scenic Rivers, designated such in 1978. Many scenes in the movie *The River Wild* were shot on the Rogue. It remains one of the most famous, scenic, and popular rivers in the United States.

Wildlife is abundant here. Paddlers often see black bear, otter, deer, and a variety of birds and other creatures. Though many boaters in a wide variety of craft use the river, its action-packed corridor remains clean, enjoyable, and secluded.

Challenging falls, technical Class III to IV rapids, ideal surf and play spots, and attractive scenery will draw folks of all generations to this sacred place for years to come. The real challenge is to allow future traffic without marring the beauty of the wilderness setting and the river experience.

The National Wild and Scenic Rivers Act was created to protect areas like the Rogue from being exploited by mineral and land development. Long ago people recognized the loss that would result from placing short-term profits ahead of long-term conservation. Placer mining along both the Rogue and Illinois rivers threatened to destroy the beauty and character of these southern Oregon streams. I am thankful to know that, because of the river protection law, I will be able to share the Rogue with friends and family in the future.

Like the other popular rivers in the United States, the Rogue requires that boaters get a permit for the Wild and Scenic section. Permits are issued annually under a lottery system. Currently, the season runs from April 15 through October 15. Get your request in during the first six weeks of every year, then cross your fingers, do your river dance, and perform luck-aiding acts that put you in favor with the River Gods. You may get lucky.

If you miss out on the wilderness permit, or just want to try other areas of the Rogue, sections of recreational Class I and II water above and below the wilderness permit section are open to boaters year-round. The river's confluence with the Applegate River signals the beginning of the official recreational corridor for the upper Rogue. Parks and campgrounds line the shores to Graves Creek, with occasional riverside businesses and residential areas. Folks preparing for a launch into the permit section of the Rogue will appreciate good campsites and launch areas in the upper stretch; campsites along the entire river often have toilets, so boaters do not have to pack out human waste. Popular launch sites for rafters include Robertson Bridge Boat Ramp, Hog Creek Boat Ramp, Indian Mary County Park, Ennis Boat Ramp, Galice Boat Ramp, Rand Boat Landing, Alameda County Park, Argo Boat Landing, and Graves Creek Boat Ramp. Shuttle services are available in Grants Pass and Galice for both the Rogue and Illinois rivers.

Going with the flow
Section 1: Grants Pass to Graves Creek (Hellgate Area)

Class: I to II	Recommended flow: 1,000 to 8,000 cfs	Miles: 33

The stretch of the Rogue River between Grants Pass and Graves Creek offers boaters Class I to II water lined with campsites, parks, and residential areas. Open year-round, Section 1 does not require Rogue Wild and Scenic River permits. It is a good place to warm-up for a wilderness run or learn river skills.

Several companies rent boats and offer lessons along the upper Rogue. Wave trains, islands, and Class I and II rapids periodically waken paddlers from a pleasant drift. Below Pierce Riffle and Riverside parks, the river rates Class I with a few islands to negotiate before Schroeder Park (on the left) and Lathrop Boat Launch (on the right). About 2 miles beyond Lathrop Boat Launch the Applegate River enters from the left, but its mouth is masked by numerous islands. **Whitehorse Riffle** (River Mile 94) ends more than a mile of island-dodging near Whitehorse Park and Boat Launch, on the right. Anchoring boats along islands in the stretch above and below the confluence with the Applegate River is prohibited.

Below Whitehorse Riffle, calm water continues for a mile to **Bedrock Riffle** (RM 93.5) at the start of Finley Bend. Matson Park makes a good picnic area on the right at the tip of the bend. After another mile, Griffin Park (left) or Upper Ferry Park (right) offer access options. In just under 2 miles, **Brushy Chutes** (RM 88) splits at an island with riffles on either side. Anchoring along the left chute is prohibited. Robertson Bridge Boat Ramp follows in just over a mile on the right past **Highway Hole,** where the last of the prohibited anchoring spots is located. Access is just upstream of the bridge. Beyond Robertson Bridge the Rogue presents primarily flatwater for 4 miles to Hog Creek Boat Ramp, on the right.

One of the most popular day trips along Hellgate Recreation Area begins at Hog Creek Boat Ramp and extends to Graves Creek Boat Launch above the Wild and Scenic permit section. The 14-mile trip takes at least a day. Boaters looking for a shorter trip may put in at one of the many access areas along the way. From Hellgate Bridge to Argo Boat Landing, Class I and II riffles occur about every mile. The actual Hellgate Canyon lies just below Hog Creek Boat Ramp and ends with **Dunn Riffle.** The rapids in order of appearance are Dunn Riffle (RM 81.5), **Ennis Riffle** (RM 77), **Upper Galice Riffle** (RM 75.8), **Lower Galice Riffle** (RM 75.5), **Rocky Riffle** (RM 75), **Chair Riffle** (RM 73), **Alameda Riffle** (RM 71.5), and **Argo Riffle** (RM 70). Graves Creek Boat Launch is the last take-out above the permit area and more serious rapids that begin at RM 68.

Section 2: Graves Creek to Foster Bar

Class: III (V)	Recommended flow: 1,000 to 10,000 cfs	Miles: 34

The Wild and Scenic section of the Rogue River begins at Graves Creek Boat Launch, but many boaters begin their trip from one of the convenient launching points farther upriver. Trailheads lead to Rainy Falls on river left or a riverside trail on the right. Immediately below the put-in at Graves Creek, a riffle leads to **Graves Creek Falls,** a Class III wave train with a small eddy on the right. This is the only warm-up before Rainy Falls in 1.5 miles.

When you hear the falls, pull out on the left shore at one of the sandy beach areas. A trail leads to a good view of the falls; spectators often gather to witness a run of the falls. Only expert boaters should attempt to run the main waterfall, since it is much more turbulent than it looks. I have seen and heard many stories of mishaps in the main left channel. At high flows a middle chute opens to allow a slightly easier passage, but it, too, is rocky and turbulent. Most opt to use the man made fish ladder at far right, but at low water lining boats down this drop can take some time. Watch for salmon jumping up the falls. The thought of being bashed by a 30-pound fish was a serious consideration on my first run over the falls, since a salmon took flight every 10 seconds! A campsite on the right above the falls provides a place from which you can contemplate the falls or watch others run them.

Once the excitement of Rainy Falls is behind you, Class II **China Gulch** rapids in 0.25 mile seem like no big deal. Whiskey Creek Campsite follows in 1 mile; it's a good place to recover from mishaps at the falls or call it a day. Paddlers can take the short jaunt to historical Whiskey Creek Cabin, just across Whiskey Creek. Other campsites line both shores below Whiskey Creek, but competition for good sites can be fierce during peak boating seasons.

Boaters will run into a small Class I riffle at **Big Slide** (RM 64.6) before reaching **Tyee** rapid (RM 65.7). Scout Tyee, since at some water levels it can rate a Class IV, with ledges that lead to a large midstream boulder. **Wildcat** rapids follow in about 0.5 mile, where an island splits the current; most of the water leads to the right, where this Class III rapid banks sharply right after some large waves and holes. **Russian** rapids, **Montgomery** rapids, and **Howard Creek Chute** are all Class II rapids that follow in 0.5-mile intervals below Wildcat. **Slim Pickins** (RM 61) is a more formidable rapid with narrow chutes through some large holes at higher water. Though it is rated only Class III, it is more technical than many other rapids of similar class. Look for the remains of an old dredge on the left bank if you get the chance.

Over the next 1.5 miles, more Class II rapids occur between stretches of flatwater. They include **Washboard** (RM 60.8), **Plowshare** (RM 60.3), and **Windy Creek** rapids (RM 60). At Class III **Upper Black Bar Falls** (RM 59.5), an easy scout along the right shore reveals a ledge-drop followed by boulders and holes that lead to **Lower Black Bar Falls,** just around the right bend. The lower rapids are an easier straight shot along the right bank through large standing waves with an eddy on the left. Since the floods of 1996, much wood and debris has collected along the banks here. Black Bar Lodge, along the left shore in 0.2 mile, is private. Be respectful of anglers here.

In 0.5 mile **Little Windy Riffle** presents surf waves just below a creek and campsite on the left. More than a mile of drift leads to the next Class III challenge at **Horseshoe Bend.** Here a tight right bend has created rapids spaced with calmer water. They build to a more difficult finale. Novice paddlers should keep to the inside to avoid faster water along the outside edges.

The next Class II riffle (RM 57) has been called many names, including **Telephone Hole, Mary's Hole, Dugan's Hole,** and **Surprise Hole.** More Class II rapids follow. **Dulog Riffle** (RM 56.2), **Entrance** rapid (RM 55.8), **Kelsey Falls** (RM 55.4), **Battle Bar Riffle** (RM 53.9), and **Winkle Bar Riffle** (RM 53.4) lead to Winkle Bar, on the right, where Zane Grey purchased the land for a cabin. The cabin still stands. Though it is on private property, visitors are welcome to stop at the cabin and sign its log book. Take only pictures and leave only footprints, since the owners have been gracious enough to allow such visits. Blackberries line the riverbanks here in season.

Visitors can sign a log book at this cabin, originally owned by the western author Zane Grey.

Below Winkle Bar more Class II rapids lead to the historic Rogue River Ranch. They include **Long Gulch Riffle** (RM 50.7), **Big Boulder** rapids (RM 50.4), **Island** rapids (RM 50.2), **John's Riffle** (RM 50), **Maggie's Riffle** (RM 49.6), and **China Bar** rapids (RM 48.7). Be sure to include a stop at the historic ranch on your itinerary. There are two campsites here on the right shore (the Mule Creek Campsites), but competition is heavy since a visit to this nationally registered lodge is a must on any Rogue River trip. Plan to make a lunch stop or visit to this well-kept treasure. Marial Lodge (reservations required) and Mule Creek Guard Station are just below the ranch.

Beyond Rogue River Ranch, three Class II riffles lead into **Mule Creek Canyon.** Class III+ and IV- rapids sit between the narrow rock walls. Two huge boulders here have been called the "horns" or "jaws" of the canyon mouth. The narrow canyon winds sharply, creating turbulent holes and swirls. Paddlers should avoid potentially bad holes on the inside of the sharp bends. A swim in the turbulent water known as **The Coffeepot** can push swimmers under in the surging waters for long periods. Stair Creek, along an eddy in the left bank, makes a wonderful break spot within the canyon confines.

Blossom Bar rapids occur before boaters leave Mule Creek Canyon. Scout these Class III+ to IV rapids by scrambling up the rocky right bank to a good viewing spot. In early times, the rapids were blasted on several occasions to allow boat passage. Today paddlers can run either side of a huge rock obstruction at river center. At low flows, the most common route is along the left side of the center rocks to a chute that runs behind the obstruction. At flows below 3,500 cubic feet per second, rocks line the left of the channel and are known as **Picket Fence**. Most raft pins occur along the fence when boaters miss the crux move to the right behind the rocks. Below the initial rapids are holes and boulders known as **Devil's Stairs**. Passages are available center or right, leading away from the main currents that pull left into more large boulders.

In another mile, Paradise Lodge offers lodging, a cafe, a landing strip, and a store for supplies (or T-shirts) when boaters find themselves short on ice, beer, or treats. Be prepared to pay the price, though, since these supplies must be delivered by jetboat from Gold Beach. The floods of 1996 inundated the grassy area just below the lodge, coming close to the infamous water levels of 1969.

Below Paradise the river eases to flatwater with the Class II riffles of **Tichenor** and **Solitude**. Half Moon Lodge (RM 43.7) is a private facility on the left. It marks the entrance to Huggins Canyon and a scenic mile of floating. Many good campsites line the banks here; the most popular are Solitude, Tate Creek, and Tacoma Camp. These campsites are equipped with electric fences and pulley systems for hanging food, since many black bears hang out in the area. Take proper precautions and do not leave food in your tent or on your boat. A rigorous hike up a trail at Tate Creek (or up the creek itself) leads to Tate Creek Slide, a natural chute along a rock wall that drops into a pool. It is great fun to climb up to the lip of the drop and slide into the pool below. Keep your head down when sliding, though, since a small protrusion at head level threatens to cause damage before you plunge into the pool below.

Beyond the campsites near Tate Creek, Class II **Tacoma** rapids make a good warm-up for **Clay Hill** rapids, beyond a private lodge on the right. Though the rapids are generally listed as Class III, the lower river rapids are wider and more forgiving than those upstream, with wave trains and some boulders to negotiate. Plan a stop at Fall Creek Falls along the left bank about 1 mile below Clay Hill Rapids for a short hike to the spectacular waterfall. Just below on the right is Flora Dell Creek and Falls, where a trail leads to two wonderful plunge pools for a quick dip on hot days.

Class II **Payton Riffle** (RM 36.9) occurs before Wild River Lodge on the left, followed by Class II **Burnt** rapids (RM 36) above Watson Creek, also on the left. The creek marks the lower boundary of the Wild and Scenic section, but few boaters other than permit-holders reach water above Foster Bar. **Watson Riffle** follows the creek and leads into historical Big Bend, where the last of the Rogue River Indians surrendered. The tribe was relocated to the Siletz Indian Reservation in 1856.

In less than a mile **Brewery Hole** sits near an island where jetboats travel the far right channel. Stay clear of the far right passage, since motorized boats must use that channel to navigate. Billings Creek and Illahe Lodge are visible on the right bank, indicating that Foster Bar Boat Ramp is less than 0.5 mile downstream

Tate Creek Slide on Section 2 of the Rogue. JEFF JACOB PHOTO

on the right. Take out at Foster Bar or continue through two-part **Illahe Riffle** to Agness Boat Landing (RM 27) on the right in another 6.5 miles. A longer trip can include all or part of Section 3.

Section 3: Foster Bar to Gold Beach

Class: I to II	**Recommended flow:** 1,000 to 5,000 cfs	**Miles:** 33.8

Below Foster Bar the Rogue River is unregulated, recreational water to Lobster Creek. The river and canyon widen here for many miles of easy rafting or paddling. Countless Class I and II riffles allow surfing and help beginning boaters learn to read the water. Less popular than Section 1, this stretch offers similar boating experience with good access and campsites in places. Look for boat ramps at Foster Bar Boat Landing (RM 33.8), Agness Boat Landing (RM 27), Quosatana Campground and Boat Ramp (RM 13.5), and Lobster Creek Campground and Boat Ramp (RM 10.7). Below Lobster Creek the river flattens and presents only a few riffles to Gold Beach.

The Siskiyou National Forest boundary is just beyond Lobster Creek; paddlers must camp above the line. Plan on floating the last several miles to Gold Beach in one day. Roads parallel the river on both sides below Quosatana Campground, but these do not interfere with a pleasant float. Take out on the right at Jots Resort just beyond the US 101 bridge.

Rapids and Campsites by River Mile (Toilets provided at all sites)

RM	Rapid/Other	Class	Campsite	R/L
67.9	Trail to Rainy Falls		Graves Creek Boat Launch	
67.8	Graves Creek Riffle	III		
67.7	Graves Creek Falls	III		
66.3			Rainy Falls	R & L
66.2	Rainy Falls	V		
64.9	Whiskey Creek Cabin	Hike	Whiskey Creek	R
64.4			Dog Creek	L
63.6	Tyee	IV		
63.4			Tyee	R
63.2	Wildcat	III		
62.9			Wildcat	L
61.8	Howard Creek	Pool		L
61.1	Slim Pickins	III		
59.8			Big Windy Creek	L
59.5	Upper Black Bar Falls	III		
59.4	Lower Black Bar Falls	III		
59.2	Black Bar Lodge	Private		L
58.7			Little Windy Creek	L

continued on next page

RM	Rapid/Other	Class	Campsite	R/L
57.9			Jenny Creek	L
57.6	Horseshoe Bend	III		
57.5			Horseshoe Bend	R
57.3			Lower Horseshoe Bend	R
56.5			Meadow Creek	R
56.1			Dulog Creek	L
55.0			Kelsey Creek	R
54.6			Lower Kelsey Creek	L
54.1			Battle Bar	L
53.2			Hewitt Creek	L
52.8	Zane Grey Cabin		Winkle Bar	R
52.0			Missouri Creek	L
51.0			Long Gulch	L
48.5	Rogue River Ranch		Tucker Flat & Mule Creek	R
48.3	Marial Lodge	Private		R
48.2	Mule Creek Canyon	IV		
45.4	Blossom Bar	IV		
45.1	Devil's Stairs	III		
44.9			Gleason Bar	L
44.6	Paradise Creek	Pool		R
44.3	Paradise Lodge	Private	Store & supplies	R
43.7			Lower Paradise Bar	R
43.7	Half Moon Lodge	Private		L
42.0	East Creek Cabin			L
41.9			Brushy Bar	R
41.7			Brushy Bar Creek	R
39.8	Hike to natural slide		Tate Creek	R
39.7			Tacoma	R
39.1	Clay Hill Lodge	Private		R
38.9	Clay Hill	III		
37.8	Fall Creek Falls	Hike		L
37.5	Flora Dell Creek Falls	Pools		R
36.8	Wild River Lodge	Private		L
35.5	Watson Creek Pool	Pool		L
35.6	Watson Creek		Ends Wild & Scenic (permits-only) section	L
34.3	Illahe Lodge	Private		R
33.8	Foster Bar/Boat Ramp		Road access	R
27.1	Agness Boat Landing		Road access	R

61 Rogue River, North Fork

Woodruff Bridge to North Fork Reservoir

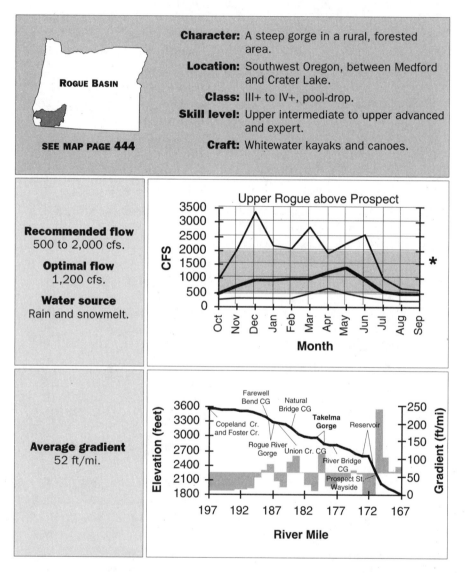

ROGUE BASIN

SEE MAP PAGE 444

Character: A steep gorge in a rural, forested area.

Location: Southwest Oregon, between Medford and Crater Lake.

Class: III+ to IV+, pool-drop.

Skill level: Upper intermediate to upper advanced and expert.

Craft: Whitewater kayaks and canoes.

Recommended flow
500 to 2,000 cfs.

Optimal flow
1,200 cfs.

Water source
Rain and snowmelt.

Upper Rogue above Prospect

*

Average gradient
52 ft/mi.

No depth measurement available.

Hazards: Always be alert for log hazards on either section of the North Fork Rogue River. **Takilma Gorge** is very hazardous, containing numerous Class IV+ rapids that require a scout from the left trail before entering. Section 2 contains many Class III+ boulder gardens and pourovers.

Access: From Interstate 5 at Medford, take Exit 30 to Oregon Highway 62 (the Crater Lake Highway) and head northeast. Follow OR 62 past Lost Creek Lake and turn on Forest Road 64 (River Road) before reaching the community of Prospect. FR 64 leads to the upper North Fork Reservoir, River Bridge Campground, and farther north to Woodruff Bridge and Campground.

Overview: The North Fork Rogue River is what most paddlers call the upper Rogue River, beyond the confluence with the South Fork Rogue at Lost Creek Lake. The upper Rogue is a classic southern Oregon river that makes an excellent one-day destination for Class IV paddlers looking for year-round action. It makes a great warm-up run before a lower Rogue, Illinois, or Umpqua river trip.

The area is relatively unpopulated but home to abundant wildlife. Brush and old-growth forest line the riverbanks. The North Fork Rogue's frigid, crystal-clear water originates as snowmelt from the Cascade Range near scenic Crater Lake. Adequate flows are available year-round, since snowmelt and groundwater seep through the riverbed's porous volcanic rock. A trail along river left allows scouting and hiking access for the length of the river.

The North Fork Rogue provides technical, pool-drop Class III+ and IV+ water divided into two sections, above and below Woodruff Bridge Campground. Advanced to expert paddlers can tackle the upper Class IV+ Takilma Gorge run (Section 1); with proper caution, intermediate paddlers can try the lower River Bridge run (Section 2).

Expert paddlers have run below North Fork Reservoir to Lost Creek Lake. This lower run is reported to be Class IV+ and requires a long, steep hike to the river below Mill Creek Falls. Adequate flows make it possible year-round. Class V boaters may also wish to check out the Middle Fork Rogue River, which contains logs, brush, a steep gradient, unportagable rapids, and plenty of pinning potential. Consult the whitewater guidebook *Soggy Sneakers* for more details.

Going with the flow
Section 1: Woodruff Bridge Campground to River Bridge Campground
(Takilma Gorge)

Class: IV+	**Recommended flow:** 500 to 1,500 cfs	**Miles:** 3.7

Known to local paddlers as the **Takilma Gorge** run, the upper stretch of the North Fork Rogue River is hazardous. The waterway is contained in a magnificent, vertical-walled gorge of sharp lava rock. Within the gorge paddlers have no way of portaging many of the Class IV+ drops, and scouting is seldom an option. Scout the entire gorge from the trail on the left before entering, since log hazards are a serious concern. One log hazard currently suggests a portage.

Above the gorge the river rates Class I+ for about a mile. Where the water begins to pick up speed, look for two Class II riffles. Here, you are about 100 yards above Takilma Gorge. Once the river turns left, catch an eddy on the left to scout. Scramble up the hillside about 30 feet to the trail and walk 0.75 mile along the gorge to scout its five major rapids. The last two rapids are the toughest drops.

Below the gorge the river eases to Class II water as it heads to River Bridge Campground and a take-out. The 3.7 miles of upper river make for a good day's run, with required scouting. Paddlers may continue along Section 2 for a longer day.

Section 2: River Bridge Campground to North Fork Reservoir

Class: III+	Recommended flow: 800 to 2,000 cfs	Miles: 5

The lower stretch of the North Fork Rogue is a fun, technical run through boulder gardens and pourovers of up to 4 feet. Unlike those of the upper section, the rapids here all can be scouted from either bank or boat (for those who are comfortable doing so). Always watch for wood hazards along this stretch, since new and shifting wood is likely. You'll have to paddle a flat mile along the North Fork Reservoir before reaching the take-out, where the highway crosses the aqueduct on the left.

—Kale Frieze

62 Row River

Wildwood Falls to Log-Scaling Bridge

UPPER
WILLAMETTE
BASIN

SEE MAP PAGE **452**

Character: A shallow, brush-lined river through farmlands.

Location: West-central Oregon, south of Eugene.

Class: II to III (IV), pool-drop.

Skill level: Upper beginner to advanced.

Craft: Kayaks and canoes.

Recommended flow
350 to 1,500 cfs.

Optimal flow
1,200 cfs.

Water source
Rain.

Average gradient
24 ft/mi.

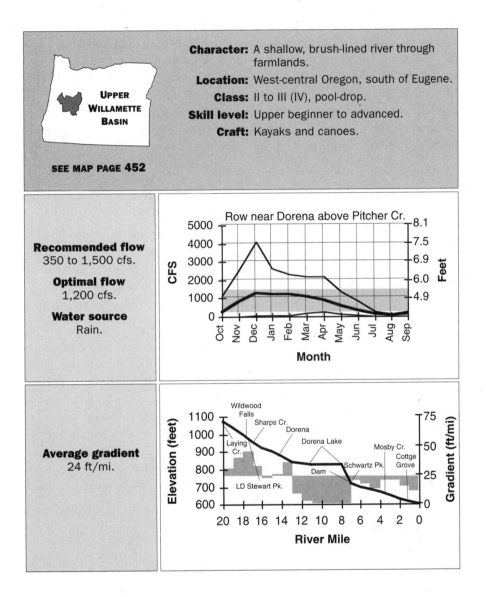

271

Hazards: There is brush in the lower Row River channel and many shallow ledge-drop rapids. Staying upright is important at a couple of the rapids, where a shallow riverbed can impede recovery. Higher flows ensure deeper channels. There are few other hazards on the river.

Access: To reach the upper section of the Row River from Interstate 5, take Exit 174 at Cottage Grove and turn east. Make a left at the stoplight, then follow signs along Row River Road to Dorena Reservoir. Drive along the southern shore of the lake, then cross the Row River; there's a covered bridge visible just upstream. To reach your take-out on the Row, turn left and head downstream a short distance on the north side of the river, taking another left into a small access area and take-out. To reach the put-in, go back upstream and drive past Sharps Creek Road, where the confluence of Sharps Creek is visible. At the next fork you can go either way, but the put-in at Wildwood, to the right, offers better access. Continue a short distance to a small park on the left. Turn into the park and drive to the river. The base of Wildwood Falls provides a nice put-in.

To reach the lower Row River, take Exit 174 and turn onto Row River Road at the first stoplight. Follow this road through Cottage Grove to the first bridge over the river just past a log-scaling station. This is the take-out; park and take out on river left. To reach the put-in, continue another 3 miles on Row River Road to a Y-intersection. Take the right fork and go about a mile to Schmidt Park and the put-in, on your left.

Overview: The lower Row River has long been a stepping stone for new Eugene-area paddlers. The river is very close to Cottage Grove and flows through farmlands in the lower Willamette Valley. Small and shallow most of the time, the river is usually hazard-free, though brushy banks must be avoided on occasion. Most of the land along the riverbanks is private, so be careful where you stop.

The Row's flows are controlled by Dorena Dam and are often subject to drastic changes. Fall, winter, and spring are the usual runnable seasons, but summer does bring occasional releases. Rafters will have more fun on a larger river with a lot more water, but the Row is popular with beginning kayakers and canoeists, plus local innertubers in warmer weather.

Going with the Flow
Section 1: Wildwood Falls to Dorena Reservoir

Class: II+ to III (IV)	**Recommended flow:** 350 to 2,000 cfs	**Miles:** 5

The upper Row River put-in is right at the base of impressive **Wildwood Falls.** After leaving the nice warm-up pool at the waterfall base, paddlers face a slew of Class II rapids with an occasional Class II+ to III rapid, depending on flow. Just below the confluence with Sharps Creek on river left is **The Weir,** which offers a few rocks to dodge (or holes at high flows) before dropping over a small ledge into a hole. This lower hole is easy to punch through, but aggressive paddlers like to try surfing here.

Around the corner, the river flows by an old lumber mill. In front of the mill are two good rapids. The first is **The Narrows,** which waits just above the mill where the river squeezes through a 10-foot-wide slot with boils. The second rapid, a tricky unnamed drop, is below The Narrows and just above a bridge.

Throughout the remainder of the run, the Row has many good rapids. Watch for a couple of rock outcroppings that divide the river into two channels just above the covered bridge. **The Falls,** the run's most difficult rapids by far, are up next. The right channel makes a 90-degree left turn followed by a 4-foot drop. The drop is easy to scout or portage on the left.

Below the covered bridge the river develops some fantastic surfing spots at high water. This is a great river to explore as a beginner or intermediate paddler, since it offers good play and challenges. If the run seems too tame, try nearby Laying Creek and Brice Creek for more advanced water.

Section 2: Dorena Dam to Log-Scaling Bridge

Class: II (III) **Recommended flow:** 350 to 1,500 cfs **Miles:** 5

Below the lower section put-in the Row River relaxes for a stretch, allowing boaters to warm-up and practice their eddy turns. About 0.5 mile below the first bridge is the first major rapid. Scout on the left, since it is a maze of ledges with an overall drop of 5 to 6 feet. Just below this first rapid is a second, similar one. A third rapid occurs just below that, with a very tricky diagonal hole at some flows. Run it pointing a little to the left, since the hole kicks from left to right—it usually manages to flip paddlers.

A short distance downstream is the last major rapid in Section 2. Visible from the drive to the put-in, it presents a short drop with rocks to avoid at low water. Other than that, the lower Row is mostly Class I and II water with some small waves for surfing along the way. If this lower run doesn't pack enough punch for you, the upper river offers greater challenges.

—*Jason Bates*

63 Salmon River
Upper Bridge to Sandy River

SANDY BASIN

SEE MAP PAGE **454**

Character: A shaded mountain river running from forest to a rural residential area.

Location: Northwest Oregon, east of Portland.

Class: III (III+), pool-drop.

Skill level: Intermediate.

Craft: Rafts at high water; kayaks and canoes year-round.

Recommended flow
300 to 1,000 cfs.

Optimal flow
800 cfs.

Water source
Rain.

Average gradient
53 ft/mi.

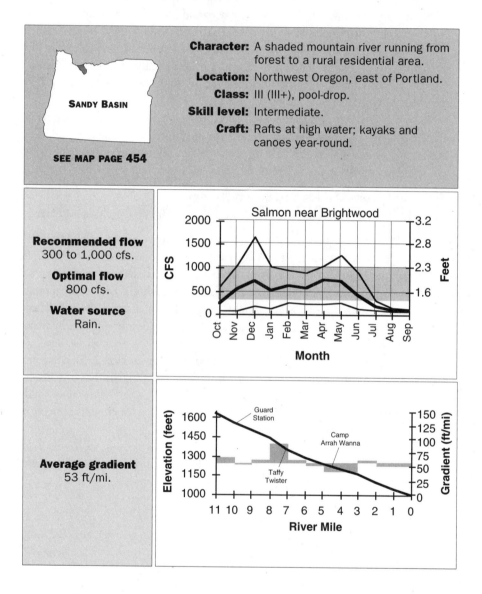

Salmon near Brightwood

Hazards: Logs are common on the Salmon River, making one or more portage likely. **Taffy Twister** is a respectable Class III+ rapid; watch for it halfway between U.S. Highway 26 and the upper bridge put-in. At or near flood stage, the rapids jump up an additional class level.

Access: From Portland, follow U.S. Highway 26 east past Sandy to the small community of Brightwood. Just west of Brightwood and the Salmon River crossing, follow a road to the right. The take-out is under the US 26 bridge along a paved bike path with easy access to the river. This is also a good place to check flow, since the river is wider here (adequate levels here indicate good flow for the rest of the trip).

To reach the put-ins, return to OR 26 and continue east to the small town of Wemme (or, from the east, to Zigzag) where roads connect to Forest Road 2618 along the Salmon River. Most of the river is not visible on the drive up. Before you cross the river's upper bridge, look for a pullout on the left; this is the usual put-in. A trail leads upstream for a longer creek run or hike for shuttle drivers. Not far up the trail are numerous large waterfalls that mark the upper boundary of boatable water.

Overview: The Salmon River is an exciting Class III trip when the Sandy River is running between 10 and 12 feet at the gage near Bull Run. The water in this tributary of the Sandy is clean and clear with a rocky bottom and wide bed that allows passage for small rafts when the gage reads 11 feet or more. Boaters on the Salmon rarely feel the sun, due to the close proximity of tall trees and mountains. The riverbanks are wooded and overgrown, but evidence of recent floods is obvious; piles of logs wait along river bends. Expect to make at least one portage around logs in the river.

Houses along the banks in the lower section seem to have weathered the recent floods, but waterlines are still apparent in yards and along steeper banks where trees cling to their moorings and threaten to block passage in the not too distant future. Private property lines the lower river, so be considerate when making portages or stopping. Various rock outcroppings make nice break spots in the lower portion of the run, since they are sunny spots in an otherwise shaded trip.

The upper half of the river is surrounded by the Salmon–Huckleberry Wilderness in the Mount Hood National Forest. Trails follow the river to higher destinations, taking hikers past several waterfalls. The drops look as if they might make a great creek run, but I have not heard of anyone running the Salmon above the upper bridge and have yet to investigate it myself.

Going with the Flow

Class: III (III+)	Recommended flow: 300 to 1,000 cfs	Miles: 7

Continuous Class II water fills the upper and middle portions of the Salmon River, though occasional pool-drop Class IIIs keep boaters at attention at all times. One rapid of particular interest is **Taffy Twister,** which occurs near River Mile 3.5 where Class II water builds to Class III then drops suddenly. The Class III+ drop folds in from both the right and left sides of the river. The easiest route is down the middle tongue between the folds, with a wave train following. Eddies on both sides of the river allow for some great surfing here. Many other surf waves punctuate the river, usually at the base of the larger Class III drops. Logs are a particular concern on this river, due to an ample supply of piled-up wood along the outside banks. Watch out for the numerous undercut, leaning trees.

Below some apartments on river right, the Salmon eases up for a more casual float with some occasional Class II rapids. The US 26 bridge marks one possible take-out. Paddlers can continue along the Sandy River for a longer trip and more action; however, most find that the 7 miles or more on the Salmon usually provide a full day of fun.

64 Salmonberry River

Beaver Slide Road to the Nehalem River

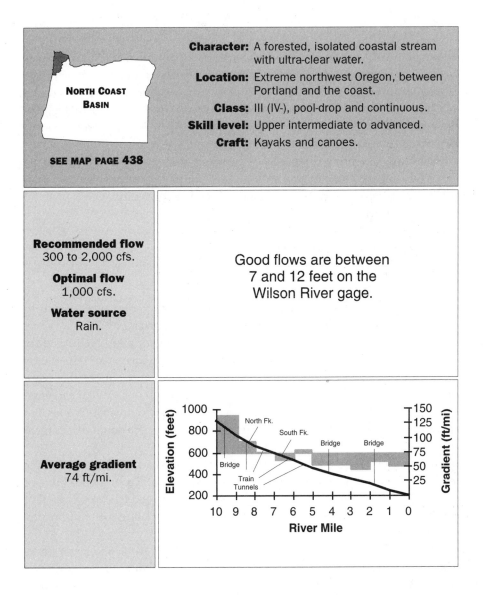

NORTH COAST BASIN

SEE MAP PAGE 438

Character: A forested, isolated coastal stream with ultra-clear water.

Location: Extreme northwest Oregon, between Portland and the coast.

Class: III (IV-), pool-drop and continuous.

Skill level: Upper intermediate to advanced.

Craft: Kayaks and canoes.

Recommended flow
300 to 2,000 cfs.

Optimal flow
1,000 cfs.

Water source
Rain.

Good flows are between
7 and 12 feet on the
Wilson River gage.

Average gradient
74 ft/mi.

Hazards: The upper half of the Salmonberry River contains continuous Class II+ and III technical whitewater. Watch for logs at all times. **Chew-Chew** is a difficult Class IV rapid about 1 mile below the confluence with the North Fork Salmonberry River. The shuttle is long and four-wheel drive is mandatory along Beaver Slide Road.

Access: To reach the put-in, follow U.S. Highway 26 west from Portland to Salmonberry Road, a dirt road on the left between mileposts 31 and 32 (1 mile before Sunset Rest Area). Follow Salmonberry Road for several miles (making sure to stay on Salmonberry at forks in the road) until you reach Beaver Slide Road. Now the driving fun begins. As you descend this four-wheel-drive road, turning back is not an option. The steep road drops 1.5 miles to the river.

You can shorten the trip by using the North Fork Road access, continuing along Salmonberry Road to North Fork Road. The roads are easier, but the put-in is not as convenient as off Beaver Slide Road, and paddlers miss some wonderful action and scenery.

To reach the take-out, backtrack to US 26 and continue west roughly 12 miles to Nehalem Road. Turn left (south) on Nehalem Road and follow it about 13 miles to the Nehalem River's confluence with the Salmonberry. Take out at the bridge.

Overview: The Salmonberry is one of the most overlooked rivers in the Portland area, perhaps for good reason. The shuttle for this run deserves a Class V rating. Since it's a long drive, you may wish to recruit someone to shuttle vehicles from the put-in to the take-out, where a day of fishing or hiking awaits the shuttle driver. Some paddlers camp near the put-in the night before to shorten the length of the drive the following day. Others have hired drivers in or around the town of Timber to take their vehicles to the take-out. The Lower Columbia Canoe Club was able to locate out-of-work loggers at the Timber Tavern to do shuttle for them in 1993.

All roads are in good shape except Beaver Slide Road. Do not attempt the steep drop down Beaver Slide without a four-wheel-drive! Recent floods brought debris onto the road (and into the river). Although the road has been cleared of downed trees, the loosely packed dirt makes it a muddy mess in the rainy boating season.

Despite the difficulty in getting to and from the river, the Salmonberry offers rewards that are well worth the trouble: continuous Class III rapids, several Class III+ to IV pool-drop sections, and ample surfing holes and waves. Outstanding scenery includes steep, evergreen-covered mountains and abundant moss, ferns, and deciduous trees along the banks. Various side streams cascade into the river's upper portion. The Salmonberry is one place you won't want to forget your camera.

Although the river is remote, a railroad follows the entire length of the river, crossing in several places. The tracks were destroyed in the 1996 floods, which even washed cement from the numerous tunnels, but the rail line has since been

Jeff Jacob heads into Chew-Chew rapid.

rebuilt. The once-blue river may take some time to clear again due to excess fill from the rail reconstruction.

Going with the Flow

Class: III+ (IV)	Recommended flow: 300 to 2,000 cfs	Miles: 9

The Salmonberry rapids start right below the put-in off Beaver Slide Road. The river offers continuous Class III drops and holes in its first several miles. About 2 miles below the put-in, the North Fork Salmonberry River enters on river right, where the floods of 1996 gouged out the tributary's bed to create a large gravel bar. More Class III action continues, in pool-drop fashion, before paddlers reach a Class IV section about a mile below the North Fork confluence. Following a left bend in the river, this rapids section (named Chew-Chew) has various routes weaving down the middle, plus a couple of holes worth scouting. The rapid is chopped into two sections, with a protruding rock in the center of the first drop. Current can push boaters into the center rock, and routes on either side contain turbulent passages. Portage or scout from the left bank, but stay clear of the railroad tracks there. Trains travel this section daily, and the Tillamook Railroad does not take kindly to trespassers.

More Class III rapids follow Chew-Chew. The gradient then eases and the river widens, giving boaters a breather for the next several miles. The water in this section rates Class II overall. A water tower used for steam engines still stands along the tracks, a reminder that trains have used this route for years. The river

passages. Portage or scout from the left bank, but stay clear of the railroad tracks there. Trains travel this section daily, and the Tillamook Railroad does not take kindly to trespassers.

More Class III rapids follow Chew-Chew. The gradient then eases and the river widens, giving boaters a breather for the next several miles. The water in this section rates Class II overall. A water tower used for steam engines still stands along the tracks, a reminder that trains have used this route for years. The river rebounds to Class III status and stays there until its confluence with the Nehalem River. The take-out bridge is just before the confluence. To avoid trespassing on private property, take out along the muddy banks near the bridge. Paddlers can lengthen the trip by continuing along the Nehalem for a few more miles, but the 9-mile stretch along the Salmonberry is usually more than enough considering the lengthy shuttle.

65 Sandy River, Upper
McNeil Campground to Marmot Dam

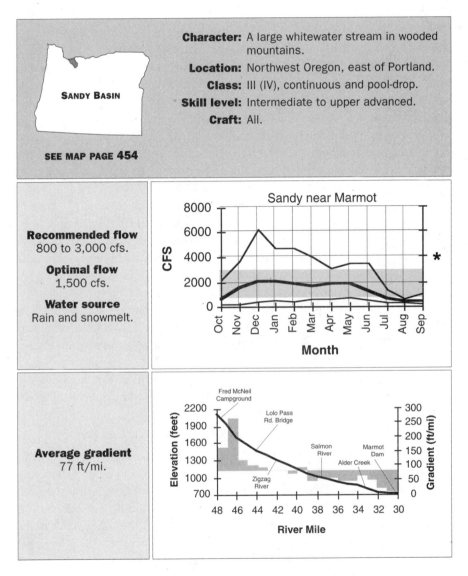

Character: A large whitewater stream in wooded mountains.

Location: Northwest Oregon, east of Portland.

Class: III (IV), continuous and pool-drop.

Skill level: Intermediate to upper advanced.

Craft: All.

SANDY BASIN

SEE MAP PAGE 454

Recommended flow
800 to 3,000 cfs.

Optimal flow
1,500 cfs.

Water source
Rain and snowmelt.

Sandy near Marmot

Average gradient
77 ft/mi.

* No depth measurement available.

Hazards: The Upper Sandy River offers continuous whitewater. From McNeil Campground to Zigzag, the upper river rates Class IV; a swim would be long and dangerous here. Logs are a serious concern along the entire upper river. **Alder Creek** rapid is the most difficult Class IV rapid in the lower section. High water raises the difficulty by at least one class.

Access: From Portland follow U.S. Highway 26 (the Mount Hood Highway) east to Sandy. To reach the take-out above Marmot Dam, watch for a sign on the east side of town that points to parks along Ten Eyck Road on the left. Turn here, toward Bull Run and Oral Hull parks. Keep left at the first intersection and follow Ten Eyck Road east of Revenue Bridge over the Sandy River. Beyond the bridge, take either Marmot or Shipley roads to the right. Where the roads intersect, continue east along Marmot Road. Not long after passing the diversion channel from the Sandy and Bull Run rivers, take a right turn onto a gravel road to the river. This road leads to the take-out at Marmot Dam.

For other access points, continue along US 26 past Sandy for about 11 miles to Sleepy Hollow Road. Turn left (north) and go about 1 mile to Brightwood. Marmot Bridge crosses the river here, and a second bridge crosses not far downstream. Take a left at the intersection just across the first bridge. Either bridge can be used as a put-in or take-out. Another bridge also crosses near Brightwood on a left (north) turn along Brightwood Loop Road.

About 4 miles beyond Brightwood is the town of Zigzag, where Lolo Pass Road leads north just beyond the store and crosses the Zigzag River in a short distance. A bridge crosses the Sandy River less than 0.25 mile beyond the Zigzag River for access.

To reach the uppermost put-in, continue along Lolo Pass Road 3.5 miles to Forest Road 18 and Forest Road 1825, heading east to a bridge before McNeil Campground.

Overview: From its headwaters high on volcanic Mount Hood, the Upper Sandy River runs steep and continuous all the way to Marmot Dam. The upper river starts in Mount Hood National Forest below McNeil Campground, but soon leaves public lands. Though private property lines its banks, this rural river still has a wilderness feel. Roads follow the river to Alder Creek, but they are far enough away to allow only occasional views of the river. Forests line much of the river, so logs can present hazards—particularly in the upper section. The upper river from McNeil Campground to Zigzag is an advanced-to-expert run where a swim would be long and dangerous. The lower section picks up in volume below the confluence with the Zigzag River, where the Sandy River widens to present a good challenge for intermediate boaters. Nonstop rapids keep boaters entertained for the duration of any trip to the Upper Sandy.

At very high water levels, the entire Upper Sandy River, along with neighboring Salmon and Zigzag rivers can easily jump an entire classification in difficulty. Boaters who would have had an enjoyable learning experience can get into trouble, although advance boaters will be rewarded with some great surfing waves and respectable holes.

Going with the flow
Section 1: McNeil Campground to Zigzag River Confluence

Class: IV+	Recommended flow: 500 to 3,000 cfs	Miles: 5.5

Below McNeil Campground, the Upper Sandy River starts off with a rush. The gradient measures more than 150 feet per mile where you launch; just when you start to get used to the pace, it picks up to more than 250 feet per mile! This type of gradient would normally mean a hair-raising run that only top boaters would dare attempt. However, because of the even distribution of this insane gradient and the fair visibility here, the Upper Sandy run can be made by advanced boaters with good self-rescue skills. No keeper holes are present at normal flows, but you'll have to be good at rock-dodging, wave-crashing, and continuous maneuvering. Watch for the few, very small eddies to scout or stop. Prepare to boat-scout most of what you run, and keep your nose pointed downstream as much as possible.

After the second mile, the gradient begins to drop to a more reasonable level. It continues to drop as paddlers approach the community of Zigzag. The action never seems to let up in spite of the reduction. For a mile or more above the bridge near Zigzag, the river assumes a Class III nature. Boaters may wish to take a break and catch their breath at Zigzag, but the quick run is nearly done, allowing boaters to consider continuing to Marmot Bridge for a longer day and more play.

Watch for logs in Section 1. In fall 1996, we had to portage around logs that spanned the river in two places. We also skirted a river-wide log just below the McNeil Campground bridge. Stumps in the river collected debris and were present in at least three places, a reminder that the riverbed is continually changing. Look for routes around or between the stumps, which present particularly bad hazards for swimmers.

No stream gage exists for this stretch of river, but the water level is usually good when the Lower Sandy River gage near Bull Run reads between 12 and 13 feet.

Section 2: Zigzag River Confluence to Marmot Dam

Class: III (IV-)	Recommended flow: 800 to 4,000 cfs	Miles: 13

Paddlers often divide Section 2 in half to cut the length of the trip, but the entire stretch can be done in a day with adequate flow and an early start. Marmot Bridge marks the alternate take-out.

Below Zigzag, this Upper Sandy River maintains a gradient between 50 and 75 feet per mile. This would normally have intermediate boaters a little worried, but the even water distribution buffers the drop to a forgiving, yet technically busy ride.

From Marmot Bridge to Marmot Dam the river starts to get a little slow. This lower stretch is a good place for beginners to develop technical skills. Once you are proficient here, simply move upriver to the next step. Watch that last step (Section 1), though, since it is more of a jump!

A little more than a mile above Marmot Dam, Alder Creek rapid wakes up unsuspecting boaters as the river drops more suddenly. An A-frame house on the left bank signals the approach to the rapid. Scout or portage on the right bank. At low water the rapid can disappoint, since easy routes to the right miss the worst part. At high water the rapid becomes more respectable; boaters should be prepared for a Class IV ride through pushy water. Beyond Alder Creek Rapid, the river eases and becomes flat in the last mile to the dam. The mandatory take-out is on river right before the dam.

66 Sandy River, Lower
Marmot Dam to the Columbia River

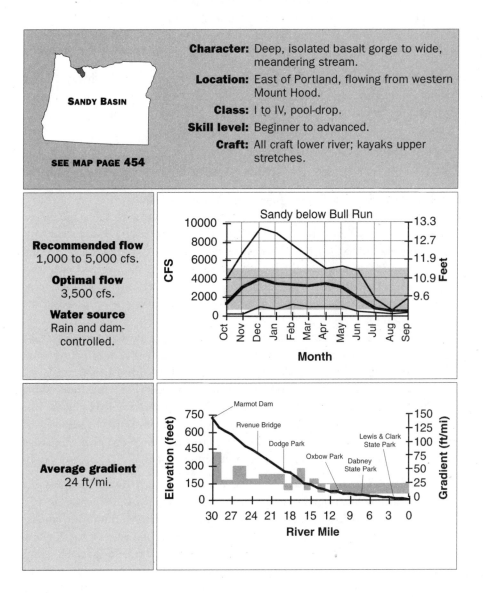

SANDY BASIN

SEE MAP PAGE **454**

Character: Deep, isolated basalt gorge to wide, meandering stream.

Location: East of Portland, flowing from western Mount Hood.

Class: I to IV, pool-drop.

Skill level: Beginner to advanced.

Craft: All craft lower river; kayaks upper stretches.

Recommended flow
1,000 to 5,000 cfs.

Optimal flow
3,500 cfs.

Water source
Rain and dam-controlled.

Sandy below Bull Run

Average gradient
24 ft/mi.

Hazards: The **Sandy River Gorge** (Section 1) contains several Class IV rapids that are difficult to scout. Hiking out from these spots is a near impossibility. Section 2 contains several Class III rapids, occasional logs, and some sharp bends in the river. **Pipeline** rapid ends Section 2; intermediate boaters on the Sandy should scout it. Section 3 contains several Class II rapids in the first 7 miles, but few other river hazards.

Access: Reach the access at Revenue Bridge by following U.S. Highway 26 (the Mount Hood Highway) from Portland or Gresham to the town of Sandy. Watch for a sign on the east side of town that points to parks along Ten Eyck Road on the left. Turn here toward Bull Run and Oral Hull parks. Keep sharp left at the first intersection and follow Ten Eyck Road to Revenue Bridge on the Sandy River. The access is on river left.

For upper access, continue up the road to Marmot Dam after crossing the Sandy River at Revenue Bridge. Take either Marmot or Shipley roads to the right. Where the roads intersect, continue east along Marmot Road. Not long after passing the diversion channel from the Sandy and Bull Run rivers, take a right turn onto a gravel road to the river. This road leads to the put-in below Marmot Dam. Paddlers who wish to avoid the log-jam rapid below the dam should park at a pullout where a gated road leads to the right. Carry craft and gear along trails heading left from the road past the gate to reach steep put-ins that avoid the hazardous rapid.

To reach the lower access, take Interstate 84 east of Portland to Troutdale. Follow signs to Lewis and Clark State Park, where there is a boat ramp take-out. The Crown Point Highway follows the river's east bank from Lewis and Clark State Park to Dabney State Park Boat Ramp, another access point. Continue along the Crown Point Highway (also called the Columbia River Scenic Highway) to a put-in at a parking area across from Oxbow Park. A trail leads to the river. Boaters may also follow signs to Oxbow Park after crossing the bridge over the Sandy River at Dabney. Park access fees are charged in summer.

Overview: Portland-area boaters often run the Lower Sandy River. The three sections described below offer a range of difficulty, from a narrow, isolated Class IV+ gorge to big-water Class I float trips. The upper river below Marmot Dam courses through an almost inaccessible canyon with moss, ferns, and vertical basalt walls. House-sized boulders restrict the flow, gather debris, and create respectable drops in the lower half of the gorge. From Revenue Bridge just outside the town of Sandy to Dodge Park outside Portland, the river widens and takes on a Class III character. Residential areas dot the banks. Below Dodge Park, several other parks are separated by larger water flow, lower gradient, and easier rapids. The Bull Run River joins the Sandy River below Pipeline rapid, returning water that was diverted above Marmot Dam to the powerhouse on the Bull Run. Here the Sandy flattens out before merging with the Columbia, allowing some Class II rapids or a peaceful float through the parks.

Though near a populated area, this designated Wild and Scenic River makes boaters feel as though they were in the wilderness. Buildings and roads are usually not visible from the upper portion, and only near the parks do boaters encounter many people. Anglers cast from shoreline beaches and small rapids; avoid their lines when passing.

Going with the flow
Section 1: Marmot Dam to Revenue Bridge (Sandy River Gorge)

Class: IV	Recommended flow: 500 to 3,000 cfs	Miles: 6.5

The uppermost section of the Lower Sandy River, beginning below Marmot Dam, is referred to as the **Sandy River Gorge** section. Boaters often put in below the dam and face a Class IV rapid that contains vertically pinned logs and an exposed root system on the right side. Though the rapid has become easier in recent years, with routes down the middle, the potential for a pin here is still severe. Paddlers would do better to put in below the rapid; look for a roadside pullout on the right at a gated road. By carrying around the gate and down a trail to the left, and staying left at a fork in the trail, you can reach a put-in pool just below the log-jam rapid. The trail is steep above the pool, so you will need to line boats to the river.

Below the log-jam, the walls close in and the pool-drop rapids begin. The first half of the gorge trip contains Class III+ rapids at higher water levels. The rapids are evenly spaced between flatter sections. Logs can jam in tighter slots or lurk underwater here, so stay alert. Most of the Class III rapids begin with boulder gardens at the top that converge to a tighter, steeper runout at the bottom. Several small beaches line pockets in the rock below the various rapids. The dramatic scenery can steal your attention until the next sudden drop wakes you up again.

In the lower third of Section 1, paddlers encounter four major Class IV rapids roughly 0.5 mile apart from each other. The first, **Boulder**, occurs around a left bend in the river just downstream of an overhanging left bank with a tree on top. An upstream eddy circles near a nice beach. At Boulder several house-sized boulders choke the river, which backs up into a narrow pool behind them. The far left channel is easiest, with a tight channel and a sharp scramble around a megaboulder, leading into the huge undercut. At lower water paddlers can walk this left route to a lower eddy, and then run the lower part of the rapid. The middle route is preferable at higher water, but logs have lodged here in the past. Any log jammed in the tricky center chute would be impossible to avoid. The rapid cannot be scouted, unless the first boaters in a group go left and tell others what the center looks like. At lower water an island in the center of the river allows scouting.

The next rapids, **Rasp Rock** and **Drain Hole**, are similar in nature. Scout both from the upper right side, where a partial portage around the lead-in will secure a safer line to the lower right. Both rapids have narrow channels that can be blocked by logs. At Rasp Rock, routes drop down the center and plow into a huge rock tooth in the middle of the main flow. The water is turbulent, and channels require some hard moves. Portage along either bank. Drain Hole leads into an eddy on the

Jeff Jacob eddies out at Drain Hole.

right before dropping sharply to the left around a mammoth boulder. Debris (which may include kayaks and canoes) collects in the three slots that fence off the eddy. Portage the upper drop on the right to secure a more direct shot at the exit chute, to the right.

After some easier water, the canyon begins to open up. Now **Revenue Bridge** rapids come into view. Pull off at a beach area on far left at the top of the rapids and walk along the rocky bank to view your route. The series is more difficult than it looks from either the bridge or the top of the rapids. The usual route is to take the rocky right-of-center path, which leads to the far right around a boulder. Lean onto the pillow off the bank as you round the bend and prepare for a face full of water before hitting an eddy on the left. Just below the eddy is a fast stretch of water that contains a couple of holes that can ender boaters. Revenue Bridge is just downstream, and the steep, rock take-out is on river left.

Section 2: Revenue Bridge to Dodge Park

Class: III to III+	**Recommended flow:** 800 to 4,000 cfs	**Miles:** 5

Below Revenue Bridge, the Lower Sandy River starts out narrow. Soon the river and its canyon widen, letting more sunlight in. The rapids here are mostly easier Class III pool-drops, narrowing at the bottom. One more difficult rapid waits midway down the run, where the river narrows to an S-turn and slams into the right bank. For practice catching a difficult eddy in turbulent water, try for the small eddy against the right wall just above where the main current bashes against it. There are also a couple of larger holes to avoid.

More rapids and fun surfing waves continue to Pipeline rapid, a short distance beyond the confluence with the Bull Run River. Scout this long rapid from Dodge Park before starting your trip, since it is difficult to scout from the river. The rapid includes a series of holes and boulders that drop in sections and converge as the river turns left. Paddlers can find several routes here, but center-to-left routes are most common (though they contain some good-sized holes at higher water). Near flood stage, several of Pipeline's drops wash out, but larger holes develop with respectable hydraulics.

Take out at Dodge Park on the left or continue to Oxbow Park or farther for a longer day.

Going with the flow—Section 3: Dodge Park to the Columbia River

Class: I to II+	Recommended flow: 1,000 to 5,000 cfs	Miles: 15.5

Beginning whitewater boaters frequent the Lower Sandy River. Its close proximity to Portland makes it convenient for many local residents, who hit the river after work. From Dodge Park to Oxbow Park, Class II rapids are frequent and evenly spaced. Boaters often hike back up a rapid to run it again. The short rapids are pool-drop in character, allowing for recovery at the bottom. Some are tight enough to cause trouble. Beginners should start by paddling with more advanced boaters before attempting the Class II rapids here.

Below Oxbow Park the river eases up, making a nice afternoon float trip for better boaters and a good place to practice handling currents and eddies for beginners. There are no real rapids in the section below Oxbow Park, where Class I water flows to various take-outs, including those at Dabney and Lewis and Clark state parks, but banks are brushy and logs are present.

67 Santiam River, Little North
Jawbone Flat to North Santiam River

Character: Paradise. A clearwater run from canyon to posted residential lands.

Location: Western Oregon, east of Salem.

Class: II to IV (V), continuous and pool-drop.

Skill level: Beginner to expert.

Craft: Kayaks and canoes.

MIDDLE
WILLAMETTE
BASIN

SEE MAP PAGE **436**

Recommended flow
500 to 3,000 cfs.

Optimal flow
1,200 cfs.

Water source
Rain and snowmelt.

Average gradient
60.8 ft/mi.

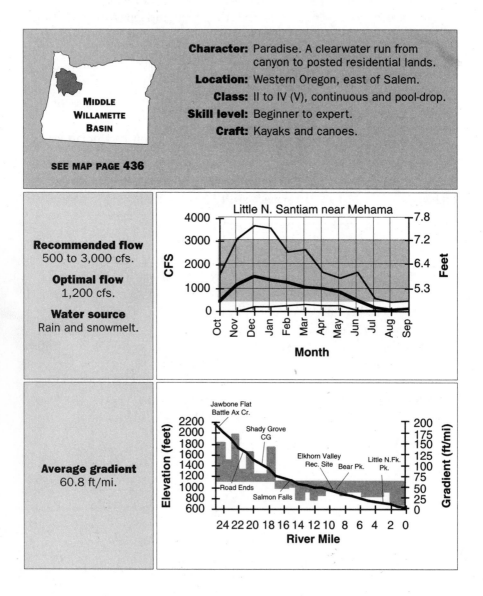

Hazards: Section 1 of the Little North Santiam River contains two 15- to 20-foot waterfalls, a huge log-jam, and many tight, technical Class IV rapids. Logs are always present. Hiking out is difficult in many places. Avoid the Class V+ gorge below the Three Pools Recreation Area take-out. Paddlers must run **The Slot** (Class IV) in the Section 2 below **Salmon Falls**. Section 3 has fewer logs and contains only one major Class IV rapid, **Troll's Tooth**.

Access: From Interstate 5 near Salem follow Oregon Highway 22 east past Mehama and turn onto North Fork Road, which runs along the Little North Santiam River. A sign points toward the Little North Santiam Recreation Area just north of the Swiss Village restaurant. Follow North Fork Road to the desired bridge or park take-out for lower runs. The take-outs in Mehama are across the North Santiam River on the south side of the bridge, or at a boat launch just across the river from where the Little North Santiam joins the main North Santiam River.

To reach the upper take-out, continue along North Fork Road beyond where it becomes gravel. Take the right fork where a sign on the left fork indicates the road ends in 4 miles. The right fork leads to the Three Pools Recreation Area take-out.

Find the upper put-ins by following the left road at the fork mentioned above, which ends in 4 miles at a locked gate. Shoulder, drag, or buddy-carry boats past the gate to the desired put-in. The first access is down a trail just before the bridge in 0.7 mile. Other locations are at a road, marked with a cable, in another 0.7 mile; below the waterfall, another 2 miles in; or at Jawbone Flat, 0.25 mile beyond the upper falls.

Overview: In a popular hiking and mountain biking area, the Little North Santiam River has only recently been discovered as a boating paradise. The pristine upper river is protected by mining claims that date back to the 1800s. The hike to the river will discourage many paddlers, but the efforts are well rewarded by ultra-clear green water set in a steep, smooth basalt canyon. Much of the picturesque river can only be accessed by boat or hiking in the riverbed at low summer flows. Large redcedars stand tall along the upper river, where heavy undergrowth lines moss-covered banks. Many deep pools separate technical pool-drop rapids and waterfalls.

The lower river widens below Three Pools Recreation Area, but a very difficult Class V+ gorge lies just below Salmon Falls. As a result, boating between Sections 1 and 2 is impractical. Below Salmon Falls, residential areas alternate with more secluded stretches. Much of the land is posted "No Trespassing," and trash, violence, and vandalism attest to problems caused by summer swimming-hole seekers and late-night partygoers.

Going with the flow
Section 1: Jawbone Flat to Three Pools Recreation Area

Class: IV+ (P)   **Recommended flow:** 500 to 2,000 cfs   **Miles:** Up to 7

Section 1 is often referred to as Opal Creek, but Opal Creek and Battle Ax Creek join the Little North Santiam River more than 3.5 miles above where the road in is blocked. How far you'll paddle on this section of river depends on how far you hike. Some paddlers put in after only a 0.7-mile trek past the roadblock. Most find it rewarding to continue to a side road, another 0.7 mile. Hard-core boaters can hike an additional 1.5 miles to a waterfall or to Jawbone Flat, 0.25 mile farther. This river is worth the extra effort. The scenery is unmatched, meeting my definition of paradise. PLEASE respect this area and keep it clean of litter or other refuse. I had serious reservations about putting this wonderful place in the book.

Below Jawbone Flat, the river narrows and develops pool-drop rapids. Many of the drops in the upper river are steep and difficult to scout. Be wary, since it would be impossible to avoid hitting any log stuck in the tight chutes. Only advanced boaters should attempt the upper river, and only experts should venture above and/or over the falls. Scout the upper falls on your hike in to get an idea of what the drop looks like. The pool at the bottom is plenty deep—I have jumped in at low summer levels and only lightly touched the gravel below. The trick is to have enough water flowing over the top of the drop, since the rock ledge can be too shallow to boof off at lower water. Penciling in could land boaters on the rocks at the bottom; you may risk breaking more than a valuable boat.

Below the falls, the river continues in pool-drop fashion through a variety of narrow channels, ledges with deep pools, and continuous Class III to IV+ drops. There are several memorable spots to take photos or a break. One log spanned the river before reaching the 1.5-mile put-in, but paddlers could roll under it. This and many other logs may shift at any time, so boat defensively!

The 1.5-mile put-in is at a side road marked "Keep Out" due to mines at the bottom. Friends of Opal Creek volunteers indicate that passage is allowed for put-in purposes only. The road leads to a deep pool off a 5-foot ledge-drop with mines on both sides of the river. Class IV pool-drop rapids follow, with longer slides of Class III water in places. Watch for metal pipe and debris in the river below the mines. You may have to dodge or limbo over and under logs in places. Horizon lines can often be boat-scouted, but get out to look at what you cannot see.

In about 0.4 mile, paddlers have faced a monster log-jam. It has occurred at the bottom of a Class IV double drop that bends right before a small pool backs up behind the jam. If the hazard exists, carry over this rapid and log-jam on the right to avoid paddling into the hazard. And I mean carry over, not around, since the canyon walls are nearly vertical. It's not as bad as it sounds, but exercise caution.

Not far below the log-jam, **Big Fluffy Falls** follow in less than a mile. Here a Class III+ rapid drops down and to the right around a corner before winding over

Daren Jacob seal-launches into the pool below Big Fluffy.

an 18-foot waterfall. Scout or portage on river right before the rapid. You'll have to make a 15-foot seal-launch into a narrow channel to get around the falls. A sloping "launching pad" slides off the rock ledge just before a log that spans the river, high above. The falls have been run, but the approach is an S-turn that makes it difficult to get enough speed to boof. A deep and dangerous pencil-in is more likely. Also, a log spanning the river above the lead-in to the falls blocked a clean route in the spring of 1997. More recently, the upper log jam has wedged below the falls, scout carefully.

From Big Fluffy Falls to Three Pools, the river becomes a continuous Class III+ technical ride. The steady barrage of action lets up in places. Before reaching the take-out, paddlers must get through one last difficult Class IV rapid, known as **Thor's Playroom.** It starts with a variety of lead-ins, labeled **Doors One, Two, and Three.** I've taken the narrow slide down Door Two, in the middle, to make a short drift to a small pool on the right before committing to the final left-to-right double drop. The second of the drops can make a dramatic rear-ending to a wonderful trip. Stay right of the first drop to make it down the second facing downstream. Spectators usually wait at a recovery pool at the bottom, offering encouragement. Paddlers can hike up the rocks on river left for more plunges down this fun finale.

Take out at Three Pools Recreation Area, since a difficult Class V+ rapid waits just downstream. Scouting or portaging this turbulent canyon is difficult (if not impossible) once you have committed to the run.

Section 2: Salmon Falls to Elkhorn Valley Recreation Area

Class: II (IV)   **Recommended flow:** 600 to 2,000 cfs   **Miles:** 6.5

Section 2 is the least-run on the Little North Santiam River, since it contains mostly Class I and II water with a narrow, turbulent Class IV- canyon in the middle. **The Slot,** about 3 miles into the run, can be a formidable Class IV- or greater. Paddlers may be able to use a gravel bar (which may have changed since recent floods) to get a view of The Slot entrance. Look to see that it is free of debris. You won't be able to portage, regardless, since the area is posted private property. For this reason, most paddlers should consider boating a different section. Paddlers who want more action can travel farther upriver or downriver to Sections 1 and 3. Those looking for a mixture of action, play, and relaxation in a longer day may chose to combine portions of Sections 2 and 3, since bridge crossings provide alternate take-outs. If you want easier water, go elsewhere. The entire 16.5-mile stretch from Salmon Falls to Mehama is slow-going, so get an early start.

At Elkhorn Valley Recreation Area, paddlers may choose to take out above or below two Class III rapids. Scout them and decide when arranging your shuttle.

Section 3: Elkhorn Valley Recreation Area to North Santiam River

Class: II (IV)   **Recommended flow:** 600 to 3,000 cfs   **Miles:** 6.5

Except for two Class III rapids at the put-in, which can be avoided, most of the river below Elkhorn Valley Recreation Area rates a Class II. The exception is

Troll's Tooth, a Class IV rapid that drops suddenly after a left bend in the river. It occurs 3.5 miles below the recreation area put-in. Scout on river left before rounding a left bend in the river that comes soon after a sharp S-turn. The rapid is just below a concrete bridge that is roughly 0.5 mile upstream. The preferred route through Troll's Tooth is far right behind a large boulder. The center route drops over a ledge into a potentially nasty hydraulic before the current splits to the center and left. The center flow slams into a huge undercut boulder, and the far left chute has had a log jammed in the slot. Once you are behind the boulder on the right, ferry facing upstream across the current to avoid the undercut and finish down the center.

Above and below Troll's Tooth, many play waves spice up the trip. Once the Little North Santiam converges with the North Santiam River, look for the take-out at Mehama, less than 0.25 mile downstream on river left under a bridge. Alternately, take out across the North Santiam River at a boat launch just across from the confluence.

68 Santiam River, Middle Fork

Willamette National Forest to Green Peter Reservoir

MIDDLE
WILLAMETTE
BASIN

SEE MAP PAGE 436

Character: A technical run through isolated wilderness, clearcuts, and gorges.

Location: Western Oregon, east of Corvallis.

Class: IV, pool-drop.

Skill level: Upper advanced and expert.

Craft: Whitewater kayaks and canoes.

Recommended flow
500 to 3,500 cfs.

Optimal flow
1,500 cfs.

Water source
Rain and snowmelt.

Average gradient
62 ft/mi.

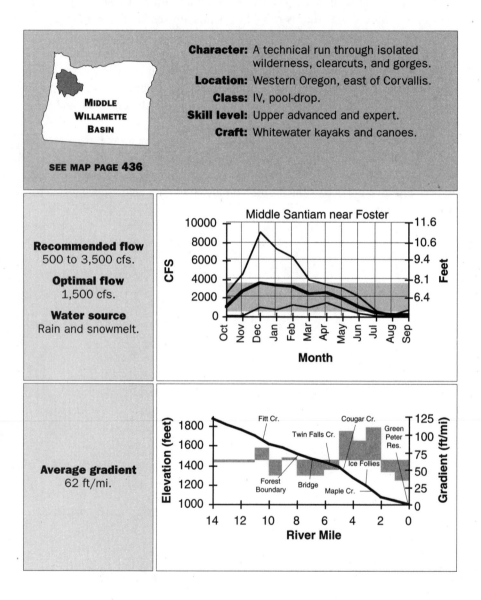

Hazards: With log portages and Class IV rapids, the Middle Fork Santiam River is a multiday adventure. Even if you plan on running the wilderness section in just one day, take overnight gear; time or hazards may force a longer-than-planned trip. Since help may be far away, paddlers should take extra gear, food, and equipment for self-rescue. Weather can be cold during the runnable season. Take extra clothing and gear for cold water even if fair weather has been forecast.

One of the most demanding aspects of an upper Middle Santiam trip is the hike to the river. Paddlers must line boats up and down numerous road blowouts for roughly 3 miles to reach the put-in. If you plan it well, the paddle is worth the effort.

Below the national forest boundary the river becomes continuous pool-drop Class III and IV water with several long, demanding stretches above Green Peter Reservoir. Paddling out from the reservoir is pure hell. For a shorter shuttle, contact the Cascade Timber Company and inquire about possible access through the gate on the far side of the dam.

Access: From Interstate 5 at Albany, Exit 233 leads to U.S. Highway 20, heading east. Follow US 20 to Foster Reservoir, then turn north onto Quartzville Road along the upper reservoir. Quartzville Road leads east to Green Peter Reservoir. The take-out is on the south side of the reservoir, reached by crossing the dam. The road across the dam is also the access route to upper river bridges—if Cascade Timber opens the gate. Don't count on getting access here, but give the company a call to remind them of recreational desires.

Access on the north side of the reservoir is available at either Thistle Creek or Whitcomb Creek boat ramps, along Quartzville Road to the east.

Note: Paddlers will have to make a long, arduous paddle (7+ miles) on still water to take out at either ramp location.

Boaters can run the lower Middle Fork Santiam River in summer below Green Peter Dam by hiking to the river, passing through (or over) two gates along a road 0.5 mile below Green Peter Dam. The take-out for the lower river is at a pullout roughly 2 miles back down the road, where a trail at another gate in the fence leads to the river.

Overview: The upper Middle Fork Santiam River lies within the Middle Santiam Wilderness. Since roads no longer lead directly to the river, paddlers must make a grueling 3-mile hike to reach the upper access. The upper Middle Fork Santiam is spectacularly scenic before dropping into private clearcuts. The Middle Fork Santiam between Green Peter Dam and Foster Reservoir is a guaranteed run even in hot summer. The lower river is classic Class IV whitewater over a 2-mile run.

The upper river was once divided into two runs above Green Peter Reservoir, but the Cascade Timber Company now blocks the road to the south side of the reservoir on weekends, and it may not be accessible during the week. An armed guard is stationed up the road to keep people out. This forces a 15-mile run with several Class IV rapids and possible log portages, plus a long paddle to a take-out across the reservoir. Advanced paddlers who can run self-contained through Class III to IV water will find plenty of challenges on this multiday trip.

Paddlers make their way through an otherwise-inaccessible forested area to reach clearcuts above the reservoir formed by Green Peter Dam, which backs up both the Middle Fork Santiam and Quartzville Creek (River 66), along separate fingers. Motorized craft do not frequent the reservoir during the runnable season, but paddlers should paddle near shore while on slack water nevertheless. If you plan to take out across the reservoir at Thistle Creek Boat Ramp, remember that you have a long, 7-mile paddle on still water. This paddle can take as long as the entire river run!

Going with the Flow
Section 1: Upper Access to Green Peter Reservoir

Class: III+ to IV	Recommended flow: 350 to 2,000 cfs	Miles: 14+

Getting to the Middle Fork Santiam River means a demanding 3-mile hike that takes roughly 2.5 hours. Paddlers must line boats and gear across several washouts on the wilderness road/trail in. Once at the river, you'll find the going much easier than expected following such devastation along the road and side creeks.

From the put-in where the road/trail meets the river, the run starts with a nice warm-up set of Class II to II+ rapids interspersed with pools for reflection and rest. Watch for otters, deer, and other wildlife along the upper river. Before long, you'll encounter more distinct pool-drop rapids that have fairly obvious routes upon boat-scouting. Check everywhere for log obstructions, recognizing that debris will move around with changing flows.

After the first few miles, the rapids gradually get more difficult with more demanding routes and scouts. As paddlers progress downstream, the pools and calm stretches between Class III and III+ rapids become shorter and the rapids get more technical.

Below the Willamette National Forest boundary and a bridge across the river (once an access bridge), roughly midway down the run, the river begins to build to Class IV technical pool-drop rapids separated by short Class II stretches. **Ice Follies** rapid occurs at an old log bridge. Scout it from the right to see that routes are clear of debris. The central drop is steep within a narrow chute. The far right is easier, but rocky at low flows.

A few more rapids lead to Green Peter Reservoir, where a 7-mile paddle leads to take-outs across the lake. If you find a better spot to take out, let me know. The marathon paddle will make your already-worn arms ache as the horizon seems never to change. Look to an island just beyond the confluence with the Quartzville and Middle Santiam fingers to keep your bearings. The boat ramps on the north side of the reservoir are roughly 2 miles beyond the island. Take your flashlight in case you reach the take-out in the dark.

Section 2: Green Peter Dam to Foster Reservoir

Class: IV	Recommended flow: 2,000 to 4,000 cfs	Miles: 2+

The lower Middle Fork Santiam River is a Class IV summer paddlers' mainstay. Green Peter Reservoir bleeds either 2,000 or 4,000 cubic feet per second (using one or two turbines) year-round, guaranteeing a Class IV run here when other rivers and creeks are at a bathtub flow. The run requires hiking both to and from the river through gates.

The upper mile of river is not as demanding as the lower, allowing a warm-up before the major Class IV rapids. In the second mile lie **Swiss Cheese, Scrawley's Wall,** and **Concussion.** Each rapid is a demanding Class IV pool-drop with short pools between; for details, see the Willamette Kayak and Canoe Club's guide to Oregon whitewater, *Soggy Sneakers*. The final drop ends at Foster Reservoir at usual reservoir levels. Take out up the bank near the pullout or continue along the reservoir to Sunnyside Campground and Boat Ramp after more than 1.5 miles of stillwater paddling. The ramp and campground are along the right shore of Foster Reservoir, just east of the Quartzville Road bridge. Campgrounds around the reservoir close in September and do not open until spring.

69 Santiam River, North Fork
Big Cliff Dam to Main Santiam River

Character: A large, wooded, roadside stream.
Location: Northwest Oregon, south of Salem.
Class: II to III+ (IV+, V), pool-drop.
Skill level: Beginner to advanced and expert.
Craft: All.

MIDDLE
WILLAMETTE
BASIN

SEE MAP PAGE 436

Recommended flow
1,000 to 4,000 cfs.

Optimal flow
2,500 cfs.

Water source
Dam-controlled.

Average gradient
25.5 ft/mi.

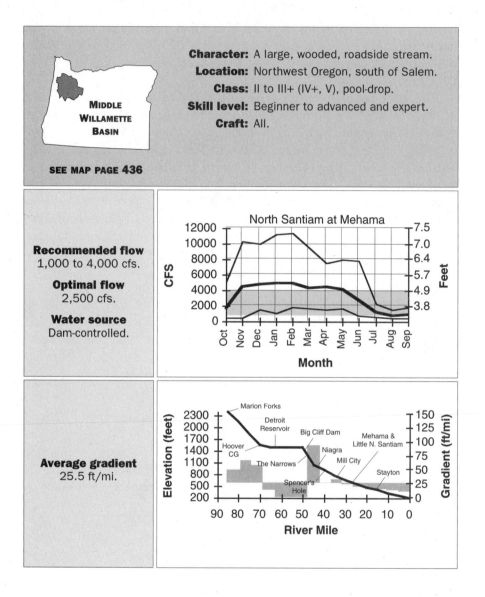

300

Hazards: Two rapids along Section 1, **The Narrows** and **Niagara,** begin with Class III+ lead-ins and deserve special attention. The Narrows offers very turbulent water in a narrow rock funnel with a nasty hole that can be run far left at high flows. Scout (with some difficulty) from an upstream right eddy within the Class III rapid just above the drop. Niagara is a Class V rapid in a narrow, twisting, rocky gorge with huge swirling hydraulics and reaction waves that lead to a huge eddy beyond with very strong eddy lines. Scout it at the nearby park before putting in.

Lower sections contain Class III rapids and holes that flow in pool-drop fashion between Class II stretches. A weir less than 2 miles beyond Niagara requires a portage on the right. **Spencer's Hole** is 1 mile beyond the weir, where water funnels into a steeper drop and hole. **Mill City Falls** is a 4-foot, river-wide ledge-drop at the bridge in Mill City.

Access: For access points above Stayton, follow Interstate 5 to the south end of Salem and take Exit 253 to Oregon Highway 22, heading east. OR 22 intersects the Cascade Highway above Stayton. Continue east along OR 22 to the desired access areas.

For access at and below Stayton, take I-5's Exit 238 near Jefferson and go east on Jefferson–Scio Drive. Seek out the stream gage and access area just downstream at Greens Bridge. The bridge marks the last take-out above the North Fork Santiam's confluence with the main Santiam River. To reach other access areas, continue east along Jefferson–Scio Drive to Shelburn Drive, turning north at the fork. Follow this road past Shelburn to Hess Road, turning left (north) to reach Buell Miller Boat Launch. Beyond Shelburn the main drive jogs its way to Stayton–Scio Road, heading northeast. Before you cross the Stayton Bridge into town, look for an access area just downstream to the west.

Overview: The North Fork Santiam River is a popular destination for boaters at all skill levels. Only advanced to expert boaters should attempt the upper stretches below Big Cliff Dam, since two Class IV to V rapids (The Narrows and Niagara) present difficult portages there. The stretch of river from Packsaddle Campground to Mill City is a favorite for playboaters. Within it, **Spencer's Hole** is a fun rodeo spot at most water levels, with numerous waves to surf. Beginning and intermediate boaters enjoy the river below Mehama. From Stayton to Jefferson the water eases to mostly Class I with occasional Class I+ areas.

The North Fork is heavily forested within its open upper canyon, changing to flatter agricultural lands beyond Mehama. While the upper river is bordered by steep basalt banks, the lower river is lined with brush. The river level is controlled below Detroit Reservoir, where two large dams disperse the flow. The reservoir is a popular recreational area with many campgrounds and boat launches for power boats. In early fall the reservoir is drained of its storage water, providing good flows on the lower river at a time when other area runs are dry. Check the Web or flow lines for late summer releases. See Appendix B.

OR 22 follows the river's right bank in the upper stretches, but stays far enough away from the river to keep from intruding. Paddlers get only occasional views of the river from the road, making the North Fork Santiam impractical to car-scout except at parks and bridges.

Going with the Flow
Section 1: Big Cliff Dam to Mill City

Class: III (IV, V)	Recommended flow: 1,200 to 3,500 cfs	Miles: 12

The first few miles of Section 1 provide the North Fork Santiam River's most exciting and dangerous whitewater below Detroit Reservoir. Most of the river is continuous Class II water with small waves and pourovers. Stretches of Class III to III+ rapids dot the river in places, most notably before the two more difficult rapid confines and below the diversion weir.

On a left bend in the river, The Narrows is a Class IV to IV+ drop where water funnels into a narrow, turbulent rock channel. Class III rapids lead to the 6-foot drop with a nasty roostertail left of center. A right diagonal hole feeds off current from the right wall, creating a keeper hole. Scout or portage the drop by taking out along the right bank before (or just into) the Class III rapid. An eddy on the right just above the drop could be a good scout or portage option, but it is a must-make move within large waves and holes. You'd regret a mishap here. At higher flows, paddlers can take a sneak route past the roostertail at far left. At any flows, the far left or left of center route is preferred; at lower flows, you'll have to portage. Beyond the drop, turbulent water banks off the wall, left to right, with the lots of pinning potential for swimmers. Anyone who wants to run The Narrows needs to have a good roll.

More fun Class II water with Class III spots leads to Class V Niagara. Scout this rapid on the drive up by stopping at the nearby park area, marked by a sign on the right. A long Class III+ lead-in rapid contains large holes and waves that require several moves before pooling above the narrow entrance to the hazard below. Swimmers and gear can easily get swept into the rapid without quick aid from fellow paddlers. Portage or scout up the steep bank on the right at the old dam construction site. Inside the narrow channel, a large eddy swirls along the left bank. Water at the entrance drop and throughout the rapid is turbulent, with strong eddy lines and pounding reaction waves off deeply undercut walls. One swimmer lost his boat, with full floatation, for more than 15 minutes. The boat eventually resurfaced and was later recovered. We were thankful that the swimmer made it to the right bank before being swept into the rapid himself.

From inside Niagara's steep basalt confines, you can make a portage around the turbulent, undercut channel. Portage over the rocky, left divide at the large eddy. Below the channel, another large eddy presents itself on the right with a powerful eddy line. Beyond the eddy a large wave hole leads to easier water. The portage within the channel avoids the powerful eddy and wave hole, but boaters must be sure and capable of making the eddy. Niagara is much easier at lower flows, becoming far less turbulent at flows below 2,000 cubic feet per second.

Beyond Niagara, more Class II and III water with fun surf and play spots leads to a diversion weir in 2 miles. Portage this deadly cement structure on the right when you see it. Water pours over most of the river along an otherwise relaxing stretch. The gentle looks are deceiving, however, since the water goes into a regular keeper hydraulic at the bottom. Look for a trailer house along the right shore as a cue to take out. Packsaddle County Park is just downstream of the weir on the right for a take-out. Alternately, paddlers may continue through more fun Class III rapids to Spencer's Hole and beyond.

Below Packsaddle Park the water eases to Class II with many play spots, but Class III rapids punctuate the river in several places. An area known as **The Swirlies** is not far downstream. The river narrows here, creating good surf waves at higher flows. At a right bend in the river, Class III **Fake Spencer's Hole** looks similar to the lead-in for the real Spencer's Hole farther downstream. Both rapids present large standing waves and holes with excellent surf. At the real Spencer's Hole, paddlers get nice play waves just above the drop. A turbulent, fast wave train follows, with a pool on the right that lets you make a return trip to the hole. At higher flows, turbulent water makes access tricky. At lower flows, the hole is stickier but easier to catch. The rocky bank has trails that lead to a pullout along a side road near Gates. This makes a good take-out for paddlers who have run the upper stretch and want some play in the hole before calling it a day.

At an island 0.25 mile beyond Spencer's Hole, much of the current leads to the preferred right side. The left side contains **Carnivore**, a turbulent, twisting channel. Beyond the island the river maintains its Class II character to Mill City with many play waves at higher water. Take out at Mill City on the right above **Mill City Falls,** or run this last Class III river-wide drop just before the bridge. Make an easy scout of the falls from the bridge in Mill City before you put in. Take out along the grassy bank beyond the bridge and falls, on the right. Some boaters float another mile to the gravel boat ramp at Fisherman's Bend Campground, in season.

Section 2: Mill City to Main Santiam River

Class: I to II+ (P)   **Recommended flow:** 1,200 to 4,000 cfs   **Miles:** 34

Below Mill City, the North Fork Santiam holds no seriously hazardous rapids. The riverbanks slowly open to rolling hills and agricultural lands where more sunlight reaches the water. Numerous eddies, small waves, and pourovers provide a good training ground for beginning whitewater paddlers. Watch out for narrow constrictions with sharp bends in places. At lower flows the river becomes shallow, rocky, and more technical. A ledge-drop near Fisherman's Bend Campground is one of the most difficult drops below Mill City Falls (Class III). Avoid it on the right. Above Stayton, paddlers get many surf waves within Class II water. The current can be fast at higher flows, creating more challenging eddy lines and larger waves. Keep an eye open for islands, making passage on either side.

The Little North Santiam River is the North Fork's largest tributary, joining the flow above Mehama. Look for access points on the left just below the confluence at John Neal Park or at the Mehama–Lyons Bridge, just beyond. Less than 0.25 mile beyond the bridge, **Beginner's Hole** provides a small pourover and hole on the left. You can easily miss it if you're not watching. Powerlines cross the river in two places between Mehama and Stayton. Above the first set the river narrows and banks to the right into the right bank. Try catching the eddy on the inside left to avoid the far bank. About 0.25 mile below the powerlines is a Class II rapid; run it on the left.

The rest of the trip rates Class I and I+, with a required portage around a dam above Stayton. Follow the left channel above the dam and portage to continue downstream. Class I+ or II riffles occur after the dam as the river gets wide and shallow. An island breaks up the stream above Stayton; just beyond it, Stayton Bridge hovers over the river. An access area on the left just beyond the bridge is a possible take-out.

Below Stayton the river passes several gravel bars and is braided by many islands. Brush and debris line the banks, blocking some island channels. There are many sharp bends in the river. The current moves faster near Stayton. The North Fork retains its isolated, open feel in spite of the area's population, since there are no roads or residences along the river. About 4 miles downstream from Stayton, Buell Miller Boat Launch provides another possible take-out. The next access area is at Greens Bridge, roughly 10 miles downriver. Plan on a long day if you intend to float from Stayton to Greens Bridge at lower flows.

70 Santiam River, Upper South Fork
Upper Soda Creek to Foster Reservoir

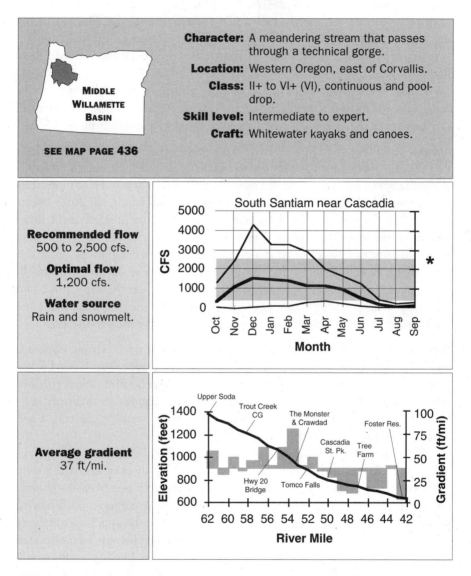

MIDDLE WILLAMETTE BASIN

SEE MAP PAGE **436**

Character: A meandering stream that passes through a technical gorge.

Location: Western Oregon, east of Corvallis.

Class: II+ to VI+ (VI), continuous and pool-drop.

Skill level: Intermediate to expert.

Craft: Whitewater kayaks and canoes.

Recommended flow
500 to 2,500 cfs.

Optimal flow
1,200 cfs.

Water source
Rain and snowmelt.

South Santiam near Cascadia

CFS — 5000, 4000, 3000, 2000, 1000, 0

Month — Oct, Nov, Dec, Jan, Feb, Mar, Apr, May, Jun, Jul, Aug, Sep

*

Average gradient
37 ft/mi.

Elevation (feet) — 1400, 1200, 1000, 800, 600

Gradient (ft/mi) — 100, 75, 50, 25, 0

Upper Soda, Trout Creek CG, The Monster & Crawdad, Foster Res., Cascadia St. Pk., Tree Farm, Hwy 20 Bridge, Tomco Falls

River Mile — 62 60 58 56 54 52 50 48 46 44 42

* No depth measurement available.

Hazards: Above Foster Reservoir, the Upper South Santiam River contains many demanding, technical rapids and drops. Paddlers must scout frequently to determine routes. **The Monster, Crawdad, Tomco Falls,** and **Tree Farm** rapids require mandatory scouts or portages. Scout **Slot Machine** on the drive up at a gated bridge downstream of Cascadia Park and the stream gage bridge. Slot Machine is one of the easiest rapids below the U.S. Highway 20 bridge. If it looks too demanding for your skill level, avoid the stretch between US 20 and Cascadia State Park.

Be alert for wood hazards in any section. Swims on the upper river can be hazardous due to undercut ledges, narrow chutes, and weird rock formations in the basalt river channel. Keep your feet up to avoid foot entrapment.

Access: From Interstate 5 at Albany, take Exit 233 and head east on U.S. Highway 20. All Upper South Santiam River access is along US 20. Reach take-outs along the South Santiam Fork of Foster Reservoir near where US 20 intersects Quartzville Road. For upstream access, continue upstream on US 20. A bridge beyond Deer Creek has a visual stream gage downstream on river left; check flows here or use the steep bank access. Access along river right is available at Cascadia State Park, east of Cascadia, and at a bridge over the river. Longbow Road, which leads along river left below the US 20 bridge, offers good access at small, undesignated pullouts. Trout Creek Campground, Fernview Campground, and the bridge at Upper Soda Creek near the Mountain House restaurant and store offer upriver access. Many pullouts along US 20 also have trails to the river.

Overview: I avoided the South Santiam River for years, since existing write-ups and the proximity of US 20 did not make the river sound appealing. When I at last visited, I was pleasantly surprised to find that the Upper South Santiam contains one of the most spectacular gorges I have ever seen. Though the highway stays close to the river, it is far enough away to keep from intruding. In only a few locations are paddlers aware that the road is there.

The scenery along the South Santiam is outstanding. Bearded moss hangs like tinsel on a Christmas tree. Huge boulders, carved basalt channels, and a deep gorge entertain paddlers' senses. Fall colors intermix with evergreens to provide the full spectrum of earthtones, dazzling the eyes. You won't have much time to notice your surroundings, though, since the rapids along the upper river are very demanding Class IV, V, and VI drops. Many are on the plus side of the scale at moderate to high flows. Scout carefully and run cautiously, looking out for wood. Some drops require difficult scouts or portages. For advanced and expert paddlers, it's a wonderland.

If you're looking for excitement and challenge, the Upper South Santiam above Foster Reservoir will fit the bill after a gentle warm-up below Upper Soda Creek. If you're just starting out or want a more relaxing adventure, Lower South Santiam below Foster Reservoir offers a variety of stretches in which you can build your skills, surf, or drift slowly along a peaceful stream.

Going with the Flow
Section 1: Upper Soda Creek to US 20 Bridge

Class: II+ (III)	**Recommended flow:** 500 to 2,500 cfs	**Miles:** 7

The Upper South Santiam River contains steep banks and an impressive gradient through an initial Class II+ stretch. Numerous Class II pool-drop rapids dot the river, with stretches of easier water in between. The only exception to the Class II character of the upper reaches is **Longbow Falls**, about 2 miles below Trout Creek Campground. Here the river drops over a 3-foot ledge that rates a Class III. View the falls on your drive up from a pullout just below a fishing platform, walking upstream to see the drop.

Paddlers can make the trip from Upper Soda Creek to the US 20 bridge in a short day at moderate flows. At higher flows the same stretch would probably take half a day to complete. Always watch for wood along the upper river! River currents can be strong, and the riverbed is narrow and winding.

Take-out along Longbow Road on the right or at the US 20 bridge. Do not continue below the bridge unless you are prepared to face demanding rapids. If you plan on running below the bridge, using Section 1 as a warm-up, get an early start to allow time to scout and/or portage. Paddlers who want a shorter warm-up can put in at Trout Creek Campground, running the 3-mile stretch to the US 20 bridge, which includes the Class III falls.

Section 2: US 20 Bridge to Cascadia State Park

Class: IV+ (V, P)	**Recommended flow:** 500 to 2,000 cfs	**Miles:** 5

Section 2 includes the most demanding water on the South Santiam River. The scenery and rapids are outstanding, so bring plenty of film and respect to this awesome place. The highway is always near the river, but it is seldom seen and often inaccessible.

Like the Sandy River Gorge, this run on the Upper South Santiam contains huge boulders, small amphitheaters, and several demanding, narrow-slotted rapids. The first 2 miles are continuous boulder gardens with short spans between pool-drop rapids. Scout frequently as needed, from both bank and water. Choose routes carefully, since there are potential strainers along the entire river.

After 2 miles of fun, technical boating, paddlers face The Monster. Portage on the left, or run this Class VI rapid along the right. Do not run the very narrow and hazardous left and central slots. Crawdad is connected to The Monster just downstream through a narrow passage. Here the river makes a nasty S-turn through a very narrow slot. Both sides are grooved and undercut at lower flows. A small log across the exit lies just underwater at higher flows. The log will wash free sometime, but you'll want to scout to make sure it's gone. Scouting is difficult; it's better to portage both The Monster and Crawdad on the left.

More fun boulder gardens and drops follow Crawdad, covering about a mile of river above Tomco Falls. The falls contain a deep, narrow slot along the left bank. This has severe entrapment potential, with undercut and grooved rock. It would be a nasty place to swim or roll. At higher flows, a rock ledge separates the

The author seals into his kayak and readies for a launch along Section 2 of the Upper South Santiam. RON KILLEN PHOTO

left slot and a tributary on the right. The right side is a steeper drop but a safer one, running directly into the river gorge below. Portage far right or up the steep bank on the left. Walk far enough above the falls to stay safe in case of a slip!

Below Tomico Falls the river enters a long, narrow gorge. Easier rapids follow for 1 mile to a narrow slot called **The Plug,** which has gathered wood in the past. At higher flows watch for a hole above The Plug; you won't see it at lower water levels. The Plug drops straight into a turbulent pool. Scout on the right to make sure it is free of debris.

More rapids continue to Cascadia State Park. These are easier to run and scout than those upstream. Though a large tree spans the entire river in one location, it's easy to spot in advance; portage along the left. At higher and faster flows water may flow over parts of the tree, creating a more severe and less visible hazard. Take out at Cascadia State Park, on the right beyond the bridge, or continue along Section 3 for a longer day. The bridge is less than 0.5 mile downstream of the Canyon Creek confluence.

Section 3: Cascadia State Park to Foster Reservoir

Class: III (V)	**Recommended flow:** 500 to 3,000 cfs	**Miles:** 10

Section 3 is a good choice for intermediate boaters, with a portage of **Tree Farm** rapids. The stretch begins with Class III to III+ rapids that alternate with flatter Class I and II stretches. A variety of boulder gardens require some technical paddling. Check the stream gage on the downstream left side of a bridge (Short Bridge) 1.5 miles below Cascadia Park.

Below the bridge, more rapids continue for a couple miles to the Class V rapids known as Tree Farm; scout or portage is along the right bank. Like The Monster in Section 2, Tree Farm contains narrow, turbulent slots. Here, too, the far left and center slots are very narrow and dangerous. Run the far right side for a Class IV+ route, or portage. Scouting the central slot, which may contain wood, is difficult from either bank at high flows. Opt for the far right unless you wish to portage left or make the expert run down the difficult left slot.

Below Tree Farm, the river eases to Class II+ with a more difficult Class III rapid at a bridge we call Slot Machine. This rapid is similar to Tree Farm, though on a much smaller scale; three slots at lower water contain narrow chutes. The easier route is again along the far right. At higher flows, the slots may fill and become less demanding. More rapids continue to Foster Reservoir, becoming progressively easier and spaced farther apart. One rapid contains a twisting route from right to left around a more shallow ledge on the left. Below this, drops continue to ease until reaching slack water at the reservoir.

The down side to taking out at Quartzville Road is the several-mile paddle you'll have to make along the reservoir. You may be able to take out up a steep bank near Menemes Campground, which is on the left after you reach the reservoir; if you can do so, you'll avoid the last 2.6 miles of still water. Otherwise, hug the left shore and paddle to Quartzville Road on the left.

71 Santiam River, Lower South and Main
Foster Reservoir to Willamette River

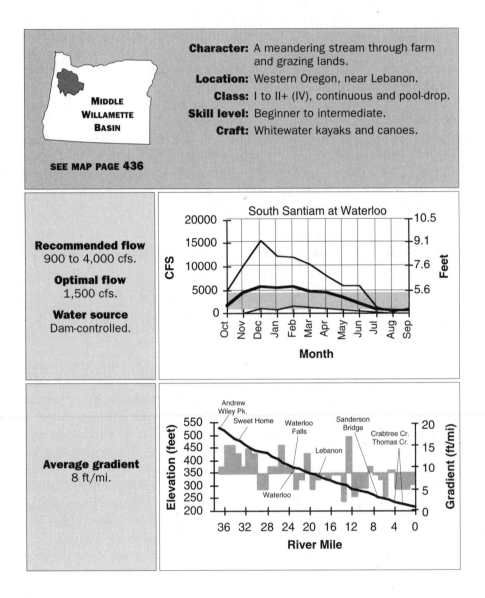

**MIDDLE
WILLAMETTE
BASIN**

SEE MAP PAGE **436**

Character: A meandering stream through farm and grazing lands.

Location: Western Oregon, near Lebanon.

Class: I to II+ (IV), continuous and pool-drop.

Skill level: Beginner to intermediate.

Craft: Whitewater kayaks and canoes.

Recommended flow
900 to 4,000 cfs.

Optimal flow
1,500 cfs.

Water source
Dam-controlled.

South Santiam at Waterloo

Average gradient
8 ft/mi.

Hazards: The Lower South Santiam River contains gravel bars, pool-drop Class II rapids, and **Waterloo Falls** near Waterloo Park. The falls are Class IV+; scout before running from the park. The river banks sharply at **Highway 20** rapids at the US 20 bridge. Scout from the bridge on the drive.

The water in the Santiam is cold, originating from the depths of Foster Reservoir. Banks are brushy in many places, with log hazards in places. Always be alert for wood.

Access: From Interstate 5 at Albany, Exit 233 leads to US 20 to the east. All Lower South Santiam River access above Jefferson is off US 20. To reach the first access site below Lebanon, turn off US 20 to follow Oregon Highway 226 left to where it crosses the river. Access is at Gills Landing. For sites upstream, follow Brewster Road east from town. Waterloo Campground, on the south side of Waterloo, has a boat landing on the river. Waterloo Park, upstream of the campground, is the take-out for the run above Waterloo Falls. At Sweet Home, Santiam Marine Park has a boat ramp. Cross the bridge at the west end of Sweet Home to reach access points off North River Road and at Andrew Wiley Park, below Foster Dam and the Wiley Creek confluence.

Below Jefferson, river access is available along the main Santiam River. From I-5 take Exit 240 and head east to Jefferson Junction Boat Ramp on the north side of the river. Upriver access is also available north of Jefferson by taking Exit 238 and heading east along Jefferson Highway, then north to Talbot Road, heading west. Follow Talbot Road to the first crossing of Morgan Creek and the Jefferson Site Boat Ramp.

Overview: If you're looking for excitement and challenge, the Upper South Santiam River above Foster Reservoir will fit the bill. If you're just starting out or want a more relaxing adventure, the Lower South Santiam offers a good variety of stretches to build your skills, surf, or drift slowly along a peaceful stream.

Below Foster Reservoir, the river features a low gradient and pleasant scenery in farm and grazing lands. The narrow basalt gorges and boulder gardens of the upper river are replaced with gravel bars, easier pool-drop rapids, and lazy stretches of flatwater. There are exceptions to the rule, however, particularly **Waterloo Falls.** Here the river raises its loud Class IV voice one last time, giving paddlers an adrenaline rush before it calms to join the North Santiam. Foster Dam releases a minimum flow that allows year-round paddling.

Going with the Flow
Section 1: Andrew Wiley Park to Waterloo Park

Class: II (IV+)	Recommended flow: 900 to 4,000 cfs	Miles: 13

Section 1 is the most action-packed stretch on the lower river. Below Foster Reservoir, paddlers see frequent Class I+ to II pool-drop rapids that are evenly distributed. Some fun warm-up rapids lead for 2 miles to Class II S-Turn, where the river banks right, then left. This rapid is the most difficult above Waterloo and requires more maneuvering than those above or below it. Most rapids are quick ledge-drops with a short runout.

The rapids above Sweet Home are more difficult than those between Sweet Home and Waterloo. Just above the access at Sweet Home is a rapid that has been called **Bogeyman**. It makes a good spot for beginners to practice eddy turns and surf, since there is a boat ramp near the water treatment plant at Sweet Home just below the rapid. Paddlers looking for a short trip can take out here.

Below Sweet Home the river contains several Class I+ to II rapids. The 10+ mile float from here to Waterloo is slow. Paddlers running from Andrew Wiley Park to Waterloo Park should plan on a long day to complete the entire run. The most difficult rapids below Sweet Home occur at the US 20 bridge and have been called Highway 20 rapids. Look for fun waves as the river banks right, bouncing off the embankment. Practice your eddy-turns, surf skills, or peelouts before continuing downstream.

The river above Waterloo Falls contains some rapids and divides at an island. Take out at Waterloo Park or scout the falls here, on the right. The Class IV+ falls can be run at higher water, but most paddlers choose to portage or end their run here. Those who seek more action can continue downstream from Waterloo Campground.

Section 2: Waterloo Campground to Jefferson Boat Ramp

Class: I+ (P)	**Recommended flow:** 900 to 4,000 cfs	**Miles:** 5.6 to 30+

Flows in Sections 1 and 2 are dam-controlled; Foster Dam provides adequate flows year-round, making the Lower South Santiam an attraction for paddlers looking for low water summer floats. The scenery downstream of Waterloo Park is similar to that of the previous section, but the river changes. Rapids are replaced with gravel bars, and the water slows after the first 2 miles. Paddlers should plan on running from Waterloo to Lebanon (5.6 miles); from Lebanon to Crabtree Creek (14.7 miles); or from Crabtree Creek to Jefferson (10 miles) on long day trips. There are few campsites along the mostly private lands along the lower river, so forget about running multiday trips here unless you have obtained permission to camp along the way.

There are few rapids of concern below Waterloo Falls, but at higher flows waves and debris may present some difficulty for beginners. Kick back and take in the day and scenery, but always be alert for logs. You must portage **Lebanon Dam,** 2.8 miles below Waterloo Campground. Take out on the right. Never attempt to run this death machine, since the regular hydraulics can recirculate paddlers and gear indefinitely.

Beyond the dam lie miles of easy water to soothe your soul. Take out at boat ramps north of Jefferson or below Jefferson at Jefferson Junction near I-5. Paddlers may continue along the main Santiam River from Jefferson to the Willamette River, taking out at the Buena Vista Boat Ramp, but doing so makes for a long day.

72 Sauvie Island and the Multnomah Channel

Character:	A meandering channel through sloughs and island lakes.
Location:	At the confluence of the Willamette and Columbia rivers.
Class:	FW.
Skill level:	Beginner.
Craft:	Canoes and sea kayaks.
Recommended flow:	Any.
Optimal flow:	N/A.
Water source:	Rain and Willamette River; levels maintained.
Average gradient:	Less than 1 ft/mi.

Hazards: Few hazards exist along the various channels, sloughs, and interconnected lakes of this island at the Willamette and Columbia river confluence. The water is muddy and filled with waste, so bring your own drinking water and do not practice self-rescue rolls here. Debris can congest smaller channels, as can low flows. Currents can change with rising or falling water levels.

Access: From Portland, follow U.S. Highway 30 northwest toward Astoria. Roughly 10 miles from downtown Portland, follow signs leading to Sauvie Island, crossing a bridge over the Multnomah Channel. Sauvie Island Road leads along the island's west side. Oak Island Road and Reeder Road lead to the central and eastern portions of the island. See map for access roads and sites.

Overview: The Oregon Department of Fish and Wildlife has maintained and regulated the Sauvie Island Wildlife Management Area since 1947. Though new land purchases have expanded the WMA boundaries in more recent times, most of the southern island and patches along the Columbia River remain private, as does an area near Cunningham Lake and Slough.

Migrating waterfowl and resident wildlife are abundant on the island. Hikers and paddlers often see great blue herons, kingfishers, sandhill cranes, ducks, and geese. More than 250 species of birds live on the island or stop here during migration. Certain areas of the WMA are restricted from use during peak hunting season, when more than 150,000 ducks and geese flock to the island on their way south. Resident animals include raccoons, red foxes, nutria, and black-tailed deer. Grazing cattle remove old forage and stimulate new vegetation.

The banks along the channels and lakes here are muddy. Low areas form large spans of cracked earth as the water recedes, stranding bottom-feeding catfish and

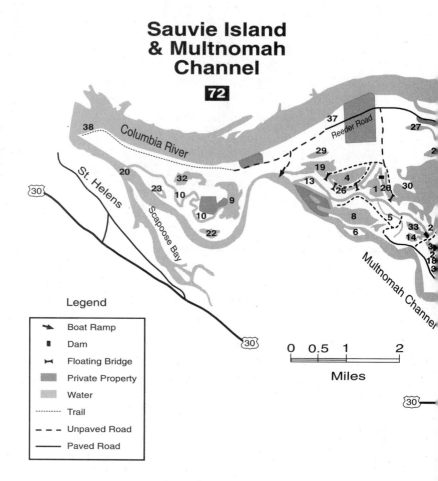

Sauvie Island & Multnomah Channel

72

Columbia River

St. Helens

Scapoose Bay

Reeder Road

Multnomah Channel

Legend

↘ Boat Ramp
■ Dam
⋈ Floating Bridge
▮ Private Property
▯ Water
········· Trail
– – – Unpaved Road
——— Paved Road

0   0.5   1   2

Miles

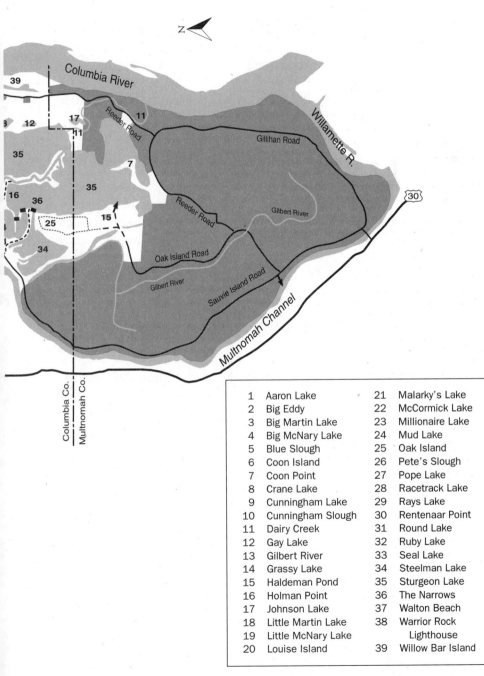

1	Aaron Lake	21	Malarky's Lake
2	Big Eddy	22	McCormick Lake
3	Big Martin Lake	23	Millionaire Lake
4	Big McNary Lake	24	Mud Lake
5	Blue Slough	25	Oak Island
6	Coon Island	26	Pete's Slough
7	Coon Point	27	Pope Lake
8	Crane Lake	28	Racetrack Lake
9	Cunningham Lake	29	Rays Lake
10	Cunningham Slough	30	Rentenaar Point
11	Dairy Creek	31	Round Lake
12	Gay Lake	32	Ruby Lake
13	Gilbert River	33	Seal Lake
14	Grassy Lake	34	Steelman Lake
15	Haldeman Pond	35	Sturgeon Lake
16	Holman Point	36	The Narrows
17	Johnson Lake	37	Walton Beach
18	Little Martin Lake	38	Warrior Rock
19	Little McNary Lake		Lighthouse
20	Louise Island	39	Willow Bar Island

carp. Anglers try for bottom fish during summer, or steelhead and salmon along the Columbia River and Multnomah Channel early in the season.

Sunbathers frequent beach areas along the Columbia River. Public beaches border private ones that have clothing-optional policies on hot summer days. Clothing is required on all public beaches, and police have issued fines to nude bathers who stray from private lands.

Visitors need permits to park along the island's roads and in designated parking areas. The permit program was enacted in 1990 to help cover costs of patrolling, maintaining trails, providing toilets, and arranging waste pick-up. Be sure to bring drinking water, since only small stores near the bridge provide food or fluids. The water in the Multnomah Channel is polluted with upstream waste; do not drink the water or practice self-rescue rolls here.

Going with the Flow

Class: Flat water   **Miles:** Various

Paddlers can take numerous routes along the channels and inland lakes of Sauvie Island. Passage is not continuous, however, since small dams control the lake levels. Plan your routes to avoid the dams, or portage around them as necessary. Slow channel waters can make finding your route difficult. Pay close attention to the route you've chosen, so that you can find your way back.

Sturgeon Lake, in the center of the island, is the largest of the inland lakes. Paddlers can easily spend an entire day at this lake, which is divided into northern and southern sections by small islands. The area is closed to recreation during the long waterfowl hunting season, which begins in October. Check with local stores or the Oregon Department of Fish and Wildlife, (503) 872-5268, for exact closure dates.

There are many floating homes along the Multnomah Channel. Be considerate of residents as you pass.

73 Siletz River

North and South Forks to Mowry Landing

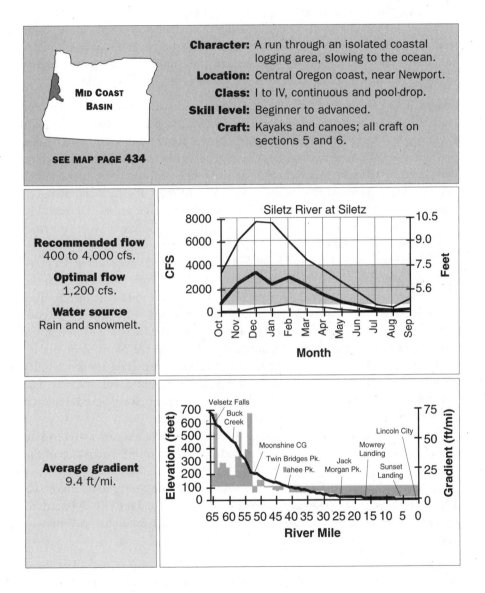

MID COAST BASIN

SEE MAP PAGE 434

Character: A run through an isolated coastal logging area, slowing to the ocean.

Location: Central Oregon coast, near Newport.

Class: I to IV, continuous and pool-drop.

Skill level: Beginner to advanced.

Craft: Kayaks and canoes; all craft on sections 5 and 6.

Recommended flow
400 to 4,000 cfs.

Optimal flow
1,200 cfs.

Water source
Rain and snowmelt.

Siletz River at Siletz

Average gradient
9.4 ft/mi.

Hazards: Several rapids on the Siletz River demand respect. Scout or portage **Silache, Powdershack, Quarry Drop,** and other Class IV and V rapids along the upper river and forks. Higher water makes for enjoyable play spots but also brings larger hydraulics, faster current, and higher classification.

Watch for wood hazards along the upper river and brushy banks in the lower stretches. Anglers often work the lower river; respect them and stay clear of lines and fishing areas. Private property lines much of the upper river. Respect it so that we may keep the weekend access that we have worked hard to obtain.

Access: From Interstate 5 at Albany, take Exit 233 and head west along U.S. Highway 20. Go beyond Philomath to Blodgett, then turn right onto Rock Creek Road and follow it to the town of Logsden. Travel about 5 miles north of Logsden on Upper Farm Road to reach access points at Moonshine Park. From Moonshine Park, drive up the private gravel road (currently open only on weekends) about 7 miles to Buck Creek. After crossing the creek, turn right at a fork and drive 0.2 mile to a gated bridge over the river; this is the Buck Creek access. To reach Elk Creek stay left at the fork and drive about 6 miles to the only spot where the road comes close to the water.

To reach the North Fork and South Fork Siletz rivers, continue about 4.5 miles upstream from Elk Creek to the bridge over the South Fork Siletz. To reach the same bridge from Salem, take Oregon Highway 22 west to Dallas, then turning south on Oregon Highway 223. OR 223 continues south to Falls City Road. Follow Falls City Road west to Falls City and take BLM Road 34 through the Valsetz townsite to the same take-out bridge. To reach the North Fork put-in, drive up the South Fork to the first left turn. Turn left and drive another 5 miles along the North Fork to the access at a locked gate adjacent to Boulder Creek. The put-in for the South Fork is 4 miles upriver from the lower North Fork Bridge at a former dam site.

For lower river sections drive from Logsden about 2.5 miles downriver to Sam Creek Road (Twin Bridges). The access boat ramps are on the south side of the bridges.

Paddlers who are coming to the Siletz River from the coast should follow US 20 east from Newport to Oregon Highway 229 at Toledo. Take OR 229 north to the town of Siletz, then turn east onto Upper Siletz Road and follow it 8 miles to Logsden. From there, follow directions as given above.

Overview: Flowing off Sugarloaf Mountain in the Coast Range, the Siletz River offers more than 50 miles of free-flowing water that ranges from solid Class IV to peaceful flat but moving water. With all this within a 45-minute drive from Corvallis, it is no wonder that the Siletz is so popular. For midcoast paddlers, the Siletz is one of the best quick-fixes in the area.

Intermediate to expert boaters will find that the river's upper reaches supply a variety of options in the Class III to IV range, including the North Fork, South Fork, and two popular runs along the main Siletz River below **Valsetz Falls.** The lower river settles down, offering a Class II area between Moonshine Park and Twin Bridges, then 25 miles of easy Class I water with many access areas. It's just the place to kick back and enjoy a warm afternoon, contemplating only good things.

Fishing is another of the area's top activities, and relations between floaters and anglers are improving. Access to the river's upper sections was recently closed by corporate landowners, but various recreational groups lobbied for access on weekends. As a result, the upper Class III to IV runs are open for use on Saturday and Sunday only. Please respect landowners and be courteous to all who use this resource.

Going with the flow
Section 1: North Fork, Boulder Creek to South Fork Confluence

Class: III (IV, V)	Recommended flow: 1,500 to 2,500 cfs	Miles: 5

The North Fork Siletz River is a long way from anywhere. It is seldom run, since the access road is bad the whole way. At least paddlers can scout all rapids on the rocky drive to the put-in.

From a locked gate just upstream of Boulder Creek, the river starts with 1 mile of continuous Class II and III water leading to a smooth ledge with a very sticky hole. The next rapid, **Bombshell**, rates a Class IV. It's a 5-foot ledge-drop into a microgorge with some simple but fun moves. Not far below, paddlers will want to portage around a narrow chute that drops into a slot with undercut walls. It looks like an easy move, but the portage on the left is the best line—the author did a little cave exploration on his first run. Another mile of Class I and II water leads to the take-out at the confluence with the South Fork.

Section 2: South Fork, Valsetz Dam to North Fork Confluence

Class: III	Recommended flow: 2,000 to 2,500 cfs	Miles: 4

The South Fork Siletz River is straightforward but remote. Its primary danger is wood; there's always the possibility of a log across the narrow, alder-lined streambed. Primary joys here are the many small surfing waves. The South Fork run is perhaps best when linked to a run along the North Fork or a hike through old-growth forest near Warnicke Creek.

The South Fork's most difficult rapid is at the old Valsetz Dam site, consisting of a pile of cobble that is steepest near the top. Pick a starting point in this 200-yard rapid based on skill. Below it, enjoy the generally Class II+ series of small bedrock ledges and sharp turns that lead to the North Fork Siletz confluence. Remember to check for wood on any blind corners. Paddlers may continue past the confluence to Valsetz Falls, about 2.7 miles. Be sure to scout the take-out well before launching, since the rocky, 70-foot falls are unrunnable.

Section 3: Elk Creek to Buck Creek (Upper Siletz)

Class: III	Recommended flow: 1,000 to 3,500 cfs	Miles: 4.5

The portion of river known as the Upper Siletz has a remote feel that adds to its fun rapids and play spots. Consisting mostly of Class II rapids, the run passes through great scenery. The views and the feeling of separation make this a winter-time treat. Intermediate paddlers love this section of river, since it gives them the feeling of adventure without the extreme hazards.

Nobody waits for action on this run. The first rapid is the largest; look for a large boulder on the right and try to go around it to either side. Just make a choice then follow through, since the gravity of this boulder increases with indecision. Past the boulder is a ledge with several possible routes. Below this two-part Class III+ area, the river settles down to a steady Class II pace with several fun holes. Because the river canyon in Section 3 is remote, be sure to take a spare paddle and other safety gear that can help you avoid a much-dreaded hike.

Paddling this stretch of the Siletz means a long shuttle. Make sure you leave time for the drive, particularly if you combine Sections 3 and 4. If you are not continuing on the so-called Silache Run (Section 4), take out at Buck Creek. You'll recognize it by a large cement bridge 100 feet above where the creek enters on the right. The best place to get out is at the mouth of the creek, carrying up a path to a parking spot at the bridge.

Section 4: Buck Creek to Moonshine Park (Silache Run)

Class: III (IV)	Recommended flow: 1,000 to 3,500 cfs	Miles: 7

Section 4 is the most popular and easily accessed section of the Siletz. Built for advanced paddlers, it comes equipped with a perfect set of warm-up rapids and play waves. A fast buildup to Silache rapid, one of the great Class IV rapids in the state, is followed by still more play and gradually decreasing difficulty. Although the Silache Run is popular with intermediate boaters, it should not be taken lightly. For years one of the rites of passage among mid-Willamette Valley boaters has been this epic adventure, complete with lost gear and lost dignity in the mile-long boulder garden.

Below the put-in at Buck Creek, paddlers see several miles of peaceful floating with occasional play opportunities. This casual stretch serves as a warm-up for the action to follow. Soon a bridge signals the entrance to a rocky Class III rapid, which ends in a moving pool along a rock wall to the right. Boulder-drops and a slot at the bottom of this pool are the welcoming mat to Silache rapid. This fa-mous rock garden requires 1 mile of boulder- and eddy-hopping moves. Expert boaters can easily boat-scout Silache, but it is just as easy to scout from the road on the shuttle. The crux is the portion nearest the road, about 150 yards into the rapid. After the first 300 yards the rapid eases to continuous Class III water with great play potential at higher flows.

About a mile below Silache, a quarry on the left signals Quarry Drop, a Class III rapid with a violent but fun hole in the center. Downstream, the pace gradually slows and the water turns to Class II pool-drops. Many paddlers take out at the bedrock outcropping that is capped by the road, 0.5 mile below the quarry. Others continue on to Moonshine Park. Doing so means getting through the shallow Class III rapid named Powdershack, which occurs around an island. Take out at the boat ramp just above an island at Moonshine Park.

Note: Experts may find great play spots on this segment at higher flows, but make a close scrutiny of the lines through the first 300 yards of Silache. Several river-wide hydraulics develop here above 5,500 cubic feet per second.

Section 5: Moonshine Park to Twin Bridges

Class: I (II)	Recommended flow: 400 to 2,500 cfs	Miles: 7.5

Perfect for a canoe trip or a beginning kayak run, Section 5 offers Class I riffles with some longer or more technical rapids that can rate an easy Class II. Boaters often float the Siletz below Moonshine Park when nearby rivers have dried up; it's a good option for late spring. Be aware of brush throughout, and watch for a ledge at a hard left bend about a mile below the park. Run this drop on the inside (left) of the turn. After passing under a bridge, keep an eye out for a final 300-yard set of waves. The waves may get fairly big at higher flows. Take out at the boat ramp on the left at Twin Bridges.

Section 6: Twin Bridges to Mowry Landing

Class: I	Recommended flow: 400 to 2,500 cfs	Miles: 25+

From Twin Bridges downstream, the Siletz River mellows to moving flatwater with occasional riffles and good fishing opportunities on a warm spring day. The primary concerns here are brush and those who take fishing more seriously than floating. Please be courteous of other boaters.

Take advantage of the many public access points in Section 6 to customize the length of your float. **Butterfield Riffle** is the start of tidewater, about 4 miles above Mowry Boat Landing. Consult tide charts for flow direction. Charts are available at sports shops along the coast or from Captain's Nautical Supply in Portland, (503) 227-1648.

—Eric Brown

74 Siuslaw River
Siuslaw Falls to Pacific Ocean

MID COAST BASIN

SEE MAP PAGE 434

Character: A meandering run to fun surf before tidal flats.

Location: Central Oregon coast, near Florence.

Class: I to II+, continuous and pool-drop.

Skill level: Beginner to intermediate.

Craft: All.

Recommended flow
1,000 to 5,000 cfs.

Optimal flow
2,500 cfs.

Water source
Rain.

Average gradient
5.6 ft/mi.

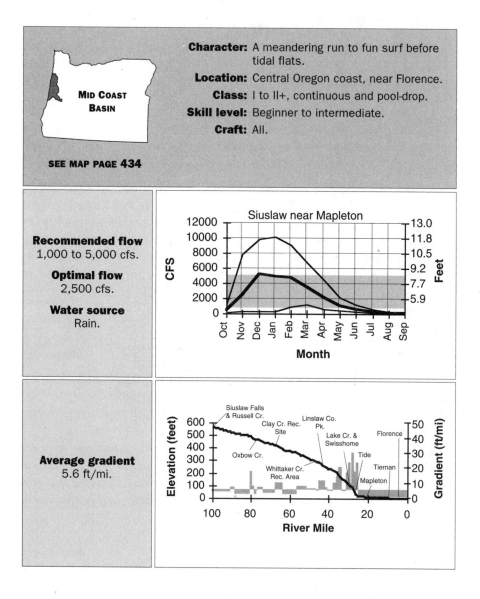

Hazards: The upper Siuslaw River meanders sharply around often-brushy banks, suggesting the possibility of wood hazards. Scout the river on the drive up for any obvious strainers. Watch for large waves and Class II rapids.

Access: From either Interstate 5 at Eugene or U.S. Highway 101 along the central Oregon coast at Florence, turn onto Oregon Highway 126. OR 126 crosses the Siuslaw River above Austa, where paddlers can use the Austa Boat Ramp south of the confluence with Wildcat Creek. To reach other access points, follow highway and river to Richardson (and Richardson Pole Slide access). Beyond this point, OR 126 leaves the Siuslaw River until it reaches Mapleton. There it joins Oregon Highway 36. OR 36/126 follows the Siuslaw River to Swisshome before branching off along Lake Creek to Oregon Highway 99 at Junction City north of Eugene. Follow the combined highways for pullout access.

Paddlers may also access the Siuslaw from Swisshome to Austa along Stagecoach Road, which follows the river and provides access to Linslaw Park between Austa and Richardson. Siuslaw River Road follows the river from Austa to Siuslaw Falls and beyond to the community of Lorane.

From Florence, heading upstream, boat launch access sites are as follows: Florence Public Ramp (River Mile 5) along the north side of the bay; Cushman RV, Marina, and Campground or Siuslaw Marina (RM 8) along the northwest side of the bay and OR 126; Midway Dock (RM 12) along the upper bay; Tiernan Boat Ramp (RM 14) in Tiernan; C & D Dock (RM 17); Mapleton Landing and Maple Lane Trailer Park and Marina (RM 19) south of Mapleton; Farnham Landing (RM 23); Tide Wayside (RM 26.5); Richardson Pole Slide (RM 41.5) near Richardson; Linslaw Park (RM 42); Austa Boat Ramp (RM 44.7); Whittaker Creek Boat Ramp (RM 46); Ford Access (RM 50); Wolf Creek Boat Ramp (RM 54); and Clay Creek Recreation Site (RM 67). Use bridges or roadside pullouts for high-water access above Clay Creek.

Overview: Beginning in Oregon's low coastal mountains, the Siuslaw River flows more than 100 miles from above Siuslaw Falls to the Pacific Ocean. It reaches the Pacific at Florence, near Oregon Dunes National Recreation Area. Meandering northwest above Lake Creek, the Siuslaw is tidal below Mapleton. The lower river and coast are windy much of year. Though the upper river is usually too low to run except after heavy rains, the lower river has a long boating season that lasts from fall through early summer.

The Siuslaw rapids are generally forgiving Class IIs at low to moderate water levels, but they can climb to Class III- at high flows. At higher flows paddlers enjoy surf spots above and below the confluence with Lake Creek. Most of the rapids are located between Linslaw County Park and 1.5 miles below Tide. The rest of the river meanders through an open landscape with trees and heavy vegetation along the banks.

Going with the flow
Section 1: Siuslaw Falls to Clay Creek Recreation Site

Class: I to II   **Recommended flow:** 300 to 1,500 cfs   **Miles:** 33

This uppermost stretch of the Siuslaw River has few access areas for larger craft. Most paddlers launch from bridges or roadside pullouts. Flows are much smaller here than downstream, with no gage information available beyond Mapleton. Try the upper river after heavy rains, anytime between early fall and late spring.

The upper river meanders through low coastal mountains with heavy vegetation along its banks. The current can be swift at higher flows. Silt washes from the often-muddy banks, creating brown water. Anglers find better fishing along the lower reaches. The river is fed by numerous side creeks, gaining flow as it goes.

Taking out near the bridge below Dog Creek (RM 97.3), or running from a pullout about a mile below Bottle Creek (RM 94.5) to Oxbow Creek (RM 78.5), makes a very long day's paddle. A good 10-mile float is from Oxbow Creek to Clay Creek Recreation Site (RM 67); most boaters can easily do this section in a day.

Section 2: Clay Creek Recreation Site to Linslaw County Park

Class: I to II   **Recommended flow:** 500 to 2,000 cfs   **Miles:** 25

In Section 2, boaters can choose from several access areas to create a run of desired length. A bridge near Wolf Creek (RM 54) roughly divides the section, with trail access upstream between Wolf Creek and the next upstream bridge. Several bridges cross the river below Clay Creek Recreation Site, at RM 63.7, 61.2, and 56.5. Paddlers also can find access at Whittaker Creek Recreation Site (RM 46) along the left shore. Austa Boat Ramp provides a launch site near the confluence with Wildcat Creek (RM 44.7), and Linslaw Park (RM 42) offers access along the left shore. Plan a float of reasonable length, recognizing that current can be slow at lower flows. A paddle of 10 miles is enough for a single day.

As in Section 1, the water in Section 2 can be a silty brown at higher flows. The river resembles a large creek along its upper portions as it meanders around sharp bends. View much of the run from the road on the drive upstream. There are no appreciable rapids along this stretch of river, but scout what you can see for debris and possible wood hazards.

Section 3: Linslaw County Park to Mapleton

Class: II+ to III-   **Recommended flow:** 1,000 to 4,000 cfs   **Miles:** 23

Paddlers find most of the Siuslaw's whitewater and surf action along Section 3. Some of the best surf spots in the northwest can be found near the Lake Creek–Siuslaw River confluence. You'll get the best action at higher flows, when the Siuslaw is running more than 3,000 cubic feet per second at the Mapleton stream gage. Avoid difficult holes and waves by paddling on the river's far right side.

The stretch from Linslaw County Park to Swisshome is a good day's paddle containing most of the fun surf and rapids. Each rapid rates Class II to II+ in difficulty, but at higher flows becomes Class III- due to swift currents. Look for clear routes through waves and small holes. Each major rapid is marked by a bridge. The first is 9 miles below Linslaw Park, after the gradient picks up to create Class II+ water in places. Near the confluence with Tilden Creek is a second Class II+ rapid; look for it on a left bend at another railroad bridge in roughly 0.3 mile. The last of the Class II+ rapids is near the confluence with Lake Creek. Just beyond this rapid is a good play hole along the left. Near a mill, it's known as **Mill Hole** and it makes for good rodeo practice.

Take-outs are available near Swisshome just below the confluence with Lake Creek, but most boaters continue to Tide and some good surf there. More Class I and II water continues to **Red Hill** rapid just above Tide. This is one of the best surf waves around, with a huge wave along center left. Skirt the wave along the right if you wish; look for a return eddy along the left for more surf attempts. At high water the turbulent eddy line can make reaching the wave challenging. Take out at Tide or continue downstream for more Class II water, taking out at Mapleton. There are a few more Class II rapids below Tide, beginning with **Davis** rapid in about a mile, followed by a second rapid 0.3 mile later. The stream gage is 1.5 miles downstream near Brickerville, along the right. Knowles Creek enters on the left at a bridge roughly 3.3 miles beyond the gage, a cue that the Mapleton access is coming up on the right.

Section 4: Mapleton to Pacific Ocean

Class: FW	Recommended flow: Tidal	Miles: 20

From Mapleton to the Pacific Ocean, the Siuslaw River is tidal. Paddlers should consult tidal charts for flow direction and be aware that upstream winds can be strong near the bay. Like other tidal rivers, the lower Siuslaw is well suited to sea kayaks and canoes. The lower reaches are popular with drift boaters, since they hold the best fishing. Chinook salmon run here from September through December. The salmon follow the clear water of Lake Creek upstream, and cutthroat trout hover in the upper river. Always be alert for anglers and stay away from where they are working the river.

Because the tidal stretch makes for slow floats, paddlers must allow more time to complete any run within this section. Do not plan on making more than 10 miles in a given day. Multiple access areas allow you to choose from a variety of put-in and take-out sites.

The river grows much larger below Lake Creek, but it still contains brushy banks and some sharp bends. Wood collects in places, so keep alert for wood hazards.

75 Smith River System, California and Oregon
North, Middle, South, Main, and Creeks

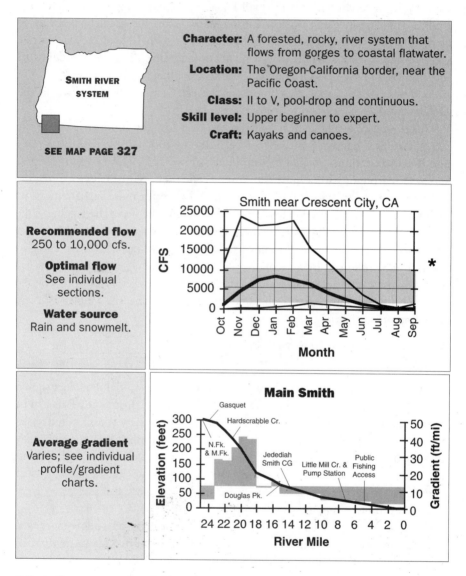

Character: A forested, rocky, river system that flows from gorges to coastal flatwater.

Location: The Oregon-California border, near the Pacific Coast.

Class: II to V, pool-drop and continuous.

Skill level: Upper beginner to expert.

Craft: Kayaks and canoes.

SMITH RIVER SYSTEM

SEE MAP PAGE 327

Recommended flow
250 to 10,000 cfs.

Optimal flow
See individual sections.

Water source
Rain and snowmelt.

Smith near Crescent City, CA

CFS — Month

*

Average gradient
Varies; see individual profile/gradient charts.

Main Smith

Gasquet
Hardscrabble Cr.
N.Fk. & M.Fk.
Jedediah Smith CG
Little Mill Cr. & Pump Station
Public Fishing Access
Douglas Pk.

Elevation (feet) — Gradient (ft/mi) — River Mile

* No depth measurement available.

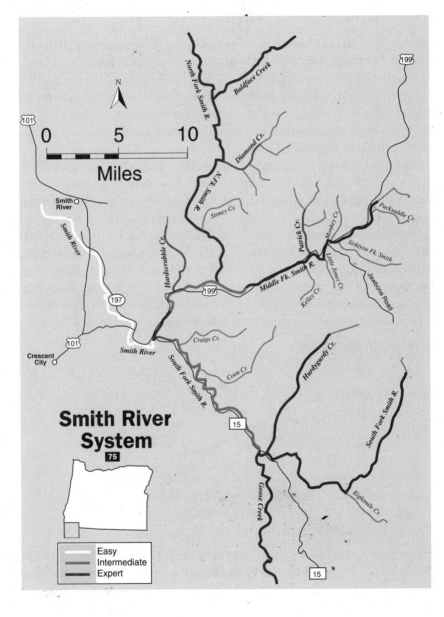

N

101

0   5   10
Miles

Smith River

Smith River

197

101

Crescent City

Smith River

North Fork Smith R.

Baldface Creek

Diamond Cr.

N. Fk. Smith R.

Stoney Cr.

Hardscrabble Cr.

199

Middle Fk. Smith R.

Patrick Cr.

Monkey Cr.

Packsaddle Cr.

Siskiyou Fk. Smith

Little Jones Cr.

Kelley Cr.

Jawbone Road

199

Craigs Cr.

Coon Cr.

South Fork Smith R.

Hurdygurdy Cr.

South Fork Smith R.

15

Goose Creek

Eightmile Cr.

15

Smith River System

75

Easy
Intermediate
Expert

Hazards: Oregon Hole Gorge, Patrick Creek Gorge, and the **South Fork Gorge** are tough sections, in order of difficulty. High water after rainstorms can make all sections (especially the gorges) more dangerous because of potentially long swims and uncertain rescue. Log obstacles are always a possibility, especially in the river's upper sections.

Overview: Named after legendary explorer Jedediah Smith, the Smith River flows mostly in California, although the headwaters of its North Fork are in Oregon. The river makes a fine boating destination in the rainy season, offering paddlers a wide variety of runs. As water levels rise, boaters can move upstream or try some of the side creeks. The Smith is the largest undammed river in California, so its flow fluctuates freely. You may run the same section many times and encounter different rapids on each trip.

With headwaters in well-managed national forests, the Smith is generally crystal-clear on all its forks, even after heavy rain. Located in a seldom-logged pygmy forest, the North Fork Smith is exceptionally clear; at times you get the feeling of being suspended in air as you float swiftly over its gravel bars.

Novice boaters may choose to run the main Smith River, rated mostly Class I with some Class II rapids. This stretch of the Smith is frequented by drift boats. Intermediate boaters can choose the Middle Fork from Gasquet to above Oregon Hole Gorge, as long as they don't miss the take-out. The slightly more difficult South Fork is another option. More experienced paddlers will find plenty of excitement in various other sections and along the river's tributaries.

SMITH RIVER, NORTH FORK

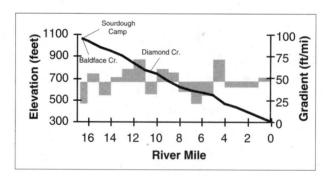

Access: To reach the Section 1 put-in, go to Crescent City, California, and take the U.S. Highway 199 turnoff toward Gasquet and the Smith River. In 2.5 miles, turn right onto Low Divide Road (Wimer Road). About 9 miles later bear right at a T-intersection with Rowdy Creek Road. Proceed uphill past Wimer Springs, over a divide, and snake downhill to a bridge. River access is available upstream on river right. To get 3 additional miles of Class IV water, continue snaking uphill for about 3 miles, then turn left on a road that goes to Baldface Creek. Drive north about 6 miles to the put-in. Only one major tributary, Cedar Creek, reaches the

North Fork between these put-ins, so if the river is runnable at the normal put-in, it's runnable at Baldface Creek.

The North Fork joins the Middle Fork Smith River 13 miles downstream. Paddlers can take out on the left above the confluence, but this involves a long carry to the road and inconvenient parking. It is easier to continue another mile to a good take-out near the Gasquet store on U.S. Highway 199. You can hire shuttle drivers through the store. Get an early start, because the 34-mile shuttle involves 21 miles of dirt road and takes nearly 2 hours.

Going with the Flow
Section 1: Upper Reaches

Class: IV	**Recommended flow:** 400 to 4,000 cfs	**Miles:** 3

The North Fork Smith River begins with a bang. Below the put-in the rapids are rocky, particularly at low flows. Expect to run several steep chutes that run against cliffs. Diamond Creek comes in on the left after 1.3 miles, significantly increasing the flow. Shortly below the confluence, the river enters a gorge containing two unnamed Class IV rapids in quick succession. The first is harder at high flows, when the second can be sneaked right. At low flows the second is harder. Class III rapids follow and continue throughout the run.

Still Creek enters on the right about 3.4 miles below the put-in. Look for the nice campsite here, a good place to stop on overnight trips in technical, low-flow seasons. A Class III+ gorge occurs 1.1 miles downstream. About 6 miles into the run, a long, curving Class IV rapid, at a landslide, contains big holes at the bottom. Peridotite Creek enters 8.5 miles down. At very low flows, you'll face a Class IV- gorge about 1.5 miles below the Peridotite Creek confluence; the gorge is Class III at moderate and high flows. Stony Creek enters on the left in 1.7 miles, and houses in Gasquet become visible.

Section 2: Above Wimer Springs to Gasquet

Class: IV to V	**Recommended flow:** 400 to 4,000 cfs	**Miles:** 14

Truly a classic Smith River run, Section 2 of the North Fork is, by itself, almost worth the long drive from population centers. The whitewater guidebook *Soggy Sneakers* says it best, gushing, "This is a run of rare isolation and beauty." The river landscape and environment inspires awe. Rare insect-eating pitcher plants grow on the banks here. At one point, you can boat into an eddy underneath an overhanging waterfall.

Generally rated at Class IV, this wilderness section of river verges on Class V at high water. Recommended flows are as follows: kayaks, 500 to 4,000 cubic feet per second; rafts, 700 to 4,000 cubic feet per second; IKs, 400 to 1,500 cubic feet per second. Flow at the take-out is about 35 percent of the flow at Jedediah Smith State Park, downstream. Flow at the put-in is about half the flow at the take-out.

SMITH RIVER, MIDDLE FORK

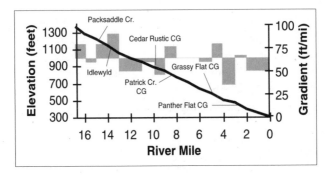

Access: To begin your trip down the Middle Fork Smith River, put in across the highway from the Idlewyld, California, maintenance station. A steep trail descends to the river, which moves swiftly past the bank. Watch out for logs throughout the run; in 1996, paddlers had to portage a log just below the put-in. Below Patrick Creek Gorge, take out near the Patrick Creek highway bridge (the Section 2 put-in), or continue on the Middle Fork Section 2, boating down to the Gasquet store and laundromat, 8.5 miles west on US 199. Paddlers put in here for Section 3; the final Middle Fork take-out is 1 mile east of Hiouchi on US 199, past the South Fork Road. Drive just beyond the tricky gorge drops, visible from the highway. Park at the next turnout, where a trail descends to the river. Walk down to the river so you recognize the take-out and avoid blundering into Oregon Hole Gorge (Section 4). Paddlers who run the gorge section can take out at Jedediah Smith State Park, just downstream along the main Smith River.

Going with the flow
Section 1: Idlewyld to Patrick Creek

Class: III+ (V)	Recommended flow: 300 to 2,000 cfs	Miles: 5 to 6

After the rigors of put-in and portage, paddlers are rewarded with tight, technical rapids on the Middle Fork Smith River. In Section 1, a scenic, narrow gorge contains some good Class III and III+ rapids, then tapers off to Class II before narrowing again into major Patrick Creek Gorge, containing four Class IV+ to V- rapids in quick succession. Boaters who wish to make a Class II run can take out at a wide trail that runs up from the river shortly before the gorge.

The Siskiyou Fork of the Smith River comes in on the left about 3 miles into the run. Shortly afterwards, the gradient flattens out and the river becomes mostly Class II water over gravel bars and boulders. The take out for the Class III+ run is an old road that leads diagonally downstream to the river. If you elect to continue into Patrick Creek Gorge, ahead, stop and scout from the road on the right bank.

Within the gorge, the first rapid is a Class IV chute with multiple holes. The second is made up of narrow slots among big rocks as the river bends right. The third is a steep drop deep in the gorge. These latter two rapids rate a IV+ or V-, but the fourth is easier.

The Middle Fork Smith might be runnable above Idlewyld, but there is no access. The scenic gorge is fairly isolated and distant from the road. Recommended flows in Section 1 are as follows: kayaks, 400 to 2,000 cubic feet per second; rafts, 600 to 2,000 cubic feet per second; IKs, 300 to 1,000 cubic feet per second. Given the narrowness of the gorge, the river quickly becomes harder here at higher flows. Flow is about 18 percent of the flow at Jedediah Smith State Park, downstream.

Section 2: Patrick Creek to Gasquet

Class: III to IV   **Recommended flow:** 400 to 2,500 cfs   **Miles:** 8.5

Many long, intricate Class III rapids and one Class IV obstacle, **Bridge Rapid,** make Section 2 of the Middle Fork one of the most enjoyable runs in the Smith River system. In his whitewater guidebook, Lars Holbek called this the "most ravaged of the three forks," since it was ruined by road construction when he visited. Vegetation has since recovered. Although the highway is often visible, paddlers are usually too busy negotiating rapids to look up at either road or scenery.

Below Patrick Creek, boulder bar rapids start almost immediately. Paddlers will need to be good at rock- and hole-dodging throughout the run. About 2.5 miles below Patrick Creek, boaters pass underneath the US 199 bridge, which marks Class IV Bridge Rapid. Scout from the left bank. The entrance drops are straightforward, but the lower part is infested with diagonal holes followed by a fast runout.

Enjoyable dodging continues for many miles. The river slows as it approaches the hamlet of Gasquet, narrowing between trees just above the Middle Fork's confluence with the North Fork Smith River, where the flow more than doubles. Big wave riding follows for another mile.

Running Section 2 is inadvisable at high flows because of brush along the banks. Recommended flows are as follows: kayaks, 500 to 2,500 cubic feet per second; rafts, 700 to 2,500 cubic feet per second; IKs, 400 to 1,500 cubic feet per second. Flow above Gasquet is about 20 percent of the flow at Jedediah Smith State Park.

Section 3: Gasquet to above Oregon Hole Gorge

Class: II+   **Recommended flow:** 250 to 5,000 cfs   **Miles:** 4.5

The Middle Fork's third run is too short to be satisfying unless you combine it with something else. The stretch of river from Gasquet to the Oregon Hole Gorge is moderate whitewater, most of it close to US 199. The highway is almost always visible from the river, and paddlers must propel themselves over flatwater stretches. Most of Section 3's rapids are simple drops through gravel bars, though there is one Class III- ledge-drop a little more than halfway into the run.

A rafter takes a wild ride through Oregon Hole Gorge. BILL TUTHILL PHOTO

Recommended flows: kayaks, 400 to 5,000 cubic feet per second; rafts, 600 to 5,000 cubic feet per second; IKs, 250 to 2,500 cubic feet per second. The flow in Section 3 is about 55 percent of the flow at Jedediah Smith State Park.

Section 4: Oregon Hole Gorge

Class: IV+	Recommended flow: 250 to 3,000 cfs	Miles: 1.5

Most paddlers combine the **Oregon Hole Gorge** run with the run from Gasquet, although you could combine it with the **South Fork Gorge** if you like doing a lot of shuttling. Many people take out at Jedediah Smith State Park along the main Smith River, or at a free boat access area just below the state park.

Oregon Hole Gorge contains sometimes-intense whitewater, though it is close to US 199. At low water, the gorge contains several distinct drops with sticky holes, then a bigger drop followed by foamy whitewater surging towards a big rock on the right. A smaller rock plugs the left exit. After this drop, the big action is over. At high water, many large waves refract off the rock walls, with huge holes everywhere. A swim might continue the entire length of the gorge. Moreover, when water is high the weather is usually bad, making everything seem worse than it is.

Recommended flows are as follows: kayaks, 500 to 3,000 cubic feet per second; rafts, 700 to 3,000 cubic feet per second; IKs, 250 to 1,000 cubic feet per second. Flow is about 55 percent of the flow at Jedediah Smith State Park.

SMITH RIVER, SOUTH FORK

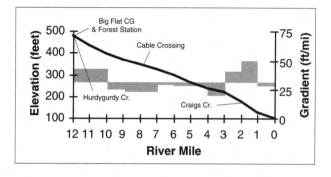

Access: To reach the South Fork Smith River, turn right onto South Fork Road off US 199 about 1 mile east of Hiouchi. Cross the Middle and South forks, then turn left and drive upriver about 1 mile. A large roadside pullout has trails leading down to the river, on the left; this is the take-out for Section 1. Walk down to the river so you can recognize the take-out and avoid blundering into South Fork Gorge. To reach the put-in, drive about 10 more miles upstream. At the third bridge crossing (High Bridge, leading to river right), park and lower your boats on a rope from the bridge. Other bridges along the way make alternate put-ins and shorten the run.

To run the South Fork Gorge, put in at the take-out described for Section 1 of the South Fork, or combine this run with the Class II to III South Fork run, making a long day. Take out at Jedediah Smith State Park along the main Smith River, or at a free boat access area shortly below the park.

Going with the flow
Section 1: High Bridge to above South Fork Gorge

Class: II to III	Recommended flow: 400 to 3,000 cfs	Miles: 12

The upper reaches of the South Fork Smith River make a pretty run that is marred in places by roadcuts. Paddlers get plenty of Class II action here, plus several Class III rapids. Aside from the main Smith River and the Middle Fork below Gasquet, Section 1 of the South Fork is the stretch most likely to have enough water to run, even if there hasn't been recent rain.

Watch for a Class III gravel bar rapid that flows straight into a large rock shortly after the put-in. Gordon Creek enters on the right after 2.7 miles. Rock Creek comes in on the left after 5.2 miles. Just above the first downstream bridge (6.3 miles below the put-in) is a long, Class III boulder garden. Coon Creek enters on the right 2.2 miles below this bridge. About 1.5 miles farther is a steep Class III waterfall, the most dramatic rapid on this run. Look for Craigs Creek on the right about 1.5 miles below the fall; the creek marks the take-out just ahead.

The South Fork Smith is runnable above the normal put-in, but the highest access point is only 2 miles farther, where Gasquet–Orleans Road turns away from the river for the last time. Flow is about 45 percent of that at Jedediah Smith State Park, downstream.

Section 2: South Fork Gorge

Class: V   **Recommended flow:** 250 to 3,000 cfs   **Miles:** 1.5

The turbulent South Fork Gorge is harder than Oregon Hole Gorge, although most guidebooks rate them the same. Not only is it longer, but the rapids are more constricted and the currents less friendly. By the time water has risen high enough for rafting, it has already started getting pushy here. Before committing to the gorge, climb down from the roadside pullout that serves as the take-out for Section 1 and scout all the rapids. One of them, called **Good Luck**, is a steep waterfall between a huge boulder and the canyon wall. This rapid is the crux of the run for rafts, because it is so narrow.

Recommended flows are as follows: kayaks, 500 to 3,000 cubic feet per second; rafts, 1,500 to 3,000 cubic feet per second; IKs, 250 to 800 cubic feet per second. Flow is about 45 percent of the flow at Jedediah Smith State Park.

OTHER SMITH DRAINAGE TRIBUTARIES AND RUNS

North Fork, Horse Creek to Wimer Road Put-In: Class IV, 9.6 miles. Reach this run from the Winchuck River valley by heading up Oregon Highway 896 then driving 23 miles on dirt roads. The put-in requires 1 mile of hiking. The gradient averages 83 feet per mile until Baldface Creek, where it falls to 51 feet per mile.

Baldface Creek, Frantz Meadow to Wimer Road Put-In: Class V, 12 miles. Reach the put-in by driving on four-wheel-drive roads past the regular North Fork put-in, carrying gear and craft 1.5 miles in. Sectional gradients in feet per mile are as follows: 120, 115, 120, 95, 150, 125, 120, and 115, dropping to 51 at the North Fork confluence.

Diamond Creek, End of Dirt Road to Gasquet: Class IV, 15.3 miles. Reach the put-in by driving on four-wheel-drive roads past the regular North Fork put-in. Sectional gradients above the North Fork confluence are 100, 80, 125, and 105 feet per mile.

Middle Fork, from Knopki Creek Bridge: Class IV, gradient 66 feet per mile. Paddlers can begin the Middle Fork run a mile above Idlewyld. To reach the put-in, drive to where a dirt road leaves US 199, crosses Griffith Creek, and winds to a bridge over the Middle Fork Smith River.

Patrick Creek, Bridge at Forks to Mouth of Creek: Class IV, 3.2 miles. Follow the gravel road along Patrick Creek for about 4 miles to where the West and East forks of the creek meet. Take out at the US 199 bridge. Sectional gradients are 150, 125, 120, and 104 feet per mile.

Hardscrabble Creek, End of Road to U.S. Highway 199: Class V (P), 4.9 miles. Access this difficult run by turning south off the Wimer Road shuttle route, which crosses this creek higher up. Sectional gradients are 150, 210, 170, 190, and 165 feet per mile.

South Fork, Island Lake Trail to South Kelsey Trail: Class V (P), 15.9 miles. Turn south off US 199 onto Jawbone Road, then proceed on dirt roads past Hurdy-Gurdy Butte, and carry craft and gear 1.5 miles. Sectional gradients are 180, 200, 185, 185, 140, 175, 132, 105, 215, 175, 125, 90, 75, 65, 55, 65, and 60 feet per mile.

South Fork, South Kelsey Trail to Put-In Bridge: Class V, 6.5 miles. Reach the put-in via a 2-mile dirt road that goes east from the Gasquet–Orleans Road, about 3 miles south from its final bridge across the Smith. There's a 0.5-mile hike to the river. Sectional gradients are 60, 79, 175 (upper South Fork Gorge), then 33 feet per mile to the take-out.

Hurdy-Gurdy Creek, Upper Forks to Mouth: Class V (P), 9.5 miles. Take a dirt road going up the creek valley from the South Fork Smith River near Big Flat, past Gordon Mountain. Requires 1.5 miles of hiking. Sectional gradients are 95, 155, 205 (Devil's Gap), 150, 130, 130, 95, 120, 80, and 70 feet per mile.

Goose Creek, Rocky Saddle to Saddle Road: Class V (P), 9.9 miles. Follow dirt roads leading south from Gasquet–Orleans Road, then west from Red Mountain Road, then north. Paddler must hike 0.5 mile to the put-in. Sectional gradients are 200, 210, 210, 175, 65, 80, 125, 80, 175 (Arn's Falls), and 95 feet per mile.

Goose Creek, Saddle Road to South Fork Put-In Bridge: Class V, 5.6 miles. Take the dirt road that turns west from Gasquet–Orleans Road 2.4 miles from its final bridge across the Smith River. Sectional gradients are 50, 110, 80, 115, and 105 feet per mile.

Mill Creek: Class II. This scenic run (watch for logs) reaches the main Smith near Stout Grove. It is accessible from Crescent City via Elk Valley and Howland Hill roads.

—*Bill Tuthill*

76 Snake River
Hells Canyon Dam to Heller Bar

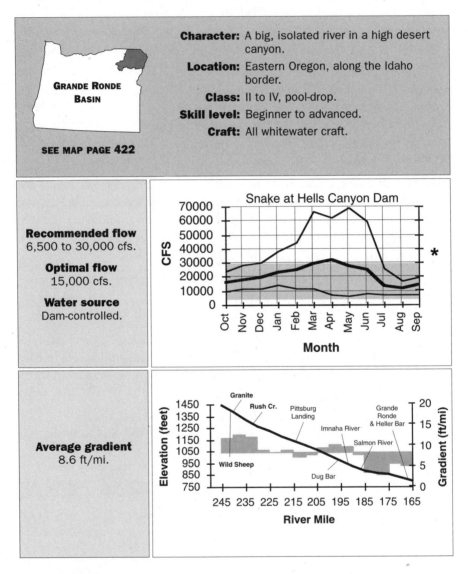

Character: A big, isolated river in a high desert canyon.

Location: Eastern Oregon, along the Idaho border.

Class: II to IV, pool-drop.

Skill level: Beginner to advanced.

Craft: All whitewater craft.

GRANDE RONDE BASIN

SEE MAP PAGE 422

Recommended flow
6,500 to 30,000 cfs.

Optimal flow
15,000 cfs.

Water source
Dam-controlled.

Snake at Hells Canyon Dam

CFS

70000
60000
50000
40000
30000
20000
10000
0

Oct Nov Dec Jan Feb Mar Apr May Jun Jul Aug Sep

*

Month

Average gradient
8.6 ft/mi.

Elevation (feet)

1450
1350
1250
1150
1050
950
850
750

Granite
Rush Cr.
Pittsburg Landing
Imnaha River
Grande Ronde & Heller Bar
Salmon River
Wild Sheep
Dug Bar

20
15
10
5
0

Gradient (ft/mi)

245 235 225 215 205 195 185 175 165

River Mile

* No depth measurement available.

Hazards: Major obstacles named **Wild Sheep** and **Granite Creek** rapids lie within the first 8 miles of the Snake River run, presenting difficult Class IV to IV+ hazards. Beyond Granite Creek, snakes, scorpions, and jet boats are larger concerns. The Snake's massive flows can create turbulent hydraulics, so boaters should wear life jackets at all times. The river has no log hazards and the water is pleasantly warm when compared to tributary streams. Jet boats commonly travel the river, creating competition for the best camps. In the future, the river permit system may be revised to help correct this inequity.

Access: Paddlers can take various routes to Hells Canyon Dam and other Snake River access points, depending on your point of origin. Most Oregon boaters drive to Baker City along Interstate 84 or other cross-state routes. From Baker City, Oregon Highway 86 leads 70 miles east through Richland and Halfway to Oxbow Dam. OR 86 continues along Pine Creek from Halfway to the dam for those with extra time in late winter and spring. From Oxbow Dam, head to the Idaho side and follow Forest Road 454 north for 23 miles to Hells Canyon Dam. The boat launch and Bureau of Land Management permit station are across the dam on the Oregon side of the river. You can find good camping facilities on the Idaho side above Oxbow Dam.

To reach Pittsburg Landing, return to Oxbow Dam along FR 454 and take Idaho Highway 71 southwest to U.S. Highway 95 at Cambridge. US 95 leads north through New Meadows and crosses the Salmon River beyond Riggins before reaching Whitebi Road. At Whitebird continue west across the Snake River to County Road 493, which leads southwest to Pittsburg Landing.

To reach Dug Bar from Oxbow Dam, return west along OR 86 to Forest Road 39, heading north. Take FR 39 across the Imnaha River, then continue north to County Road 727 (Forest Road 3955). CR 727 continues to Imnaha and beyond, remaining paved for more than 6 miles farther north. At Fence Creek, unimproved Dug Bar Road follows the Imnaha River to Cow Creek before crossing the Cactus Mountains to the Snake River and Dug Bar.

To reach Heller Bar from Oxbow Dam, follow ID 71 southeast to US 95, which heads north at Cambridge. Continue along US 95 to Lewiston, Idaho. After crossing the Snake River, take Washington Highway 129 south to Asotin. From Asotin, follow a road up the Snake River to Heller Bar.

To secure a permit, apply to Hells Canyon National Recreation Area, 3620-B Snake River Avenue, Lewiston, Idaho, 83501; (208) 743-2297.

Overview: The Snake River was once home to the Nez Perce and Shoshoni Indians. Its barren landscape, within a deep, rugged canyon, is bordered near the put-in by mountains, the Seven Devils on the Idaho side, and Summit Ridge on the Oregon side. The canyon is one of the deepest in the world, since the Seven Devils climb 8,000 feet above the river. The high ridges are only visible on occasion, blocked elsewhere by the canyon walls.

The 31 river miles above Pittsburg Landing have been protected by national Wild and Scenic River designation since 1975. In a landmark decision, Supreme Court Justice William O. Douglas chose to apply the unprecedented no-build option with respect to dam development along the Snake River. His decision prevented the flooding of the spectacular Hells Canyon stretch, and saved hundreds of archaeological sites—not to mention a few rapids.

Eastern Oregon's dry climate supports an abundance of plants and wildlife. Poison ivy is common along the upper Snake River, but it is slowly replaced by cacti as the canyon widens and drops. Black-tailed deer, mountain goats, and a variety of birds inhabit the canyon. Rattlesnakes and scorpions also reside here. Though snakes are common along the lower river, they are not directly responsible for the river's name. Instead, white explorers misinterpreted the waving motion that Shoshoni Indians used to describe themselves in sign language. The people became known as the "Snake" Indians, and their home river gained the same name.

Boaters encounter the Snake's most difficult rapids in the first 8 miles below the put-in at Hells Canyon Dam. Class II and III rapids dot the river to Pittsburg Landing, the take-out for the Wild and Scenic stretch. Below Pittsburg Landing there is only one remaining Class II+ to III rapid, near the mouth of the Imnaha River. The river then opens to rolling hills, where a drier climate attracts less wildlife. Boaters may see strong upstream winds in afternoon and evening along the lower river.

Hiking trails lead to various archaeological or historic sites from the river's many campsites. Trails also follow both sides of the canyon; the main trail is along the Idaho side of the river. Sightseers should stop at Kirkwood Historic Ranch, 6 miles above Pittsburg Landing. The ranch is a treasure-trove of historic photos, artifacts, and legends. Boaters may find Indian pictographs, wash basins, and arrowheads in many places along the Snake. These are protected by law. Take only pictures and leave only footprints.

On any Snake float, you will undoubtedly see jet boats below Wild Sheep and Granite Creek rapids. They become more prevalent near Lewiston, Idaho, which happens to be the place many are manufactured. A basic inequity regarding river permit allocation between jet boats and rafters is still unresolved. Jet boaters obtain self-issue permits for the Wild and Scenic stretch; paddlers and rafters must apply in advance and attend conservation lectures. As on the lower Rogue River (River 67), jet boats carry loads of sightseers into the canyon daily. Many would not get to see the beauty of the canyon without them, but the power boats spoil the experience for those choosing to explore wilderness on a more intimate level. We can only hope that a solution will incorporate both types of river experience.

Hells Canyon offers primo campsites.

Going with the Flow
Section 1: Hells Canyon Dam to Pittsburg Landing

Class: II to IV	**Recommended flow:** 6,500 to 30,000 cfs	**Miles:** 32.1

A designated Wild and Scenic River, the Snake River sits beneath majestic rock canyon walls at the put-in for Hells Canyon (River Mile 247). Most boaters have little time for the view—they're too busy preparing for the demanding whitewater ahead.

The first 5 miles are an easy warm-up. Battle Creek enters on the left, with a trail to historic Barton Cabin. In about 0.5 mile Wild Sheep Creek also enters on the left. The creek is the signal for boaters to stop along the left bank and scout Class IV+ Wild Sheep rapid (RM 241.2). Scout from the trail. The rapid is normally run left or right of a large hole at the top, moving toward the center to punch over the large waves at the bottom. The waves and hole become larger with increased flow.

Class IV+ Granite Creek rapid (RM 239.2) follows after 2 miles. Pull out on the left below Cache Creek to scout. The pullout is difficult, so some boaters may opt for a longer hike and easier stop at Lower Granite Creek Campsite, on the left about 0.4 mile above the rapid. A large center rock forms a formidable hole at most flows. Scout for a line through large holes and waves that change at various flows.

Below Granite Creek, only one rapid requires a scout. **Rush Creek** rapid (RM 231.5) presents Class III to III+ waves and holes. Watch for the large hole created by a central boulder at the top of the rapid, followed by big waves. Several Class II and III rapids dot the river to Pittsburg Landing (RM 214.9).

Section 2: Pittsburg Landing to Heller Bar

Class: II (III) **Recommended flow:** 10,000 to 60,000 cfs **Miles:** 46.6

Many folks consider the lower Snake River to be less scenic than the Hells Canyon portion, since the steep mountains gradually shrink to rolling, barren hills. The lower trip is usually hot, and is often windy in mornings and evenings. It also has more snakes, scorpions, and jet boats. For these reasons, more than half of all Snake River trips end at Pittsburg Landing. The nearby Grande Ronde and Salmon rivers are more popular among paddlers. Still, the lower Snake River is a good choice for novice boaters who wish to get experience on big water. Once the Salmon River enters the Snake at RM 188.3, flows can easily top 70,000 cubic feet per second. This is big water! Most novice paddlers can handle the flow, but a swim could be very long. Lost gear could leave you stranded in the middle of nowhere.

Below Pittsburg Landing the river eases to Class II water with only one Class II+ to III rapid below the confluence with the Imnaha River. **Imnaha Rapid** (RM 191.6) washes out at higher spring and early summer flows. Numerous Class II rapids keep boaters awake on an otherwise lazy float to Heller Bar. Many shorten their trip by taking out at Dug Bar (RM 196.2).

SNAKE RIVER RAPIDS AND CAMPSITES, BY RIVER MILE

Mile (RM)	Rapid/Other Feature	Class	Camp or Facility	Water	Size	Side (L or R)
247.0	Hells Canyon Dam		Boat ramp	Y		L
246.7	Cliff Mountain rapid	II				
245.2			Lamont Springs	Y	L	R
244.7	Brush Creek rapid	II	Square Beach		S	R
243.8			Rocky Point		M	R
243.7	Rocky Point rapid	II				
243.4			Chimney Bar		L	R
243.2			Warm Springs		L	R
242.3	Barton Cabin					L
242.1			Battle Creek		L	L
241.8			Sand Dunes		S	L
241.6			Birch Springs	Y	M	R
241.4			Wild Sheep	Y	L	L
241.2	Wild Sheep rapid	IV				
240.8			Rocky Bar		L	R
239.7	Hibbs Ranch		Upper Granite Creek	Y	L	R
239.6			Lower Granite Creek	Y	L	R
239.2	Granite Creek rapid	IV	Cache Creek Bar	Y	L	L
238.2	Three Creeks rapids	II to III				
238.0			Three Creeks	Y	L	R
237.7			Oregon Hole		L	L
237.2			Upper Dry Gulch		L	R
237.0			Lower Dry Gulch		L	R
236.6			Hastings	Y	M	R

Mile (RM)	Rapid/Other Feature	Class	Camp or Facility	Water	Size	Side (L or R)
236.2			Saddle Creek	Y	L	L
235.2	Upper Bernard Creek rapid	II to III				
235.0			Bernard Creek	Y	L	R
234.6	No name rapid	II				
233.7	Waterspout rapid	III to IV				
233.2	Bills Creek rapid	II				
231.6	Sluice Creek rapids	II	Sluice Creek		L	L
231.5	Rush Creek rapid	III to IV	Rush Creek		L	L
229.8			Johnson Bar Landing	Y	L	R
229.6	Sheep Creek rapid	II to III				
229.4	End navigation marks		Sheep Creek	Y	L	R
229.0			Steep Creek		M	R
228.6			Yreka Bar		L	L
228.3	Eagle Nest rapid	II				
228.1			Upper Sand Creek		M	L
228.0	Sand Creek Cabin					
227.8	Willow Creek rapids	II				
227.5			Pine Bar	Y	L	L
226.5			Upper Quartz Creek		L	L
226.2			Lower Quartz Creek		L	L
225.1			Caribou Creek		L	R
224.5			Dry Gulch		L	L
224.3	Public landing strip		Big Bar		L	R
222.9	Suicide Point Trail	Hike				R
222.5			Upper Salt Creek	Y	L	L
222.4			Lower Salt Creek	Y	L	L
222.2			Two Corral		L	L
222.1			Gracie Bar		L	R
221.6			Half Moon Bar		M	R
220.9			Slaughter Gulch		L	L
220.5	Kirkwood Ranch		Historic site; emergency phone			R
220.3			Kirkwood Bar		L	R
220.0			Yankee Bar		S	L
219.6			Russell Bar		L	L
218.9	Middle Kirby rapid	II to III				
218.7			Kirby Creek Resort			R
218.2			Cat Gulch		M	R
217.0			Corral Creek	Y	L	R
216.4			Fish Trap Bar		L	L
216.3	Upper Pittsburg Lndng		Landing; Wild & Scenic section ends		S, T	L R
216.2	Klopton Creek Lndng		Landing; road access		S	R
215.7			Silver Shed		L	L
214.9	Pittsburg Landing		Landing; road access	Y	L	R
214.8	Pittsburg Adminis.		Emergency phone			
213.8	L. Pleasant Vlly rapid	II to III				
213.7			Pleasant Valley	Y	M	R
212.4			Davis Creek		M	L
211.8			McCarty Creek		M	L
210.8			Big Canyon	Y	L	R

continued on next page

Mile (RM)	Rapid/Other Feature	Class	Camp or Facility	Water	Size	Side (L or R)
210.5			Somers Ranch		S	L
210.4			Lower Big Canyon		S	R
210.1			Somers Creek		L	L
209.8			Camp Creek		L	L
209.4			Tryon Creek	Y	L	L
208.3			Lookout Creek		L	L
205.3	Copper Bar & Resort		Special use permit campground			
204.4			Bob Creek		L	L
202.9			Wolf Creek	Private	S	R
202.0			Bar Creek		L	L
199.1			Deep Creek	Y	M	L
198.5			Robinson Gulch		L	L
198.3			Dug Creek	Y	S	L
196.7	Nez Perce Crossing		Interpretive site			
196.6	Dug Bar Landing		Road access		M	L
196.2	Dug Bar		Road access		M	L
195.3			Warm Springs	Private	L	R
195.2	Warm Springs rapid	II to III				
194.1			Zigzag		S	R
193.2			Divide Creek	Y	L	R
192.4			China Bar		L	L
191.9	Mountain Chief Mine		Mine tunnel & trail			
191.7			Imnaha		M	L
191.6	Imnaha rapid	I to III; gone at high flows				
191.4			Eureka Bar		L	L
190.4			Knight Creek	Y	L	L
188.3			Salmon Mouth		L	R
188.0			Salmon Falls		L	R
187.8			Salmon Bar		L	L
184.6			Geneva Bar		L	L
183.4			Cook Creek	Y	M	L
182.0			Lower Jim Creek		L	L
181.8			Meat Hole		S	R
181.5			Cactus Bar		M	R
181.1			Uppr Cottonwood Crk	Y	L	R
180.9			Lowr Cottonwood Crk	Y	L	R
180.2	Scenic area boundary					
179.8			Upper Cougar Bar		M	R
178.6	Historic cabin		Museum; Coon Hollow Campground		L	L
178.2		Hike	Cochran Island		L	L
178.1			Garden Creek		S	L
177.5			Upper Cache Creek		L	L
176.9	Cache Creek Ranch		Day use; visitor center	Y		
176.8			Lower Cache Creek		S	L
176.0	Oregon/Washington border		State & national forest boundary			
168.4	Heller Bar		Landing; road access	BLM		L

77 Squaw Creek
Sisters to Deschutes River

DESCHUTES BASIN

SEE MAP PAGE **418**

Character: A low-water run through a narrow, secluded desert canyon.

Location: Central Oregon, near Bend.

Class: II+ to IV (V+, P), continuous and pool-drop.

Skill level: Intermediate to advanced and expert.

Craft: Whitewater kayaks and canoes.

Recommended flow
80 to 300 cfs.

Optimal flow
150 cfs.

Water source
Snowmelt and springs; diverted.

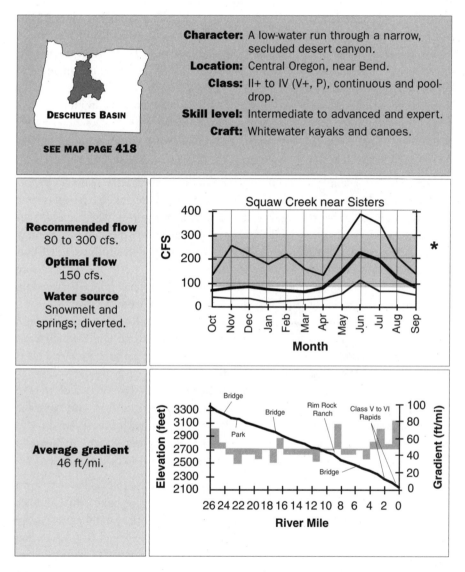

Squaw Creek near Sisters

Average gradient
46 ft/mi.

* *No depth measurement available.*

Hazards: Section 1 rates a Class II+ because of fence hazards and log portages. Most of the creek is continuous Class II water, but paddlers must keep alert. Be skilled enough to pull off the creek and/or maintain a motionless position on the water upon encountering various limbos or obstacles. Section 1 contains some Class III rapids near the take-out and a few Class II+ rapids at higher water. Make sure you have plenty of time to make it to the take-out, since Ron Killen and I enjoyed a cold, unexpected night in the basalt canyon after putting in late. We heard several rattlesnakes while trying to hike out along the left bank, where thick brush and vertical walls forced an overnight stay.

Section 2 contains more Class III water with a long stretch of continuous Class V and V+ water in the last 2 miles before the confluence with the Deschutes River. Scout or portage along the left bank. Rattlesnakes are common along Squaw Creek; take your snake-bite kit!

Access: There is a small park on the east end of the town of Sisters, along Oregon Highway 126. Squaw Creek runs on its southern end. One possible put-in is near the arched bridge across the creek at the park. A better put-in, which avoids two fence portages as well as farmland near Sisters, is 5 miles downstream at the Forest Road 2610 bridge. To reach the bridge or other access areas follow Wilt Road (Forest Road 900) northeast from Sisters off U.S. Highway 20 (Oregon Highway 126) about 1 mile beyond Indian Ford Creek and turn onto FR 2610, heading southeast. FR 2610 crosses Squaw Creek roughly 1 mile from the turn.

To reach midstream access points, continue along Wilt Road another 8.5 miles to Forest Road 63. Follow FR 63 to unimproved Forest Road 6360, which leads to an unofficial campground and ford across the creek in about 2.5 miles. This is the last access to the creek above Lake Billy Chinook.

Paddlers who continue their float down the Deschutes River may wish to take out at the bridge at Lake Billy Chinook. To get there, return to and continue northeast along FR 63. Stay straight at the intersection with Forest Road 64 to reach the bridge. Alternately, head south from Madras along Culver Highway to Gem Lane, then turn west. Gem Lane connects with FR 63 at the lake.

Overview: Squaw Creek is a small stream that enters the Deschutes River to form **Squaw Creek** rapids along the Steelhead Falls section above Lake Billy Chinook (see the Central Deschutes description for details below the confluence). Above the confluence, Squaw Creek flows through the remote Crooked River National Grasslands with hiking trails along the creek's left bank. Squaw Creek's watershed is large enough to support a year-round boating season, but most of the creek's water is diverted above the town of Sisters. The remaining flows allow boating through June, with rock-scraping levels to August. The lower creek swells with water from grazing lands (Note: Don't drink the water), small side streams, and springs. Thus the lower section can become pushy despite a slow rock-dodge in the beginning. The stream narrows to allow runs at unusually low flows. In places fallen trees and brush choke passage, but the majority of the creek is passable.

Below the FR 2630 bridge, the creek enters a wide gorge with views of newer homes along the rim. The gorge gradually narrows, opening to small ranches, above the access points along FR 6360. Sagebrush and grasslands surround the lower stretches. The lower creek suddenly narrows into a steep gorge with beautiful basalt rock formations. Metamorphic intrusions and ash layers add to the striking vistas beneath generally clear blue skies.

Going with the Flow
Section 1: Sisters to FR 6360 Bridge

Class: II+ (III)	Recommended flow: 100 to 300 cfs	Miles: 16

Squaw Creek begins at the park on the eastern side of Sisters, where an arched bridge makes an easy put-in. Below the bridge, the small creek meanders past farms and sparse residential areas with some narrow passages around brush and downed trees. Expect at least one portage around fallen trees, and be alert for fences. Above the alternate put-in at the FR 2610 bridge, paddlers will have to negotiate two fences and one wire across the stream, plus small Class II- rapids in a couple of spots.

Below FR 2610, boaters paddle 11 miles to reach the next take-out. Beautiful vistas fill the trip, with occasional newer homes along the creek. Watch for one fence and a couple of log limbos and portages in this stretch. The creek gradually enters a basalt canyon that closes in on both sides. You'll run through several small Class II rapids in the last several miles, with busy Class III drops over the last 2 miles. The road that can be seen traversing the canyon wall near Rim Rock Ranch is on private property and cannot be used for access.

As the canyon begins to open, boaters may see cattle along (and occasionally in) the creek. About 1.5 miles beyond Rim Rock Ranch watch for a fence on the left with steps built over it. This stile signals the take-out on the left at the upcoming ford. The area makes a great spot to camp if you plan on a two-day self-contained trip.

—Robb Keller

Section 2: FR 6360 Bridge to Deschutes River and Lake Billy Chinook

Class: III and IV (P)	Recommended flow: 100 to 300 cfs	Miles: 11.6

The second section of Squaw Creek is continuous Class II water with some Class III features after the first mile. Narrow slots contain numerous broach possibilities for the unwary. At low water paddlers will drag over rocks and dodge branches to the put-in, where Squaw Creek meanders along the canyon floor. At an estimated flow of only 50 cubic feet per second, the streambed is still full to its banks—though it is often as narrow as a boat length.

Watch for a tributary coming in from the right. In a few hundred yards, a gorge begins where a large vertical cliff forms an undercut headwall on a sudden

The action is fast and technical along lower Squaw Creek. RON KILLEN PHOTO

left turn. The channel along the headwall contains a log that completely blocks the channel, so you'll have to portage. High-water marks along the wall indicate that flows of 3 feet or more would make this difficult. Not far below the portage, a root ball on the right strains most of the flow, forming a serious hazard.

As paddlers progress into the gorge, both gradient and flow increase. Two trees that have fallen from the left bank lean against the right canyon wall, forcing a limbo passage. About 1 mile above the confluence with the Deschutes River is a twisting Class IV rapid. Scout and run this rapid on the left. Within the next 0.5 mile springs quickly increase the stream flow, leading to a long right bend and horizon line drop. It's time to scout! Get out on the left, since the talus slope on the right ends at a sheer wall. The scout reveals a set of Class IV entrance rapids leading into Class V ledge-drops with several slots clogged by either logs or jagged rocks. Portage this stretch by bushwhacking to a path that looks as if it might lead along the Deschutes River to the lake along the left.

At low summer flows, many of the Class IV drops downstream on the Deschutes River turn into picket fences with flows pouring through piles of boulders. These same rock piles form rapids at higher water. If run at higher levels, the Deschutes provides several Class IV- rapids before the long paddle to the take-out on Lake Billy Chinook. Take out on the left at the bridge over the lake.

—*Gus Stinstrom*

78 Sweet Creek

Beaver Creek Trailhead to Homestead Trailhead

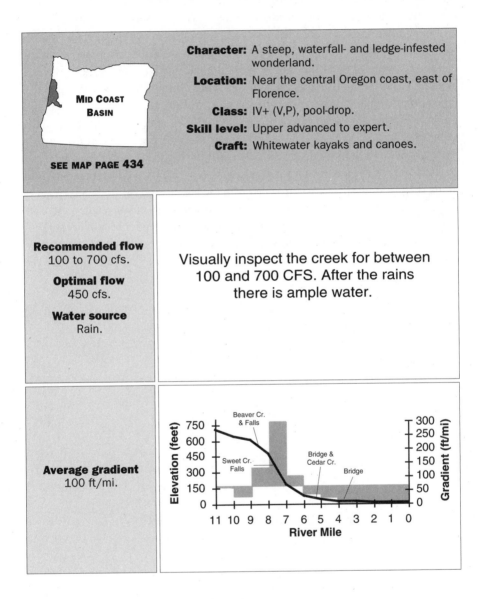

MID COAST BASIN

SEE MAP PAGE **434**

Character: A steep, waterfall- and ledge-infested wonderland.

Location: Near the central Oregon coast, east of Florence.

Class: IV+ (V,P), pool-drop.

Skill level: Upper advanced to expert.

Craft: Whitewater kayaks and canoes.

Recommended flow
100 to 700 cfs.

Optimal flow
450 cfs.

Water source
Rain.

Visually inspect the creek for between 100 and 700 CFS. After the rains there is ample water.

Average gradient
100 ft/mi.

Hazards: First Screen is a difficult Class V rapid at the Sweet Creek–Beaver Creek confluence. Scouting is mandatory. Paddler must portage around 90-foot **Sweet Creek Falls,** which is preceded by rapids. Scout before attempting to run this stretch! Throughout the creek run, many ledges have shallow landings with pinning potential.

Access: From Mapleton, east of Florence on Oregon Highway 126, drive 0.2 mile east over the Siuslaw River and turn south onto Sweet Creek Road. Continue on Sweet Creek Road along tidal water, then head up Sweet Creek itself to Homestead Trailhead. This is the take-out (or put-in if you are only interested in running the last 300 yards).

For upper access continue up Sweet Creek Road another 0.5 mile to Sweet Creek Falls Trailhead, another possible access. Do a quick spot-check of the falls area by driving 0.4 mile farther to a pullout on a faint left bend and peer down to the falls and lead-in drops. Continue another 0.2 mile to a bridge at Wagon Road Trailhead, another put-in.

To reach the uppermost put-in, drive upstream from the bridge toward Beaver Creek Trailhead, stopping to scout First Screen from a pullout on a hard right bend 0.1 mile below the gate in the road. Park at the trailhead and put in under the bridge.

Overview: When Dan Coyle, a fellow kayaker, first spoke of Sweet Creek, it seemed unlikely that anything so promising existed right under our noses. He was right, and we who championed Lake Creek were wrong. This little stream may be short, but it has quality.

Sweet Creek is the boating video game of midcoast Oregon. The action is fast paced, and when the game is over it only takes a minute to walk back up and do it again, and again, and again. There are more than 2 miles of runnable stream, but the creek is not really a "run"; it is more like a boater's playground. Park at the paved parking area, walk 5 minutes to the gorge on an immaculate gravel hiking trail, then navigate the series of seven 6- to 10-foot drops leading back to your car. The only difference between real life and a video adventure is that if you miss a critical move on this screen, the toll will be much greater than a quarter or two. Despite its advanced character, Sweet Creek lives up to its name.

Certain of the creek's traits are not unlike a waterpark ride, right down to the walkway built into bedrock canyon walls for your scouting, gawking, and photographic pleasure. In the heart of the canyon, you may stand on a steel path almost directly above one of the best drops, with full spitball access to your boating buddies below. You'll watch friends play around like children in a wave pool. This is not to say there are no worries: you'll have to do some careful scouting and recognize that one person's playground is another's battlefield. Be on the lookout for Class V obstacles, pin spots, and the unrunnable Sweet Creek Falls, not to mention the wood. Sweet Creek is fun and beautiful, but it's no free ride.

Going with the Flow

Class: IV+ (V, P)	**Recommended flow:** 100 to 700 cfs	**Miles:** 2.2

Though the last 300 yards of Sweet Creek make up the bulk of the action, the entire run is worth a taste. From the put-in at Beaver Creek Trailhead, 150 yards of fast bedrock slots lead to the first major loss of elevation. Here Sweet Creek and Beaver Creek join forces as they both drop over an 18-foot ledge, meeting in the pool at the base. This Class V rapid may be the best single drop on the run; it has been called First Screen. After running the main drop, you may find it worthwhile to hike up the bank and run the Beaver Creek variation of the falls. This side is more straightforward—and more vertical. If First Screen looks unappetizing, put in at its base or at the bridge 0.6 mile below. Some paddlers return to the take-out and do the set of drops again, since the mile of river leading to the portage around Sweet Creek Falls is easier Class II water.

A bridge about 0.6 mile downstream of First Screen offers possible river access. About 0.5 mile below the bridge, a series of small ledges leads to 90-foot (unrunnable!) Sweet Creek Falls. Take out above the ledges on the left and follow the hiking trail around the falls to continue downstream. The falls' second and third tiers have been run with success, but not style. Below the portage, the river travels through a series of log-jams and ledges. When the trail becomes suspended from the canyon wall, stop and scout on the right. This is the start of the lower fun section, ending in 300 yards at the take-out. Again, some paddlers walk back up and repeat the series of drops and slides. Remember to scout carefully before you commit, since there are pin spots and shallow landings on several of these ledges. At higher flows hydraulics become a serious issue.

—Eric Brown

79 Thomas Creek
Hill Creek to South Santiam River

Character: A run under covered bridges on a basalt-lined stream.

Location: West-central Oregon, near Albany.

Class: I to III (IV), continuous and pool-drop.

Skill level: Beginner to advanced.

Craft: Whitewater kayaks and canoes.

MIDDLE
WILLAMETTE
BASIN

SEE MAP PAGE 436

Recommended flow
400 to 1,000 cfs.

Optimal flow
700 cfs.

Water source
Rain and snowmelt.

Average gradient
35 ft/mi.

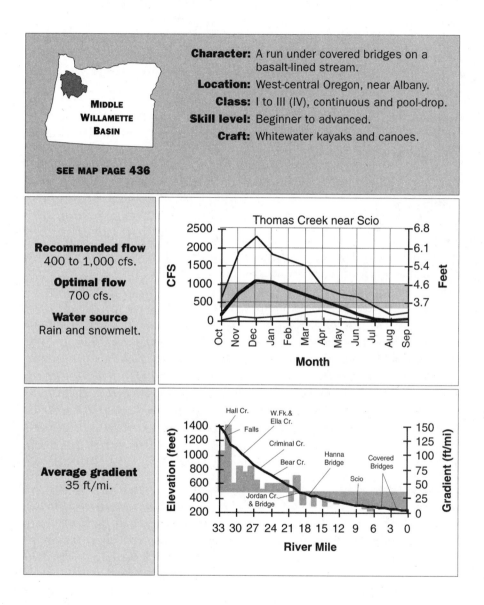

Hazards: Upper Thomas Creek contains steep Class III water with a few Class IV to IV+ drops. Though roads cut along the upper creek like spaghetti on a plate, access is difficult in most places. Portage the old Jordan Dam near Jordan. You'll need to know where you are if you put in above the Hall Creek confluence, since a 40-foot waterfall lies just below the uppermost access point. Lower Thomas Creek (Section 2) offers wonderful floats along Class I and I+ water and under three covered bridges. Banks along the entire creek are brushy, with currents. Paddlers must have good boat-handling skills.

Access: From Interstate 5 between Salem and Albany, Exit 238 intersects with the Jefferson Highway (Oregon Highway 226), heading east. Follow the Jefferson Highway across the Santiam River to Jefferson. Continue east along Jefferson–Scio Drive to Scio and possible access sites there. Two covered bridges lie below Scio; one is to the south along Kelly Road; the other is south along Robinson Drive to Goar Road, then south to where it crosses the creek. From Scio, OR 226 leads east to Richardson Gap Road. Take this road north to the creek for possible access. Farther east along OR 226, Bridge Drive leads south before the highway crosses the creek; there's a stream gage just upstream of the bridge. Hanna Bridge is located another 2.5 miles beyond the OR 226 crossing. Turn south from OR 226 to reach the bridge.

Reach upper access areas from Jordan, farther east along OR 226. Thomas Creek Drive leads east to several spur roads that head south to access bridges. A common take-out for the upper run is a bridge 4.6 miles along Thomas Creek Road. Beyond this access, the creek climbs. Bridges below Bear Creek and above Criminal Creek are possible access points.

Farther upstream, paddlers will find little access until they reach Hall Creek. Follow the north side of Thomas Creek for 9.8 miles from Jordan. Watch for an intersection on the left at the top of the ridge. At the next road to the right, descend to the river below Hall Creek. Another road leads to an access on Hall Creek near a 40-foot waterfall. Be sure to put in below the drop.

Overview: Upper Thomas Creek is remote, and its banks are steep with little access except at bridges. Roads are gravel and dirt along the upper creek. Several branches loop and intertwine throughout the area, evidence of logging activity. The most difficult gradients and water lie in the 5 miles of creek above the Criminal Creek confluence. The upper creek contains mostly Class III water with two Class IV drops and a portage at Jordan Dam.

The lower creek is a lovely float on Class I to I+ water with several historic covered bridges. The area is thick with brush. The creek banks sharply in a couple places. Current can push paddlers toward the outside shore, so keep alert as you float. Paddlers can choose from several access points to make a trip of desired length. One possible trip goes from Shimanek Bridge above Scio to Jefferson Boat Ramp near Jefferson, continuing on the South Santiam River below the Thomas Creek confluence.

Though I have not seen the creek since the floods of 1996-1997, neighboring streams were hammered by the high water. Be alert for new debris in the river.

Going with the Flow
Section 1: Below Hall Creek to Hanna Bridge

Class: III (IV+, P)	**Recommended flow:** 400 to 900 cfs	**Miles:** 13.2

Paddlers are sure to see clearcuts along the banks of Thomas Creek, evidence of past logging activity here. The upper creek pool-drops its way to Hanna Bridge, with most of the rapids located above Bear Creek. The drops are mainly Class III, with more difficult rapids in places.

The first Class IV drop is about 0.5 mile below the upper access, where large boulders force the creek into the right bank. Scout or portage left. This area is likely to collect debris, so watch for wood. Class II and III drops entertain boaters for the next 3 miles. Then comes **Criminal** rapid, named after the creek nearby. Here Thomas Creek narrows and banks sharply right along a steep wall on the left.

The last major rapid in the upper stretch is a ledge-hole that extends across the creek. This Class IV drop, known as **The Bear,** is near the creek of the same name. Scout it ahead of time, since it is visible from the road on the drive upstream. At higher flows this could be a terminal hole. Scout or portage left.

Beyond The Bear, the creek eases for 0.5 mile to the bridge below Bear Creek, a possible take-out. From here it is roughly 5 miles to Jordan or 6.8 miles to Hanna Bridge. The entire stretch is easier Class II+ water with horizon line drops that have clear routes. Portage **Jordan Dam** and the following chute near Jordan; the creek drops 20 feet at the old dam site. A series of fun rapids lead to the access at Hanna Bridge. Take out here or continue to Section 2.

Section 2: Hanna Bridge to South Santiam River (Covered Bridges)

Class: I to I+	**Recommended flow:** 500 to 1,000 cfs	**Miles:** 17.3+

Lower Thomas Creek drops in gradient and is far more manageable for beginner and intermediate paddlers. The lower creek passes under three historic covered bridges as it weaves its way to the South Santiam River. A good day trip is from Hanna Bridge to the lower covered bridge. Though there are no particularly difficult rapids, banks are brushy and current can sweep paddlers into brush in places. Be alert for debris in the creek.

The creek meanders by an island below some powerlines and above Shimanek Bridge (River Mile 12). The town of Scio (RM 8.8) roughly divides this section; a bridge there marks the halfway point. The lower covered bridges are located at RM 4.7 and RM 2.2. Some paddlers combine this trip with a float along the Santiam River, taking out at Jefferson Boat Ramp near Jefferson.

80 Trask River
Upper North Fork to Tillamook

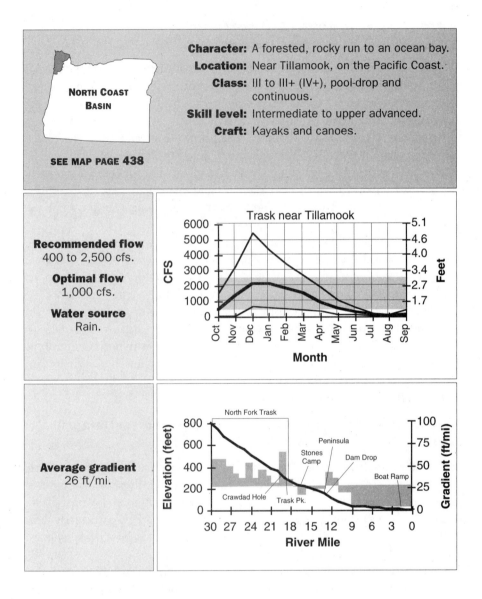

NORTH COAST BASIN

SEE MAP PAGE **438**

Character: A forested, rocky run to an ocean bay.
Location: Near Tillamook, on the Pacific Coast.
Class: III to III+ (IV+), pool-drop and continuous.
Skill level: Intermediate to upper advanced.
Craft: Kayaks and canoes.

Recommended flow
400 to 2,500 cfs.

Optimal flow
1,000 cfs.

Water source
Rain.

Average gradient
26 ft/mi.

Trask near Tillamook

CFS: 6000, 5000, 4000, 3000, 2000, 1000, 0
Feet: 5.1, 4.6, 4.0, 3.4, 2.7, 1.7

Month: Oct, Nov, Dec, Jan, Feb, Mar, Apr, May, Jun, Jul, Aug, Sep

North Fork Trask
Peninsula
Stones Camp
Dam Drop
Crawdad Hole
Trask Pk.
Boat Ramp

Elevation (feet): 800, 600, 400, 200, 0
Gradient (ft/mi): 100, 75, 50, 25, 0
River Mile: 30, 27, 24, 21, 18, 15, 12, 9, 6, 3, 0

Hazards: The upper North Fork Trask River contains continuous Class II and III whitewater with a handful of Class III+ pool-drop rapids along the way. Above the confluence with the South Fork Trask, **Crawdad Hole** presents a Class IV+ drop. Portage right or run along the middle right channel. Class III **Dam Drop** occurs just after The Peninsula, where the river funnels into a turbulent passage between jagged rock walls. Always be alert for log hazards and courteous toward anglers.

Access: From U.S. Highway 101 south of Tillamook, cross the Trask River and head west on Long Prairie Road. Taking the first left along Long Prairie Road leads you to Lower Trask Boat Launch. An even lower access area is located at Carnahan Park, off the Netarts Highway on the west side of Tillamook. The park is on the eastern bank of the river (river right), south of the bridge.

Reach upstream access by heading back along Long Prairie Road across the river to Trask River Road. Take this road east along the north bank of the river to the North Fork–South Fork confluence. Many access areas and roadside pullouts are available along the way.

North Fork Trask Road leads left along the North Fork Trask River. Follow it to a pullout near the upper forks in roughly 8 miles. The road was washed out during the 1996 floods but has since been repaired. You'll want to take a vehicle with good clearance and four-wheel drive, since areas of rough dirt can get muddy during boating season.

You can reach an access near the mouth of the North Fork Trask by taking the right fork in the road near the confluence, following it across North Fork to a good take-out on the south shore.

Overview: The Trask River flows through a steep coastal canyon and ends in Tillamook Bay. The canyon is heavily wooded with a mixture of evergreen and hardwood trees. In fall, the river corridor is ablaze with color as leaves from deciduous trees turn brilliant autumn shades. Mist-covered mountains rise sharply from the valley, giving paddlers breathtaking views on the drive up. Most of the river's commonly traveled stretches are shaded by the folded hills and tree-lined banks. Many waterfalls pour into the flow.

Anglers have long known about the Trask River. Yearly runs of chinook salmon (also known as Trask hogs) make their way up the North Fork Trask to spawn. Boaters may see 30-pound fish jump the rapids or spook upstream as they drop into pools from above. The size and majesty of these fish became apparent to me when I saw one shoot upstream onto the bank. It forcefully flipped itself back into the water after several pounding attempts. Other creatures live here, too. On one trip we witnessed a raccoon being attacked by a large cat, either a mountain lion or bobcat. The poor animal put up quite a fight before playing its necessary role in the food chain.

The Trask is a favorite day-trip destination among Portland-area boaters. Most run it during the rainy season from late October through early June. Flows vary depending upon rain. Even advanced boaters will enjoy the continuous technical North Fork or the challenging, rocky drops of the lower river. Intermediate paddlers should avoid Crawdad Hole and may wish to portage Dam Drop. Beginners will enjoy stretches below Dam Drop to Tillamook.

Going with the Flow
Section 1: Upper North Fork to South Fork

Class: III to III+	Recommended flow: 400 to 1,500 cfs	Miles: 8

The upper North Fork Trask River begins with continuous Class II+ rapids below the confluence with the Middle Fork. (We've eyed the Middle Fork for some time, wondering about a high-water run from Barney Reservoir. Someday . . .) Rapids continue for nearly 3 miles; some of them are steeper Class III ledge-drops. The first river-wide rock ledge drops 4 feet. Below it, the river continues its steady action, pooling in places. Two more technical ledge-drops occur after about 0.5 mile. These are similar to the first rapids below the put-in, with technical drops over rock ledges followed by eddies.

Pool-drop rapids dot the river beyond the third rocky drop, but are less dramatic. A steady pace of smaller boulder gardens, ledges, and waves leads to the access area above the confluence with the South Fork Trask. This stretch is lots of fun for intermediate paddlers! Take out on the left above the bridge, or continue along Section 2.

Section 2: North Fork to Cedar Creek Boat Ramp

Class: III (IV+)	Recommended flow: 500 to 1,500 cfs	Miles: 11

The North Fork Trask combines with the South Fork in less than a mile. The same continuous Class II to II+ rapids—ledges, technical chutes, and boulder gardens—continue along this stretch. This technical stretch is fun for intermediate paddlers, but it contains a Class IV+ ledge-drop known as Crawdad Hole (River Mile 18.9) above Trask Park. Scout the rapid on the drive up at a pullout on a left bend in the road, about 0.5 mile above Trask Park. Those wishing to portage the drop should flag the area just upstream of the right bend in the river. Those running the drop should choose the central right chute, since the larger far left chute is badly undercut on both sides. The narrow rocky chute drops 8 feet into a narrow, converging slot. It is easy to get shoved into the left wall by the converging water. If in doubt, remember that the portage here is easy.

In less than 0.5 mile, paddlers will see Trask Park and the access there on the right. The river continues with Class II water to Stones Camp, in 2 miles; look for the boat ramp on the right, a possible take-out. Upper Peninsula Boat Launch follows in 1.5 miles, with Lower Peninsula Launch just downstream. Both are on the right.

About a mile below Upper Peninsula Launch, watch for Dam Drop rapid (RM 12.4). It's a narrow, turbulent chute within jagged basalt rock. Scout or portage on the right. Dam Drop marks the last of the big drops above Tillamook.

The author lines up for Crawdad Hole on the upper Trask River. JEFF JACOB PHOTO

Downstream access areas are available at Cedar Creek Boat Ramp (RM 11) on the right and Loren's Drift Boat Ramp (RM 9.5) on the left. Class I water soon changes to flatwater. The gradient drops to less than 4 feet per mile before the river reaches Tillamook Bay. Take extra time to paddle this flat stretch along farms and grazing land. Between RM 4 and RM 2, houses line the banks. A good take-out is on the left at Lower Trask Boat Ramp, above the US 101 bridge. The last take-out before you reach the bay is on the western end of Tillamook on river right at Carnahan Park.

81 Tualatin River

Tigard to Willamette River

Character: An easily accessible run with a rural feel.

Location: Near Tillamook, on the Pacific Coast.

Class: I on upper section; II on last 3 miles.

Skill level: Beginner to Intermediate.

Craft: Kayaks and canoes.

LOWER WILLAMETTE BASIN

SEE MAP PAGE 430

Recommended flow
500 to 5,000 cfs.

Optimal flow
700 cfs.

Water source
Rain.

Average gradient
1.7 ft/mi.

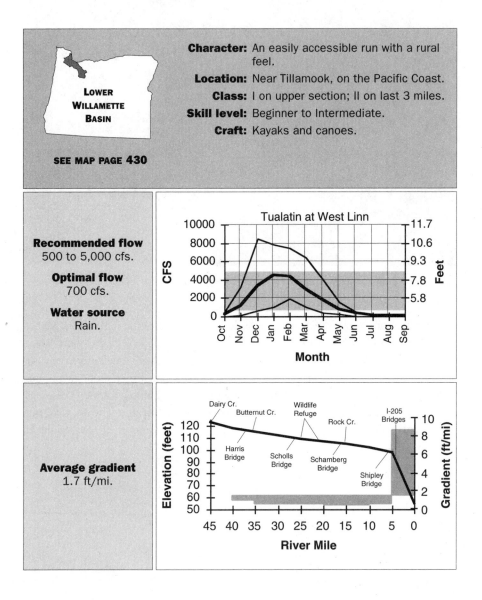

Hazards: There are few hazards at recommended flows on the upper Tualatin River. The lower river contains a weir that should be run on the right and a couple of Class I+ rapids that lead to a long Class II to II+ rapid above Willamette Park, at the Willamette River confluence.

Access: From Interstate 205 near West Linn, take the 10th Street exit and head south on 10th to a T-intersection. Turn right and go 2 blocks to 12th Street, then turn left. Follow 12th to Willamette Park and the river. This is the final take-out. To reach the put-in for the lower river, follow the road back out of the park to Borland Road, heading west. Borland and Stafford roads intersect at Wankers Corner, where there is a store, bar, and gas station. Turn right (east) onto Stafford Road and follow it over the bridge to a road that leads down on the right. A short distance down this road, a pullout provides good access to the river.

Upper river access can be had at several bridges and parks. Common put-in spots are Cooks Park in Tigard, Scholls Road, Schamberg Bridge, and the Oregon Highway 210 bridge. There are endless other possibilities; consult a Portland-area roadmap to find other access locations.

Overview: Portland paddlers often overlook the Tualatin River since it flows between major metropolitan areas. The river provides area residents with easy access at many parks, bridges, schools, or even golf courses. Residential areas line most of the upper river, but the float has a rural feel despite its proximity to urban sprawl. Some friends and I paddled the upper river at peak flood stage during the floods of 1996, witnessing the flooding of several residences, apartments, and parks.

Vegetation is heavy along the Tualatin between developments. The upper river includes nice stretches of easy water with more seclusion than one would imagine. The lower river passes through less development, with steeper banks that shield one from residential areas in places. It also holds more hazardous and exciting water.

On the down side, the Tualatin is not the place to practice your rolls. Its water is always murky and infested with algae. Raw sewage often dumps into the river during or after heavy rains, giving the water a strange odor. Head to the local pool to practice your technique before putting on the river, and keep your mouth closed if you have to make an emergency swim.

Going with the Flow
Section 1: Scholls to Stafford Road Bridge

Class: I	Recommended flow: 1,000 to 5,000 cfs	Miles: 21

The upper Tualatin River meanders past many residential, park, and school areas. There are few hazards along this stretch , but banks are brushy between developments and the shoreline is generally muddy. The river passes beneath several bridges between Scholls and Lake Oswego. Cooks Park offers easy access on the left in Tigard, but the banks can be muddy at low water.

Watch for a diversion on the left at the entrance to Lake Oswego. The gate normally controls the level of the lake. It was dramatically breached during the

High water on the Tualatin River.

floods of 1996, bringing high water into the nice homes along the lakeshore. A road leads to the gate for alternate access. Another nice take-out for the upper flatwater stretch is just below the Stafford Road bridge, on the left.

Section 2: Stafford Road Bridge to Willamette River

Class: I+ (II)	Recommended flow: 1,000 to 5,000 cfs	Miles: 5.5

The lower Tualatin is more secluded, with lush vegetation along muddy banks. Residential areas line the river in places. Keep your eyes open for a dangerous weir along the upper middle portion of this section. Paddlers cannot see the weir from any access road. Concerned citizens who live on the left bank informed us that they have had to call 9-1-1 on several occasions when unprepared paddlers drifted over the weir. Always wear your life jacket and carry proper floatation gear in your boat if you intend to paddle this section. The weir is not a bad drop on the right side, where water slides down a rocky ramp, but the left side drops off to form a small reversal that could hold paddlers and gear at higher flows. Stay right of center.

Beyond the weir, flatwater fills the next mile. Next come some Class I+ rapids that wind down washboard ramps at bends in the river. At one ramp, a headwall greets paddlers at the bottom; the river is sharply diverted left here. This diversion signals the beginning of more difficult Class II to II+ rapids. These finish off the trip, ending at the park near the Tualatin's confluence with the Willamette River. Take out on the left.

82 Umpqua River, North Fork
Tigard to Willamette River

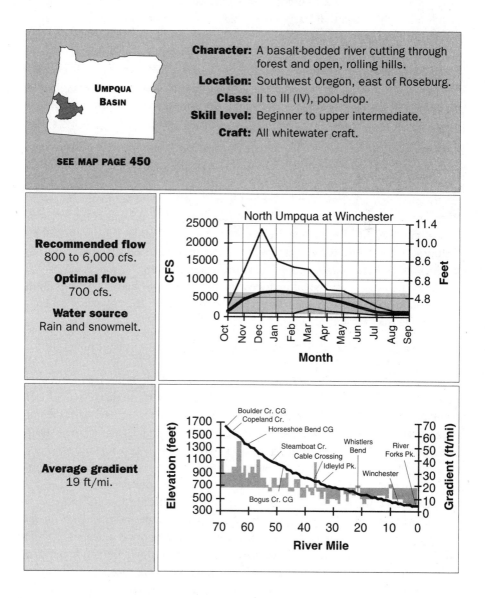

UMPQUA BASIN

SEE MAP PAGE **450**

Character: A basalt-bedded river cutting through forest and open, rolling hills.

Location: Southwest Oregon, east of Roseburg.

Class: II to III (IV), pool-drop.

Skill level: Beginner to upper intermediate.

Craft: All whitewater craft.

Recommended flow
800 to 6,000 cfs.

Optimal flow
700 cfs.

Water source
Rain and snowmelt.

Average gradient
19 ft/mi.

North Umpqua at Winchester

Boulder Cr. CG
Copeland Cr.
Horseshoe Bend CG
Steamboat Cr.
Whistlers Bend
Cable Crossing
River Forks Pk.
Idleyld Pk.
Winchester
Bogus Cr. CG

Hazards: The North Fork Umpqua River has few unusual hazards unrelated to its general classification level. **Pinball** is a Class IV- boulder garden that can potentially pin boats in narrow, technical routes. **Bathtub** contains a narrow passage at low flows, with a potentially large hole at higher flows. **Sleeper** is a turbulent rapid with large holes around a sneaky right bend. **Upper and Lower Island** rapids contain good-sized waves and wave holes at most flows. Portage **Deadline Falls** or make your mandatory scout and possible cheat along the right channel. The turbulent passage known as **The Narrows** also requires a scout or portage along the right. Logs or debris may collect in the chute, so scout the drop before committing to it.

Access: From Interstate 5 at Roseburg, drive east and south through town to take Oregon Highway 138 east along the North Fork Umpqua River. OR 138 parallels the river, leading to all upstream access sites.

Reach the river below Winchester by taking Exit 129 off I-5 and heading west. Winchester Road leads west to Wilbur–Garden Valley Road, a left at the intersection with Cleveland Road. This leads you to Hestnes Landing. Continue along Wilbur–Garden Valley Rd. to Garden Valley Road, turning left at the intersection, to reach River Forks Boat Ramp. This is the lower take-out.

Alternate access can be had by following the Oakland–Shady Highway south across the river to Winchester, where roads lead east from Page Road to the boat ramp along the river left bank.

Overview: The North Fork Umpqua River has long been a prime fishing spot for summer steelhead and spring chinook salmon. In 1988 it became known for its wildness too—the 34-mile stretch from Rock Creek to Soda Springs Dam was designated a Wild and Scenic River. The river runs west to the main Umpqua River from its origins at Maidu Lake in the Cascade Range. Evergreen trees and volcanic rock spires line the upper river; sparsely vegetated, rolling hills and grazing sheep line the lower reaches. On hot days the upper river country provides ample shade from the blazing sun, but boaters on the lower river get better suntans (or sunburns) and more relaxing floats. Riverside trees change from evergreen to deciduous near Roseburg and the North Fork's confluence with the main Umpqua.

The water on the North Umpqua is magical. Its blue hue and clarity are due to underlying lava rock, which filters much of the water before it reaches the river. Numerous springs feed the river year-round for ample flows into summer. The upper river corridor is narrow, but the lower river widens, exposing smaller rock ledges and narrow passages at low flows. Paddlers in small craft can negotiate the entire river year-round, though rafts are best in all seasons except late summer. Rapids are short, steep, pool-drop encounters along the upper and central river, gradually easing in difficulty and spreading out on the lower river. Exceptions are Deadline Falls and The Narrows. Both of these Class V areas on the lower river require a scout. Most boaters opt to portage these obstacles.

Frequent campsites and access areas allow boaters to choose from a variety of runs. Most campgrounds charge a fee for camping or parking, with heavy competition on busy holiday or prime fishing weekends (particularly below Steamboat Creek). The Forest Service has limited floating on the lower river at certain times of year due to conflicts between anglers and boaters. The voluntary closure area runs from Gravel Bin to Bogus Creek Campground from July 15 to October 31. Boats are not allowed on the stretch from July 1 to July 15 before 10 a.m. and after 6 p.m. on any stretch of river. Both anglers and boaters can enjoy the river without conflict by keeping to this rule. If you see people fishing along the banks, pass on the far side of the river in the area that they are working, making as little disturbance as possible. If in doubt, politely ask where they would like you to pass.

There's fun for the entire family in the North Umpqua Basin. Diamond and Crater lakes lie to the southeast, and a wildlife park near Winchester or hikes to Toketee Falls provide enjoyable excursions in the area. Ask for one of the recreational guides that is available free at the store near Soda Springs beyond Boulder Flat Campground.

Going with the Flow
Section 1: Boulder Flat Campground to Island Campground

Class: II to III (IV)   **Recommended flow:** 800 to 3,000 cfs   **Miles:** 19.2

The upper North Fork Umpqua River is wide enough for rafts at adequate spring and early summer flows. You'll want to have plenty of water in this technical upper stretch. From Boulder Flat Campground (River Mile 68), an easy Class III rapid known as **Boulder Hole** starts the run. Class II pool-drop rapids **Snag Rock** and **The Wall** lead to the confluence with Copeland Creek (RM 66.6). About 1 mile below the creek confluence, OR 138 crosses the river and cues paddlers to Class II **Weeper** rapid, nearby. An easy Class I float follows to Class II **Lunch Counter** just before Dry Creek comes in on the right.

Beyond Dry Creek, the river contains several Class III pool-drop rapids. The first is **Dog Wave**, followed in 0.5 mile by **Cardiac Arrest**. The second bridge, below Happy Creek, provides an alternate access in roughly 3 miles. Once you see it, watch out for upcoming Class III **Weird Weir**. This natural rock ledge forms a river-wide ledge-drop with a narrow chute on the right along a rock wall. At lower water, most of the flow goes through the chute. In less than 1 mile, paddlers reach Horseshoe Bend Campground (RM 60.5) and another river access point, on the right. The river slowly makes a 180-degree right turn to the north at Horseshoe Bend, then makes a 90-degree turn back west. A river-spanning log was washed clear in the 1996-1997 floods.

Section 1 continues with more Class II and III pool-drop rapids. Beyond Horseshoe Bend, **Toilet Bowl** and **Frogger III** rapids lead into a Class III stretch that is followed by **Frogger I**, near Dog Creek. About 2 miles below the campground at the bend, Class III **Rollout** precedes a long Class III boulder garden that has been called **Amazon Queen** (or **Eiffel Tower**).

Apple Creek Campground (RM 57.6), marked by a bridge, provides access for a take-out above Class IV Pinball rapid, a short distance downstream. Watch for the river to bend to the right, then take out on the left to scout or portage the rapid. Pinball is the most difficult rapid on the upper river and one of few that cannot be seen from the road. Its long boulder garden contains several large holes at high water and technical routes at low water. Rafters may have a hard time negotiating the minefield of boulders at lower flows. A trail follows the left bank; it leads to Applegate Bridge and Campground if you have to hike out.

Below this crux rapid, 4 miles of easier pool-drop rapids lead to Island Campground (RM 54). The stretch below Pinball starts with Class II **Alligator** rapid, followed in about 1 mile by three easy Class III rapids known as **Silk's Hole, Headknocker Moe,** and **Headknocker Curly,** with routes down the center. These three rapids are closely separated by Class I stretches leading to Island Campground and Gravel Bin Boat Ramp in roughly 2 miles. This is the lowermost take-out between July 1 and October 31, when boating is restricted downstream. Anglers congregate around Steamboat Creek, another 1.5 miles downriver, during the fishing season.

Section 2: Island Campground to Susan Creek Campground

Class: III (IV)	**Recommended flow:** 800 to 3,000 cfs	**Miles:** 11

Paddlers are not allowed to float Section 2 of the North Fork Umpqua between July 15 and October 31. In addition, they are asked to limit trips to the hours between 10 a.m. and 6 p.m. from July 1 to July 15. Keeping to this schedule will ease tensions between anglers and boaters. Keep in mind that the fishing season is already restricted, and the boating season extends throughout most of the year.

This stretch of river contains many pool-drop rapids that are created by resistant underlying rocks. The basalt riverbed creates steep, short Class III drops that are evenly distributed between long stretches of Class I+ and II water. Large boulders remain in a couple of locations.

Steamboat Creek (RM 52) enters on the right about 1.5 miles below Island Campground and the Gravel Bin access, contributing to river volume. Class III+ **Steamboat** rapid narrows into a left chute below Steamboat Creek, where observers dining at the Steamboat Inn can watch your run. Remember your manners and stay below the high-water mark when scouting! More pool-drop action leads to an alternate take-out at Bogus Creek Campground (RM 48.8), where there is a gravel access area and trail on the right.

Wright Creek Bridge (RM 48) follows Bogus Campground in less than 1 mile. A Class III rapid known as **Burial** waits near here. The covered bridge is a historic landmark and signals upcoming **Bathtub** rapid (also known as **Drop-Off**). This Class III+ rapid divides into narrow channels before dropping over a ledge. The passages can be tight; paddlers and rafters are sure to get a good soaking. Scout or portage on the left. In about 1 mile a drop creates a large wave above the confluence with Fall Creek. This is the **Mailbox** (also known as **Curl Back**). Fall Creek Picnic Area (RM 46.5) is on the right bank for a pit stop.

Between high cliffs, the river drops through more pools for less than a mile to reach **Island** rapids. At a large island, most of the current flows to the right with boulders near the top. The stairstep slide ends in a narrow channel at the bottom, particularly thin at low flows. Rafts have a technical squeeze at the top. Scout the rapid from the road on the way upstream. The left channel is easier, but has less water. Paddlers get a short break before the lower, action-packed part of Island, where a narrow runout contains some large fun waves. Smaller Class II **Roostertail** rapid follows in about 0.25 mile.

After 2 miles of easy Class I water, boaters face **Ledges** rapid, a fun Class III drop that can contain a nasty hole at higher water. In another mile, Class III+ **Sleeper** sneaks up around a right bend in the river. This rapid contains a narrow passage into a double drop with respectable holes. Punch through with speed left of center. About 1.5 miles downstream, Susan Creek Campground (RM 43) appears. The boat ramp and take-out here is not obvious, so look carefully to avoid missing your shuttle. A small sign signals the upcoming access less than 0.25 mile below Sleeper; both sign and access are on the right.

Section 3: Susan Creek Campground to Cable Crossing

Class: II (III)	**Recommended flow:** 800 to 3,000 cfs	**Miles:** 7

Below Susan Creek Campground and Boat Launch, the river gradually increases in difficulty. In roughly 3 miles it changes from an easy Class I float to Class II water with **Hogback** and **Wailing Wall** rapids. The rapids are straightforward pool-drops with calm stretches between them. Smith Springs County Park (RM 41) is on the right above Wailing Wall.

Another 3 miles of Class I water leads to Richard G. Baker Memorial Park (RM 38) on the right. At the park, a Class III drop known as **Upper Baker** rapid warns of upcoming **Baker Falls** (**Little Niagara**), which drop 5 feet and give boaters one last thrill before taking out at the park.

Some paddlers may wish to continue downstream another 2 miles to Cable Crossing (RM 36), on the right. Cable Crossing is the last take-out above Class V to VI **Deadline Falls** (also called **Rock Creek Falls**) at RM 35.5! Do not miss the take-out! Though expert paddlers could run the falls and perhaps cheat on the right side, a mistake here could be deadly. Also, anglers congregate near Rock Creek to watch steelhead and salmon jump the falls. Many cast a line here during the fishing season.

Between Deadline Falls and Idleyld Park lies another Class V rapid known as The Narrows. Here, the river is constricted by a natural rock dam into a narrow, turbulent passage. You can view the constriction from a small pullout along the road, but you'll need to hike to view the full channel before running the drop. Portage or scout along the right bank if you plan to make the run to Idleyld Park.

Section 4: Idleyld Park to Winchester Dam

Class: II to II+   **Recommended flow:** 800 to 3,000 cfs   **Miles:** 13

Both the river and the surrounding mountains widen in Section 4. The evergreen-forested banks of the upper river give way to rolling hills that are sparsely dotted with hardwoods. The lower river flattens and opens up as spacious farmlands cover the landscape. Rapids ease from Class III pool-drops to more technical Class II to II+ slides through narrow basalt rock formations at lower water. Higher flows cover the basalt, creating Class II to II+ wave trains.

From Idleyld Park (RM 34.5) on river right, paddlers see Class II rapids that become more frequent. Class II to II+ **Salmon Hole** is just below Idleyld Park, providing waves down the middle. Above the confluence with the Little River (RM 29), a Class III+ to IV narrow drop through a carved channel will entertain more proficient paddlers. The easier route is to the left of the left channel. The North Fork Umpqua heads straight into Little River to form **Colliding Rivers** rapid, on the left. Class II rapids lead into the main bend, where large waves and turbulent Class III to IV water are more difficult at higher flows. Scout the rapid on the way up from the left just across the bridge over the Little River.

Several miles of easier Class II pool-drop rapids lead to Whistler Bend Campground (RM 21.3). Take out above or below **Whistler Falls,** a long Class II rapid that bends to the left around the campground. About 4 miles beyond Whistler Bend an island splits the current, with most of the water leading to the right down

The lower North Umpqua gets slow and shallow in the summer.

a Class II+ slide at **Dixon Falls.** The left side is easier, but has little water at summer flows. More Class II spots dot the river to Winchester. About 1.5 miles above the take-out, Umpqua Community College becomes visible along the right bank. Look for the access site on the left in Winchester above the dam.

Section 5: Armacher County Park to River Forks Park

Class: I (II+)   **Recommended flow:** 800 to 3,000 cfs   **Miles:** 6.5

Below Armacher County Park, the North Fork rapids are easy Class I riffles with some Class II wave trains and bends. Section 5 makes an easy float for beginners, and is often done in innertubes during summer. Pack your waterproof suntan lotion, since the exposed river gets little shade. A stream gage and bridge near Riversdale (on the left) mark the beginning of slow flatwater. The lazy float continues for 2 miles above the confluence with the South Fork Umpqua River at River Forks Park.

The most exciting rapids along this stretch are located just a mile above the take-out. Here **Burkhart** rapids present a diagonal ledge-drop at lower water and a large diagonal wave at higher flows. The drop is followed by Class II waves and smaller rapids. The take-out at River Forks Park is on the right. Floaters may continue along the main Umpqua River for more Class I and II rapids.

83 Umpqua River, South Fork

Campbell Falls to Main Umpqua River

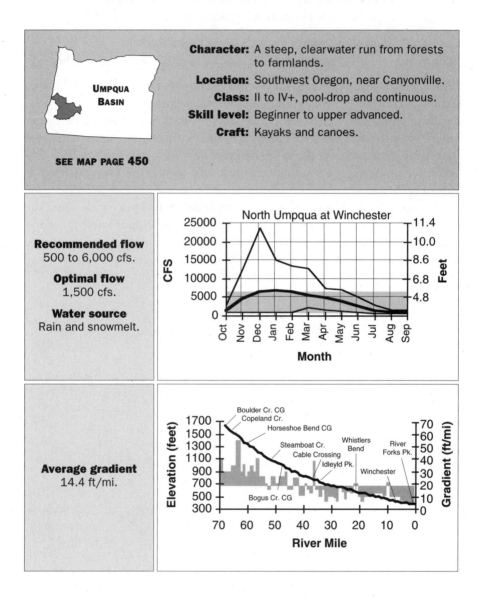

UMPQUA BASIN

SEE MAP PAGE 450

Character: A steep, clearwater run from forests to farmlands.

Location: Southwest Oregon, near Canyonville.

Class: II to IV+, pool-drop and continuous.

Skill level: Beginner to upper advanced.

Craft: Kayaks and canoes.

Recommended flow
500 to 6,000 cfs.

Optimal flow
1,500 cfs.

Water source
Rain and snowmelt.

North Umpqua at Winchester

CFS / Feet vs. Month (Oct–Sep)

25000 — 11.4
20000 — 10.0
15000 — 8.6
10000 — 6.8
5000 — 4.8
0

Average gradient
14.4 ft/mi.

Elevation (feet) / Gradient (ft/mi) vs. River Mile

Boulder Cr. CG
Copeland Cr.
Horseshoe Bend CG
Steamboat Cr.
Cable Crossing
Whistlers Bend
River Forks Pk.
Idleyld Pk.
Winchester
Bogus Cr. CG

1700 — 70
1500 — 60
1300 — 50
1100 — 40
900 — 30
700 — 20
500 — 10
300 — 0

70 60 50 40 30 20 10 0

River Mile

Hazards: The South Fork Umpqua River begins with 12-foot Campbell Falls. Scout before deciding to run, or put in below the drop. An additional ledge-drop occurs 2 miles below the falls, where a terminal hole develops along the left at high water. Watch for the Class IV ledge hole 3.5 miles below Three C Rock Picnic Area. Scout or portage on the left. About 2 miles above Days Creek, be on the lookout for a Class IV drop in a boulder-infested area. Run or portage on the left. Wood hazards exist throughout the entire river.

Access: From Interstate 5, take Exit 98 at Canyonville and head east on Oregon Highway 227 (the Tiller Trail Highway) along the South Fork Umpqua River. At Tiller, Forest Road 28 (the Tiller–South Umpqua Road) branches northeast along the river to Boulder Creek Campground and Campbell Falls. Boaters can choose from several access sites at campgrounds, bridges, and picnic areas.

To reach the take-out at River Forks Park, take Exit 129 at Akin and head north of Roseburg. Turn west on Winchester Road, continuing along Winchester Rd. to the intersection with Cleveland Road. Take the left fork here, which becomes Wilbur–Garden Valley Road. Stay left and follow this road to the main Garden Valley Road. From the intersection, follow Garden Valley Rd. left to River Forks Park. Alternate lower river access areas are within Roseburg at parks or at a boat ramp south of town near the fairgrounds.

Overview: The South Fork Umpqua River originates in the foothills of the Cascade Range not more than 15 miles from the upper Rogue River. This beautiful river contains brilliant blue water that cuts through serpentine rock. Its banks are steep and heavily vegetated along the upper sections, where the nearby highway stays far above the waterway. The lower river cuts through pastoral farmlands and clearcut hills before reaching the main Umpqua River at River Forks Park.

Adequate snowmelt feeds year-round flows, but most paddlers run the South Fork during spring runoff. The rapids here range from Class I to V depending on the stretch selected. Riverside campsites are plentiful, allowing longer stays and floats down multiple sections.

Going with the Flow
Section 1: Campbell Falls to Three C Rock Picnic Area

Class: III (IV+)	Recommended flow: 500 to 4,000 cfs	Miles: 10

The South Fork Umpqua River begins with 12-foot Campbell Falls, a vertical ledge followed by a narrow, turbulent exit. The drop is runnable, but those who wish to avoid it can put in below the falls on the right. Boulder-choked rapids, ledge-drops, and nasty holes follow in the next 2 miles.

The next major rapid, a 5-foot ledge, drops toward the left into a hole. At higher flows the left-hand ledge-drop creates a terminal hole, but an alternate route lies on the right. Below this nasty drop, all of Section 1's rapids can be boat-scouted or viewed along either bank. Wood is always a serious concern. Keep alert for new or shifted logs.

Section 2: Three C Rock Picnic Area to Tiller

Class: III (IV)	Recommended flow: 500 to 4,000 cfs	Miles: 5

Most of the South Fork is continuous Class II water with a few Class III rapids sprinkled along the way. The river courses through a nice canyon below Three C Rock Picnic Area, keeping a good pace throughout the run. About 3.5 miles into the stretch, watch for a large Class IV ledge hole. Scout or portage on river left. More Class II and III action will entertain you to the take-out on river right under the bridge at Tiller. Paddlers who want longer runs may continue downstream.

Section 3: Tiller to Days Creek

Class: II (III+)	Recommended flow: 800 to 4,000 cfs	Miles: 17

Section 3 has a wonderful scenic character. Here the South Fork cruises through sharp turns among gravel bars. Many of the chutes are fast and contain good-sized waves at higher flows. About 15 miles into the stretch is a surprising Class IV rapid. Watch for it where the river narrows and big boulders sit on either side of the stream. The flow splits into a hole, with most of the current going right. Run or portage the drop on the left.

The river remains busy and fun to the take-out at Days Creek. Practice your surf and eddy turns!

Section 4: Days Creek to River Forks Park

Class: I to II+ (III)	Recommended flow: 800 to 4,000 cfs	Miles: 59

Below Days Creek, the river rates a Class I or II, with an occasional Class II+ to III rapid. Several access locations allow boaters to chose various lengths of trip along the remaining 59 miles of river above River Forks Park.

—Kale Frieze

84 Washougal River, Washington
Timber Creek to Camas Slough

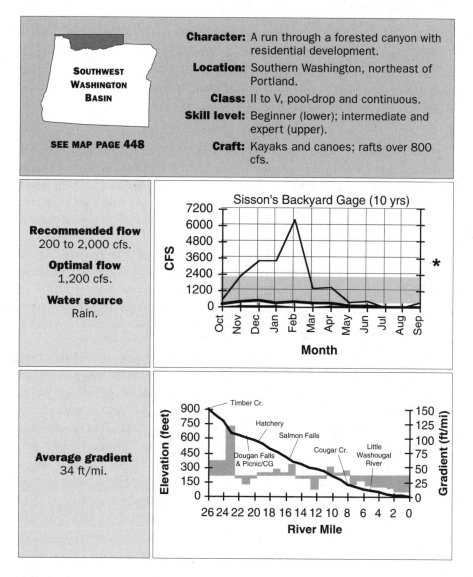

SOUTHWEST WASHINGTON BASIN

SEE MAP PAGE **448**

Character: A run through a forested canyon with residential development.

Location: Southern Washington, northeast of Portland.

Class: II to V, pool-drop and continuous.

Skill level: Beginner (lower); intermediate and expert (upper).

Craft: Kayaks and canoes; rafts over 800 cfs.

Recommended flow
200 to 2,000 cfs.

Optimal flow
1,200 cfs.

Water source
Rain.

Sisson's Backyard Gage (10 yrs)

CFS: 7200, 6000, 4800, 3600, 2400, 1200, 0

Month: Oct, Nov, Dec, Jan, Feb, Mar, Apr, May, Jun, Jul, Aug, Sep

*

Average gradient
34 ft/mi.

Elevation (feet): 900, 750, 600, 450, 300, 150, 0

Timber Cr.
Hatchery
Salmon Falls
Dougan Falls & Picnic/CG
Cougar Cr.
Little Washougal River

Gradient (ft/mi): 150, 125, 100, 75, 50, 25, 0

River Mile: 26 24 22 20 18 16 14 12 10 8 6 4 2 0

No depth measurement available.

Hazards: Above River Mile 13, the Washougal River drops through four hazardous waterfalls. These are seldom run; those who do so use inflatable (rather than hard shell) boats. Portage the weir at RM 20 on the right. Only 0.5 mile below the weir is a fish diversion dam. Portage this in the fall, when it is completely set up; in other seasons, the left-hand section is removed. **Salmon Falls,** at RM 15, is difficult to portage legally.

Below RM 13, the main hazard is **Big Eddy** rapid, which can and should be scouted from the road during the shuttle. Wood can be a problem, particularly now that development is occurring along the entire river corridor. There are few choke points, however, so boat-scouting is possible.

Access: From Portland, cross the Columbia River and drive east on Washington Highway 14 about 3 miles past the city of Camas. Turn left at a stoplight, where a sign indicates "15th Street Washougal." Drive north on 15th Street, which soon crosses the Washougal River and becomes Washougal River Road (Washington Highway 140). The first river bridge, at 17th Street, is near milepost 0.4. If you wish to take out at the Sandy Swimming Hole, drive west on Shepherd Road 0.6 mile to the small park.

The take-out for the regular run is 2.6 miles up Washougal River Road. On the way up, scout **Cougar Creek** rapids at milepost 5, and scout Big Eddy at milepost 7.4. Afterwards, continue upriver to the public fishing access at milepost 8.4 or Canyon Creek Road at milepost 9.8. At Canyon Creek Road, turn right and cross the river. Go 150 yards, then turn right again onto Sportsman Road. The put-in is 200 yards downstream.

To run **The Gorge,** drive up Washougal River Road just past Salmon Falls Road, at milepost 11.8. This is the take-out. Continue up Washougal River Road 6.3 miles to **Dougan Falls.** On the way, scout most of The Gorge by hiking in at the bottom of the slide area.

To run or view the upper part of the river, turn right just past Dougan Falls onto DNR Road 2000. Here the pavement turns to gravel. The uppermost access is 5 miles farther, at Timber Creek. Locked gates prevent further upriver travel.

Overview: Fed by rain, the Washougal River rises and falls quickly. The varying levels bring new dimensions to the run, making each trip different from the last. At most levels boaters find frequent play spots. In June, paddling the 100 cubic feet per second can be easy, but technical. In winter, boaters enjoy flows exceeding 4,000 cubic feet per second. Typical flows range from 200 to 1,500 cubic feet per second.

Above RM 13, the river is punctuated by waterfalls and Class IV rapids. The upper section is less frequently run, usually by advanced boaters. The road stays high above the water, and there are only a few access points. Although much of the upper run seems like wilderness, the road is close enough for rescue. Cabins and homes dot the riverbanks.

Below the Canyon Creek Road bridge (RM 13), most of the Washougal's rapids are Class II, with an occasional Class III. The exception is Big Eddy rapid, which is, at most levels, a solid Class IV. Washougal River Road follows closely on river right, providing intermediate access and exit points. Many homes, backyards, and decks overlook the run. During winter, you are likely to see anglers trying for steelhead, in boats and on the bank.

Going with the flow
Section 1: Dougan Falls to Salmon Falls (The Gorge)

Class: IV	Recommended flow: 200 to 1,000 cfs	Miles: 6

To run Section 1, put in at the bridge just below Dougan Falls. A Class III plunge takes you under the bridge and downstream. For several miles, the river flows over shallow bedrock ledges and around boulders, passing a series of houses on the left bank.

Just above the salmon hatchery (an alternate access point), watch for a Class III drop. A river-wide weir waits just below it. Portage this weir on river right. Downriver, channels braided in rock lead to another drop. Around the corner and below the bridge is a dam used for fish diversion. Most of the year, boaters can run it on the left, where a portion of the dam is removed. In fall, however, the dam runs the width of the river. Portage on the right.

Pleasant Class II and III drops fill the next several miles. Then, on the right bank, a cluster of cabins appears and the river swings left. This bend marks the start of The Gorge, a long Class IV rapid. At low and moderate water levels, boaters can pull out toward the left on a gravel bar island to scout the upper part. The Gorge has three parts. First, the river drops abruptly over large boulders. After a little slack water, it drops again over a bed of smaller boulders. Finally, it enters a short gorge of sculpted bedrock, veering back and forth. Several large boulders clog the exit; the best run is to the right. Scout the lower part of The Gorge by hiking in from the road at the point where the road surface is rough due to continuous subsidence and repair. The slow slide that damages the road also forms the rapids.

Below The Gorge, the river lets up to Class II water until the take-out above Salmon Falls. Be sure to study the take-out closely during your shuttle, to avoid inadvertently running the falls.

Section 2: RM 14 to RM 13 (North Fork Play Hole)

Class: IV (V)	Recommended flow: 500 to 1,500 cfs	Miles: 1

About 0.5 mile below the confluence of the North Fork Washougal with the main Washougal River, paddlers often enjoy a good play spot. Unfortunately, access is difficult. One approach is to put in close to the bridge at milepost 10.8, where Washougal River Road passes over the North Fork. Another approach is to drive 0.6 mile up the North Fork Road and down to the Skamania Steelhead Hatchery, then put in. This means running about 0.5 mile of the North Fork before you get

to the fun. This short run requires boofing a 4-foot ledge and portaging a slot waterfall on the left.

Below the North Fork confluence, the main Washougal rates a Class II. Below a cliff on the right bank, a convenient eddy provides good access to several play holes and waves. Take out on the left just past the Canyon Creek Road bridge or continue down Section 3 for a longer run.

Note: We cannot recommend running the upper North Fork Washougal, sometimes referred to as the West Fork. This beautiful, challenging, 5-mile Class IV trip includes two mandatory waterfall portages and has become dangerously congested with trees knocked down by an ice storm in December 1996. It may take years before this run is cleared of the constant deadly threat of sweepers. We hope to include it in *Paddling Oregon's* second edition.

Section 3: RM 13 to RM 6 (The Regular Run)

Class: III (IV)	Recommended flow: 200 to 1,500 cfs	Miles: 7

Most Washougal River paddlers put in at the fishing access on river left, 200 yards downstream from the bridge at the Washougal River Mercantile. Catch the wave at the put-in if you can, since you won't see another for a while. About 2 miles of easy Class II paddling follow, taking you past a number of homes and an alternate put-in at road milepost 8.5. You may see drift boat anglers taking out here, hinting at things to come.

Several Class II+ rapids follow, with some likely play spots. Next comes the large pool at the confluence with Winkler Creek, where the right bank holds a

A paddler introduces himself to Big Eddy. DICK SISSON PHOTO

county park. Big Eddy rapid, rated a Class IV, flows out to the left from this pool. Most boaters will take at least a quick look at this one from the road on the drive up, since routes change drastically at different flows. At lower flows, the common route is to pass just right of the **Twin Rocks,** then cut left with the main flow. Many eddies provide an exciting slalom challenge. It is easy to carry up the right bank and make multiple runs. At moderate to high flows, look for a sneak path on the right. At high water, scout carefully to pick a path through the holes and exploding waves.

Below Big Eddy, the river swings right and accelerates into a Class III rapid. A powerful hole forms just below where it turns back to the left. Although this hole will provide an exciting ride for the adventuresome, many boaters will want to avoid it by cutting sharply left. Enjoy the next mile of Class II+ water.

At the Mount Norway bridge, where Northeast Vernon Road crosses the river, the Washougal lets up. This bridge is an alternate access. In about 2 miles, as the river sweeps right and is split by a gravel island, the Cougar Creek rapids begin. About 50 yards below the end of the island, the river swings back left; a rock ledge extends out from the right bank here. There is usually a strong reversal behind it, with a tongue near the left bank. At moderate to low levels catch the eddy on the right, then peel out crossing the river. First-timers may want to scout this one from the road on the way up. Watch for a couple of surf waves partway down the little gorge.

Past Cougar Creek, the river eases up to mainly pool-drop Class II water. There is one notable drop, 1 mile downstream. A rock island sends most of the river right, creating a play hole as it passes over a small ledge. As the river turns back to the left, it drops over a large but shallow ledge. The best run is down the left bank.

A popular take-out is the fishing access site at milepost 3. It sits right at the bottom of a Class II+ rapid.

Section 4: RM 6 to the City of Washougal

Class: II (III)	Recommended flow: 200 to 2,000 cfs	Miles: 3

Put in at the fishing access site on river right. When the flow is high, you'll find good surfing waves in Section 4. Otherwise, it's a mild beginner run. Steelhead anglers frequently drift this section. About 0.25 mile below the put-in, watch for a large hole at the remains of **Cottrell Dam.** Easy passage is on the left. Take out at the Sandy Swimming Hole, on the right at RM 2.

—*Dick Sisson*

85 White River

Barlow Crossing to Deschutes River

Character: An isolated, forested canyon with vertical rock walls.

Location: North-central Oregon, south of The Dalles.

Class: III to III+ (IV), continuous and pool-drop.

Skill level: Intermediate to advanced.

Craft: Kayaks and canoes.

DESCHUTES BASIN

SEE MAP PAGE **418**

Recommended flow
400 to 2,000 cfs.

Optimal flow
1,000 cfs.

Water source
Rain and snowmelt.

Average gradient
60 ft/mi.

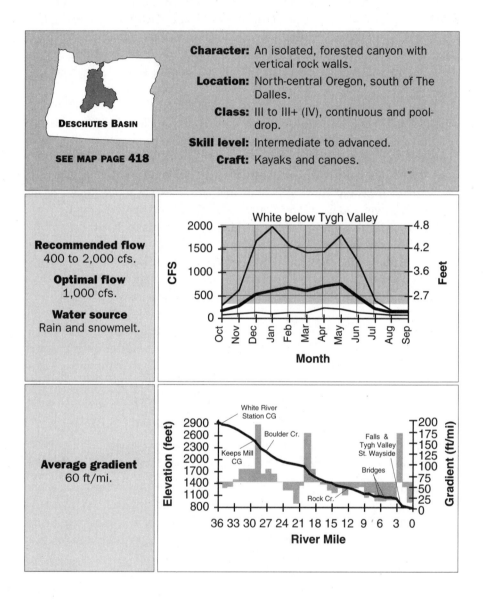

Hazards: Log-jams and log hazards are always a concern. Section 1 comprises continuous Class III rapids with two Class IV rapids in the middle. Section 2 is mostly pool-drop Class IIIs, but also has a Class IV rapid near the middle with a portage around a river-wide log. **White River Falls** precedes Section 3. Paddlers must portage three waterfalls if they wish to continue to the Deschutes River. The first is 90 feet, the second, **Celestial Falls,** is 40 feet, and the third is 20 feet. The last two have been run.

Access: From the Portland area, follow U.S. Highway 26 east past Sandy and Government Camp to the intersection with Oregon Highway 35. To reach the Barlow Pass put-in, follow OR 35 east to Forest Road 43 (Barlow Road). Continue along FR 43 to a bridge over the White River. This is the upper put-in. An alternate put-in can be reached via a road that turns into campgrounds along river right below the bridge. This avoids some of the log mess immediately below the upper put-in.

To reach Keeps Mill Campground, return to US 26 and continue southeast past Clear Lake to Oregon Highway 216 (the Wapinitia Highway). Follow OR 216 about 3 miles to Keeps Mill Road, on the left. Bear Springs Ranger Station is beyond if you miss the turn. Follow Keeps Mill Road to the campground and access area.

For downstream access, return to OR 216 and continue southeast past Pine Grove to a sign designating Victor Road to Wamic and the White River. Turn left onto the dirt Victor Road and follow the signs toward Wamic, turning left at an intersection indicating the White River Crossing Road. The road becomes steep and narrow as it descends to the White River, with access on river left. This is the usual take-out for the Keeps Mill section, or the put-in for the lower section.

Return to OR 216 and continue east to the intersection with U.S. Highway 197. Follow OR 216/US 197 north to the White River for a take-out. Reach another bridge upstream by following Tygh Valley Road to the left before you cross the White River. The bridge crosses the river about 1 mile upstream of US 197 for a shorter run. Alternately, continue along the dirt road heading north toward Wamic and turn onto the paved road leading to Tygh Valley. It is easy to miss your turns here, so take a map or use the OR 216/US 197 route.

If you wish to take out on the Deschutes River, turn right at the OR 216/US 197 intersection and follow US 197 to Maupin and the Deschutes. Follow the road along the right bank to a take-out near **Surf City** rapids.

Overview: The White River is one of three major rivers that originate as snowmelt from Mount Hood. In the spring, melting snow washes finely ground glacial silt down the mountain, clouding the river water. At such times the river gains a milky appearance, revealing the origin of its name.

The upper river begins in open forest with glimpses of Mount Hood in the distance. After several miles of flatwater, the river slowly picks up speed and gains volume before reaching Keeps Mill Campground. As the river steepens, walls begin to close in. Below Keeps Mill Campground there is no river access for 12 miles. Hiking out of the deep canyon is a near impossibility. The river remains secluded and inaccessible to the high desert of Tygh Valley. Spectacular waterfalls cascade into the river, but your attention will be focused entirely on the whitewater from Keeps Mill to the first bridge. Below the bridge, the river changes from absolutely continuous Class III+ water to pool-drop Class III rapids, allowing time to gander at the marvelous canyon walls.

Every trip down the lower White River is different, since the ever-present wood moves around. On my first trip to the White I had to contend with numerous log-jams; on my most recent trip, there was only one spot where a log forced a por-tage. The river is a good choice for paddlers who want seclusion on a multiday, self-contained journey. There are many campsites interspersed with private prop-erty. Be careful with fire, since the dry ground is covered with pine needle tinder.

Except for a long carry around three large waterfalls—90, 40, and 25 feet respectively—paddlers who run the White to the Deschutes face only a couple of rapids that can be boat-scouted. The view of White River Falls and the old power-house near the base of the second set of falls are well worth a photo stop. View them from Tygh Valley State Wayside along OR 216 between Tygh Valley and the Deschutes River.

Going with the Flow
Section 1: Barlow Crossing to Keeps Mill

Class: II to III (IV)	Recommended flow: 400 to 1,200 cfs	Miles: 6.5

Logs and debris collect in the first several miles of the White River, where the gradient is low. Expect Section 1 to take longer than you think, due to numerous portages. To make a shorter trip, put in along the dirt road that follows the river on the right to two campgrounds below Barlow Bridge.

The river picks up speed 3 miles below Barlow Crossing at a Class IV double drop called **Sliced and Diced.** Scout or portage on the left along the rocky shore. The upper part of the rapid squeezes into a narrow, twisting chute with sharp rocks. It leads into a lower drop of jagged basalt, which bounces boaters to a bottom pool. The lower drop is a real boat-scraper at low to moderate water, hence the name.

Below this Class IV drop, the river changes to continuous Class III water that gradually increases in difficulty to Keeps Mills. Take out at the park, camp, or continue on. Do not begin Section 2 unless you have ample daylight, since there is no take-out for 12 miles, with few campsites or eddies.

Section 2: Keeps Mill to White River Bridge

Class: III+ (IV)   **Recommended flow:** 500 to 1,500 cfs   **Miles:** 12

This is the longest continuous stretch of whitewater that I know. It is pure pleasure for those comfortable with Class III+ water, but pure terror for anyone having a bad day. Section 2 is not the place to swim, and it's not the place to be caught without a paddle or other gear. Be prepared for the worst; carry an extra paddle, emergency blanket, lighter, food, and whatever you need for an unplanned stay along the river.

None of the water is really that difficult, with the exception of two Class IV- rapids that must be scouted. These can be viewed from your boat, but if you are in doubt as to what lies ahead, check from shore. Most of the river rates an easy Class III, but the whitewater is so continuous that I have given it a III+ rating. Eddies are rare at low flows, nonexistent at high water. On one trip we decided to pull out at the next eddy, and 3 miles later had to grab a tree root to exit the river, one at a time.

Ron Killen and I did this section in 3.5 hours after reaching Keeps Mills late. The rest of the party walked out, hoping to hitch a ride. Ron and I ran what felt like a slalom race as we paddled to beat the darkness to the White River Bridge. As we pulled into our camp there, Gus Stinstrom greeted us with a cold beer, a delicious warm meal, a hot fire, and a necessary clothesline. Truly a welcome sight. Thanks, Gus!

Section 3: White River Bridge to Deschutes River

Class: III (IV, P)   **Recommended flow:** 500 to 1,500 cfs   **Miles:** 11

The lower White River is a beautiful trip within spectacular canyon walls. It's the more popular section on the river, and is appropriate for intermediate paddlers. There are good campsites along the waterway for self-contained trips, but boaters can easily run the 11 miles to the Tygh Valley Bridge in a day if they start early. Like Section 1, Section 3 is isolated and inaccessible, so take the same precautions.

The rapids here are pool-drops, allowing you to divide your attention between the scenery and your route. Don't gaze up at your surroundings too long,; logs are constant dangers here, particularly at higher flows with faster current. The upper section contains more frequent rapids, but they are scattered throughout the run. Two Class IV- rapids occur toward the end of this section, with technical horizon line drops that weave through megaboulders. Scout for logs before running, since one of these rapids almost always has wood somewhere within it.

After the second long Class IV drop, Tygh Valley Road bridge is not far ahead. Take out here or continue to the OR 216 bridge. Paddlers who wish to float through flatwater can go on to Tygh Valley State Wayside. The take-out beach at the wayside is on river left, just above a weir. **Do not continue beyond this take-out, since an unrunnable 90-foot waterfall waits just downstream!**

A trail leads to the park and bottom of the falls, where an old powerhouse once thrived. It is worth the hike to see it, even if you don't plan on continuing downriver. If you do plan to continue to the Deschutes River, make sure you put in below the second and third waterfalls, which lie just downstream of the powerhouse. A 25-foot waterfall is just around the bend, and the extra hike is easy enough. Paddlers from Bend have reported running the 40-foot fall Celestial Falls between the deadly 90-foot falls and the lower 25-foot falls, but I wouldn't recommend it. Access is difficult, and it may not even be legal.

The water below the falls is an easier Class II to II+, running in pool-drop fashion over the 1.5 miles to the Deschutes River. The White River enters the Deschutes just above Surf City, where paddlers play at the edge of the big water. Take out on the right below this play spot or continue downstream.

86 White Salmon River, Washington

Above Trout Lake to Northwestern Day Use Area

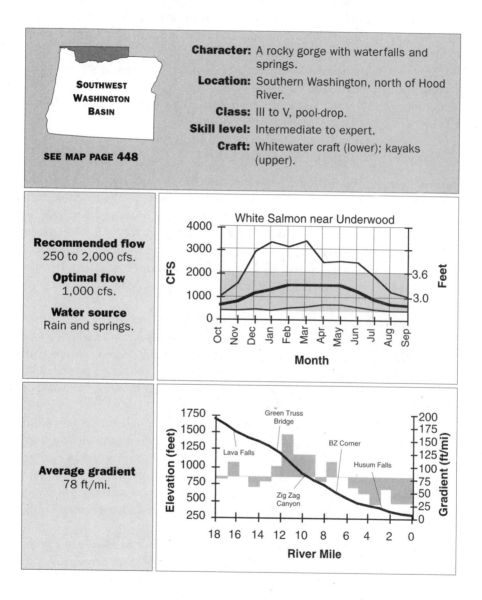

SOUTHWEST WASHINGTON BASIN

SEE MAP PAGE 448

Character: A rocky gorge with waterfalls and springs.

Location: Southern Washington, north of Hood River.

Class: III to V, pool-drop.

Skill level: Intermediate to expert.

Craft: Whitewater craft (lower); kayaks (upper).

Recommended flow
250 to 2,000 cfs.

Optimal flow
1,000 cfs.

Water source
Rain and springs.

White Salmon near Underwood

Average gradient
78 ft/mi.

Hazards: Sections 1, 2, and 3 of the White Salmon River are serious Class IV and V runs for experts only. They contain many Class V waterfalls, rapids, and difficult portages. All possible hazards exist on the upper runs, so take precautions. First-time paddlers should run with knowledgeable local paddlers or at least contact them for guidance along the upper sections. Contact Alder Creek Kayak, (503) 285-0464, for recommendations.

The lower White Salmon River (Section 4) is more popular, since it is enjoyable for intermediate paddlers. Locals run guided trips in this stretch, which holds continuous Class II water and some tough Class III pool-drops. **Husom Falls** is a Class V- drop that most boaters should portage.

The White Salmon River is extremely cold year-round; even a summer swim could lead to hypothermia. Bring warm clothes.

Access: From Interstate 84 at Hood River, Oregon, cross the toll bridge over the Columbia River to reach the community of White Salmon, Washington. Turn west onto Washington Highway 14 here, then turn right in about 1.5 miles onto Washington Highway 141. To reach the Section 4 take-out, follow WA 141 about 3 or 4 miles to Northwestern Lake Road, heading west to where a bridge crosses the White Salmon River. The road to the right just beyond the bridge leads to a day use area and boat ramp on recently drained Northwestern Lake. This is the take-out.

To reach upstream access areas, return to WA 141 and follow it another 2 miles to Husom Falls and the town of Husom where access is available at or above the second bridge near Husom Falls. Continue 4 miles to BZ Corner. Many paddlers use a private boat access just down the road from the bridge on the right; you'll have to pay a small fee for lowering boats to the river on a cable winch or using the access trail to carry to this put-in.

Expert boaters may continue north up WA 141 for 2 more miles and a dirt road to the right. This road ends at the bridge and a pullout area where a steep access means lining boats in or out of the water just downstream of the bridge. An alternate access point is about 8 miles past BZ Corner, off Warner Road. Turn right on Warner Road and continue 1 mile to a bridge. Put in upstream just across the bridge. Ask permission from landowners to park across from a barn on the right, near an easier put-in.

Farther up WA 141, Section 1 ends at Trout Lake, but paddlers can run the river can be paddled to Section 2 if desired. For the uppermost access, continue north from Trout Lake along Forest Road 17. Turn left on Forest Road 23 in about a mile. Follow FR 23 roughly 7 miles to Forest Road 8031, on the right, which leads to the access bridge across the river.

Overview: The White Salmon is one of the region's most popular rivers, set in a beautiful, deep gorge that separates boaters from populated lands. Although roads are not far from the river in any section, access is next to impossible except at a few specific locations where boaters could scramble up steep banks. The water is always icy cold here, usually 40 degrees Fahrenheit, which can catch summer boaters unprepared. The water is exceptionally clear, filtered underground and emerging in numerous springs. It's amplified with snowmelt from Mount Adams, providing adequate flows throughout the year.

Rapids in the canyon are steep, technical pool-drops separated by easier stretches. There are numerous play spots, spaced near enough to keep boaters busy at all times. The lower river, from BZ Corner to Husom Falls, is a good run for intermediate to advanced boaters and guided trips. The upper stretches are for expert paddlers only, since hazardous waterfalls and turbulent, constricted stretches pose serious dangers. Slalom and downriver races are held on the White Salmon in June.

Going with the flow

Section 1: Upper Bridge to Trout Lake (Green Canyon)

Class: IV to V	Recommended flow: 400 to 800 cfs	Miles: 9

The upper reaches of the White Salmon River were not explored until spring 1996. This was not because of lack of interest. An assortment of paddlers had eyed the 9 miles of remote canyon, each hoping to make the first descent. Access was the problem. When the upper river has enough water, the road is usually blocked by snow. By the time the snow melts, the river is virtually bone dry.

On an early 1996 reconnaissance mission, Doc Loomis and I were happy to find the road had been plowed and the river was full. We wasted no time in gearing up and putting on the newly deemed Green Canyon Run (not to be confused with the Green Truss Bridge Run of the lower river). What we found in this stretch was classic White Salmon boating: beautiful canyons, big ledge-drops, huge hydraulics, and lots of mellow floating. Unfortunately, we also found a few log-jams and limbos, some of which required split-second decisions.

Putting in at the bridge, paddlers immediately encounter fast, shallow water moving through a maze of small rocks. If this stretch were really pumping, the drops downstream would be terrifying. Around a sharp bend to the left is the entrance to a beautiful canyon, dotted with Class II to III rapids. You will know when you have arrived at the first major drop, known as **Triple Drop**. A horizon line marks this tight, twisting affair with three runnable ledges. It gets the heart pumping, but not for long.

More easy water leads into **Too Close for Comfort**. This is a very tight slot. The left bank threatens to do some serious facial damage; a face mask is a prerequisite for anyone running this drop. Not far downstream is a meaty ledge-drop. Run this one just off the right bank.

After a log-jam or two, you will find yourself heading into an imposing gorge. This whole canyon deserves a scout to make sure it is totally clear of wood. The whitewater here is not difficult, but it is a blind situation. Keep your eyes peeled for a big double drop downstream we called **The Envelope**, because this is what Doc was pushing when he ran it. Much to his chagrin he flipped his inflatable in the first part and found a log wedged just under the surface in the bottom half. I opted for the portage.

The logs on this run are always changing. Most of them are concentrated toward the end of the run, where the river begins to meander through gravel beds. Some of these log-jams have sneak routes, and some require short hikes. The quality of whitewater increases toward the end of the run as well. A short section after The Envelope offers plenty of enjoyment for advanced boaters. Big sloping ledges, chutes, and slides make this a playground worth visiting.

High water would create many keeper holes in Section 1. Be careful and scout as frequently as you need to. The view downstream is generally unimpeded, with horizon line ledge-drops as standard fare.

Note: Due to severe wood hazards that have collected in the river since the 1996-1997 floods, we deem this section too dangerous to run. The log hazards sit in particularly bad places, so don't try to run the section until it clears out with more high water. Check with the folks at Alder Creek Kayak for updated information.

–Andrew Wulfers

Section 2: Warner Road Bridge to Green Truss Bridge (The Farmlands)

Class: IV+ (P)	**Recommended flow:** 500 to 1,200 cfs	**Miles:** 5.1

The Farmlands section is a notch below the Green Truss Bridge Run (Section 3), but it contains the same hazardous conditions: steep walls, difficult scouts, and probable portages around one or more Class V drops. Put in below the Warner Road bridge or ask permission to park on private property just past a small barn on the right for an easier put-in. Initial Class II and III pool-drop rapids lead into longer **Sidewinder,** the first rapid requiring a scout or portage on river left. The current in this Class IV rapid is easy to misjudge, and staying on line can be difficult. Avoid the undercut left bank and the bottom right bank. Complicating matters, a roostertail rock at the bottom just right of center divides the main current at moderate flows.

Boat-scout the few Class III drops, which take you into a pool above **Lava Falls.** Scout or portage this drop from the right bank, taking particular notice of the boil at the bottom. Boaters have run Lava's center right tongue at higher to moderate flows, but the door disappears at lower water when much of the water flows through a lava tube into the pool below. (This could be the source of the strange boil effects.)

Continuing downstream is 0.5 mile of Class III to III+ pool-drop rapids. You can boat-scout these from eddies at moderate flows, but a couple of the drops require complex moves on the way down. These become pushy and contain bigger holes at higher water. As the river eases its pace, Class II rapids spaced farther apart allow some surfing in the 2 miles above **Off Ramp.** Scout or portage this 12-foot waterfall from a pool on the left; in June 1996 it contained a vertically pinned log, making a portage mandatory. At higher water, look for a possible route on the right. A few more rapids follow, ending above Green Truss Bridge.

Use this section as a warm-up for the more difficult Section 3, or take out just below the bridge on river right. Taking out here means making one of the steepest climbs that I would wish to attempt without climbing gear. Boats must be lined up from the top. Don't forget to keep your helmet on at the bottom, since climbers often dislodge rocks and send them onto those below.

Paddlers usually run Section 2 at higher water levels than Section 3, since numerous springs keep water levels higher on the lower sections. Boaters often use a makeshift gage located upstream from the lower bridge at Husom Falls, where a good flow for Section 2 is 3.5 feet. Section 3 is preferred at 3 feet or lower, especially for first-time runs.

Section 3: Green Truss Bridge to BZ Corner

Class: V (P)	Recommended flow: 250 to 1,000 cfs	Miles: 5

The Green Truss Bridge Run is one of the most classic Class V runs around. Cascading underground springs, awesome rapids, and big drops complement the beautiful scenery. The first World Kayak Federation Class V downriver race was held here in July 1996. Invariably, the first question asked by expert area boaters is, "Have you run the Green Truss?"

Paddlers must make an intense descent into the canyon, lining boats down to the river on the steep slope just below the Green Truss Bridge on river right. For an easier put-in and a longer day, you may wish to combine this section with Section 2. Below the bridge, the first mile of river is dotted with some nice Class III and IV warm-up drops with calm pools between. The first major drop is **The Meatball,** which begins with a jagged eight foot sloping drop into a swift pool. The exit is blocked by a large rock (the Meatball itself) with narrow chutes on either side. The chutes lead into a twisting 6-foot drop into a large pool. Wood perpetually gathers in one of the chutes, so scout carefully above the first ledge on river left.

The pool below The Meatball is the entry to **Bob's Falls,** a river-wide 10-foot drop with a very large boil in the turbulent pool below. At low flows this drop is straightforward, but at higher levels both the extreme right or left sides can be used to sneak the boil. Beware, however, since Bob's Falls has consumed more excellent boaters than any other drop I know of on this section. Portage on river left.

Two short drops lead to the calm entry above 24-foot **Big Brother,** the biggest drop on this river. Although paddlers have run this drop, it has many factors that compound risk. The top of the drop is very technical; the current is misleading. An undercut cave threatens the bottom river right wall, and the pool below has shallow spots. Portage is on river left and put in below the plunging 12-foot fall known as **Little Brother** (or **The Faucet**). To run Little Brother, ferry across the pool to river right and hike back up the other side.

A couple more Class IV drops mark the entry to **Double Drop,** an intimidating, narrow, 18-foot double falls. Running these is equal to a roll of the dice. Once you are over the lip, only the river itself will determine the outcome. The fun, 6-foot, seal-launch portage is on river left. Below Double Drop, an innocent-looking 5-foot ledge-drop has a wicked hole on the left at higher flows. Stay right!

The river eases into Class III and IV water. It also increases in flow and decreases in temperature after passing springs that cascade down the canyon walls. The next main drop, known as **Cheese Grater**, is marked by an obvious outcropping of basalt on river left. The drop has wild currents and an undercut bank on river right, with jagged walls on both sides. Scout or portage on river right.

Upper and lower **Zig Zag Rapids** are the next main obstacles, where the river flows powerfully and spectacularly through a narrow, steep canyon. The water here is intense and very fast, with powerful hydraulics and virtually no eddies. Advanced boaters will have difficulty negotiating these two areas. Some boaters have portaged up the steep right bank before Zig Zag Canyon, but the area is private property; get permission from the owner before you take out here. Scout Zig Zag carefully and portage the upper canyon from river right. Portage the lower drops from river left by ferrying across on the pool between the rapids. The portages are arduous but possible. A submerged boulder right of center blocks the exit of lower Zig Zag, forcing what has been called "The Move," a shift or ferry to the left of the rock. Water is forced on the right into an undercut area.

More Class III and IV rapids dot the river on the approach to **The Flume.** This Class IV chute with wild waves and hydraulics is marked by a series of water pumps on the river left bank. The pool below is the last calm water before the Class IV entry to **BZ Falls.** This dynamic and violent 16-foot sloping drop has a powerful hydraulic below. Hike down the right bank from the pool, or catch one of the small eddies on river right. The scout is on river right, as is the portage 50 yards farther, requiring an exhilarating 15-foot seal-launch or jump after your boat into the pool below.

A few more fun drops follow before the BZ Corner launch site is visible around a right bend in the river. Take out on the river right trail here, or continue through Section 4 to Husom Falls and the Northwestern Reservoir Boat Ramp.

Note: Section 3 has very steep, forested sides that make hiking out difficult or impossible in most places, so carrying extra gear is a good idea. This section is notably more difficult at higher flows and is usually run during summer and early fall. Property along the river is private, with the owners allowing access. Please respect their generosity and their property. Don't forget to pay the fee at BZ Corner if you take out at the private trail.

-Ron Blanchette

Section 4: BZ Corner to Northwestern Reservoir Boat Ramp

Class: III+ (V-)	**Recommended flow:** 500 to 2,000 cfs	**Miles:** 8

Below BZ Corner, nicely spaced pool-drop rapids keep the action coming. Paddlers get no warm-up before **BZ Rapid** at the put-in. More aggressive paddlers may choose to wash up in **Maytag** hole by following the trail right to an alternate put-in just upstream. Maytag is permanently stuck in the wash cycle; it occurs just before two ledge-drops that can complicate a recovery. Boaters can choose to run these rapids or carry below BZ Corner along the rocks.

Downstream, there are a couple of places where undercut ledges could pose a hazard, particularly along the right bank. Watch out below a couple of Class II warm-ups, and beware of getting pushed too close to the walls of the canyon. **Shark's Tooth, Grasshopper, Siwash, Corkscrew,** and **Waterspout** are Class III rapids that follow in quick succession, separated by Class II water. The many named rapids can be boat-scouted, but most contain a twist before pooling at the bottom. Just below a footbridge, watch for a cave on river left; it appears to be partially manmade. After a short float, look for the large eddy and sandbar that mark a great break spot midway to Husom Falls. Respect private property above the high-water mark. Play spots are frequent in this section, and the river has one of the best ender spots in the northwest at **Stairstep,** just a short distance downriver from the sandbar. Catch an eddy after the second step to wait your turn, then pirouette for the camera and/or get scraped down step number three.

Before reaching Husom Falls, the river eases up and flattens out. Listen for the falls after rounding a right bend, then pull out on either bank to scout and make your decision. Rafters usually line their craft down the left chute from the left bank. Boaters often run Husum Falls, which provided the first waterfall experi-

Dennis "Cat-Man-Do" Schultz manages a clean run at Husum Falls.

ence for many local area boaters. Even though mishaps are common here, serious injuries are rare for properly protected and prepared boaters. The maul at the bottom center-right chute tends to spit people out quickly into the deep pool.

Worse trouble usually occurs in Class III **Rattlesnake** rapid, just under the bridge and around the corner. Here swimmers encounter rocks and holes as the rapid snakes around a hard right-to-left bend. More Class II water and good play waves continue to the take-out, as riverside homes come into view (including a small castle on the left). The once-flatwater stretch along Northwestern Reservoir recently has been drained, providing action to the take-out. When and if the dam is removed, paddlers may be able to run the extra whitewater to the Columbia River.

—Robb Keller

⟦87⟧ **Willamette River**
McKenzie River to Columbia River

Character: A long, large-volume river between metropolitan areas.

Location: Northwest Oregon, between Eugene and Portland.

Class: FW to I, continuous.

Skill level: Beginner and experienced flatwater paddlers.

Craft: Canoes and sea kayaks.

WILLAMETTE BASINS

SEE MAPS PAGES **430, 436 & 452**

Recommended flow
2,500 to 50,000 cfs.

Optimal flow
10,000 cfs.

Water source
Many tributaries.

Average gradient
1.9 ft/mi.

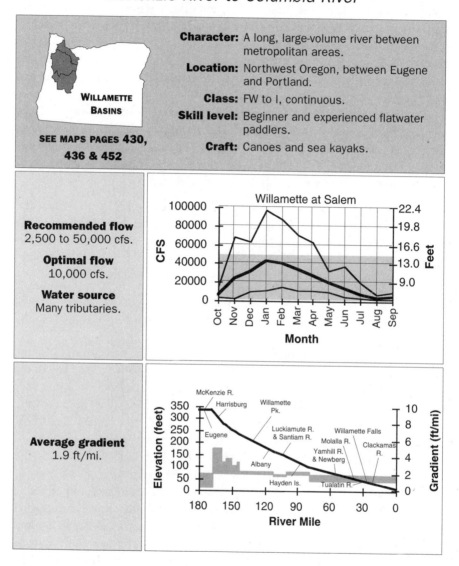

Hazards: Wood, channels, current, and power boats constitute the main hazards on the Willamette. The upper river is best suited to experienced flatwater paddlers, but the middle river is larger, slower, and easier for novices. High flows can create strong eddy lines and currents with choppy water along open stretches. Only experienced paddlers should put in at flows above 20,000 cubic feet per second. Make sure you plan a trip of appropriate length, since slow water and headwinds can add time. Do not try to cover distances of more than 10 miles in a single day in an open canoe.

Below Newberg, watch for power boats and jet skis. Beyond Willamette Falls, shipping traffic and tour boats are also a concern. Paddle near the shallow banks to ensure a safe trip along the lower river. Boaters along river right have the right-of-way when passing. Keep a steady course while being passed by faster craft, though slower craft have the right-of-way when overtaken.

Access: There are a plethora of places to camp, park, or access the Willamette River. The main areas are listed in the chart below by river mile. Paddlers should pick up a Willamette River Recreation Guide and/or a copy of DeLorme's *Oregon Atlas and Gazetteer* for access roads. The guide is available from Oregon State Parks; get the *Oregon Atlas and Gazetteer* where books and maps are sold.

Overview: The Willamette River is the longest free-flowing river that lies entirely within the state of Oregon. It is also one of the few rivers of its length in the country that flows almost entirely north.

Oregon City, on the Willamette's banks, was one of the first cities west of the Rocky Mountains to be incorporated, in 1844. Steamboats were the main transportation of the time, traveling first to Willamette Falls and later to Eugene after completion of wooden locks to circumnavigate the 41-foot falls. The locks were the first of their kind in the country; built in 1873, they still operate today. Communities relying on river transportation and shipping thrived until roads and railroads surpassed river transport in the early 1900s. Historically and presently, the river has provided the Willamette Valley with ample water to irrigate a variety of crops. The area is one of the nation's leaders in hops, a main ingredient of beer.

The six wildlife refuges along the main river are temporary home to migrating birds. Blue and green herons, eagles, kingfishers, osprey, hawks, and owls live and thrive along the river. Look for heron rookeries and osprey nests in the trees. Raccoons, nutria, beaver, deer, and otter can be seen along the banks. Chinook salmon and steelhead make runs up the river in fall and spring. Trout, walleye, and even white sturgeon can be found along the lower river.

The Willamette Greenway Project, established in 1967, has created several parks, boat ramps, and camping areas along the main Willamette River. Making the river more user-friendly, the project has restored habitat areas and cleaned up the river corridor. The river was deemed unsafe to swim in after pollution levels soared in the early 1960s. The Willamette has since been one of the nation's success stories, showing that water treatment facilities and strong legislation against dumping toxic wastes can dramatically improve water quality and help restore dwindling fish populations.

Ample flows are available year-round on the Willamette. Most people float during the warm summer months with lower water levels. Higher flows in fall, winter, and spring make distances easier to cover in a shorter time span, but increase the difficulty and add chop to the water. Be prepared for wet and cold conditions if you plan a run during these seasons. Fall colors are particularly enjoyable, since colored leaves show a palette of colors on the river canvas before you.

Camping is a matter of preference. Locations with no road access ensure a quiet, serene experience. Paddlers will find many riverside campsites with beautiful scenery and level ground. Low-impact camping is the rule; bury all waste far from the river at sites where facilities are not provided. Camp only along areas that are marked for public access, since private lands line much of the main river. Though paddlers can legally stop on any bank within the high water mark, landowners do not always understand this. River miles are conveniently marked with signs, allowing you to check your progress and location. It is a good idea to monitor your speed along a short stretch before venturing too far in a single day.

The Willamette River Recreation Guide, offered by Oregon State Parks and the Oregon Marine Board, is an excellent resource. It includes good maps of access areas and state parks, with recreation suggestions. The maps are indispensable for paddlers who seek places to camp on multiday adventures. They also help you keep track of your progress downstream.

Going with the flow
Section 1: McKenzie River to Harrisburg (Upper Mainstem)

Class: I+ (II)	Recommended flow: 2,500 to 25,000 cfs	Miles: 18

The McKenzie River has often been called the third fork of the Willamette River. The river runs fast, winding to its confluence with the Willamette. The banks are lined with cottonwood, willow, alder, and maple trees. Many side channels tempt paddlers, but it is better to stay in the main channel, which presents its own challenges. Watch for fallen trees or "strainers" that dot the river. You'll hardly notice the transition from the McKenzie to the Willamette due to numerous channels and islands near the confluence.

Above Harrisburg, the Willamette really moves and requires quick decisions and maneuvering more suited to experienced paddlers. Canoes and sea kayaks are the craft of choice. The 18 miles by river to Harrisburg make a long day's paddle; it's better to divide the trip over two days if you have the time, since camping and swimming spots are excellent on this stretch.

Armitage Park, off Coburg Road near Eugene, is the access point for the last 5 miles of the McKenzie River. Only day parking is available at the park. Look for access areas along the Willamette to plan a manageable day trip. Keep alert for a Class II rapid near a footbridge at Alton–Baker Park in Eugene.

Section 2: Harrisburg to Albany

Class: FW to I   **Recommended flow:** 2,500 to 25,000 cfs   **Miles:** 42

Section 2 is a recommended multi-day trip. Headwinds can make getting downriver difficult work here. The river meanders around many bends with tempting side channels that are best avoided. The side channels are shallower and slower than the main river, collecting fallen trees and debris. Paddlers who investigate side channels may face portages around blocked areas along tree-lined banks and open farmland. The channels create wonderful habitat for fish and wildlife, however. Osprey populations decrease as the river slows, while blue and green heron sightings increase along slower water.

Above Corvallis, the Willamette is matched to more experienced paddlers or novices on one of the many guided excursions. From Corvallis to Salem, the water is deeper and slower. Inexperienced paddlers can travel this area with ease. Remember to always watch the water, since changes in current or sudden riffles indicate rocks and logs that can capsize a boat and entrap paddlers. Infrequent sandbars remind boaters that the river is not all open flatwater.

Camping near Albany is limited and unpleasant. The stretch contains several mills along the river. The constant roar of pumps and machinery, bright lights, and occasional smell of paper-in-the-process deter boaters from the otherwise beautiful scenery. It's a reality-check for anyone who has forgotten about mankind's historic abuse of the river.

Section 3: Albany to Newberg (Middle Mainstem)

Class: FW   **Recommended flow:** 2,500 to 25,000 cfs   **Miles:** 69

The river continues to slow below Albany and no longer contains actively changing river channels. The river maintains a 12- to 15-foot clearance, with areas that are as much as 80 feet deep. The slower river is still entertaining; stay alert for changes in water patterns. Riffles can indicate a log hung up below the surface. Obstructions in the river cause occasional strong currents and shallows. The river moves slowly enough for alert paddlers to prepare for and avoid hazards.

Look for a favorite campsite at Luckiamute Landing (River Mile 109), surrounded by remnants of a gallery forest. Birders will catch an eyeful, with bald eagles, kingfishers, and nighthawks frequenting the area. The water is shallow and swift near the banks. The confluence with the Santiam River is just beyond Luckiamute. It is fun to paddle up and explore the Santiam. The water along its rock bed has greater clarity than that of the Willamette, which hauls silt from muddy upstream contributors.

Both the Wheatland and Buena Vista ferries still operate within this stretch, in operation since the early 1850s.

Section 4: Newberg to Willamette Falls

Class: FW	Recommended flow: 2,500 to 25,000 cfs	Miles: 22

This short section of river has fewer access areas, but there are still enough spots to let you plan a trip of appropriate length. It is possible to float the entire stretch in one day, but it's a long paddle even without headwinds or stops. There are a number of islands in Section 4's lower half, with signs of the north valley's increasing population in places.

You must stop before you reach **Willamette Falls**, 1.5 miles beyond the confluence with the Tualatin River on the left. On the north bank at the confluence, Willamette Park (Berhert Landing) makes a good last take-out above the unrunnable falls. It is possible to circumnavigate the falls, though we don't recommend it. The Willamette Falls Locks will accommodate paddlers, but you may be forced to wait for commercial vessels.

Section 5: Clackamette Park to Columbia River

Class: FW	Recommended flow: 2,500 to 25,000 cfs	Miles: 25

Below **Willamette Falls,** the river is busy with recreational and business traffic. Watch for barges and other large shipping traffic, sternwheeler tour boats, jet skis, and waterskiers along this stretch. Beginning paddlers should stay farther upriver, due to the extensive traffic hazards. If you wish to float this stretch, stick near the banks and wear bright colors to help fast-moving traffic see you on the water.

Willamette Falls at night. JEFF JACOB PHOTO

Tidal waters flow to Willamette Falls, making currents unpredictable. Consult tide charts available at Captain's Nautical Supply in Portland. Tides can take some time to reach the Portland and Willamette River areas, so expect a delay from the published tide times.

Aside from its many hazards, residences, and businesses, the lower river offers islands to explore, wildlife, and beautiful views of the downtown Portland area. Dragon Boat races are held each spring near Waterfront Park. Sculling is also popular along the waterfront. Beyond the downtown area, shipping and industrial areas line the shores with countless smokestacks, lights, and storage containers making up the main view. Beyond the industrial area, near Multnomah Channel and Sauvie Island, the river returns to a more natural setting. Kelley Point Park on the eastern shore of the Willamette River marks the last access above the Columbia River confluence. The Columbia Slough, which has been cleaned up in recent years, has become popular among paddlers. The slough drains Smith and Bybee lakes, entering the Willamette River one mile upstream of Kelley Point Park.

—*Field Blackard* and *Robb Keller*

Willamette River Public Access Areas by River Mile

Access	RM	Right/Left Side
Kelley Point Park	0	R
Cathedral Park	6	R
Tom McCall Waterfront Park	13	L
Oaks Bottom	15	R
Willamette Park	16	L
Sellwood Riverfront Park	16	R
Powers Marine Park	17	L
Jefferson Street Boat Ramp	18	R
Roehr Park	20	L
Oak Grove Boat Ramp	21	R
George Rogers Park	22	L
Cedar Oak Boat Ramp	23	L
Mary S. Young State Park	24	L
Meldrum Bar Park	24	R
Dahl Park	25	R
Clackamette Park	25	R
Westbridge Park	25	L
Bernert Landing	28	L
Rock Island Landing	30	L
Coalca Landing	30	R
Fish Eddy Landing	33	R
Hebb Park	34	L

Access	RM	Right/Left Side
Molalla River State Park	36	R
Willamette Meridian Landing	37	L
Wilsonville Memorial Park	38	L
Boones Ferry Boat Ramp	39	R
French Prairie Access	41	R
Champoeg State Park	45	R
Parrett Mountain Access	46	L
Rodgers Landing	50	L
Hess Creek Landing	53	L
San Salvador Park	56	R
Yamhill Landing	57	L
Jackson Bend Landing	64	R
Eldridge Bar Landing	69	R
Willamette Mission State Park	70	L
Willamette Mission Boat Ramp	72	R
Spring Valley Access	74	L
Windsor Island Access	76	R
Lincoln Access	77	L
Spongs Landing Park	78	R
Darrow Bar Access	78	L
Darrow Rocks Landing	79	L
Beardsley's Bar Access	79	R
Palma Ciea Park	81	R
Sunset Park	81	R
River's Edge Park	82	R
McLane Island	83	C
Wallace Marine Park	84	L
Downtown Riverfront Park	84	R
Minto–Brown Island	86	R
Halls Ferry Access	91	R
E. Mark/L.Strange Fishing Hole	91	L
Independence Riverview Park	95	L
Independence Island	96	L
Independence Bar Landing	97	R
Sidney Access	101	R
American Bottom Landing	104	L
Wells Island Park	105	C
Buena Vista Park	106	L
Luckiamute Landing	109	L
Black Dog Landing	112	R
Takena Landing	117	L
Bowman Park	118	R

continued on next page

Access	RM	Right/Left Side
Montieth River Park	119	R
Bryant Park	120	R
Bowers Rock State Park	121	R
Hyak Park	122	L
Riverside Landing	125	R
Half Moon Bend Landing	126	L
Truax Island Access	127	R
Michael's Landing	131	L
Waterfront Park (Corvallis)	131	L
Martin Luther King Jr. and Alan Berg Parks	131	R
Pioneer Boat Basin	132	L
Willamette Park	134	L
River Jetty Landing	136	L
Kiger Island Landing	137	L
Peoria Park	141	R
Hoacum Island Landing	143	L
Buckskin Mary Landing	145	L
Sam Daws Landing	146	R
Irish Bend	151	L
Harkens Landing	153	L
Anderson Park	154	L
McCartney Park	156	R
Harrisburg Park	161	R
Blue Ruin Island	165	R
Scandia Landing	166	L
Brown's Boat Skid	167	L
Christensen's Boat Ramp	169	R
Marshall Island Park	169	L
Beacon Landing	172	L
Hileman Boat Ramp	173	L
Rogers Bend Landing	174	L
Whitely Landing	175	R
Whitely Boat Ramp	176	L
Armitage State Park	178	L
Beltline West Boat Ramp	178	L
West Bank Park	180	L
Maurie Jacobs Park	181	L
Skinner Butte Park	182	L
Alton Baker Park & Waterway	183	R
West D Street Greenway	185	R
Island Park	186	R

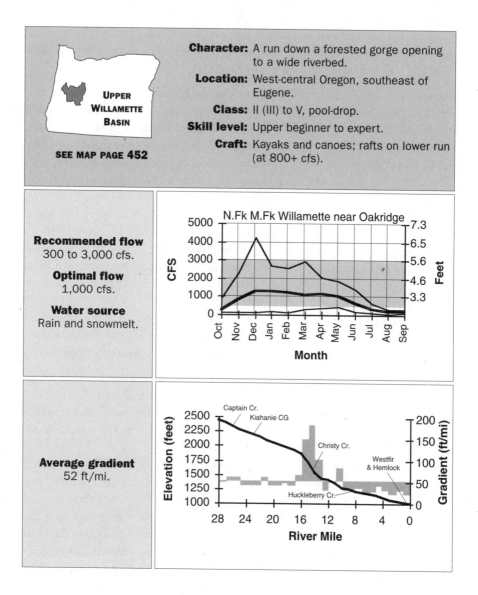

UPPER WILLAMETTE BASIN

SEE MAP PAGE **452**

Character: A run down a forested gorge opening to a wide riverbed.

Location: West-central Oregon, southeast of Eugene.

Class: II (III) to V, pool-drop.

Skill level: Upper beginner to expert.

Craft: Kayaks and canoes; rafts on lower run (at 800+ cfs).

Recommended flow
300 to 3,000 cfs.

Optimal flow
1,000 cfs.

Water source
Rain and snowmelt.

Average gradient
52 ft/mi.

N.Fk M.Fk Willamette near Oakridge

CFS / Feet / Month

Elevation (feet) / Gradient (ft/mi) / River Mile

Captain Cr.
Kiahanie CG
Christy Cr.
Westfir & Hemlock
Huckleberry Cr.

Hazards: Logs are a concern on the North Fork of the Middle Fork Willamette River, and they tend to move after high water. The upper section has severe pinning potential in continuous rapids. At press time, there was a nasty trap in the middle of **Whoop-De-Doo**. Several logs have jammed the normal S-turn from left to center, but are only visible once you are very close to the drop. Eddies are small if you go too far into the rapid. **Dragon Slayer** is a nasty keeper hole just below Christy Creek Bridge. Scout it from river right.

Access: From Interstate 5 at Eugene, take Oregon Highway 58 to the Westfir exit, which is about 2 miles north of Oakridge. Continue on North Fork Road through the town of Westfir. In about 0.5 mile you'll see an old weigh station, which is the first take-out. The road continues upstream, following the river closely and providing lots of put-in and take-out options. Where the road crosses the river, paddlers put in for the lower run; between this bridge and the next, about 1 mile upriver, is the Class IV lower gorge.

There are several put-ins in the 2-mile flat section above the gorge for those who want to add excitement to their day. The next road to the left crosses Christy Creek Bridge, where a stream gage is located. This bridge is often used as a take-out for those who just want to run the **Miracle Mile** section (perhaps two or three times in a day). You can also put-in at the bridge, but you'll want to scout or portage **Dragon Slayer**, just downstream.

Continue upstream on North Fork Road for another mile. On the way, you'll get glimpses of the Miracle Mile. As soon as the road comes level with the river, look for a couple of turnouts on the left side of road. This is the Duck Pond put-in.

Overview: The North Fork of the Middle Fork Willamette River has been designated a Wild and Scenic River for good reason. Thick forests and steep mountains make this a favorite of mine. The lower gorge has beautiful, steep, moss-covered cliffs and a spectacular waterfall that drops in from river left. The transition between upper and lower river keeps boaters' interest.

Below the upper Duck Pond put-in, the river stays shallow and flat over gravel bars and logs. Just around the corner it starts to drop steeply for about a mile, then gradually flattens to Class II+ water for about 2 miles. The river then changes again as it drops through the Class IV lower gorge. Below the gorge, the river has a more open feel with lower gradient (about 30 feet per mile) and Class II and III pool-drop rapids. The lower section to Westfir is a good intermediate run, although rapids such as **Shotgun** and **Bullseye** can be intimidating.

The best way to check out the flow is to look at the stream gage on the river right pillar of the Christy Creek Bridge. Here, one foot equals 1,000 cubic feet per second, a highly scientific equation devised by very unscientific kayakers.

Going with the Flow
Section 1: Duck Pond to Lower Gorge (Miracle Mile)

Class: V	Recommended flow: 300 to 1,200 cfs	Miles: 5

Putting in at the Duck Pond gives paddlers a mellow start with a nice Class III+ warm-up rapid and some nice eddies for practice. The first bridge signals the start of the steep stuff. The next mile is affectionately called the **Miracle Mile** for all its whitewater. Watch for a big log-jam on the right just below the bridge. Stay far left and you will immediately be thrown into **Initiation**. The hazing lasts for about 0.25 mile with lots of small drops and some tough eddy-hopping.

After this straight section, the river mellows briefly and bends to the right. Get out on the left to scout **Ricochet** rapid. One short drop below Ricochet, watch for a big eddy on river right. This is a good place to get out and look at the top of **Confusion**, a long, tight, technical rapid. Below where the river bends back to the right is a drop called **Shark's Tooth**. The crux move here is visible from the eddies at the top, but it's a tough one. After the crux move at the top, you will have to negotiate a big runout.

Next keep your eyes peeled for two islands on the right, marking the start of Whoop-De-Doo. Eddy out on the left when you come to the first island and scout on the left. The sneak route between the islands is the recommended line, due to logs left and center. Below Whoop-De-Doo paddlers have better visibility. With smaller boulders and drops, the river is tough all the way to the Christy Creek Bridge. Beware of a very dangerous, nearly invisible log in the middle of a long

A paddler looks deep into Dragon Slayer. JASON BATES PHOTO

399

straight stretch; look for an old dead snag on river right as a sign, then stay far left or take the small slot left-of-center. Do not go down the main channel right-of-center.

Once you make it to the bridge, get out on river right to scout Dragon Slayer. Better yet, go down the little rock garden on river left as far as you can and portage to the bottom of the rapid. After two long Class IV rapids that follow, look for a cliff on your right with a steep drop just in front of it. Scout on the right; this is the **Boat Abuser.**

Below Boat Abuser, the river has a few more Class III and IV rapids before settling into a mellow Class II float for about 2 miles. The third bridge signals the start of the lower gorge. The gorge rates a Class IV, with about four good rapids before the really big one. The boulder garden here ranges from Class IV to V, depending on flow and route. Around the corner, a big slab of rock has fallen off the left wall at the second biggest rapid. Scout all of the lower gorge from the road before you run it.

The fourth bridge signals the end of the gorge and the start of the next section.

Section 2: Lower Gorge to Westfir

Class: II to III+   **Recommended flow:** 500 to 3,000 cfs   **Miles:** 8.5

Section 2 is a great run for intermediate paddlers, allowing them to hone their skills amid lots of play spots and numerous good rapids in a scenic location. Reliable flows during the rainy season make this a standard winter run. Rapids that stand out are Shotgun and Bullseye. Both of these big ones plus most of the other main rapids can be scouted from the road.

Shotgun has a fun vertical drop at low to medium flows, and a big hole at high flows. Bullseye is tricky, with several lines available. The main current on the left drops through two slots, one aiming right and one aiming left. The slots converge and slam into the Bullseye rock. Good luck here. Watch out for the sneaky rapid just below Bullseye, especially at high water when a nasty hole forms on the right.

Some paddlers use the next bridge as a take-out for a shorter run. Below the bridge, the river is mostly Class II water with a couple of tricky, shallow ledge-drop rapids. The run below the fifth bridge would be suitable to novice paddlers who have a good roll and are guided by those more familiar with the run. Take out at the old weigh station in Westfir or continue down to the Middle Fork Willamette River for easier Class I and II water.

—*Jason Bates*

89 Wilson River
Drift Creek Bridge to Tillamook

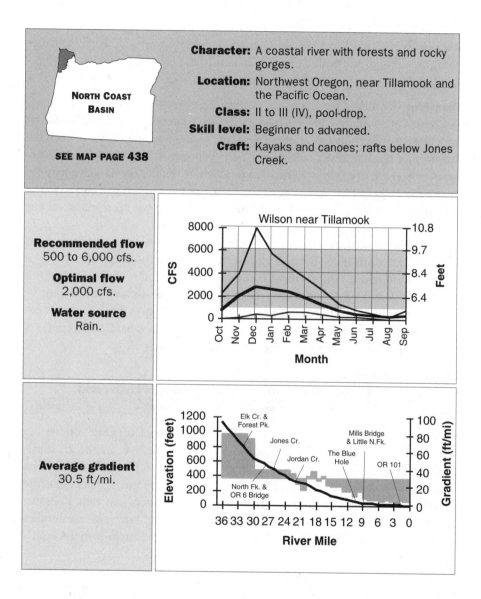

Character: A coastal river with forests and rocky gorges.

Location: Northwest Oregon, near Tillamook and the Pacific Ocean.

Class: II to III (IV), pool-drop.

Skill level: Beginner to advanced.

Craft: Kayaks and canoes; rafts below Jones Creek.

NORTH COAST BASIN

SEE MAP PAGE **438**

Recommended flow
500 to 6,000 cfs.

Optimal flow
2,000 cfs.

Water source
Rain.

Wilson near Tillamook

Average gradient
30.5 ft/mi.

Elk Cr. & Forest Pk.

Jones Cr.

Jordan Cr.

Mills Bridge & Little N.Fk.

The Blue Hole

OR 101

North Fk. & OR 6 Bridge

Hazards: Watch for logs on the Wilson River. The upper Class IV+ rapids in the Devil's Lake Fork section, and various Class III and IV drops are the major water hazards. Rafters should stick to the lower Wilson (Sections 2 and 3), where the river widens and gains in flow.

Access: The Wilson River follows Oregon Highway 6 from U.S. Highway 26 to Tillamook. From Portland, follow US 26 east to the OR 6 intersection, then follow OR 6 southeast to any of various put-ins and take-outs along the road.

Overview: The Wilson River is one of northwest Oregon's standard spring through fall runs. On any particular weekend in season, boaters can be found here. The water can change from a clear blue-green gem to a raging, muddy mess when the stream gage reads at levels higher than 9 feet. Though OR 6 parallels and sometimes crosses the river, allowing many access sites, it remains far enough above the river gorge to keep from interrupting the beauty of this run through carved basalt rock. Deciduous trees line the banks, shielding views of weekend traffic on this major coastal route.

Paddlers often encounter deer along the road and the river; every year, at least one accident occurs involving deer along OR 6. Anglers also frequent the Wilson on all its stretches, but are most common between Jones Creek Bridge and Tillamook. Stay away from fishing holes when you are picking a surf spot or boating past anglers with lines in the water. On Class II stretches, drift boats become the popular means of casting. Private property inhibits bank fishing options along much of the lower river, except at boat launch areas.

Going with the flow
Section 1: Drift Creek Bridge to Jones Creek (Devils Lake Fork)

Class: III+ to IV	**Recommended flow:** 350 to 1,500 cfs	**Miles:** 8+

On the upper Devil's Lake Fork of the Wilson River, below Drift Creek Bridge, the river rates a Class IV+. It drops through an old landslide here, and debris sometimes makes this section unrunnable. Since the floods of 1996, the section has cleared out enough to run. Be prepared for technical drops through tight, narrow stretches. By scouting from the road at the put-in, boaters can view the most demanding stretch of whitewater. Two notable rapids that flow into one another are called **The Big One** and **The Little One**. These rapids approach a Class V rating at higher flows.

Below this initial rapid stretch, the river keeps its Class IV character but begins to widen. As the gradient eases, logs and debris require mandatory portages. Boaters soon reach a second bridge, where an alternate put-in avoids the more difficult Class IV water. Below this point, flows are increased by the addition of the South Fork Wilson River. Class III rapids continue for about 0.5 mile, after which the river eases to Class II+. A more significant pool-drop rapid occurs at just over 0.5 mile below the bridge. Here the water funnels into a turbulent chute after dropping over a 5-foot ledge; scout on the right.

Not far downstream, Elk Creek also brings up the flow. Here, Class III+ **Elk Creek** rapid first shows itself as a horizon line less than a mile below the confluence with the South Fork Wilson. Scout or portage on the right bank well above the drop. The left side drops into a keeper hole over a boat-scraping edge, then slams into a wall in the eddy below. The drop looks more innocent than it is. Having been stuck in this hole, I can report that its river-deep hydraulic could bounce a swimmer off the bottom. Escaping can be tricky; swimmers must work toward the edges of the hole and the outflow. It's better to take the recommended route down the center-to-right chutes. At low water, the center route is mandatory, since the right side becomes too rocky.

Below Elk Creek, the river maintains a continuous Class II+ character where boaters can play among many great surf spots. At islands and channels in the next few miles, stay center and right. About a mile below Elk Creek is another steeper drop where turbulent water drops sharply into a pool that makes a right-hand bend. Scout or portage on the right.

Jones Creek rapid is the most difficult on the river below the South Fork confluence. Scout this Class IV drop from the island that separates the rapid into two channels. Choose one of the two channels, depending on water level. The left side is shorter but more turbulent. The right side makes three stairstep drops as it winds to the left. Beware of a sharp rock in the lower center, which often forms a roostertail. Current can push boaters away from their intended route into this rock. The bridge at Jones Creek is another good scouting point and a popular take-out. If the rapid looks too intimidating, Jones Creek makes a good put-in for the easier section below.

Section 2: Jones Creek to Milepost 8 Boat Ramp

Class: III (IV)   **Recommended flow:** 800 to 6,000 cfs   **Miles:** 15

If the rapids farther upstream are not your cup of tea, try Section 2. It has a high thrill factor, with less-complex routes through Class III water. Pool-drop rapids are spread evenly throughout this section, separated by Class II water with many play spots. Rafts can negotiate the river from Jones Creek to Tillamook but may have trouble at **The Narrows,** which is only 10 feet wide!

Just over a mile into this section, boaters encounter **The Gorge.** Here the river narrows into turbulent pool-drop rapids around blind corners. Holes exist on the inside and outside edges, with good surf waves at the bottoms at some levels. Class II water separates larger Class III to III+ drops, allowing recovery and good return eddies for surfing. At very high water The Gorge approaches Class IV-.

Jordan Creek enters on the left about 5 miles below Jones Creek. Boaters who want a more technical float can put in up the creek at flows over 6 feet on the Wilson River gage. A nice surf wave and wave hole marks the confluence. An alternate take-out here is near the bridge.

The Narrows are more difficult than other rapids on this section and demand a scout. The rapids occur just 1 mile below the confluence with Jordan Creek and cannot be viewed from the road. Scout along the right bank before entering the Class III lead-in. Pull out on river right and scramble along the bank to view the narrow passage as it twists left, ensuring that it is free of debris. Longer kayaks and canoes could easily wedge here if caught sideways at low water. Since private property lines the banks, portaging is difficult or impossible. Rafters may wish to take out above the narrow confine, but take-outs are up steep banks or narrow trails. Houses come into view below this rapid, and posted private property borders the waterway.

The river eases to Class II water with occasional Class II+ rapids. Surf spots and small holes entertain boaters to the Section 2 take-out at the milepost 8 boat ramp. Another common take-out is at a roadside pullout at milepost 15.

Section 3: Milepost 8 Boat Ramp to Tillamook

Class: I to II	Recommended flow: 800 to 7,000 cfs	Miles: 9

In its lower reaches, the Wilson River is wider and slower than sections upstream. Anglers find this section particularly good for drift boats, since there are several boat launches in the lower river. The Wilson is a good producer of salmon and steelhead in any given year. Homes and trailer parks line its banks in places, but the river still maintains a secluded feel as it meanders to the coast. Fog often greets boaters in spring and fall.

When the river begins to change from its usual clear blue color to a murky brown, this signals that the current will be stronger. Find a nice eddy to park in for breaks or fishing.

90 Wind River, Washington

Above Trout Creek to Columbia River

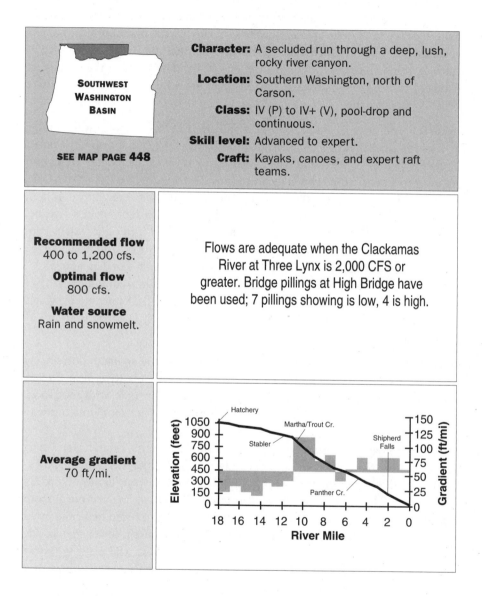

Character: A secluded run through a deep, lush, rocky river canyon.

Location: Southern Washington, north of Carson.

Class: IV (P) to IV+ (V), pool-drop and continuous.

Skill level: Advanced to expert.

Craft: Kayaks, canoes, and expert raft teams.

SOUTHWEST WASHINGTON BASIN

SEE MAP PAGE 448

Recommended flow
400 to 1,200 cfs.

Optimal flow
800 cfs.

Water source
Rain and snowmelt.

Flows are adequate when the Clackamas River at Three Lynx is 2,000 CFS or greater. Bridge pillings at High Bridge have been used; 7 pillings showing is low, 4 is high.

Average gradient
70 ft/mi.

Hazards: Section 1 contains continuous boulder gardens and ledge-drops from **Initiation** to **Climax**. Paddlers could get pinned in many places throughout this area. Eddies are small, so you should allow plenty of room between boats while running. On Section 2 the lead-in rapids to the two mandatory portages at **Shipherd Falls** and **Beyond Limits** are deceptively fast. Unwary or over-confident boaters could quickly find themselves in a life-threatening situation if they are tempted to catch "just one more eddy." Snow, ice, or wet conditions make the portage at Shipherd Falls nearly impossible. Luckily, trees are less of an issue on the lower broad, pool-drop run.

Access: From Interstate 84 between Portland and The Dalles, cross the toll bridge at Cascade Locks and follow Washington Highway 14 east for about 8 miles. Cross the mouth of the Wind River, then turn left on Old Hatchery Road and follow it to a boat ramp. This is the lowermost take-out.

To reach the put-in for the lower run or the take-out for the upper section, return to WA 14. Head west, then turn right (north) on Hot Springs Avenue. Proceed 2 miles to the stop sign at Wind River Road and turn right (east) again. Proceed 2 miles to High Bridge Road, on the left. Take this road and then take the first right onto Old Detour Road, following it to the river in less than a mile.

To reach the upper put-in, return to Wind River Road and continue north 5.3 miles to Hemlock Road. Follow Hemlock Road west for 0.25 mile to Edgewater Drive, heading right. Follow Edgewater Drive to the river. The land is private at this put-in; please respect it and the owners.

Overview: The Wind River is a classic stream with plenty of action. It flows freely down the southern flanks of Mount Adams to the Columbia River near Carson Hot Springs. The springs make a wonderful end to a day's paddle, with good food, lodging, and clawfoot tubs for soaking. Don't miss this "hot spot" on your way home.

Though boaters have run the Wind River in paddle rafts, catarafts, and even an open canoe (Richard Frenzel), I can only recommend kayaks and decked canoes here. In open craft, the river's continuous obstacles can be negotiated by experts only. The pool-drop rapids of the lower Wind River make it much more forgiving than the upper section. Strong intermediate boaters can make the run if they go in the company of more advanced boaters. Few run the lower stretch, due to the extremely strenuous portage at Shipherd Falls. Those who make the effort are rewarded with Class III to IV rapids, a beautiful and isolated canyon, and hot springs to console trembling muscles.

Get a good feel for water level and difficulty by looking at the river from High Bridge along Wind River Road, several miles north of Carson. If the huge boulders in this Class IV section are sticking out of the water with slow to moderate current, the level is good for a first run. If the same boulders are making holes and the river sounds like a freight train, go elsewhere. Paddlers usually run the upper section in the fall and from spring to early summer. The lower river is best run at lower water on a warm, sunny day.

Going with the Flow
Section 1: Edgewater Drive to High Bridge

Class: IV+ (V)	Recommended flow: 400 to 1,200 cfs	Miles: 6

At the Section 1 put-in and take-out, the Wind River looks much easier than it does between the two points. The upper section begins with Class II and III pool-drop rapids that have carved the riverbed's basalt walls. The walls begin to open and the rapids pick up pace before Trout Creek enters on the right. Some paddlers take time to paddle Trout Creek as a warm-up. Just past Trout Creek, the rapid known as **Initiation** looms below. Scout on the right below the confluence. This long series of boulders, holes, and ledges continues for some distance before easing up.

After getting initiated, paddlers face boulder gardens that continue for more than 2 miles of nonstop action. Steep horizon line drops here contain tricky routes over ledges and around wrap rocks. Scout frequently from your boat at small eddies along the way. Many eddies will hold only one or two boats at a time, so space yourselves appropriately. Somewhere near the lower middle of this continuous stretch lies **Ram's Horn.** Scout on either side, but portage on the right. At higher flows, a sneak route along the left misses the protruding rock horn, but a nasty river-wide keeper hole forms just before the obstacle. Punch the hole with speed on the far left or right, or portage along the right rock ledge and seal-launch into the pool along the bottom right.

More action continues to **Climax,** another horizon line drop. For all practical purposes the stretch from Initiation to Climax is one continuous, 2.5-mile rapid. You'll enjoy a waterfall cascading from the right, if you get a chance to see it. After the action lets up, there remain only Class II and III pool-drops to the take-out. Take note of the take-out area as you drop your shuttle vehicle, since you'll find yourself running Section 2 if you miss it!

–Robb Keller

Section 2: High Bridge to Columbia River

Class: IV (P)	Recommended flow: 400 to 1,000 cfs	Miles: 5

In Section 2, less than 0.5 mile of Class II water precedes Class IV **High Bridge** rapid. Eddy out just above the bridge on the left your first time down to check out a nasty river-wide hole. Less-confident boaters may choose to walk around this one. The rest of rapid can be eddy-hopped, with a variety of routes to choose from.

Beyond a short gorge, Panther Creek enters from the left and adds substantially to the flow. About 1 mile of enjoyable Class III to III+ rapids follow. Most of these can be read and run from the boat; all can be easily examined from the right bank if you so desire. As the river slows and disappears to the left over an obvious horizon line, get out on the right to scout **The Flume.** This Class IV+ drop is steep but straightforward through some intense hydraulics. A relatively easy portage on the right requires a squirrelly seal-launch into the foaming runout.

The Flume marks the beginning of the most spectacular and dangerous stretch of river. A couple of drops below it is Beyond Limits, a serious Class VI waterfall marked by a concrete fish ladder on the left. Eddy out early on the left and portage. Many excellent Class III to IV rapids follow. A sweeping left turn begins a long, pushy Class IV rapid that first-timers will want to scout on the right. Start center and work far left to avoid some big holes center and right.

Shortly after this drop, a footbridge over the river indicates the approach of Shipherd Falls. This impressive cataract drops 50 to 60 feet in five steps. Eddy out on the left after a Class III drop but before the Class II water that leads into the falls. A screw-up here would likely be fatal. Follow the steep trail up and over the cliff on the left bank. Ropes and teamwork make the endeavor manageable. The reward for hardy paddlers who survive this ordeal comes in the form of a hot spring about 0.25 mile down on the left. The rest of the run gradually tapers from Class II to flatwater as you approach the take-out boat ramp.

–Rob Cruiser

91 Yamhill River, South Fork
Grand Ronde to McMinnville

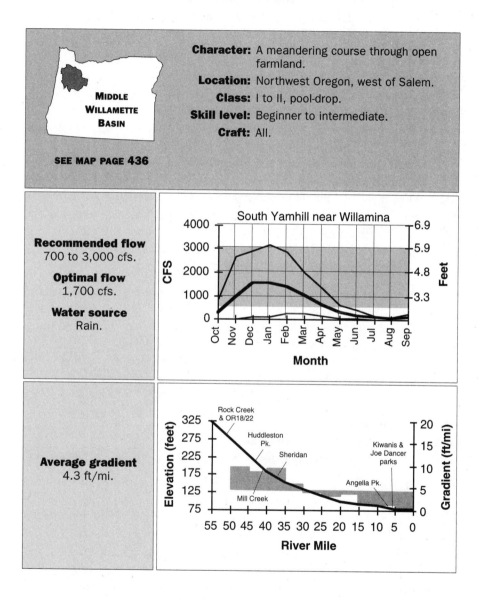

Character: A meandering course through open farmland.

Location: Northwest Oregon, west of Salem.

Class: I to II, pool-drop.

Skill level: Beginner to intermediate.

Craft: All.

MIDDLE
WILLAMETTE
BASIN

SEE MAP PAGE **436**

Recommended flow
700 to 3,000 cfs.

Optimal flow
1,700 cfs.

Water source
Rain.

South Yamhill near Willamina

Average gradient
4.3 ft/mi.

Hazards: The upper South Fork Yamhill River contains brushy areas with narrow passage around islands, plus two difficult ledge-drops above Sherman. The lower river is mostly flatwater with brushy banks. Currents are much swifter at higher flows. Give yourself plenty of time to paddle the flat stretches, since currents are almost nonexistent at lower flows and between steeper drops.

Access: From Oregon Highway 99W at McMinnville, follow Three Mile Lane to Kiwanis Marine Park, on river left. This is a good take-out for the lower stretch of river. Continue along OR 99W (the Pacific Highway) west beyond McMinnville, taking Oregon Highway 18 at the intersection. Follow OR 18 to Bellevue, then turn left onto the Bellevue Highway and head toward Amity. The highway crosses the South Fork Yamhill River in about 1 mile for access.

For upriver locations, continue west along OR 18 to Sheridan. Cross the bridge at Sheridan and park in a suitable location near the store. Access is below the bridge down the steep bank. The upper put-in is farther west along OR 18 near the community of Grand Ronde. On Grand Ronde Road, heading south, a bridge crosses the river; this is the upper put-in. There are many spots along the road for take-out access. Make sure you mark the bank or take note of geographic indicators, since much of the bank looks the same from the river.

Overview: The South Fork Yamhill River is a great place for beginning paddlers or advanced beginners moving toward Class II rapids. Most of the river meanders though rural farmland with thick vegetation along its banks. In fall, beautiful deciduous trees drop colorful leaves into the reflective flatwater.

Always allow plenty of time to make your way along longer stretches of the South Yamhill, since there are few access locations on the lower river and current can be extremely slow at normal flows.

Going with the Flow
Section 1: Grand Ronde to Sheridan

Class: II (II+)	Recommended flow: 700 to 3,000 cfs	Miles: 15

The South Fork Yamhill River flows lazily for several miles below the put-in at Grand Ronde. Class II ledge-drops of 1 to 3 feet occur in places, separated by miles of flatwater. At higher flows some waves develop, allowing paddlers to practice surfing skills; at lower flows they are too small to surf.

About 7.5 miles below Grand Ronde, a larger ledge-drop leads to a pool and flatwater. This drop is similar in appearance to a more difficult ledge-drop, known as **The Ledge,** about 2 miles downstream. The area between the two drops requires some tight maneuvering around brushy islands. Narrow passages here are not recommended for beginning paddlers with little experience.

Mill Creek enters from the right about 1 mile below The Ledge, signaling that the take-out at Sheridan is 3 miles downstream. Take out under the bridge and hike up the bank to the road and store.

The upper South Yamhill is a good place for paddlers to tackle Class II waters.

Section 2: Sheridan to McMinnville and the Willamette River

Class: I   **Recommended flow:** 700 to 3,000 cfs   **Miles:** 45.6

The lower South Yamhill continues to meander through open farmlands, but offers paddlers fewer access options. Most boaters divide this stretch at the Bellevue–Amity Road bridge. The upper stretch is brushy and contains faster water with some Class I riffles. The lower reaches are mostly flatwater and can be very slow.

Always give yourself plenty of time to paddle these meandering stretches of slow water. There are few hazards and few signs of habitation except for farms along the way. Banks are muddy and brush lined. Take out at Marina Park on the left at McMinnville beyond the bridge.

Boaters can continue to the Willamette River from McMinnville on Class I water. The 17-mile trip takes one long day and includes the main Yamhill River.

Eddyville to Pacific Ocean

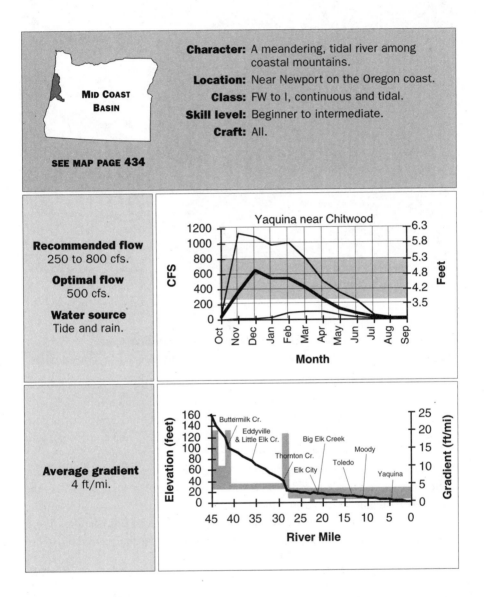

MID COAST
BASIN

SEE MAP PAGE **434**

Character: A meandering, tidal river among coastal mountains.

Location: Near Newport on the Oregon coast.

Class: FW to I, continuous and tidal.

Skill level: Beginner to intermediate.

Craft: All.

Recommended flow
250 to 800 cfs.

Optimal flow
500 cfs.

Water source
Tide and rain.

Average gradient
4 ft/mi.

Yaquina near Chitwood

Buttermilk Cr.
Eddyville & Little Elk Cr.
Big Elk Creek
Thornton Cr.
Moody
Elk City
Toledo
Yaquina

Hazards: There are few hazards along the Yaquina River, with the exception of brushy banks and wood in places. The lower river is tidal below Thornton Creek above Elk City; paddlers who go beyond this point should review tide charts for flow direction. Travel can be slow-going, and upstream winds are common along the lower river. Plan on covering a shorter distance than you would on a faster stream.

A large number of ocean-going fishing boats travel into Yaquina Bay. Always give these boats plenty of room, since they must follow certain tidal channels. Respect anglers all along the river, and paddle on the opposite bank from where they are working. If you can, ask where they would prefer you pass.

Access: From U.S. Highway 101 in Newport, U.S. Highway 20 leads east to Toledo. For midriver access, turn and follow onto Toledo's Main Street, heading southwest. This road eventually becomes Elk City Road, which leads to Elk City. Upstream access is available at Moody; south of Toledo just off of Elk City Road; Toledo Boat Launch; Cannon Park and Boat Launch between Toledo and Elk City; and Elk City Dock and Ramp in Elk City.

Elk City Road eventually returns to US 20 before reaching Thornton Creek. US 20 follows the Yaquina River from below Chitwood to Eddyville, where it then follows Little Elk Creek to Ellmaker State Park. Access in Eddyville is possible near the bridge along US 20, but no boat launch facilities are available above Elk City.

From Eddyville, the Eddyville–Blodgett Highway follows the Yaquina River upstream to the mountain summit that divides the Yaquina and Marys rivers. Use bridges or roadside areas for a launch along the upper river.

Lower access areas are located in Newport at the Newport Marina near the bay; South Beach Marina just across the US 101 bridge along south Yaquina Bay; Idaho Point Marina, east of the community of South Beach; and River Bend Moorage near Oneatta Point Campground, south of US 20 along Yaquina Bay Road.

Overview: The Yaquina River is a mostly tidal stream that empties into Yaquina Bay. The bay is also known as Newport Bay, since the large metropolitan center of Newport lies along its northern shore. Ocean fishing, oyster beds, and timber mills sustain the area's population. Tourism is popular in and around Newport, where good seafood, colorful kites, saltwater taffy, seagulls, and big fishing boats are attractions. Sea lions, seals, lighthouses, and beautiful surfing beaches draw tourists along the coast.

The river is best suited to sea kayaks and canoes. It slowly meanders from Eddyville to the Pacific Ocean. The small upper river contains little water except during the rainy season. Watch for logs and brush above Elk City. Along the tidal reaches, the river widens and slows. Give yourself plenty of time to complete a desired run. If you are used to flowing streams, double the time you expect you'll need to complete a trip.

The upper river is more isolated from population and boat traffic; it's also more scenic. At the small community of Eddyville, Little Elk Creek joins with the Yaquina to nearly double the flow. Clearcuts stand as evidence of the logging activity that feeds local mills. A historic covered bridge marks Elk City and the confluence with Big Elk Creek. Salmon fishing is popular during fall runs of chinook; expect to see anglers along the lower river from Elk City to Yaquina Bay. They often gather along the bay or near Elk City around Big Elk Creek.

Going with the Flow

Class: FW to II   **Recommended flow:** 250 to 700 cfs (with tide)   **Miles:** 36

The upper Yaquina River earns a Class II rating due to its small streambed, sharp bends, and sometimes rocky flows. The river drops from the coastal mountains just a few miles above Eddyville, above which the current and difficulty increases. I have not explored the upper river beyond Eddyville, though I have listed profile and gradient information for those interested in checking it out.

From Eddyville to Elk City the river is small with more frequent bends in the riverbed. Keep alert for debris, particularly along the outside of each bend. Before reaching Elk City, you'll see the large, red covered bridge. Look for the boat ramp above the bridge on river left, one possible access site. A small store in town can provide food and drink.

Below Elk City, the river makes wide undulations to Yaquina Bay. Cannon Park lies a little more than halfway to the ocean, making possible a reasonable division of the stretch from Elk City to the bay. Beginners should float to or from this access on a one-day venture.

There are no hazards along the tidal river, but upstream winds can make the going slow. Choppy water and power boats can be a problem along the wider reaches of the bay. At low tide, muddy tidal flats flank both sides of the river, with deeper water toward river center. Large seagoing fishing boats leave and enter the bay frequently during the regular season; watch for them and give them plenty of room to pass.

Seagulls and seals frequent the area, cleaning up fish tailings thrown into the bay. Crabs also feed on fish remains. Do not mess with crab pots placed by local commercial fishermen, but do sample the seafood cuisine at nearby Newport restaurants.

More details at: www.paddling.oregon.com
Profile/Gradient charts and hydrographs are available for most of the streams.

River	Class	Flow CFS	Gradient ft./mi.	Water Source	Trip Type	Basin
Applegate River Flume Flat to Rogue River	II to III+	800-2500	20.1	Dam	Day	R
Large Rogue tributary with residential areas.						
Big Butte Creek Butte Falls picnic area to Rogue R.	III+(IV,V)	350-1000	62	Rain/Snow	Day	R
A rapid-filled creek through forested mountain canyon.						
Blue River Above Blue Lake	IV+ &V	250-900	79	Rain/Snow	Day	UW
Technical, small river with Class V tripple drops.						
Canton Creek Upper creek to North Umpqua River	III to IV (V)	250-2000	93	Rain/Snow	Day	U
Steep creek with clear-cuts, ledge drops, and falls.						
Chewaucan River Upper reaches to Paisley	Exploratory	250-800	50	Rain/Spring	Day	G&SL
A descent from forested canyon through steeper drops to open high desert.						
Clackamas, Oak Grove Fork Below Timothy Lake to Clackamas R.	III+ to V	350-800	115	Dam	Day	LW
Isolated, steep river fork in log-choked, deep, forested canyon.						
Columbia Hat Rock and McNary Dam to Astoria	FW	5-20 ft.	<1	Dam	Day/Multi	Various
A long, wide, island and channel filled river with refuges between large dams.						
Copeland Creek NFD 300 Bridge to N.Umpqua R.	IV(V)	400-1000	160	Rain	Day	U
A scenic, exciting, forested tributary of the North Umpqua River.						
Cow Creek I-5 near Galesville to Lawson Bar	I(II) to III-IV	500-2500	18.4	Rain/Snow	Day	U
Long isolated tributary of the South Umpqua River.						
Crooked, North Fork Deep Creek CG to Main Crooked R.	II+(P)	500-1000	37.5	Rain/Snow	Multi	D
Isolated, multi-day trip with basalt gorges, containing two waterfalls.						
Crooked, Upper Above and below Prineville Reservoir	II to III	800-3500	10.3	Dam/Rain	Day/Multi	D
High desert stream with camping and abundant wildlife.						
Fish Creek 4+ miles above Clackamas River	III+ to IV-	500-1500	180	Rain	Day	LW
A forested, rocky tributary of the upper Clackamas River popular with anglers.						

River	Class	Flow CFS	Gradient ft./mi.	Water Source	Trip Type	Basin
Granite Creek Granite to North Fork John Day River	II & III(V,P)	250-600	59	Rain/Snow	Day/Multi	JD
Dredged creek to forested, isolated wilderness.						
Grays (WA) South Fork to Grays Bay	FW to IV+	500-1500	24	Rain	Day	WA
Short Class IV+ canyon below the south fork to Class I and tidal flats to the bay.						
Humbug Creek US Hwy 26 to Nehalem River	I to II	250-700	20	Rain	Day	NC
A small creek meandering from forest to open river valley.						
Joseph Creek Hwy 46 to Grande Ronde River	II to IV	250-800	50	Rain/Snow	Day/Multi	GR
An isolated wild and scenic trip from deep forested canyon to desert.						
Lewis and Clark Upper boat launch to Youngs Bay	FW	Tidal	<1	Tidal	Day	NC
A trip through coastal farm/grazing lands past historical Fort Clatsop.						
Long Tom Cheshire Road to Willamette River	I+	200-2000	3.5	Dam	Day	UW
Slow, meandering stream with dams.						
Luckiamute Foster Creek to Willamette River	I to III+(V,P)	300-2000	5.2	Rain/Dam	Day	UW
Narrow, brushy stream meandering to the Willamette. Log choked upper run.						
Malheur Above Drewsey to Snake River	I to II	500-3000	9.7	Dam	Day/Multi	M
A long rural high desert river with dams and weirs.						
Marys Blodgett to Willamette River	I to I+(II)	250-1200	12	Rain	Day	UW
Scenic, meandering, isolated river flowing east off the coast range.						
McKenzie, South Fork Frissell Crossing CG to Cougar Res.	III+ to IV	400-2500	65	Rain/Snow	Day	UW
Exciting, forested run with campgrounds above Cougar Reservoir.						
Millicoma, West Fork Above Henry Falls to Allegany	III(IV)	250-1300	27	Rain	Day	SC
Scenic, playful, tree-lined coastal stream.						
Minam Red's Horse Ranch to Minam Rec. Area	III to III+	1000-4000	45	Rain/Snow	Day	GR
A continuous Class III wilderness run through steep, forested canyon.						
Mohawk Private Road to McKenzie River	II(III)	250-1200	30	Rain	Day	UW
Logged and forested river along residential areas.						

River	Class	Flow CFS	Gradient ft./mi.	Water Source	Trip Type	Basin
Powder Thief Valley Res. to Brownlee Res.	III	400-1000	16.5	Dam	Day/Multi	P
Long, desolate river with diversion dams and canyons.						
Sharps Creek Mineral Campground to Wildwood Falls	II(III)	250-800	76.5	Rain/Snow	Day	UW
Exploratroy upper creek with intermediate, logged lower stretch.						
Silver Creek Silver Falls Park to Silverton Reservoir	IV(P)	250-800	48	Rain/Snow	Day	MW
Isolated steep creek with falls in a deep V canyon.						
Smith, Oregon Above Smith Falls to Umpqua River	FW	Tidal	8.3	Tidal/Rain	Day	U
Exploratory intermediate upper river to tidal flatwater tributary of the Umpqua.						
Sprague Above Sycan River to Williamson River	FW & I	500-3000	1.6	Rain/Snow	Day/Multi	K
Long, meandering isolated high desert river.						
Steamboat Creek Above Cedar Creek to North Umpqua	IV(V,P)	500-2000	43.2	Rain/Snow	Day	U
Forested creek with camping, falls and Class V rapids.						
Umatilla Cabbage Hill to Columbia River	II to IV(P)	800-2500	14.6	Rain/Snow	Day	UM
Steep, forested stream to open fields through farmlands with dams & surf.						
Umpqua, Main River Forks Park to Winchester Bay	FW to II(II+)	1000-5000	3.4	Rain/Snow	Day	U
Long, large river from coastal mountains to tidal Pacific Ocean.						
Wallowa Enterprise to Grande Ronde River	II to III+	500-2000	34	Dam/Rain	Day/Multi	GR
Majestic snow-capped mountains to agricultural lands and narrow canyons.						
Wiley Creek 14 miles upstream to S.Santiam River	III to IV(V)	250-800	99	Rain	Day	UW
Long isolated creek with clear-cuts, canyons and rocky drops.						
Willamette, Coast Fork Cottage Grove Res. to Willamette River	I(II)	700-2500	9.4	Dam	Day	UW
A rural, meandering stream among transit routes.						
Williamson Klamath Marsh to Upper Klamath Lake	FW to III/IV?	600-2500	11.8	Rain/Spring	Day/Multi	K
Isolated, rapid-filled canyon to open rural stream.						
Youngs Klatskanine River to Youngs Bay	FW	Tidal	<1	Tidal	Day	NC
A tidal stream meandering through coastal rainforest and farmlands to open bay.						

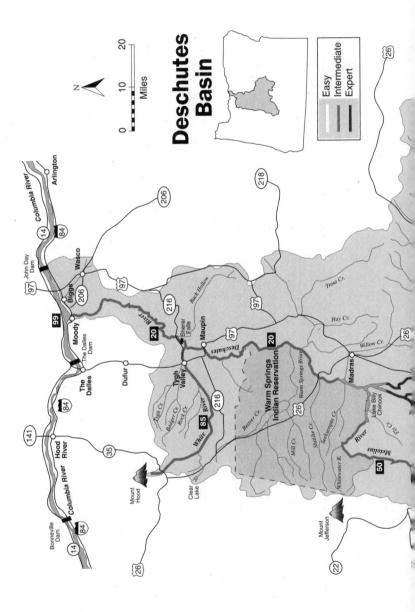

Deschutes Basin

N

0 10 20
Miles

Easy
Intermediate
Expert

Columbia River
Arlington
14
84
John Day Dam
97
Wasco
206
Biggs
206
97
99
Moody
The Dalles Dam
20
Sherar Falls
Maupin
Buck Hollow
Trout Cr.
97
216
Deschutes River
97
218
206
Hay Cr.
Willow Cr.
26
The Dalles
Dufur
Tygh Valley
216
Warm Springs Indian Reservation
20
Warm Springs River
Madras
Lake Billy Chinook
84
141
Hood River
Columbia River
35
Reist Cr.
Badger Cr.
Rock Cr.
White River
85
Beaver Cr.
26
Seekseequa Cr.
Mill Cr.
Shitike Cr.
Fly Cr.
River
Metolius
50
26
Bonneville Dam
14
84
Mount Hood
Clear Lake
Whitewater R.
Mount Jefferson
22

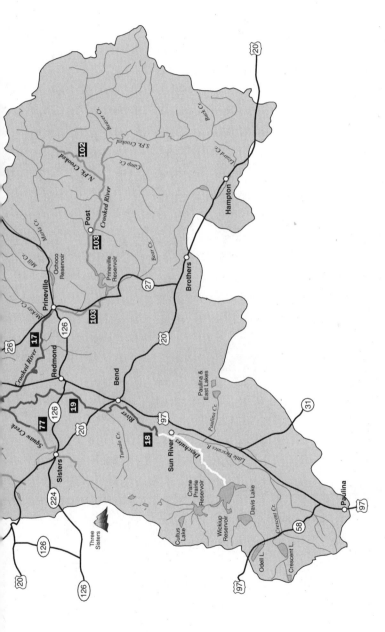

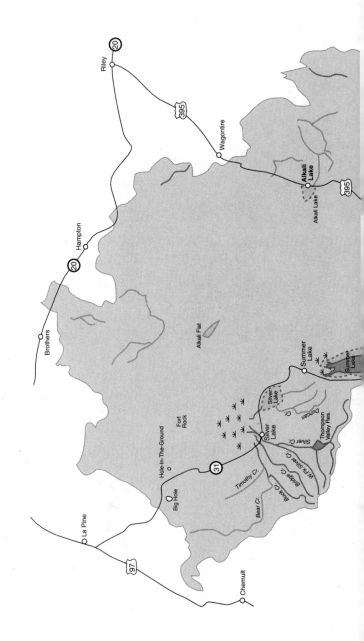

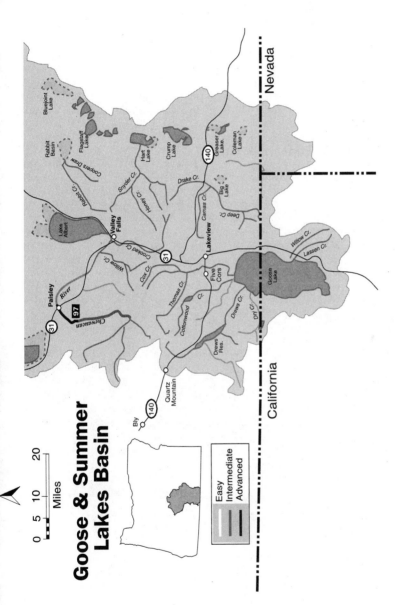

Goose & Summer Lakes Basin

Miles
0 5 10 20

Easy
Intermediate
Advanced

Bly
Quartz Mountain
140
140
Chewaucan River
97
31
Paisley
31
Willow Cr.
Lakes Albert
Bench Cr.
Valley Falls
Crooked Cr.
Cox Cr.
Thomas Cr.
Cottonwood Cr.
Drews Res.
Drews Cr.
Dry Cr.
Five Cors
Lakeview
31
Snyder Cr.
Honey Cr.
Camas Cr.
Deep Cr.
Drake Cr.
Big Lake
140
Willow Cr.
Lassen Cr.
Goose Lake
Coopers Draw
Rabbit Basin
Flagstaff Lake
Hart Lake
Crump Lake
Greaser Lake
Coleman Lake
Bluejoint Lake

Nevada
California

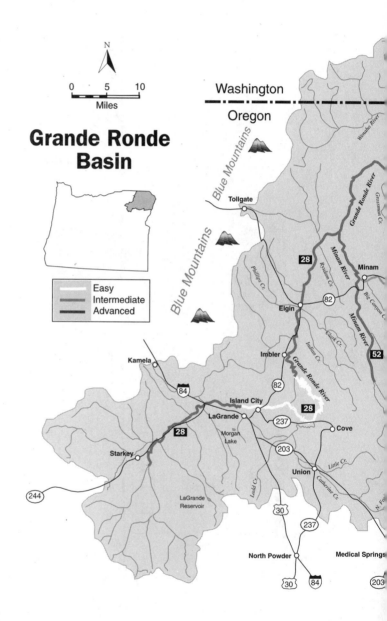

N

0 5 10
Miles

Grande Ronde Basin

Easy
Intermediate
Advanced

Washington
Oregon

Blue Mountains

Blue Mountains

Blue Mountains

Tollgate

Minam River

Grande Ronde River

Wenaha River

Grossman Cr.

Minam

Phillips Cr.

Rhinehart Cr.

28

82

Elgin

Clark Cr.

Indian Cr.

Big Canyon Cr.

52

Minam River

Kamela

Imbler

Grande Ronde River

82

Island City

28

LaGrande

237

Cove

84

28

Morgan
Lake

203

Little Cr.

Starkey

Ladd Cr.

Union

Catherine Cr.

N. Fork

244

LaGrande
Reservoir

30

237

North Powder

Medical Springs

30

84

203

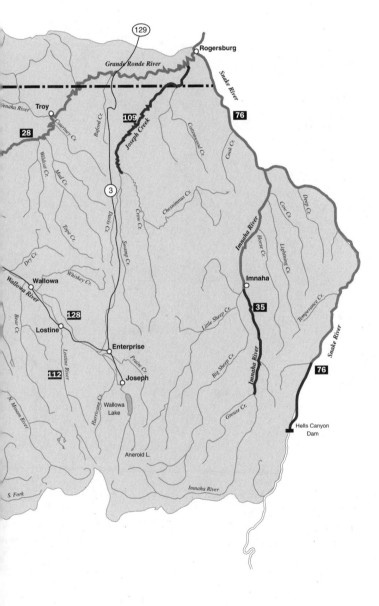

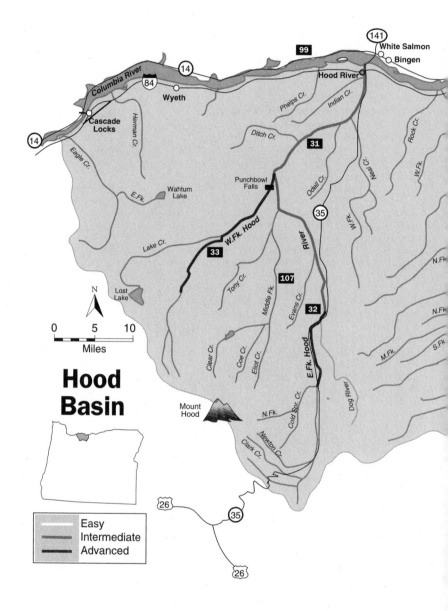

Hood Basin

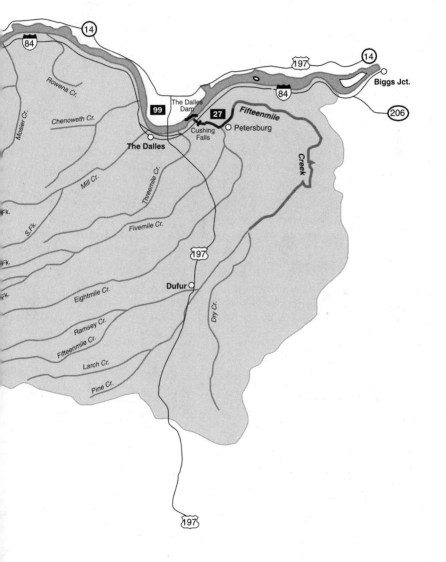

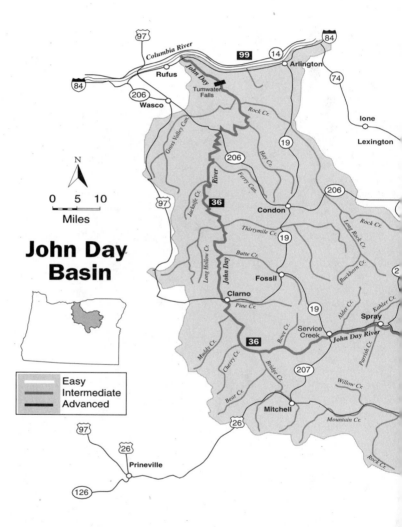

John Day Basin

N

0   5   10
Miles

Easy
Intermediate
Advanced

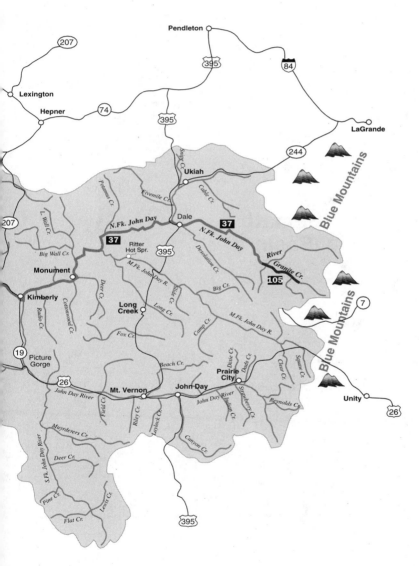

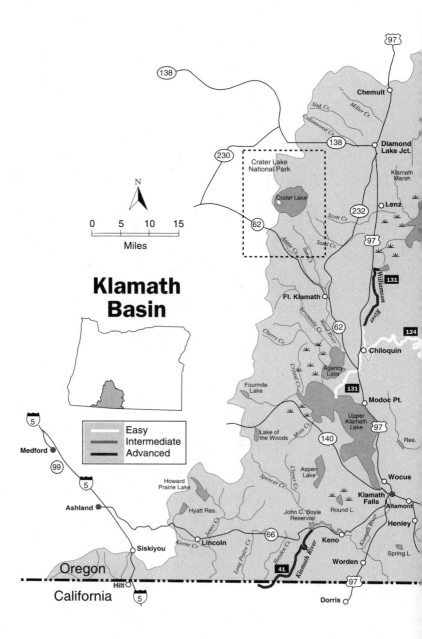

Klamath
Basin

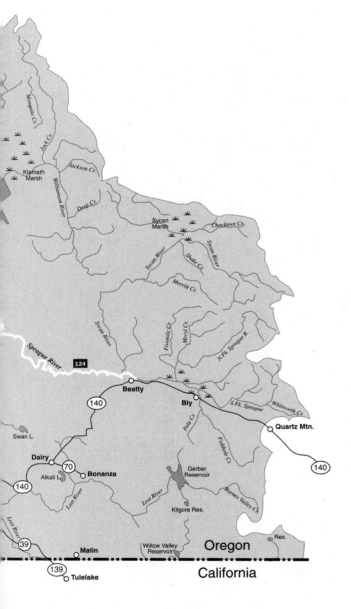

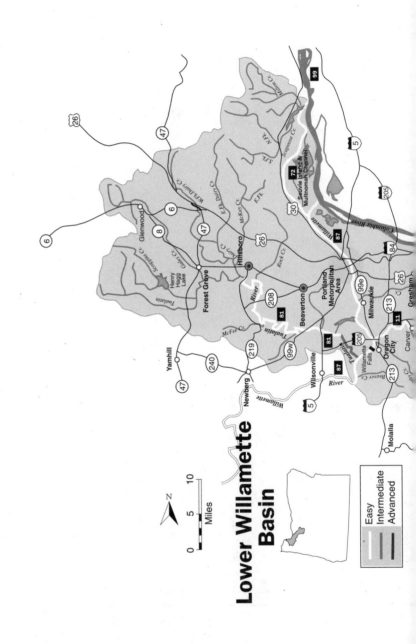

Lower Willamette Basin

Easy
Intermediate
Advanced

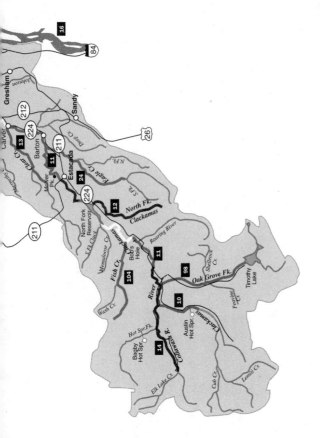

Malheur Lake Basin

N

0 5 10
Miles

Easy
Intermediate
Advanced

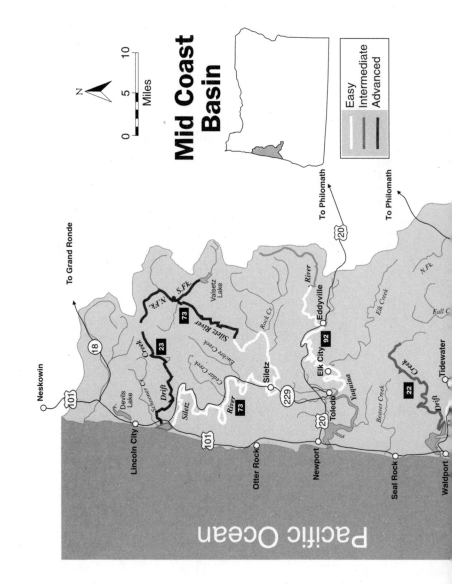

Mid Coast Basin

Easy
Intermediate
Advanced

N

Miles
0 5 10

To Grand Ronde

Neskowin

101

18

Lincoln City

Devils
Lake

Schooner Cr.

Drift Creek

Siletz

River

23

73

N.Fk.

S.Fk.

Valsetz
Lake

Euchre Creek

Cedar Creek

Siletz River

Rock Cr.

River

Eddyville

To Philomath

20

101

Otter Rock

Siletz

229

Newport

20

Toledo

Elk City

92

Yaquina

Beaver Creek

Elk Creek

N.Fk.

Fall C.

To Philomath

Seal Rock

Drift Creek

22

Tidewater

Waldport

Pacific Ocean

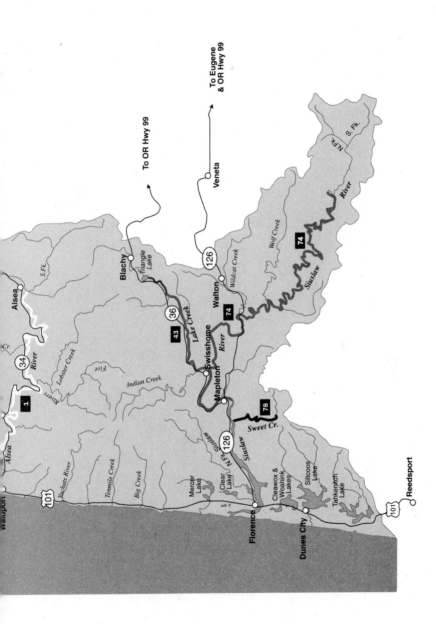

To OR Hwy 99

To Eugene
& OR Hwy 99

Veneta

[126]

Wildcat Creek

Wolf Creek

74

Siuslaw River

N. Fk.

S. Fk.

Blachly

Triangle Lake

[36]

Lake Creek

43

Walton

74

Swisshome

Mapleton

Swisshome River

Five

Indian Creek

Lobster Creek

[34]

River

Cr.

Alsea

S. Fk.

1

Alsea

Rivers

78

Sweet Cr.

Siuslaw

[126] N. Fk.

Siuslaw

Yachats River

Temmile Creek

Big Creek

Mercer Lake

Clear Lake

Cleawox & Woahink Lakes

Siltcoos Lake

Tahkenitch Lake

[101]

Waldport

Florence

Dunes City

[101]

Reedsport

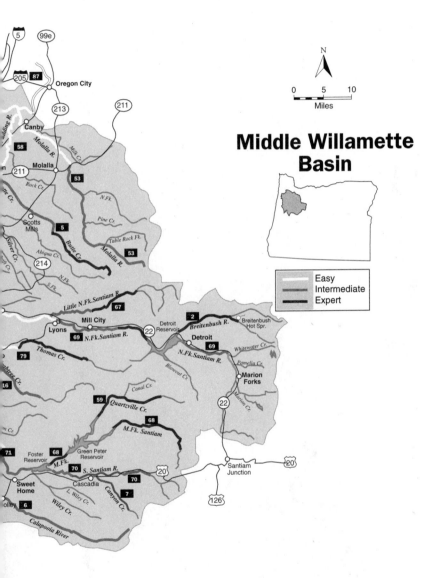

Middle Willamette Basin

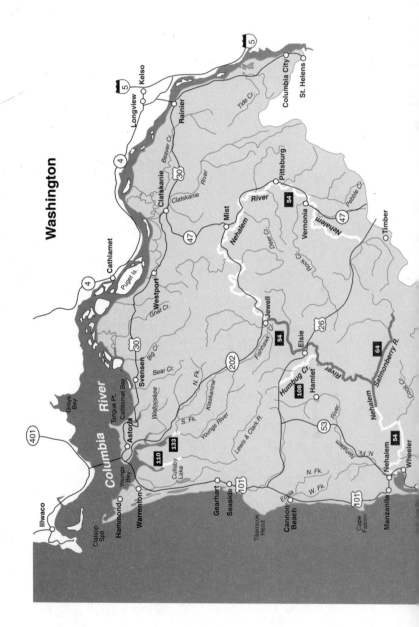

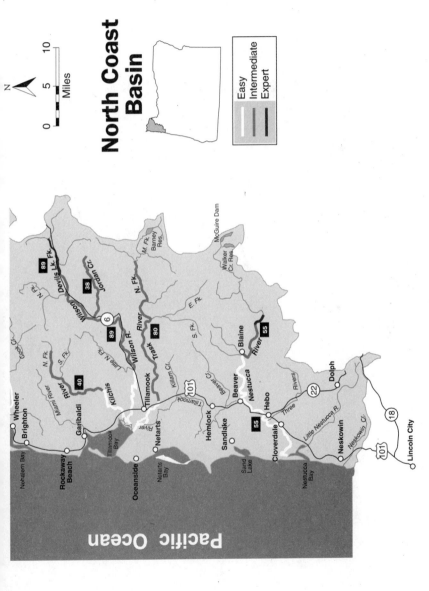

North Coast Basin

Easy
Intermediate
Expert

N

0   5   10
Miles

Pacific Ocean

Nehalem Bay
Wheeler
Brighton
Rockaway Beach
Garibaldi
Oceanside
Netarts Bay

Cook Cr.
N. Fk.
Miami River
S. Fk.
Kilchis River
Tillamook Bay
Netarts
Tillamook River
Hemlock
Sandlake
Sand Lake
Little N. Fk.
Little N. Fk.
Wilson R.
Trask River
Killam Cr.
Tillamook
Beaver Cr.
Beaver
Hebo
Three Rivers
Cloverdale
Nestucca Bay
Neskowin
Neskowin Cr.
Lincoln City

Devils Lk. Fk.
N. Fk.
Wilson River
Jordan Cr.
N. Fk.
M. Fk.
Barney Res.
E. Fk.
S. Fk.
Blaine
Nestucca River
Dolph
Little Nestucca R.
Walker Cr. Res.
McGuire Dam

89
38
6
89
80
40
101
55
55
22
18
101

439

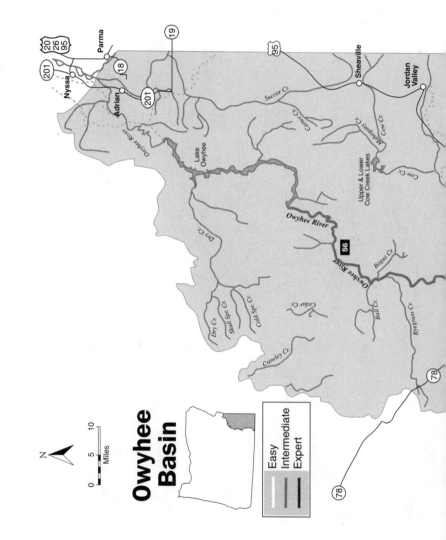

Owyhee
Basin

N

0 5 10
Miles

Easy
Intermediate
Expert

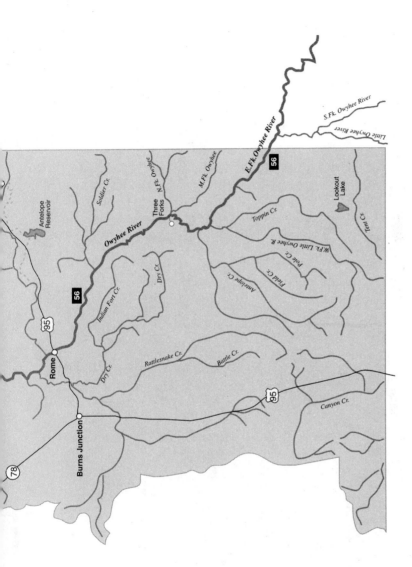

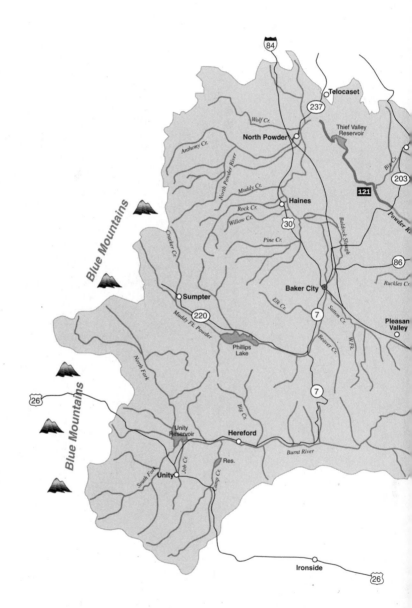

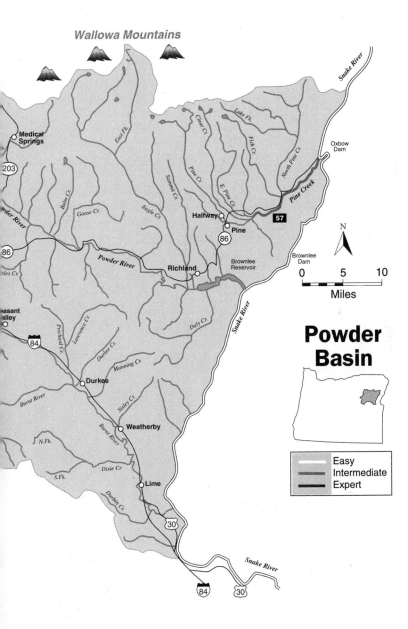

Wallowa Mountains

Medical
Springs

203

Snake River

Clear Cr.

Lake Fk.

Fish Cr.

North Pine Cr.

Oxbow
Dam

East Fk.

Pine Cr.

Summit Cr.

E. Pine Cr.

Pine Creek

Basin Cr.

Goose Cr.

Eagle Cr.

Halfway

Pine

57

86

der River

Powder River

Richland

86

Brownlee
Reservoir

Brownlee
Dam

N

0   5   10

Miles

cles Cr.

asant
alley

Pritchard Cr.

Lawrence Cr.

Daly Cr.

Snake River

84

Durkee Cr.

Manning Cr.

Durkee

Burnt River

Sisley Cr.

Weatherby

N.Fk.

Burnt River

S.Fk.

Dixie Cr.

Lime

Durbin Cr.

30

84   30

Snake River

**Powder
Basin**

	Easy
	Intermediate
	Expert

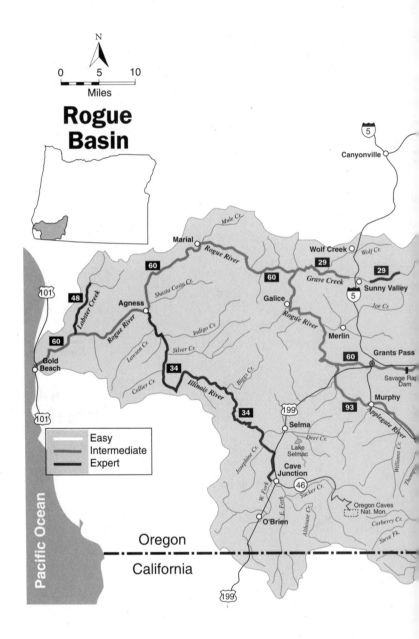

N

0   5   10
Miles

Rogue Basin

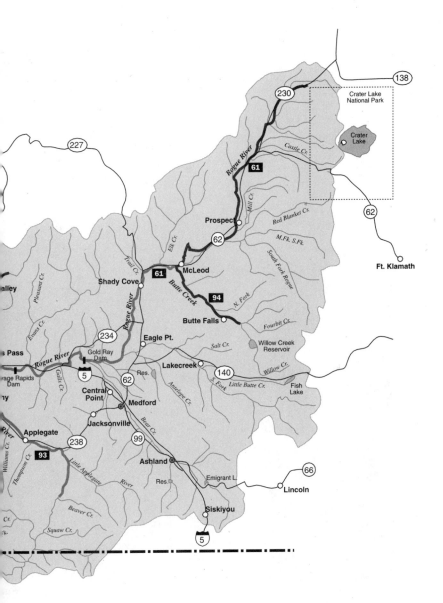

Crater Lake
National Park

Crater
Lake

138

230

227

Rogue River

61

Castle Cr.

62

Ft. Klamath

Prospect

62

Red Blanket Cr.

Mill Cr.

Elk Cr.

M.Fk. S.Fk.

Trail Cr.

61

McLeod

South Fork Rogue

Shady Cove

Butte Creek

94

N. Fork

Valley

Pleasant Cr.

Rogue River

Butte Falls

Fourbit Cr.

Evans Cr.

234

Eagle Pt.

Salt Cr.

Willow Creek
Reservoir

s Pass

Rogue River

Gold Ray
Dam

140

Willow Cr.

vage Rapids
Dam

5

Res.

Lakecreek

Little Butte Cr.

Fish
Lake

ny

Galls Cr.

62

Antelope Cr.

S. Fork

Central
Point

Medford

Jacksonville

Bear Cr.

Applegate

238

99

Williams Cr.

River

93

Thompson Cr.

Little Applegate

River

Ashland

66

Res.

Emigrant L.

Lincoln

Beaver Cr.

Cr.

Squaw Cr.

Siskiyou

5

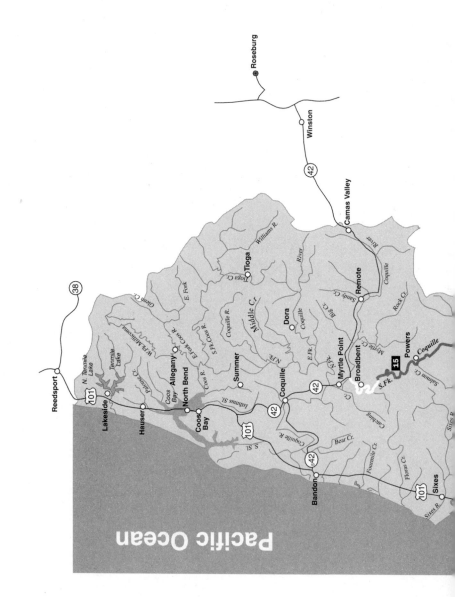

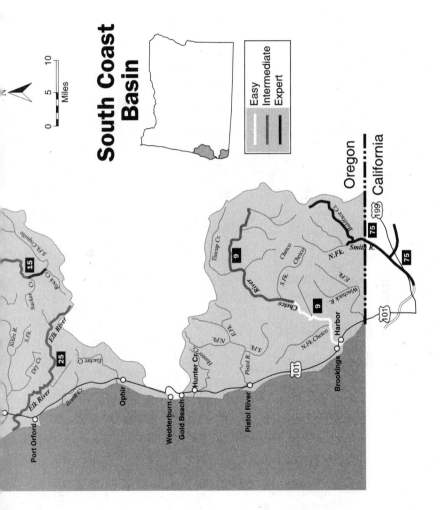

South Coast Basin

Easy
Intermediate
Expert

Miles
0   5   10

N

Oregon
California

Port Orford
Ophir
Wedderburn
Gold Beach
Pistol River
Brookings
Harbor

Elk River
Sixes R.
S.Fk.
Dry Cr.
Brush Cr.
Euchre Cr.
Elk River
Sucker Cr.
Rock Cr.
S.Fk.Coquille
Hunter Cr.
N.Fk.
E.Fk.
Pistol R.
S.Fk.
Chetco River
Tincup Cr.
Chetco
Chetco
S.Fk.
N.Fk.
E.Fk.
Winchuck R.
N.Fk. Chetco
N.Fk. Smith R.
Bollinger Cr.

15
25
9
9
75
75
199
101
101

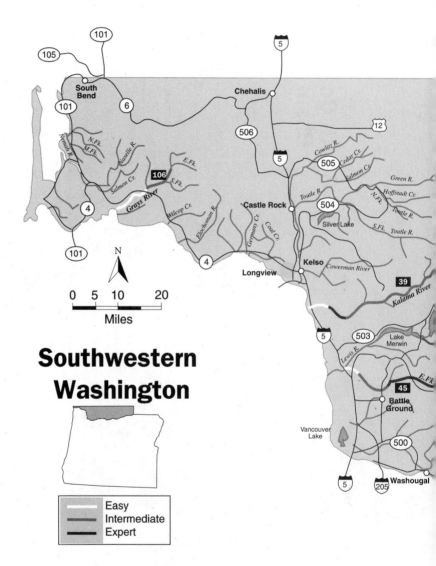

Southwestern
Washington

0 5 10   20
Miles

N

Easy
Intermediate
Expert

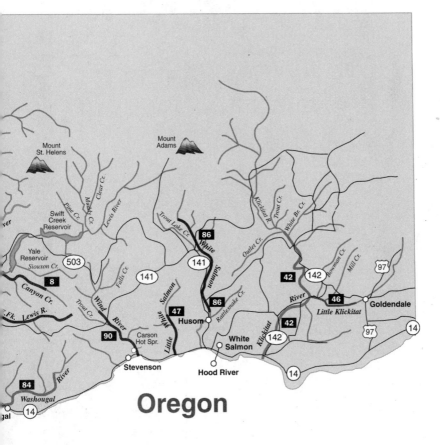

Mount
St. Helens

Mount
Adams

Clear Cr.

Pine Cr.

Middle Cr.

Lewis River

Swift
Creek
Reservoir

ver

Yale
Reservoir

Siouxon Cr.

503

8

Canyon Cr.

E. Fk. Lewis R.

Falls Cr.

Trout Cr.

141

141

Trout Lake Cr.

86

White

Salmon

Salmon

White Salmon

Little White Salmon

47

86

Husom

Rattlesnake Cr.

Klickitat

142

Klickitat R.

Trout Cr.

White Br. Cr.

Outlet Cr.

42

142

Bowman Cr.

Mill Cr.

97

46

Little Klickitat

River

Goldendale

42

97

14

Wind

River

90

Carson
Hot Spr.

Stevenson

White
Salmon

Hood River

14

14

84

Washougal

River

gal

14

Oregon

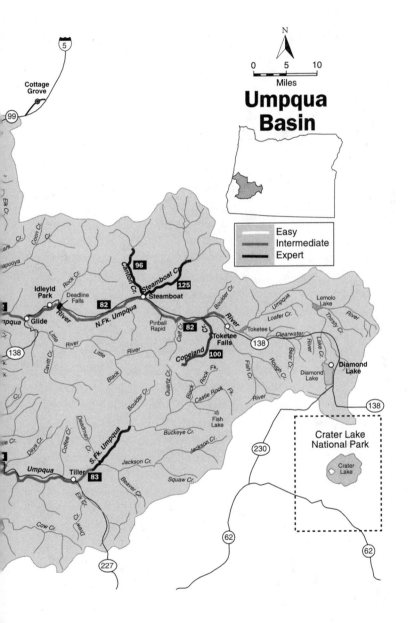

N

0 5 10
Miles

Umpqua Basin

Easy
Intermediate
Expert

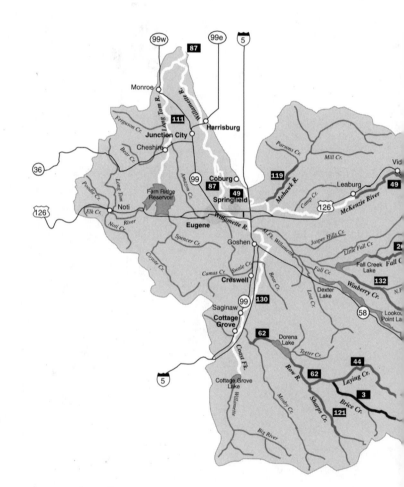

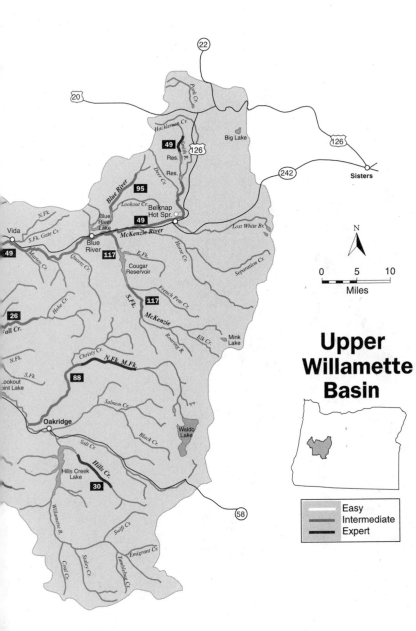

Upper Willamette Basin

Easy
Intermediate
Expert

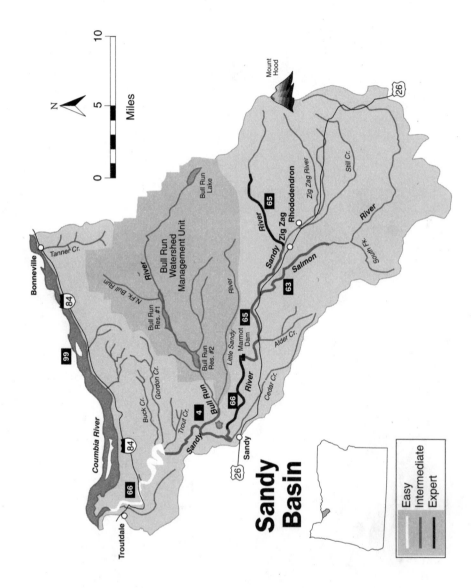

Mount
Hood

26

Bull Run
Lake

Bull Run
Watershed
Management
Unit

River

Still Cr.

Zig Zag River

65

Sandy

River

Zig Zag
Rhododendron

River

N. Fk. Bull Run

Tanner Cr.

Bonneville

84

Salmon

63

South Fk.

River

Bull Run
Res. #1

River

Alder Cr.

99

Gordon Cr.

Bull Run
Res. #2

Little Sandy

65

Buck Cr.

Marmot
Dam

Columbia River

Trout Cr.

Bull Run

66

River

Cedar Cr.

84

4

Sandy

66

26   Sandy

66

Troutdale

Sandy
Basin

N

0   5   10

Miles

Easy
Intermediate
Expert

Appendix A

GEAR CHECKLIST

Paddling gear
- ❑ Boat
- ❑ Paddle
- ❑ Spray skirt
- ❑ Life jacket/vest
- ❑ Helmet
- ❑ Dry suit or paddle jacket or wet suit
- ❑ Gloves/poggies
- ❑ Hood/hat
- ❑ Booties
- ❑ Float bags
- ❑ Food and drink
- ❑ Map and guidebook
- ❑ Sun screen
- ❑ Sun glasses
- ❑ Toiletries
- ❑ Knife
- ❑ Whistle
- ❑ Extra keys
- ❑ Wallet/ID

Rescue/safety gear
- ❑ Spare paddle/ breakdown
- ❑ First aid kit
- ❑ Throw rope
- ❑ Lighter/waterproof matches
- ❑ Flashlight
- ❑ Energy bars
- ❑ Carabiners (2)
- ❑ Pulleys (2)
- ❑ Prussic loops (2)
- ❑ Webbing (6+ feet)
- ❑ Duct tape
- ❑ Pocket tool (Leatherman)

First aid kit
- ❑ Athletic tape/surgical tape
- ❑ Band Aids
- ❑ Ace bandage
- ❑ Gauze
- ❑ Airway
- ❑ Thermometer
- ❑ Garbage bag/thermal blanket
- ❑ Snake bite kit
- ❑ Antihistamines
- ❑ Antibiotics
- ❑ Antidiarheal
- ❑ Salts
- ❑ Scissors
- ❑ Razor blade
- ❑ Needle and thread
- ❑ Water purification tablets
- ❑ Coins for phone
- ❑ Tweezers
- ❑ Antibiotic cream

Self-contained/camping Gear
- ❑ Sleeping bag
- ❑ Tent
- ❑ Tarp
- ❑ Stove/fuel/lighter fluid
- ❑ Thermarest/pad
- ❑ Change of clothes
- ❑ Hat
- ❑ Extra food/drink
- ❑ Extra batteries
- ❑ Coffee pot/pot
- ❑ Cup/plate/bowl/silverware
- ❑ Watch/compass/altimeter
- ❑ Radio/rescue signal device

Appendix B

INFORMATION NUMBERS AND WEBSITES

Getting information by phone

For more information about paddling Oregon's rivers, contact managing agencies at the telephone numbers listed below:

Oregon Bureau of Land Management
(503) 952-6001

Oregon River Levels
(503) 261-9246

US Forest Service Phone Numbers

Siskiyou National Forest

Chetco District	541-469-2196
Galice District	541-471-6500
Gold Beach District	541-247-3600
Illinois District	541-592-2166
Powers District	541-439-3011
Rand District*	541-479-3735

Umpqua National Forest

Cottage Grove District	541-942-5591
North Umpqua District	541-496-3532
Diamond Lake District	541-498-2531
Tiller District	541-825-3201

Gifford Pinchot National Forest

Mount St. Helens District	206-247-5473
Mount Adams District	509-395-2501
Packwood District	206-494-5515
Randle District	206-497-7565
Wind River District	509-427-5645

Siuslaw National Forest

Alsea District	541-757-4480
Hebo District	541-392-3161
Mapleton District	541-268-4473
Waldport District	541-563-3211
Oregon Dunes District	541-271-3611
Cape Perpetua District	541-547-3289

Wallowa-Whitman National Forest

Baker District	541-523-4476
Hells Canyon District	541-426-4978
LaGrande District	541-963-7186
Pine District	541-742-7511
Unity District	541-446-3351
Wallowa Valley District	541-432-2171

Deschutes National Forest

Bend District	541-433-5664
Crescent District	541-433-2234
Fort Rock District	541-388-5674
Sisters District	541-549-2111

Mount Hood National Forest

Barlow District	541-467-2291
Bear Springs District	541-328-6211
Clackamas District	541-630-4256
Estacada District	541-630-6861
Hood River District	503-666-0704
Zigzag District	503-666-0704

Willamette National Forest

Blue River District	541-822-3317
Detroit District	541-854-3366
Lowell District	541-937-2129
McKenzie District	541-822-3381
Oakridge District	541-782-2283
Rigdon District	541-782-2283
Sweet Home District	541-367-5168

Bureau of Land Management Phone Numbers

Salem District	503-375-5646
Eugene District	541-683-6600
Coos Bay District	541-756-0100
Roseburg District	541-440-4930
Medford District	541-770-2200
Lakeview District	541-947-2177
Burns District	541-573-5241
Vale District	541-473-3144
Prineville District	541-447-4115
Boise District	208-373-4000

Call the Rand District Ranger for Rogue River permit information

Paddling clubs and commercial websites

Many area paddling clubs and shops maintain web sites that include information on Oregon rivers. Check out the following site listings:

American Canoe Association
http://www.aca-paddler.org/

American Whitewater Association
http://www.awa.org/

Jim Reed's Kayaking Page
http://www.efn.org/~jpreed/

Lower Columbia Canoe Club (LCCC)
http://www.teleport.com/nonprofit/LCCC/

Reservoir Regulation and Water Quality
http://nppwml.npp.usace.army.mil/index.html

USGS Rating Tables (Oregon)
http://nppwml.npp.usace.army.mil/rating.html

Willamette Kayak and Canoe Club (WKCC)
http://www.peak.org/community/whitewater/

Websites, water level and flow

PDX page for weather and river conditions
http://www.ocs.orst.edu/pub_ftp/weather/river_conditions/river_levels.PDX

USGS Flows for Oregon streams
http://wwworegon.wr.usgs.gov/rt_dir/rt_list.html

USGS Flows for Washington streams
http://wwwdwatcm.wr.usgs.gov/wrd-home.html

Various Oregon, Washington, and Idaho stream levels
http://www.physics.orst.edu/~tpw/kayaking/levels.text

Appendix C

RIVER NAME ORIGINS

Alsea River: Named by explorers Meriwether Lewis and William Clark, who called it Ulseah. William P. McArthur named it Alseya in 1855. The "y" was later dropped.

Big Butte Creek: Named for nearby Mount McLaughlin, which was known as Snowy Butte.

Breitenbush River: Named after pioneer hunter John Breitenbush.

Brice Creek: A prospector named Frank Brice (or Brass) fell in the creek, which bore his full name until the "Frank" was dropped.

Bull Run River: Named for the cattle that escaped from Oregon Trail emigrants and ran wild along the river for years.

Butte Creek: Named for Graves Butte or Lone Tree Butte (today's Mount Angel), where a gigantic fir stood on the summit.

Calapooia River: An earlier spelling was Calapooya, probably stemming from the Kalapooian Indians.

Canyon Creek: Probably named for its main geographic feature.

Chetco River: Named for a small Indian tribe known as the Chetko or Chitko people. An Indian woman named Lucky Dick was the last of the Chetko tribe.

Clackamas River: Named after a large tribe of Chinookian Indians who were relocated to the Grande Ronde area.

Clear Creek: Probably named for its clear water at low flows.

Collawash River: First known as the Miners Fork of the Clackamas River, it was later named for Chief Colawash of the Columbia Basin. The original spelling of his name was probably Kalu-wass, meaning "the place where awl baskets were made."

Columbia River: Named at the coast in May 1792 after Captain Robert Gray's vessel, the **Columbia Rediviva.** Among the Indians of Minnesota, Jonathan Carver wrote of hearing tales of the great river he called the Oregon. William P. McArthur was the first to examine the river from land.

Coquille River: Coquille is the French word for shell; the name is a mispelling of the name of a Chetco Indian tribe known as the Ku-Kwil-Tunne or Kiquel.

Crabtree Creek: Named for John J. Crabtree of Virginia, who bought William Packwood's claims east of the forks of the Santiam River.

Crooked River: Noted as such on an 1838 fur-trading map drawn by Colonel J. J. Albert. Albert mentions the numerous springs found along the river's walls.

Deschutes River: First noted by explorers Lewis and Clark as the Towornehiooks River; Clark later returned, calling it Clarks River. The Klamath Indians referred to the river as Kolamkuni Koke. "Kolam" stood for wild root; "keni" was a place, and "koke" stood for stream. French fur traders prevailed, though, named the place the Riviere des Chutes in reference to the rapids and falls nears its mouth on the Columbia. Dams have since covered the rapids, and the name was shortened to des Chutes, then combined into its current form.

Drift Creek: Named for driftwood along its banks.

Eagle Creek: Named in 1844 by Indians who observed large numbers of eagles along the stream. There are at least two other Eagle Creeks in Oregon, one in the Columbia Gorge, and one in eastern Oregon near the Eagle Cap Wilderness.

Elk River: Named for the plentiful elk herds that were standard provisions of early pioneers and fur traders.

Fall Creek: Earlier known as the Tay River, called such by local Scots who settled the area and recalled a river in their home country. The name was changed to Big and Little Fall creeks in 1885. There are several other Fall Creeks in the Pacific Northwest.

Grande Ronde River: The French named it the Riviere de Grande Ronde, the "river of the big circle."

Grays River: The ocean bay at the mouth of the river was labeled Shallow Nitche by Lewis and Clark. The river was later named to commemorate Captain Robert Gray, who discovered the Columbia.

Hood River: Lewis and Clark called it Labeasche River in 1805, after the French word for a female deer. It was later renamed Hood because of its origins on Mount Hood. Early settlers thought it was the Dog River, where starving settlers ate dogs to survive.

Humbug Creek: No known origin. A tributary of the Applegate River by the same name was called such because of a quarrel over mining claims.

Illinois River: Named by the Althouse brothers of Albany, who emigrated from Peoria, Illinois, and placer-mined for gold here.

John Day River: John Day was a Virginia backwoodsman who became a member of the Astor-Hunt overland party. He and Ramsey Crooks fell behind and became separated from the group. They befriended the Walla Walla Indians, who led them to the Columbia. There, hostile Indians robbed them of their clothes. They were eventually rescued by the Robert Stuart party. Lewis and Clark called the river Lepages River in 1805. In years past, it has been referred to as the Days River.

Jordan Creek: No known origin.

Kilchis River: Named for Chief Kilchis of the Tillamook tribe, who was friendly to white settlers.

Klamath River: Named for its origins in the largest lake in Oregon, Klamath Lake, home to the Klamath Indian people. The Indians themselves called the river the Koke, meaning "river."

Klickitat River: Named for the Indian tribe that lived along its banks. Lewis and Clark called the river the Wahhowpun. David Douglas later called the nearby tribe the Clikitats, and Wilkes referred to them as the Klackatacks. Railroaders translated the named to mean "robbers," the U.S. government said the name meant "beyond."

Lake Creek: Named for its origin at Triangle Lake.

Laying Creek: Named after George Layng, who homesteaded the area in 1892; the name was later misspelled.

Lewis River: Named for explorer Meriwether Lewis. Lewis and Clark called the river the Komoenim. Wilkes later called it the Saptin.

McKenzie River: Donald McKenzie was an explorer with John Jacob Astor's Pacific Fur Company; he named the river in 1812. McKenzie later retired in New York with wealth from fur trading. He was reportedly a good shot, skilled in Indian warfare and trade, and a good woodcrafter.

Metolius River: The Warm Springs Indians called this the Mpto-ly-as, for the white salmon that lived or spawned here. The name was later given a Latinesque spelling.

Mill Creek: Named for a sawmill operated by Jason Lee's Methodist Mission here, from 1840 to 1841.

Minam River: Local Indians called it the E-mi-ne-mah. The word "mah" refers to valley or canyon; the rest of the name reportedly alludes to an edible sunflower that grew in the area.

Molalla River: Named after a band of Indians in the Waiilatpuan Tribe, who were detached and driven west from the Cayuse Hills during wars with hostile tribes.

Nehalem River: The Salish Indians called this the Naalem, which was later respelled.

Nestucca River: Originally known as the Staga-ush by native peoples; the name Nea-Stocka in their dialect referred to only one place on the river. What is now called the Little Nestucca was once known as the Nestachee.

Owyhee River: Named after two Hawaiian men who were presumably murdered by Shoshoni Indians in 1819. Owyhee was the name for Hawaii in the 1800s.

Pudding River: Named by fur traders Gervais and Lucier, who had Indian wives that made them blood pudding or sausage from elk shot nearby. The traders called the stream the Riviere au Boudin, which was translated as Pudding River.

Quartzville Creek: Named for the town of Quartzville, which in turn was named for the gold-bearing quartz lodes found in 1860 in Dry Gulch. The town and stamp mill were laid out in 1864.

Rogue River: French traders called the river Les Coquins, which translates into "rogue." One account suggests the original name was Rouge River, which translates into "red river." Since the local Indians were troublesome to the French, they were more likely to have called it the Rogue. The Indians themselves called the river the Trashit. It was known for a time as the Gold River, named such by the local legislature, but the name Rogue River was restored in 1855.

Row River: Origin unknown.

Salmon River: Named for the fish and for the post office at its mouth, established in 1891. The post office later moved and the town name was changed to Brightwood.

Salmonberry River: Salmonberries *(Rubus spectabilis)* are found along its banks.

Sandy River: Originally the Barings River, the Sandy was named by Lieutenant W. R. Broughton of Captain Vancouver's 1792 expedition. The name honored banker and financier Francis Baring. Lewis and Clark noticed the great quantities of sand near its mouth, and named it the Quicksand River. The name stood for fifty years, until it was later shortened.

Santiam River: Named for the Santiam Indians, a Kalapooian tribe that lived near here before being relocated to the Grande Ronde Agency in 1906.

Siletz River: Named for the Siletz Indians, the southernmost coast tribe of the Salishan Nation. The river was referred to as the Celeste, Neselitch, and Sailetc in the past. The Rogue Indians knew Siletz Lake as Silis, from which the tribe and lake were named. The Siletz Reservation today includes people who speak languages in the following linguistic families: Athapascan, Yakonan, Kusan, Takilman, Sastan, and Shahaptian.

Siuslaw River: An Indian name for a chief or tribe in the Yakonan family. Lewis and Clark called the river Shiastuckle, and it was later referred to as the Saoustla, Saliutla, and Saiustla. It was changed to Siuslaw in 1852.

Smith River: Named for American fur trapper and explorer Jedediah Smith. Originally from New York, Smith was later killed by Comanche Indians on the Santa Fe Trail.

Snake River: Named for the Snake Indians (Shoshoni and Paiute) who resided in the river canyon. Lewis and Clark called the river the Choshones and Sosonees. The name "Snake" came from the Shoshonis' sign for themselves, which resembled a snake's motion. Known for their reticence and root-digging lifeways, these people were also known as the Digger Indians, Nez Perce, Sahaptin, and Kimconim. The river was briefly known as the Lewis or Louis River.

Thomas Creek: Named after Fredrick Thomas, who settled on its banks in 1846.

Trask River: Elbridge Trask settled in Oregon after coming from Massachusetts in 1834. He worked in a sawmill at Hunts Mill Point until moving to the Trask River area in 1852.

Tualatin River: An Indian name meaning "lazy" or "sluggish" or possibly "land without trees." Originally spelled Twha-la-ti or, over time, Faladin, Twality, Quality, Falatine, Nefalatine, and Tuality before its current form.

Umpqua River: An Indian name for one place on the river. There were several Fort Umpquas in the river basin, at different locations. Other names included Umptqua and Arquilas, according to David Douglas.

Washougal River: Formerly called the Seal River by Lewis and Clark, for the seals found at its mouth. Washougal is an Indian word meaning "rushing water."

White River: Named for the white glacial silt that is washed into the river from glaciers on Mount Hood.

White Salmon River: Named in 1872 for sick returning salmon that died here by the hundred with many sores, having been infected by fungi that turned them a white color. Lewis and Clark called the river Canoe Creek, after seeing many Indians fishing from canoes on the stream.

Willamette River: The largest river entirely within the state of Oregon. The Indians called it the Wal-lamt, which was said to mean "spill water" in reference to the area above Willamette Falls. There have been many spellings of the name over the years.

Wilson River: Originally the Geogia or Geogie River, it was renamed the Wilson River after the first settler to drive cattle into the area from Seaside. Wilson later founded the Tillamook dairy industry. Early explorers in the Kilchis and Wilson river country became lost, nearly starving to death before they found their way back to Tillamook.

Wind River: Lewis and Clark called this Crusatte's River, after a member of their exploring party. Governor Isaac Stevens renamed it the Wind River in 1853.

Yamhill River: The first reference to the name is at Yam Hill Falls, which gave its name to a post office in 1856. The name was combined to Yamhill in 1908.

Yaquina River: Named for an Indian tribe in the Yakonan family, which lived near the bay. Lewis and Clark called it the Youikeones or the Youkone.

Index

About the Author

Robb Keller grew up in the eastern Oregon town of La Grande, where he learned to swim, hike, and scuba dive. He graduated from the University of Oregon after studying chemistry, biology, and physics. He also studied philosophy and computer science for fun.

Robb moved to Portland in 1989 and worked at Oregon Health Sciences University in the Department of Biochemical Genetics.

He has been kayaking, rafting, and photographing Oregon for the past eight years. He has taught basic paddling skills and rolling techniques at OHSU and is a member of several local paddling clubs, including the Lower Columbia Canoe Club (LCCC), Oregon Kayak and Canoe Club (OKCC), and Willamette Kayak and Canoe Club (WKCC). He is also a member of the American Canoe Association (ACA), the American Whitewater Association (AWA), and the Oregon Historical Society (OHS). Though he has learned how to roll an open canoe, he still prefers two paddle blades to one.

Robb considers himself privileged to have twice run the Colorado River-Grand Canyon and Middle Fork Salmon River, and to have made several trips on the Rogue, Snake, and Selway Rivers. He now works for Pacific Wave, a paddle-sport outfitter in Warrenton, Oregon, and enjoys the surf and sea in addition to streams.

FALCON GUIDES are available for where-to-go hiking, mountain biking, rock climbing, walking, scenic driving, fishing, rockhounding, paddling, birding, wildlife viewing, and camping. We also have FalconGuides on essential outdoor skills and subjects and field identification. The following titles are currently available, but this list grows every year. For a free catalog with a complete list of titles, call FALCON toll-free at 1-800-582-2665.

BIRDING GUIDES
Birding Minnesota
Birding Montana
Birding Texas
Birding Utah

FIELD GUIDES
Bitterroot: Montana State Flower
Canyon Country Wildflowers
Great Lakes Berry Book
New England Berry Book
Pacific Northwest Berry Book
Plants of Arizona
Rare Plants of Colorado
Rocky Mountain Berry Book
Scats & Tracks of the Rocky Mtns.
Tallgrass Prairie Wildflowers
Western Trees
Wildflowers of Southwestern Utah
Willow Bark and Rosehips

FISHING GUIDES
Fishing Alaska
Fishing the Beartooths
Fishing Florida
Fishing Glacier National Park
Fishing Maine
Fishing Montana
Fishing Wyoming

PADDLING GUIDES
Floater's Guide to Colorado
Paddling Montana
Paddling Okeefenokee
Paddling Oregon
Paddling Yellowstone & Grand
    Teton National Parks

ROCKHOUNDING GUIDES
Rockhounding Arizona
Rockhound's Guide to California
Rockhound's Guide to Colorado
Rockhounding Montana
Rockhounding Nevada
Rockhound's Guide to New Mexico
Rockhounding Texas
Rockhounding Utah
Rockhounding Wyoming

WALKING
Walking Colorado Springs
Walking Denver
Walking Portland
Walking St. Louis

HOW-TO GUIDES
Avalanche Aware
Backpacking Tips
Bear Aware
Leave No Trace
Mountain Lion Alert
Reading Weather
Wilderness First Aid
Wilderness Survival

MORE GUIDEBOOKS
Backcountry Horseman's
    Guide to Washington
Camping California's
    National Forests
Exploring Canyonlands &
    Arches National Parks
Exploring Hawaii's Parklands
Exploring Mount Helena
Recreation Guide to WA
    National Forests
Touring California & Nevada
    Hot Springs
Trail Riding Western
    Montana
Wild Country Companion
Wild Montana

FALCON®